HURRICANES OVER SINGAPORE

BRIAN CULL is the author of the following Grub Street titles:

AIR WAR FOR YUGOSLAVIA, GREECE and CRETE 1940-41 with Christopher Shores and Nicola Malizia
MALTA: THE HURRICANE YEARS 1940-41 with Christopher Shores and Nicola Malizia
MALTA: THE SPITFIRE YEAR 1942 with Christopher Shores and Nicola Malizia
BLOODY SHAMBLES Volume 1 with Christopher Shores and Yasuho Izawa
BLOODY SHAMBLES Volume 2 with Christopher Shores and Yasuho Izawa
SPITFIRES OVER ISRAEL with Shlomo Aloni and David Nicolle
TWELVE DAYS IN MAY with Bruce Lander and Heinrich Weiss
WINGS OVER SUEZ with David Nicolle and Shlomo Aloni
249 AT WAR
THE DESERT HAWKS with Leo Nomis
HURRICANES OVER TOBRUK with Don Minterne
HURRICANES OVER MALTA with Frederick Galea
SPITFIRES OVER SICILY with Nicola Malizia and Frederick Galea
WITH THE YANKS IN KOREA Volume 1 with Dennis Newton
BUFFALOES OVER SINGAPORE with Paul Sortehaug and Mark Haselden
ONE-ARMED MAC with Roland Symons

HURRICANES OVER SINGAPORE

RAF, RNZAF AND NEI FIGHTERS IN ACTION AGAINST THE JAPANESE OVER THE ISLAND AND THE NETHERLANDS EAST INDIES, 1942

BRIAN CULL
WITH PAUL SORTEHAUG

GRUB STREET · LONDON

Published by
Grub Street
4 Rainham Close
London SW11 6SS

British Library Cataloguing in Publication Data
Cull, Brian
Hurricanes over Singapore: RAF, RNZAF and NEI fighters in action against the Japanese over the island and the Netherlands East Indies, 1942
1. Great Britain. Royal Air Force – History 2. Hurricane (Fighter planes) 3. World War, 1939-1945 – Aerial operations, British 4. World War, 1939-1945 – Campaigns – East Asia
I. Title II. Sortehaug, Paul
940.5′44941

ISBN 1 904010 80 6

Typeset by Pearl Graphics, Hemel Hempstead

Printed and bound in Great Britain by
Biddles Ltd, King's Lynn

CONTENTS

ACKNOWLEDGEMENTS

Much of this account is based upon the memoirs of the late Jerry Parker DFC, who served with 232 Squadron at Singapore, Palembang and in Java before becoming a prisoner of war. Written originally for the benefit of his children and grandchildren, he graciously gave permission for extracts to be published herewith. He also provided the Foreword. Sadly, he passed away in 2002 before this account was finished.

Terence Kelly – distinguished author, playwright and former fighter pilot with 258 Squadron – is thanked for giving permission for the copious use of extracts from his trilogy *Hurricane over the Jungle*, *Battle for Palembang* and *Hurricane and Spitfire Pilots at War*, which effectively covers 258 Squadron's history for this period; extracts from these books will be found in all chapters and thereby have enhanced this work considerably. Similarly, many of the recollections of his former squadron colleague Art Donahue DFC (deceased) have been extracted from the American pilot's memoirs published in 1943 as *Last Flight From Singapore*, shortly after his death in action.

Many anecdotal contributions have emanated from dear Canadian friends Gordie and Edith Dunn during our visits to each other's homes. A meeting with the late Sandy Allen MBE DFM, former Chief Executive of the Guinea Pig Club, also proved most enjoyable and beneficial. Sadly, he also passed away (May 2003) before the book's completion. Other important contributions have come from the late Tom Watson DFC and Bill Lockwood (both of whom Brian and Val met in Canada in 1995); Tom Watson's widow, Rowena, is to be thanked for the loan of a video Tom made shortly before his death. When Gordie and Edith visited England a few months later, a surprise meeting was arranged for them with David and Maureen Kynman – Gordie and David had both served with 232 Squadron before spending the remainder of the war as prisoners; they had lost touch at the war's end. It proved to be an extremely emotional but happy reunion, despite David's terminal illness.

An official report submitted by Sqn Ldr Ivon Julian DFC (deceased) has proved most useful, as has a taped interview made with him by Paul, who also tape interviewed Air Commodore Ernie Gartrell CBE DFC (deceased), Sqn Ldr Jack Mackenzie DFC (deceased), the late Sqn Ldr Denis Sharp DFC (who died shortly before publication), Jim MacIntosh (deceased), Harry 'Bunt' Pettit, Perce Killick, John Vibert, Ian 'Snowy' Newlands, Eddie Kuhn DFM (deceased), Peter Gifford (deceased), Wally Greenhalgh, Collis Sharp, Rod MacMillan and Brian Stringer. Paul also wishes to acknowledge contributions from Phil de la Perrelle, Nicholas Wright and Mrs Margaret Burton. Paul has also provided, via Mike Hutcheson, an account prepared by Sqn Ldr John Hutcheson DFC (deceased); and acknowledges the late Frank Hood for access to his diary. A potted operational history of 232 Squadron compiled by the Squadron Adjutant, Flt Lt Norman Welch, has proved invaluable. Further contributions have come from Ian Fairbairn and Tom Young, both Australians, and Canadian Flt Lt John Fleming. Other personal contributions are from the memoirs of Charles Campbell-White (via Annette Campbell-White) and from correspondence with the late Air Marshal Sir Harold Maguire KCB DSO OBE, Fred Margarson, Sqn Ldr Ambrose Milnes, Bert Lambert and Sqn Ldr Doug Nicholls DFC (when Brian was researching *Bloody Shambles*). Brian also acknowledges the encouragement of the late Air Vice-Marshal Stanley Vincent CB DFC AFC, who gave permission for extracts from his book *Flying Fever* to be used.

Others who have proved most helpful include Dr David Wilson, RAAF Historical Department; Lex McAulay, author and publisher (Banner Books); Canadian author and historian Hugh Halliday; staff at AHB(RAF)MoD, particularly Mrs Susan Dickinson;

staff at the Public Record Office, Kew; staff at the Bury St Edmunds Public Library; and old friends such as Chris Shores, Yasuho Izawa, Bruce Lander, Sqn Ldr Andy Thomas (in particular for the loan of photographs), and Martin Goodman; not forgetting Jack Lee, gentleman and scholar. And, of course, our thanks to Chris Thomas for another splendid dustjacket illustration. Both authors offer their thanks to Mr John Davies and his staff – Louise and Luke – at Grub Street, and to Paul's nephew Nathan for his unstinting efforts in e-mailing copious notes from New Zealand to Britain. Paul also thanks his family for their encouragement and support throughout the period of research (many years) entailed in helping to make this account as comprehensive as possible. Last, but by no means least, Brian thanks his wife Val for her continuing support, both financial and practical, in seeing this account come to fruition on time – his seventeenth book for Grub Street in as many years.

Brian Cull – Bury St Edmunds, England
Paul Sortehaug – Dunedin, New Zealand

FOREWORD

Flt Lt B.J. 'Jerry' Parker DFC
232 Squadron, Singapore, Sumatra and Java 1942
Prisoner of war 1942-1945

After six months' training on Tiger Moths at White Waltham and Hawker Audaxes at Hullavington, I was transferred as a newly qualified pilot to the Operational Training Unit at Usworth near Sunderland in February 1941. By early April I had soloed on the Miles Master – a cantilever monoplane trainer with enclosed cockpit, oxygen, radio, flaps and retractable undercarriage – and also the Hurricane, but owing to bad weather had only one lesson in flying on wartime operations. More time was spent on the very rainy days in sitting around a stove in the Flight Office listening to the memories of pilots from whom I learnt several useful manoeuvres.

I was then posted to A Flight of 232 Squadron on a very sandy airfield just north of the town of Montrose. My first flight there in a Hurricane ended in my engine cutting out over the town with my flaps and wheels down and overturning the aircraft in a ploughed field. This was an unlooked-for lesson in the advisability of always landing with my safety straps very tight, the seat locked down in the cockpit and the canopy locked back.

Soon the Squadron transferred to Ouston, a newly created airfield on the top of a shallow hill near Newcastle with three all-weather runways, which nevertheless made it very difficult for us in the high winds prevailing to avoid the mud alongside. We carried out patrols to protect convoys navigating the North Sea but there was no real action. Otherwise we amused ourselves by practising formation flying, dogfighting, aerobatics and low-flying, although restrictions on non-operational flying were imposed. Such restrictions were probably the cause of our not practising aerial gunnery; we were allowed one short burst apiece using one of our eight guns at a ground target and another at a towed drogue target. In early June it was planned that the Squadron would support a landing in the Mediterranean and the majority of the more experienced pilots were sent on commando courses in eastern Scotland whilst half a dozen of us flew Hurricanes and Spitfires from factories to and between operational airfields. During my time with the Squadron and the delivery flight I accumulated 130 flying hours on Hurricanes. It served me in good stead later.

In early November 1941, Flight Lieutenant Landels, four sergeant pilots and I left by chartered liner for our mystery landing; but the Japanese war had broken out before we reached Durban and there we transferred to a transport that took us to Singapore. We were joined by six pilots of similar ranking to our own from each of three other squadrons and, as Jock Landels was appointed Squadron Leader, the resulting unit was designated 232 (Provisional) Squadron. The other three flight commanders of course were far senior to me but most of the other pilots had remarkably little experience. Some of the sergeant pilots had less than 20 flying hours on Spitfires, none on Hurricanes – an extraordinarily poor preparation for war.

51 Hurricanes in crates had been diverted with us in the same convoy to Singapore and the groundcrews set about unpacking them very promptly. The Hurricanes were Mark IIB, embodying a total of twelve machine guns each and the requisite ammunition and Vokes air filters under the nose of the aircraft, which, for me obviated a repeat of the accident I had suffered at Montrose. However, these modifications increased the weight of each aircraft by about half a ton. Whilst the Vokes filters prevented huge

amounts of sand from being blown into the carburettors, their weight and internal baffles considerably reduced the performance of the Hurricane II. In the equatorial heat of Java the maximum speed obtainable in level flight was reduced to about 250mph and the rates of climb and manoeuvrability diminished accordingly. The big filter was taken from one aircraft only, presumably without benefit, as that modification was not tried on other aircraft.

We had brought our own Intelligence Officer with us but, although he set about visiting Air Headquarters immediately upon landing, he was quite unable to let us have any useful information about the aircraft we would meet in combat. It was mid-January 1942 and the Japanese had been bombing Singapore in large formations, generally of 81 bombers, although from ground level I could see no fighters. But there was a machine referred to as the Navy 0, which had quite remarkable rates of turn and climb and which the pilots of Buffaloes, already stationed at Singapore, held in great respect. We were totally ignorant of the quality of the Japanese pilots but presumably, having planned the invasion of Malaya so well, their commanders had not overlooked the employment of their most experienced and dedicated men. They appeared to be well informed of the assembly and preparation of the Hurricanes and, helped by Singapore's lack of adequate radar and observer corps, were enabled to fall upon us on the first day of our operations. On our part we rarely enjoyed early warning of the height and direction of incoming raids and were generally caught napping.

Thus as a 20-year-old, combat-inexperienced pilot I arrived at Singapore. Most of my colleagues similarly lacked experience of facing the enemy in the sky – let alone the expertly flown Japanese Army and Navy fighters we were to meet over Singapore and the Netherlands East Indies in the ensuing weeks. Our group comprised 24 young pilots, many straight from Operational Training Units, and within three days of combat five were missing presumed killed including our Squadron Commander, one replacement pilot was also killed, and two others seriously injured. A dozen of our Hurricanes had been shot down or otherwise badly damaged. By the end of the first week of action our losses had risen to about 20 Hurricanes. Ten pilots were missing although two later returned, and another three were in hospital seriously injured, with two others out of commission. Fifteen out of 25 pilots lost to the Squadron in just seven days.

Following the fall of Singapore, survivors from our group and reinforcements continued to face overwhelming odds at Palembang in Sumatra and later still in Java. Our small band of pilots dwindled until there was only a handful left during the closing days of the fighting. I was one of the lucky ones and flew until practically the last day of operations before the capitulation of Java, and was shot down shortly before the end. Those of us not able to evacuate Java were destined to face life as prisoners of war for the next three and a half years. Although many thousands of Allied military personnel died in these camps, those remaining in Java were relatively fortunate, and our entire group survived.

There are not many of my flying companions left now. Faces have long been forgotten in the mists of time, while names often just ring a bell. But, through the efforts of Brian Cull and Paul Sortehaug in this excellent record, *Hurricanes over Singapore*, they ensure that their names are not forgotten. Their deeds are recorded within these pages and the Roll of Honour poignantly remembers those who made the supreme sacrifice.

Jerry Parker 1921-2002
Exmouth, Devon

A warning unheeded . . .

In the early 1920s, a British Mission under Colonel Lord Sempill AFC was sent to Japan to assist with the training of pilots of the embryonic Japanese Naval Air Service. The 30-strong party included instructors in flying, armament, technical matters, design and administration – but not psychology, it would seem:

> "One gathers from those who have returned to England that though the Japanese pilots are not very quick to learn, as was only to be expected seeing that the Japanese are not a horse-riding nation [!], they learn very assiduously whatever is taught to them and carry out their instruction with care and intelligence. The result is that their progress as pilots, though perhaps slow according to our ideas, is nonetheless steady and safe. The number of casualties to Japanese Naval aviators in training has been extraordinarily small."

Aeroplane, 1922

PREAMBLE

HURRICANES FOR SINGAPORE

November 1941 – January 1942

> "I do not pretend to have measured accurately the martial might of Japan, but now at this very moment I knew the United States was in the war, up to the neck and in to the death. So we had won after all!! We had won the war. England would live; Britain would live; the Commonwealth of Nations and the Empire would live. As for the Japanese, they would be ground to powder."
>
> Winston Churchill, December 1941[1]

With the end of 1941 rapidly approaching, Britain's fortunes in the war against Germany and Italy looked surprisingly brighter than they had done for many months. The glimmer of hope and optimism was brought about by the sudden and dramatic German invasion of the Soviet Union in June, which focused Germany's attention to the East rather than the West. At last Britain had an ally of sorts, at least one that was now bearing the brunt of the mighty German military force that only the English Channel had denied from steamrolling its way into Britain a year previous. Having stoically faced the might of the Luftwaffe for nigh on a year, the British people gratefully witnessed the German war machine change tack to the East, where the Russians and their allies fell back in total disorder as the invasion force swept all before it, as it had done through the Low Countries and Scandinavia. Until that fateful backstabbing decision by Hitler and his generals[2], Germany's former ally had, by default, been Britain's potential enemy.

Nonetheless, and despite her own deprivations, Britain was not slow in coming to its new ally's aid, albeit initially in dribs and drabs as circumstances permitted, but also with promise of more. A Military Mission was rushed to Moscow to establish just what could be done. With the crushing defeat of the Red Air Force in the opening weeks of the German offensive, the Soviets were desperate for modern aircraft as much as anything else Britain could offer. The Americans also rallied round and made available quantities of mainly fighter aircraft that had been destined for the RAF and, with Britain's agreement, would soon divert these to the new war zone: these included P-39s and P-40s, which compared favourably with the surviving fighters in the Soviet inventory. Although Britain was still at risk and, in the Middle East, where the RAF and Commonwealth units were fighting desperate air battles against the Axis, continuous steams of bombers and fighters were urgently required, Prime Minister Churchill magnanimously promised to make available to the Soviets hundreds of Hurricanes over the coming months. This decision aggrieved not only the commanders in the Middle East, but those in the Far East who, when they learned of the Prime Minister's generosity to his new-found and unlikely ally, urgently demanded Hurricanes for their own commands.

RAF Far East Command's demands were promptly dismissed. Since the Chief-of-Air Staff perceived that there was no particular threat in that area, it was therefore decided that the Command should make do with the aircraft already on strength, mainly Blenheim light bombers, Vildebeest biplane torpedo bombers, and US-supplied Brewster Buffalo fighters – a fighter type rejected by the RAF as unsuitable for operations over Northern Europe; even Middle East Command was not keen to retain the few that had been despatched to Egypt. The Japanese threat to British, American and

Dutch possessions in South-East Asia was still not taken seriously, for it was proposed that obsolete Gladiator biplane fighters currently residing in the Middle East would be sufficient to strengthen Singapore defences. Enquiries to the various meteorological and communications flights in the Middle East revealed that 21 Gladiators could be made available, while a further five were currently on the strength of a Free French fighter unit. Air HQ Middle East estimated that whilst these could be made serviceable for operational use, "... all aircraft are rather old and none too reliable for long flights." In the circumstances it was considered that it would be "uneconomical" to proceed with the venture – not to mention that the proposal would have been little short of suicidal. The offer was anyway unequivocally turned down by AOC Singapore.

On 20 July 1941, Churchill sent a message to Premier Stalin – one of a series at this critical time – part of which advised the Soviet leader of the impossibility of the British attempting immediate land invasions of France and Norway to remove the pressure from the Eastern Front (as Stalin had demanded). Churchill's lengthy communication concluded:

> "It is therefore to the north we must look for any speedy help we can give. The Naval Staff have been preparing for three weeks past an operation by seaborne aircraft upon German shipping in the north of Norway and Finland, hoping thereby to destroy enemy power of transporting troops by sea to attack your Arctic flank. Secondly, we are sending forthwith some cruisers and destroyers to Spitzbergen, whence they will be able to raid enemy shipping in concert with your naval forces. Thirdly, we are sending a flotilla of submarines to intercept German traffic on the Arctic coast, although owing to perpetual daylight this service is particularly dangerous. Fourthly, we are sending a minelayer with various supplies to Archangel. This is the most we can do at the moment. I wish it were more.
>
> We are also studying as a further development the basing of some British fighter air squadrons on Murmansk. This would require first of all a consignment of anti-aircraft guns, then the arrival of the aircraft, some of which could be flown off carriers and others crated. When these were established our Spitzbergen squadron could come to Murmansk and act with your naval forces. We have reason to believe that the Germans have sent a strong group of dive-bombers, which they are keeping for our benefit should we arrive, and it is therefore necessary to proceed step by step. All this however will take weeks." [3]

True to his word, Churchill ordered two squadrons of Hurricanes to be made available for immediate despatch to Murmansk, together with a further 200 crated Hurricanes to be delivered by sea. The squadrons selected were two comparatively newly formed units, 81 and 134 Squadrons, and these formed 151 (Fighter) Wing under the command of Wg Cdr H.N.G. Ramsbottom-Isherwood DFC AFC, a New Zealander in the RAF. The old training aircraft carrier HMS *Argus* was commissioned with the task of delivering the air party, 24 Hurricanes flying from her deck at a point north of Murmansk, all aircraft arriving safely at the newly constructed airfield at Vianga; the sea party, which included 14 more pilots, arrived at Archangel aboard the former liner *Llanstephan Castle*, while other ships of the convoy carried the crated Hurricanes among other cargo. Only six weeks had passed since Churchill had made his promise to Stalin. In the coming weeks of September and early October, 151 (Fighter) Wing's Hurricane pilots would be credited with some 15 air victories in defence of its base and surrounding area, including the occasional bomber escort; one Hurricane and its pilot was lost in action. In the meantime, 15 of the crated Hurricanes were swiftly erected and tested, allowing RAF pilots to begin instructing their Soviet counterparts in the art of flying the machine. These included Soviet ace Boris Safonov, already with at least 16 kills to his credit. One RAF pilot was killed in an accident during the training period.

The Wing was withdrawn soon after and returned to Britain by sea during early November.

Following the success of 151 (Fighter) Wing, it was decided to send another formation to assist the Soviets in their struggle against the Germans on the southern end of the Eastern Front, 267 (Fighter) Wing being established for this duty. 267 (Fighter) Wing, under the command of Wg Cdr A.W. Pennington-Legh, was formed with 17, 135, 136 and 232 Squadrons, all of which were to be equipped with Hurricane IIBs. It was planned that the Wing would take the long sea route around Africa, for initial delivery to Iraq. Its further destination was a closely guarded secret, but the squadron commanders and intelligence officers were advised that it was to be the Caucasus. When the pilots of the four squadrons learned of the news of an overseas posting, farewell parties were quickly organised. This was not to the liking of all, including Sgt Gordon Dunn, a 21-year-old Canadian of 232 Squadron, then based at Ouston, of whom newly promoted Flt Lt Ivon Julian, a New Zealander known as Taffy to his friends, had taken an instant dislike. Gordie Dunn recalled:

> "I came back to the sergeants' mess at Ouston from a trip to Sunderland – where I had been befriended by a Scots family while at RAF Usworth – and found the groundcrews had staged a bit of a riot in the canteen and had fire hoses turned on them. In the mess some of the guys were a bit beered up, and we got into quite a hassle. Some of the guys flushed billiard balls down the toilet and broke some glasses and what not. Julian, who was in change in the absence of the CO, had to make good the damage before we could leave. He came to Tom Young and me and said he had settled the bill and each share came to £6. As Tom and I hadn't been involved, we said no way, and anyway, who had authorised him to spend £6 on my behalf? He replied that he was in charge of the draft but I told him that I didn't care a damn if he was in charge or not, I wasn't going to give him a cent. I said he could sue me if he wished but I wasn't going to give him even six pennies. The officers and sergeants were not all that close at times – at least one sergeant, me, and one officer, Julian."

The four squadron commanders and the majority of the pilots went aboard the troopships *Strathallan*, *Durban Castle* and *Abossa*, while parties of half a dozen pilots from each unit, each under a flight commander, boarded the *Monarch of Bermuda*, an Admiralty-chartered luxury liner which had been on the pre-war run between New York and Bermuda. The latter vessel sailed from Liverpool on 12 November. The troopships did not leave the Clyde until the end of the first week of December. On board the *Monarch of Bermuda* with 232 Squadron was Plt Off Jerry Parker – a 20-year-old Londoner from Charlton:

> "[Flt Lt] Jock Landels and I, with [Sgts] Christian and Hardie, two other sergeant pilots [Nicholls and Lowe] and all the groundcrew… found ourselves with masses of Army people and six pilots and groundcrews of each of three other fighter squadrons. The convoy, which would be escorted by some frigates and destroyers, carried an invasion force (so we thought) to affect a bridgehead on a beach in the Mediterranean. We heard that we had 51 Hurricanes in crates with us in the convoy and we would fly these after the ground forces had captured an airstrip under cover of the fighters from *Indomitable* which would already be flying and would expect us to land there. I thought it a pretty tight schedule but we really only had rumours to guide us."

At about the same time, Convoy *WS14D* departed the Clyde bound for the Middle East, the seven ships of the convoy loaded with mainly anti-aircraft guns, both heavy and light, plus 4,000 gunners and other troops. The convoy was routed to follow the West African coast via the Cape and up along the eastern coast to Iraq via the Suez Canal. On board *Warwick Castle* and the *Empress of Australia* were HQ personnel of another newly formed wing – 266 (Fighter) Wing composed of 242, 258 and 605 Squadrons under the command of Wg Cdr H.J. Maguire. Personnel included 39 mainly inexperienced, and, in many cases, newly qualified Hurricane pilots, the majority of whom were Australians, New Zealanders, and Canadians. They were to be casualty replacements for the regular pilots for the three squadrons embarked on HMT *Athene*, an Army transport-cum-aircraft tender described by one pilot as a floating hangar, aboard which were stowed 39 crated Hurricanes. The *Athene* headed for Gibraltar, from were it was intended that the pilots would embark on the aircraft carriers *Ark Royal* and *Argus* to fly to Egypt via Malta. Hence, on arrival at Gibraltar, the pilots of 242 Squadron and the majority of those of 605 were instructed to embark aboard the two carriers, those from 258 Squadron to follow on the next trip. The pilots knew beforehand that they were to fly from the deck of a carrier, as recalled by 258 Squadron's Flt Lt Denny Sharp, a New Zealander:

> "We moved from Martlesham Heath to Debden to do what they called deck training, because they knew we were going to go on an aircraft carrier, and the intention was to fly us into Malta. So, as soon as we went to Debden, we knew that we were going to fly off an aircraft carrier, and about the only place we would be flying off an aircraft carrier would be into Malta. Deck training consisted of short take-offs and short landings. You would rev the engine up just before take-off, apply the brakes until they slipped, then let them go and slam the throttle on full power. And there it was – you would get airborne much quicker than normal. And the same applied in landing. Flaps and wheels down, come in with a lot of power generating lift from the airflow from the propeller – which was in fine pitch – over the wings. You would be able to come in at the slow speed of about 65 knots and, just holding off, over the fence, cut the throttle and sink onto the ground, braking immediately, with the joystick back in your tummy."

Fellow New Zealander Plt Off Charles Campbell-White (known to his friends as Cam) later recalled their departure from Greenoch in Scotland and subsequent arrival at Gibraltar:

> "We were going somewhere but where? Was it Russia, Malta or the Middle East? Then we were on our way, but without Wilf [Sqn Ldr Clouston, the CO], and still not knowing our final destination. We travelled by truck to Greenoch, passing through a damp and dismal Glasgow. At Greenoch, we boarded the Navy aircraft tender *Athene* for Gibraltar. The Navy and Air Force did not get along well right from the start, which wasn't surprising. We had nothing to do and they carried out their normal duties. We took up all their wardroom space. We were always there and we were getting in their hair. Eventually the Navy had had enough and it came to a head after we left Gibraltar. They decided they would put us in our places. Their attitude was, as they told us, the Battle of Britain is forgotten but Nelson still lives!
>
> The night for this putting us in our place was a formal dinner night when there were usually high jinx after dinner, which was always a pukka affair. After dinner we went back to the wardroom. The Navy gathered in strength on one side of the room. On a formal dinner night it was more or less compulsory to attend if you could attend. The RAF always gathered in strength. The Navy put their hands on each other's shoulders and started singing 'We are the King's Navy'. When they came opposite us we pounced on them. A brawl started. I was knocked over a chair and sat on a glass. The rest of the evening I spent in sick quarters having glass removed from my bottom. Apparently the duty officer lost his head and called out the guard who cleared the wardroom with fixed bayonets."

The trip from Greenoch to Gibraltar was mercifully uneventful.

> "I shall never forget my first view of the Rock from my porthole. Just as big and menacing and impregnable as in the pictures. And now all was revealed. We were to transfer to the *Ark Royal*, and fly off just before the Straits of Pantelleria, which were too narrow for the *Ark Royal* to proceed safely through without being exposed to huge attacks from land based enemy planes. The Hurricanes, with their cumbersome long-range tanks, were assumed to be able to fight their way through if attacked. Our Hurricanes, which travelled with us, would be transferred from the *Athene* to the *Ark Royal*. The type of Hurricane we were to fly to the Middle East was the Mark IIC, equipped with two 20mm cannons instead of the eight or 12 machine guns in the wings. There was a big difference when firing. The machine guns had very little effect. Just a gentle rippling sound, but with the cannons, 'pow', 'pow', 'pow', and the aircraft almost came to a stop.
>
> While we were in Gibraltar, we occasionally went on anti-submarine patrols with the Navy in their motor torpedo boats. A screen of MTBs and destroyers patrolled the Straits of Gibraltar in close formation right up to the African shore to prevent enemy submarines from getting into the Mediterranean. It was about the only time I felt seasick. The MTBs went flat out to their patrol position. Up down, up down, splash, splash over the waves. Then slow down and patrol up and down all night. While going out on patrol, I was in the tiny wardroom and next door was supper, which smelt of bacon and eggs being cooked. I knew I was going to be sick but didn't want the Navy to know. I stood up and as casually as I could say, "I think I shall go up on deck for a bit to see where we are." I was most relieved to feel the cool air blowing on my face. Then, thank God, the MTB slowed down. There was lots of talk on the R/T but as far as I knew, no submarine was attacked. It wasn't always so free of incident as demonstrated by a destroyer in Gibraltar harbour with a big gash in its bow from ramming a sub."

Shortly after arrival at Gibraltar, the pilots of 242 Squadron and the majority of those from 605 Squadron embarked aboard the aircraft carriers *Ark Royal* and *Argus*; the carriers then conveyed them to a point within range of Malta, from where they flew to the island. The intention had been for them to refuel there, and then fly on to Egypt. In the event, with the threat from a renewed Luftwaffe presence in Sicily becoming apparent, they were retained for the defence of the island. As the carriers headed back to Gibraltar for their second load – the remainder of 605 Squadron and all of 258 Squadron – *Ark Royal* was torpedoed by a German U-boat and sank shortly afterwards. It had been considered impractical and too dangerous to despatch *Argus* – an old training carrier – to Malta alone, so 258 Squadron, together with three pilots from 605 Squadron (Flt Lt Eric Wright DFM[4], Plt Off Joe Hutton and Plt Off Bill Lockwood RCAF) plus 242 Squadron's spare pilot (Plt Off Arthur Brown, a Canadian in the RAF), remained at Gibraltar awaiting the arrival of a replacement carrier.

In the meantime, the pilots formed an ad hoc fighter flight. With time and freedom on their side, some of the pilots – particularly the four Americans of 258 Squadron including the handsome American Plt Off Don Geffene – indulged in woman hunting, as Plt Off Red Campbell, another of the Americans, recalled:

> "Don was a sophisticated, attractive man with a magnetic personality. He was one of the few Eagles who had married before getting into the RAF. He had been married and divorced. When he walked into a room, you could see all the women start watching him. In Gibraltar, the only females were a few Spanish women, who came across the border in the daytime, worked in the shops, and then went home. Geffene was the only one of us who could find feminine companionship there. He set himself up with a girl who worked in a butcher shop. A young navy lieutenant from the *Athene* found out about this and asked Geffene how he managed it. 'Just put your money on the table,' Don told him. The

lieutenant tried this, and got chased down the street by a very angry Spaniard with a butcher knife.

When we first came to Gibraltar, there were half a dozen British WRENS there. We called their mess the 'Wrennery'. One of the squadron commanders said that if we would promise not to insult the ladies he would arrange a party for us. Geffene learned that the CO planned to fix himself and another pilot up with WREN dates. Don promptly went down to visit the British battle cruiser in the harbor and told the officers that everyone there was invited to a big party at the 'Wrennery'. The Squadron Leader arrived at the party he had arranged to find the place filled with Navy types."[5]

258 Squadron's Rhodesian pilot, 26-year-old Plt Off Graham Macnamara, known as Ting[6], wrote:

"The question now arose as to what would be done with us. While our future was being decided we were officially termed Fighter Defence Gibraltar and, with long-range tanks fitted to our cannon-firing Hurricanes, had the unique experience of being able to boast of flying patrols in fighter aircraft which covered two oceans and two continents! We ranged along the Med and Atlantic coasts of both Europe and Africa in one patrol. We now settled down to a humdrum life but this was interposed by various excursions.

There was a classic blunder when one day three Yanks from our squadron and myself were on a patrol when one of them, Don Geffene, force-landed on the beach at Tangiers. Cannon Hurricanes were at this time still unpublished, so his companion [Plt Off Cardell Kleckner] asked for permission from Ops if he could make a pass at the stranded machine and so destroy it. Hearing this on the intercom we, too, hurried over to the scene of the excitement to join in the fun. Ops were panicking about international territory and what not, but before they finally issued any instructions, Kleckner had noticed Spanish soldiers taking off, and knowing Tangiers was full of Germans, decided to have his pass. As he peeled off and dived down on the aircraft, his four cannons spitting angry death and destruction, the Spaniards took to their heels and seldom have I seen a crowd disappear so quickly and in such undignified haste! I'm sure some succeeded in digging themselves in the sand!

Anyhow, Kleck hit his target and we [Macnamara was flying with Plt Off Red Campbell] joined in and in no time it was a blazing wreck. Our respective patrols continued and finally we went home. Not long afterwards our friend Franco created a terrific din. As a result the whole Rock – Army, Navy and Air Force – stood at readiness for 24 hours a day for three days – then all quietened down. Of course, we don't know if we were the direct cause of the excitement or not, but we never regretted doing what we did."[7]

Cam White added:

"Don spent some time in Morocco having a jolly good time as a guest of the British Ambassador."

He continued:

"We also did anti-submarine patrols in Catalina flying boats and, occasionally, as second pilot. An amusing incident occurred while at Gibraltar. The mighty and very prestigious battleship, the HMS *Nelson*, was moored next to us. We had to go aboard the *Nelson* if we wanted to use the telephones. Though whom we would need to call, I can't imagine. Anyhow, very junior Plt Off Bruce McAlister had to board the *Nelson* to make some call or other. Now the *Nelson* personnel had to observe all sorts of rituals, as did all Naval ships to a more or less degree. For instance, one always saluted the Quarter Deck where the great man was mortally wounded on the victory at Trafalgar.

The big event was when the Admiral came aboard or left the ship – there was always lots of gold braid in evidence, particularly at the head of the gangway. The whole ship's company stood at attention. The officers saluted and the seamen of the watch piped the Admiral from the ship with their shrill whistles. All was in order and proceeding according to plan except for McAlister who was halfway up the gangway. To his horror, when he looked up, there was the Admiral giving his answering salute and glaring at McAlister whom he saw for the first time. Bruce decided to continue his climb and nervously passed the Admiral where he gave a rather perfunctory salute, avoiding his eyes and increasing his pace to avoid being grabbed, clapped in irons and probably shot.

We tried rowing the ship's boats with hilarious results. The Admiral of the Fleet sent us a signal telling us to keep out of Gibraltar harbour, where we were so busy catching crabs we failed to see him going past in his barge. We should have raised our oars aloft while the coxswain stood and saluted. We used to travel from the dock to the ship by Liberty boat, as we were moored on the other side of the harbour. As we approached the ship the coxswain would say, 'According to Naval custom, strict silence will be observed as we go alongside.' This was all a part of Navy tradition and very awe inspiring and we felt this gave us great respect for the Navy and its traditions. I always thought no Navy man could not do his duty because the Navy expected him to, as Nelson would be watching. One night the spell was broken because no sooner had the coxswain called for silence when somebody, probably Air Force, fell overboard and had to be rescued. We popped across to Spain now and then – La Linea, San Roque and Algaciras, which, as Spain was neutral, maybe we were not supposed to do. We visited all the places of interest on the Rock including the famous Rock Hotel. We drank beer in the local pubs and ate bowls of lunch counter shrimps."

When news was received of the Japanese attacks in the Far East, the pilots of 258 Squadron, plus the three stranded pilots of 605 Squadron and 242 Squadron's lone spare pilot, were ordered to re-embark on the *Athene*, which had brought them out from England; evidently the *Athene* still had her cargo of 39 crated Hurricanes intact. It had been decided that 258 Squadron would form part of the first fighter reinforcements for the new theatre of war. The transport set sail for Takoradi on the Gold Coast, to join pilots from 267 (Fighter) Wing, who had been diverted there on the outbreak of hostilities in the Far East, awaiting further orders. One of 258 Squadron's pilots, Sgt Terence Kelly, later wrote:

"I remember the magic of that week at sea, the magic of the first experience of sailing in tropical waters ... the old constellations sank and the new ones rose and the sea silvered by the moon and starlight hissed along the hull. There were duties to perform: four hour shifts manning two of *Athene*'s pom-pom anti-aircraft guns and night watches under the soft, warm, star powdered sky. There were incidents; the rebellion against rank discrimination, the stentorian yell by Kleckner: 'Submarine on port bow' bringing the Captain in a bath towel needlessly on the bridge to view a passing log, and the sickening thud of Bertie [Lambert], looping the loop in his hammock and stalling at the top."

Flg Off Art Donahue, one of 258 Squadron's American pilots[8], who had seen action during the Battle of Britain, also wrote of the trip:

"At night the sea was phosphorescent, one of the wonders of nature which most of us had never seen. Every disturbance in the water caused little flaky green lights to flash beneath the surface, so that the water churned from the ship's sides seemed full of fireflies. Every white-cap was a shower of fiery little green jewels, every fish left a trail like a small green sky-rocket in the darkness, and the wake of the ship was like a great convulsive mass of coloured fire.

It was on one of these nights, while on watch, that I got my first torpedo scare. I had been leaning over the rail by my gun for a long time, idly watching the lovely show, when suddenly I thought I heard a hissing noise. Looking up, I was terrified to see a huge trail of phosphorescence coming in a straight line toward the ship, scarcely a hundred yards away. I just seemed to freeze, inside and out, as if hypnotised by the sight, as it streaked on, cutting just beneath the waves and straight for the middle of the ship. It came straight as a die until less than twenty yards away, when it suddenly executed a sharp turn, in the most unorthodox manner for torpedoes! Then it started following along beside the ship so that I could see its outline, illuminated by the phosphorescence and then I recognised it as a big porpoise!

When my breath came back, I called the other boys to look. Soon we saw not one porpoise but several; then more and more joined up until there were all of fifty swimming beside us, mostly in pairs, gambolling about and converting the dark water for two or three hundred yards out into a fairyland of curving, swirling green sky-rockets. They followed along with us for fifteen or twenty minutes, one of the weirdest and most beautiful shows I've ever seen. Then, little by little, they dispersed and disappeared into the darkness."

The *Athene* arrived at Takoradi shortly before Christmas 1941, as Sgt Jimmy King of 232 Squadron revealed in a letter home to his wife:

"Anchored in West African port but not allowed ashore. When we anchored, we were surrounded by native vendors selling various items and fruit, particularly oranges and bananas. The natives were very patriotic and included two extra oranges or bananas above the order – one for the King and one for the Queen! The natives dived into the sea after coins thrown in by passengers, but they were only really after silver coins. Some pilots threw pennies and ha'pennies wrapped in silver paper."

It was at Takoradi that the commanding officers were informed of their new destination. 232 Squadron was detached for service in the Dutch East Indies together with 258 Squadron. The pilots of 17, 135 and 136 Squadrons were to go to Burma as 267 (Fighter) Wing. While this was happening, the pilots of the original 232 Squadron[9] commanded by Sqn Ldr Arthur Llewellin, together with those of 258 Squadron, now commanded by Sqn Ldr James Thomson, had been flown to Khartoum via Kano in Pan Am DC-3s, where a number of brand-new tropicalised Hurricane IIBs were made available. Selected pilots then flew the Hurricanes to Port Sudan via Khartoum where, to their shock, the new aircraft carrier HMS *Indomitable* awaited their arrival; others were ferried to the port in a variety of DC-2s, Blenheims, Bostons and Dragon Rapides, including Blenheim Z9671 piloted by one of the Hurricane pilots, Plt Off Mike Fitzherbert of 232 Squadron. With him were New Zealander Sgt Bill Moodie and Sgt Gordie Dunn, who recalled:

"There weren't enough Hurricanes available for all of us so anyone with experience on twins was offered a Blenheim to ferry to Port Sudan. The CO had refused to let us travel by train since there were only two types of carriage: First Class, which sergeants were not permitted to use, and cattle wagons, which the CO wouldn't allow us to travel in, so Mike volunteered to fly a Blenheim but later admitted that he had only flown twins on a couple of occasions. The Blenheim was clapped out and was due to go to an OTU. Our radio did not work. We were told not to retract the undercarriage, but to fly all the way with the wheels down. This was due to a hydraulics problem. We were delayed in setting out owing to a faulty magneto and when about 15 minutes flying time from Khartoum, it started to get dark. We were worried about landing in the dark, so decided to turn back to where we had seen a landing strip. Mike told me to raise the undercarriage to save fuel, which I did, but when we approached the strip, one wheel wouldn't come down again. In an effort to force it down, Mike tried to 'bounce' it out but we nose-dived into the ground. We bounced and then the second wheel folded up and we slid across a big field. The front Perspex was knocked out and sand came flying in right in my face. We were thrown about but no one was injured. We were some 90 miles short of our destination.

We got a message through to Port Sudan and after a day or two the RAF sent out a limousine to pick us up – a big, nine-passenger Chrysler. We travelled all through the night. There was a sequel to this when a Court of Inquiry was convened to determine the reason for the loss of the Blenheim. I was supposed to attend but, as I never used to read the Daily Routine Orders, I missed it. I was later summoned to appear before the court over which a judge, an air vice-marshal, presided – an old colonial-type 'Colonel Blimp' – and when he asked me to explain my absence, I told him I had gone fishing with Snowy Newlands. 'Gone fishing!!?' he bellowed. 'Gone fishing!!? Gone fishing!!? Bloody colonials!!' And with that he dismissed me. I guess I didn't make many friends at Port Sudan either!"

Another Blenheim (Z7778) was ferried to Port Sudan by 258 Squadron's Plt Off Ambrose Milnes, with Flg Off Harry Dobbyn, Plt Off Tom Watson and a sergeant pilot as passengers. Meanwhile, squadron colleague Campbell-White was among those who arrived at Khartoum aboard a DC-2:

"Then the big trek across Africa, my first experience of Africa. My memory is of very different people. Black, turbans, mud brick buildings, mud walls, sand, true desert, little gecko lizards, scorpions, sleeping out under the stars with mosquito nets, some very elegant guest houses or hotels, looking in our shoes before putting them on. The Dakota [*sic*] we travelled in had no seats and no seatbelts, so when the weather was bumpy we tended to lift off the ground, float in the air then drop back onto the aircraft. Some of our hardened pilots were very sick. We more or less found our own way to Port Sudan. I hitched a ride in a Boston, an American tricycle undercarriage, medium-range bomber. Our new CO, Sqn Ldr Thomson, was the pilot. Port Sudan, as I remember, was a hot, crowded, unattractive city."

New Zealander Sgt Snowy Newlands of 232 Squadron was one of those who ferried a Hurricane from Khartoum to Port Sudan:

"At Khartoum we were just getting used to flying in the desert. We would take turns going up and down and having the odd dogfight between ourselves. A whole crew of us were there including Gordie Dunn from Canada, Tom Young from Sydney, Bill Moodie from New Zealand and Fred Margarson, an Englishman. There was a little boxer chap I used to go around with – Billy Brown, also English – but he didn't actually get to Singapore, nor did Dick Swann[10], but we all eventually got to Port Sudan."

At Port Sudan, Sgt James Sandeman Allen – known to one and all as Sandy – who had been posted away from 232 Squadron a few weeks earlier for 'overseas duty', unexpectedly rejoined them. He soon found that this was to involve ferrying a Hurricane from Takoradi to Cairo, having been transported to Takoradi aboard the battleship *Prince of Wales*, which was en route to Singapore. He recalled:

"I was presented with a Hurricane to ferry across Africa. Setting off from Takoradi I, and a number of other Hurricane pilots, followed a 'mother' Blenheim to Khartoum in the Sudan. At one refuelling strip I awoke to find a giraffe inspecting the cockpit! After reaching Egypt I encountered members of 232 Squadron in a bar. Learning that they were about to be ferried from Port Sudan to the Far East aboard the *Indomitable*, I organised a posting to rejoin them."

Sqn Ldr Llewellin was only too pleased to have him rejoin the Squadron. Sgt Rod

Lawrence, a Canadian who had travelled out to West Africa on the *Prince of Wales* with Sandy Allen, also joined 232 Squadron at this time. In addition, the three 605 Squadron pilots (Flt Lt Wright, Plt Offs Hutton and Lockwood) were officially posted in, while Plt Off Leslie Emmerton arrived from 70 OTU, together with four pilots from the Middle East Pilots' Pool – 2/Lts John Stewart, Neil Anderson and Neil Dummett, all of the South African Air Force. 258 Squadron was also brought up to strength when Plt Off Brown, the 242 Squadron pilot, was attached, as was Plt Off Teddy Tremlett from the ME Pilots' Pool. At least half a dozen spare pilots were attached to the two squadrons in case of sickness or accidents. While at Wadi Safi, an airstrip located just outside Khartoum, all pilots practised short take-offs in readiness for their debut departure from the flight deck of a carrier. These completed, a number of sergeant pilots from each squadron were earmarked to taxi the brand-new Hurricane IIs from the airstrip to the docks – not an easy proposition, as 258 Squadron's Sgt Kelly remembered:

> "Port Sudan was a God-forsaken place, consisting as I recall it solely of two squares of arcaded buildings with a few shops plonked down in the desert, a hotel out of bounds to us, some salt lakes where I fruitlessly tried my hand at barracuda fishing, and docks and airfield interconnected by a road built up from the desert by sand embankments with telegraph poles staggered on either side. All this was relevant, for the job was ferrying Hurricanes (of a wingspan wider than the distance between the poles had they been directly opposite each other) from the airfield down to the docks where they would be loaded on HMS *Indomitable*, a brand new aircraft carrier about to make her maiden operational trip.
>
> The difficulty about taxiing Hurricanes was twofold: firstly, their angle of repose is such that the nose rears up and you can see nothing at all ahead and secondly that directional control is by the rudder which responds proportionately to the amount of slipstream affecting it. In other words, the faster you taxi, the more control you have. There was about a mile of curving road, a large number of Hurricanes to be delivered and the telegraph poles were spaced about fifty yards apart. And it was very, very hot – it really was quite a job."

On 14 January, the pilots embarked aboard *Indomitable*, as noted by Campbell-White:

> "At Port Sudan we boarded the spanking new *Indomitable*. We were amazed at the junk [Swordfish] on board. Very obsolete and could never have coped with Japanese aircraft, as we were soon to discover. The officers on the *Indomitable* lived in luxury with their own cabins and batmen. Other ranks had only a small part of the ship to themselves and at night were packed in like sardines swung backwards and forwards in their hammocks. The English class system. We had a luxurious dining room and wardroom, though."

Some of the ship's personnel took a dim view of the RAF intrusion on their particular way of life, as recorded by one of the carrier's Sea Hurricane pilots, Sub Lt(A) Hugh Popham:

> "The wardroom was full of RAF moustaches and RAF slang, and the ship had been reduced from a top-line carrier to a freighter, which disgruntled us."[11]

Below deck were stored 48 Hurricanes minus their wings. Unfortunately, these all featured large Vokes air filters for desert operations and had the effect of causing a relatively substantial reduction in top speed. Around 100 RAF groundcrew also embarked, their task to reassemble the Hurricanes en route to their destination: however, it transpired that very few of them had previously worked on Hurricanes, and it would fall to the Naval airmen of the carrier's Sea Hurricane unit, 880 Squadron, to ensure the task was successfully completed. The carrier's other resident fighter unit, 807 Squadron equipped with Fulmars, had flown off at Aden as had its Albacore squadron, to make room for the RAF Hurricanes. The plan called for *Indomitable* to sail to a point south of Christmas Island, from where the Hurricanes would fly to Batavia in Java (see Chapter III). Campbell-White continued:

> "We stopped for a while at Addu Atoll in the Maldives group of islands. A tropical island paradise where we swam. All this time Hurricanes were being assembled below decks and mighty hot work it was, the airmen stripped to the waist and sweating profusely. I told them: 'For goodness sake, take it easy fellas. I have to fly this off the carrier and once airborne, if something is missing, I can't get back.'"

In the meantime, the pilots of the reduced 267 (Fighter) Wing were despatched from Freetown shortly after Christmas, some being flown on Pan Am airliners to Takoradi, others being carried by the troopship *Abossa* to the same destination. One of these, Sgt Ron Cundy RAAF of 135 Squadron, was not enamoured with what he found at Takoradi:

> "...the place was swarming with mosquitoes. Despite the heat and humidity, long-sleeved shirts and long trousers tucked into the tops of our boots were essential. The sooner we could get out of the place the better. Shiploads of Hurricanes in crates were offloaded there, reassembled and then flown to Cairo, about 4,000 miles away. During the few days we were in Takoradi I lived in fear of being selected as one of the pilots assigned to fly a Hurricane to Cairo. The prospect of flying a single-engine aircraft over that vast expanse of jungle and desert did not appeal to me. My luck did not desert me. A number of us were put aboard a Sabena Airlines (Belgian) aircraft, of all things a Ju52, for the flight across Africa. Overnight stops were made at such fascinating places as Douala in the French Cameroons, Libenge in the Belgian Congo and Stanleyville, before being offloaded at Juba on the Nile in the southern Sudan.
>
> This was a bleak place virtually devoid of vegetation. For a week we were stuck in an army camp, accommodated in tents, before boarding a Sunderland flying boat for the journey north. Having received no pay since leaving England our funds had dried up which meant our thirst was quenched with either tea or water – palatable but most uninteresting. Stopping over in Khartoum, we were welcomed into the sergeants' mess but still without funds, the luxury of a beer eluded us. Next stop was Helwan south of Cairo where I was unlucky enough to be offloaded to make way for some VIP. There we spent a few boring days before being flown to Cairo in a twin-engine Bombay, a terrible old crate ready for the scrap heap."[12]

On arrival at Cairo, Cundy was amongst those posted away from 267 (Fighter) Wing and was instead transported to Mersa Matruh, where he joined a newly formed Hurricane squadron. Also joining this unit was a Canadian from 135 Squadron, Sgt Nelson Gilboe, the only one of six Hurricane pilots who had set out from Takoradi, with a Blenheim acting as navigator and guide, who safely reached Khartoum. The other five had crash-landed en route when the Blenheim became lost. Fortunately, no one was injured. Gilboe meanwhile landed near a village, from where the locals contacted the nearest RAF depot and obtained 50 gallons of petrol, sufficient for him to reach Khartoum under his own steam. Early in January, the pilots of 267 (Fighter) Wing selected to fly on to the Far East collected new Hurricanes and began the long haul to India, then across the sub continent and down through Burma to Rangoon.[13]

During this very confusing time, Convoy *WS14D* arrived at Durban, and the decision was taken to divert it to the new war zone (now codenamed *DM2*) where the anti-aircraft guns and personnel aboard the ships were desperately needed, more so than in the Middle East. Aboard the *Warwick Castle* and the *Empress of Australia* was the HQ of

266 (Fighter) Wing, the back-up Hurricane pilots and the ground personnel from the three squadrons (242, 605 and 258 Squadrons) that had been offloaded at Gibraltar, while aboard the accompanying transport *Athene* were more crated Hurricanes. The ships would leave Durban on 14 January, bound for Singapore.

The *Monarch of Bermuda* had already reached Durban, where the pilots learned for the first time of the new plan to send them to the Far East. This group comprised two-dozen pilots drawn equally from 17, 135, 136 and 232 Squadrons, each with a flight commander, together with the groundcrews of the latter unit. The senior flight commander, Flt Lt Jock Landels of 232 Squadron, was immediately promoted to Acting Squadron Leader and given command of the reconstituted 232 (Provisional) Squadron, as the assemblage was now designated: there now existed two 232 Squadrons! The 24 pilots selected were:

232 Squadron
Sqn Ldr L.N. Landels[14]
Plt Off B.J. Parker
Sgt H.T. Nicholls
Sgt C.D.G. Christian
Sgt P.D. Lowe
Sgt G. Hardie

17 Squadron
Flt Lt H.A. Farthing
Plt Off W.N. McCulloch RAAF
Sgt K.H. Holmes
Sgt E.M. Porter
Sgt R.L. Dovell
Sgt A.V. Coutie RAAF

135 Squadron
Flt Lt T.P.M. Cooper-Slipper DFC
Plt Off B.P. Daniel
Plt Off J.G. Gorton RAAF
Sgt I.S. Fairbairn RAAF
Sgt G.W. Schaffer RAAF
Sgt C.F. Marsh RCAF

136 Squadron
Flt Lt E. Murray Taylor
Plt Off N.M. Williams
Plt Off R. Mendizabal RCAF
Sgt S.N. Hackforth
Sgt J.H. Leetham RCAF
Sgt J.P. Fleming RCAF

The party was very inexperienced, with only Landels and the three flight commanders having flown operationally[15]. They were promptly transferred to an Army troopship, the Dutch vessel *Aoranji*[16], bound for Singapore, while 51 crated Hurricanes (see Appendix III) were aboard the cargo transport HMT *Sussex*, with the intended destination of Tjilatjap on Java's south coast. From there it was planned that the crated Hurricanes would be taken by road and rail to Batavia, where they would be assembled and then flown over to Singapore. In the event they were offloaded at Singapore. The convoy was codenamed *DM1* and departed Durban on Christmas Eve. Jerry Parker recalled:

> "Our convoy was now much reduced but still contained several troopships and cargo vessels laden with military equipment and artillery. We had no trouble crossing the Indian Ocean and passed through the Sunda Straits between Sumatra and Java, with Krakatoa on our left. Here we were joined by several Dutch warships and HMS *Exeter* escorting us for the next two days to Singapore. We were rarely out of sight of land and the brilliant green jungle and plantation country, washed with heavy showers behind the blue-green seas, appeared most attractive and inviting."

Their peace and tranquillity was soon to be shattered.

CHAPTER I

HURRICANES ARRIVE AT SINGAPORE

January 1942

> "We had a great thrill when we saw our first Hurricane overhead. And to see the squadron in the air was a sight for sore eyes. They are indeed sleek looking creatures – streamlined, speed personified."
>
> A New Zealand Buffalo pilot

Having been assured by their British commanders that Buffaloes were good enough for Singapore, the mainly Commonwealth pilots of these fighters soon found they were outperformed, once war had broken out, by both the Japanese Army Air Force's fixed-undercarriage but highly manoeuvrable Ki-27 and the more potent Ki-43, and also by the A6M of the Japanese Navy Air Force – known to the Allied pilots as the Navy 0 or Zero – when the latter appeared over Singapore, although it was often mistaken for the Army's Ki-43 Oscar[17]. The importance of sending quantities of modern fighter aircraft to Singapore was soon deemed paramount and Air Vice-Marshal C.W.H. Pulford CB OBE AFC[18], AOC Singapore and Commander of the RAF in the Far East, was greatly relieved when advised that Hurricane reinforcements were on their way from the United Kingdom, and were due to arrive by the second week of January 1942. It was the performance of the Japanese fighters, particularly the Ki-43 and the A6M, which had created the greatest initial impression. They could out-climb, outmanoeuvre and were much faster than the Buffalo, which had difficulty in reaching heights of over 27,000 feet. During their initial battles up country in December, the two RAAF Buffalo squadrons had been overwhelmed, a fate now being experienced by the two resident Singapore-based units, 243 and 488 Squadrons. Six Buffaloes were shot down on 12 January alone. Hurricane reinforcements were arriving in the nick of time.

Bad weather prevented a heavy raid by Japanese Navy bombers on Singapore during the morning of 13 January, just a single chutai (squadron) from the Kanoya Ku reaching Keppel Harbour. Another formation, comprising 27 G3Ms of the Mihoro Ku, was intercepted over Johore by Buffaloes from 488 Squadron but came under concentrated fire from the bombers' rear gunners, three being hit and forced down, one of which ditched in the sea. All three pilots survived, however. A fourth Buffalo ran out of fuel and its pilot baled out and he, too, survived. Fourteen more Buffaloes, from 21/453 Squadron, provided cover for the advance convoy, including the *Aorangi* and the *Sussex*, as it approached Singapore but did not make contact with the bombers that headed for other ships berthed in the Straits, as Plt Off Jerry Parker, one of the Hurricane pilots aboard the *Aorangi*, recalled:

> "Whilst we were being manoeuvred into Keppel Harbour there was an air raid alert, and I saw for the first time a formation of 27 Japanese bombers at about 15,000-20,000 feet. They kept very tight formation and bombed the *Empress of Britain* [sic] also in the harbour, but I did not hear of any casualties."

The 232 Squadron Adjutant, Flt Lt Norman Welch, was also travelling with this party:

> "The Squadron disembarked at Singapore narrowly escaping destruction in a determined bombing attack made on the convoy as it was entering harbour, but a severe tropical rainstorm saved the convoy."

Air Vice-Marshal Paul Maltby DSO AFC, Assistant AOC Singapore, in his subsequent report, wrote:

> "It is difficult to adequately convey the sense of tension which prevailed as these convoys approached Singapore, and the sense of exultation at their safe arrival. The feeling spread that at least the Japanese were going to be held on the ground if not driven back, whilst many confidently expected that the Hurricanes would sweep the Japanese from the sky. On their arrival they were immediately unloaded and the majority dispersed to previously selected concealed positions, where they were erected and wheeled to nearby a airfield for testing; the remainder proceeded direct to 151 MU for erection at other dispersal points. The speed with which these aircraft were erected was a very remarkable achievement.
>
> Twenty-four pilots arrived. When AHQ first heard of their diversion to the Far East, it had been planned to give the aircrew a [rest] spell before employing them in operations. This spell was obviously desirable, not only because of their time at sea, but also because of the need for acclimatising pilots to local conditions. However, events moved too fast and the stake was too high for delay to be acceptable. The Hurricanes had to be used immediately they had been erected and tested."[19]

The pilots were sent first of all to a transit camp in the rubber plantations to await the Hurricanes, which, still in their crates, were quickly offloaded and despatched to Seletar during the night. As the first batch arrived, however, a senior officer ordered the crates to be removed from the airfield. They were to be dispersed amongst the rubber trees to avoid being destroyed on the airfield by a bombing attack. Slowly the vehicles with their cumbersome loads turned around, only to run straight into the second convoy. The point of meeting was a narrow road with monsoon ditches either side, giving little room for the vehicles to manoeuvre. As there was a full moon any raider would have been presented with a most tempting target. However, fortunately for those on the ground, the moon was shrouded most of the night by clouds, from which heavy rain fell almost continuously. The convoy commanders and their men laboured all night in these appalling conditions and, by dawn, the heavy crates had been manhandled into relative security. When news of their arrival filtered through to the hard-pressed Buffalo pilots, all were elated. A Buffalo pilot wrote in his diary:

> "Hurricanes are being assembled at Seletar. I hope I get one. I am glad the Hurrybirds are almost ready because the Buffs can't cope with these Jap kites."

Next day he added:

> "We haven't seen any Hurricanes yet – I hope they hurry up. We have been having unusually bad weather lately, a thing we are to be very thankful for."

Within 48 hours the first Hurricanes were assembled and ready for air testing. This was a most notable achievement by the men of 151 Maintenance Unit, who received a special message of appreciation from the Chief-of-the-Air Staff for their efforts. Two of the crated Hurricanes were found to be damaged and were presumably used for spares. Soon Hurricanes were to be seen flying over the Island, an Australian flight lieutenant noting:

> "At the sight of those planes, morale sky-rocketed 100 per cent, and the sun shone again and the birds sang. That evening at all the nightspots the gay topic of conversation was Hurricanes. The miracle had happened. The Hurricanes were here and their world was saved."

American broadcaster Cecil Brown, one of the many correspondents and war reporters based at Singapore, agreed:

> "This afternoon six Hurricanes flew back and forth over Singapore. It was a sort of pep show for the people. They look good, and that means that now they have been assembled they will crack back at the Japs."[20]

Having listened to tales of woe from some of the Buffalo pilots they had come to help, Jerry Parker and others wondered if the Hurricanes would perform much better:

> "The Hurricanes were IIBs with the more powerful engine than we'd had at RAF Ouston, but their radios were the old, almost useless TR9Ds. Also they were equipped with heavy filters on the air intakes. It was a pity that they could not apparently be removed, except in one case of a plywood panel being fitted locally to replace that which in the main carried the filter. We never got a good performance from our Hurricanes in Singapore.'
>
> Another disability of our aircraft in terms of manoeuvrability was that they were equipped with 12 machine guns instead of eight. Although for marksmen of our calibre a congregation of machine guns was desirable, the extra four guns and their ammunition must have weighed at least half a ton. The Hurricanes became not only slow, particularly in the climb, but also very heavy and unwieldy in manoeuvre. However, we were most anxious to get amongst the formations of bombers which daily flew over Singapore. This did not prevent me – and the others, I suppose – from growing nervousness about the approaching series of battles, which must be fought out in the air."

With 21 Hurricanes assembled by 17 January, and currently being air-tested, 232 (Provisional) Squadron was almost ready to join the action. The Squadron was divided into three flights:

A Flight was based at Seletar under Flt Lt Hugh 'Penny' Farthing with the ex-17 Squadron pilots (Plt Off Sandy McCulloch and Sgts Ken Holmes, Mark Porter, Ron Dovell and the Australian Alan Coutie), plus Plt Off Jerry Parker and Sgt Geoff Hardie from the original 232 Squadron.

B Flight was also to operate from Seletar under Flt Lt Edwin Murray Taylor (a former flying instructor at 53 OTU) with the ex-136 Squadron pilots (Plt Offs Norman Williams and Rudolpho 'Dizzy' Mendizabal (of Canadian mother and Bolivian father), Sgts Sam 'Dean' Hackforth, Joe 'Jigs' Leetham and John Fleming, the two Canadians), plus Sgt Henry Nicholls and Plt Off Alphonso 'Tex' Marchbanks RCAF, the latter an American who had arrived a few days earlier at Singapore and was awaiting a posting.

C Flight settled in at Kallang, where the ex-135 Squadron pilots (Plt Offs Brian Daniel and Australians Plt Off John Gorton, Sgts Ian Fairbairn, and Geoff Schaffer, and Canadian Carl 'Swampy' Marsh) plus Sgts Charles 'Chris' Christian and Peter Lowe, were to be led by Flt Lt Mike Cooper-Slipper, who had won a DFC during the Battle of Britain.

It was however, another two days before the Squadron was ready for operations. CBS's Cecil Brown optimistically wrote:

> "Forty-eight[21] Hurricanes are almost ready to go up. They are getting the stiffness out of them now. The tragedy is that only one [*sic*] of those Hurricane pilots has had combat experience. This one has had five hours in combat. But all the pilots are very confident. These Hurricanes will enable the British to change their tactics and go directly after the bombers. Some of the Hurricane boys tell me they're convinced not a single Jap bomber will get back."[22]

The services of one of these Hurricanes (BG828) was immediately lost when Jerry

Parker narrowly missed colliding with a large truck:

> "During the evening I took up one of the Hurricanes for testing and while I was airborne was told to hunt for a Jap reconnaissance plane. I didn't find him and came into land at Seletar down a short runway, which had been added to the airfield by carving a long strip from the surrounding rubber plantations and jungle. I was just on the point of touching down when, out of the trees on my left, and ahead, appeared a large truck filled with coal. Peering round the side of the engine I could only kick on port rudder and hope to ease round the back of the truck. It wouldn't be possible to lift the plane over it. There was a sickening swing to the left and the nose and the starboard wing reared, although I had evidently missed the truck. However, the port wing smashed down at such an angle that it hit the ground before the undercart did, and the plane ground-looped with the port undercarriage leg buckling under the strain. I never did discover why the coal truck should have appeared at that moment but there was no criticism of me after all the evidence had been taken – a great relief. I suspect there might have been something behind it as there was a very strong atmosphere in Singapore about the activities of Japanese intelligence, not unfounded, and we were not allowed to wear our pilots' brevets. I'm not sure whether this was to avoid assassination in dark alleys, or to hide the fact of our being here."

Assembled pilots of A and B Flights at Seletar were informed that a dozen Hurricanes would be ready for action on the morning of 20 January, and what was expected from them. As noted by Parker:

> "Jock [Landels] told us we would be on standby and explained his tactics. These seemed to be that we should go off in three flights of four aircraft and take the bombers in beam attacks, breaking downwards and returning to attack in individual sections. Aircraft should not attack in formation for fear of collision but should space their attacks to ensure a free field of fire. This seemed simple, straightforward and the best that could be hoped for in view of our ignorance (and Singapore Air HQ's) of the armament and vulnerability of the Japanese aircraft. I was to be Jock's No.2.
>
> I just did not know how I would react in combat although I comforted myself with the knowledge that I was spiritually and mentally prepared to die and that, since I was protected in front by the hulk of the engine and windscreen of armoured glass, and in the rear by armoured plate, the chances were that I would live. Even so, I had far more upon which to support my optimism and resolution – my Catholic faith and 130 Hurricane flying hours – than did the rest of the pilots except those originally from 232 Squadron. Some of the others had less than 20 hours on Spitfires and none on Hurricanes!
>
> Dovell, Porter and Holmes were the only sergeants who registered with me. Dovell was a well-balanced young fellow, steady and thoughtful, although no more experienced than the other two. Porter and Holmes had very little opportunity to gain experience on the Hurricanes before being put into combat. They were very decent fellows."

A Buffalo pilot wrote in his diary:

> "We tried to bolster up the courage of the Hurricane boys today, with the result that they suggested they look after the bombers and we take on the fighters – maybe! Tomorrow will be a big day and here's hoping I live through it."

CHAPTER II

HURRICANES INTO ACTION

20-29 January 1942

"The RAF Hurricane pilots fought gallantly and courageously against overwhelming odds and during their brief period of operation in Malaya they scored several brilliant victories and shot down many Japs. But they too took the knock."

An RAAF Buffalo pilot

20 January 1942

As predicted, this day was to see the heaviest raid yet on Singapore, a force of about 80 bombers approaching just before 0900, having been preceded by the daily early morning reconnaissance aircraft, as noted by Cecil Brown:

"At 8.30 this morning the anti-aircraft began firing in the distance rather heavily, even rattling the house. Evidently it was a reconnaissance plane. I finished shaving. Then about 8.40 the siren and a few minutes later the all-clear."[23]

The crews of the Ki-21s of the 12th and 60th Sentais had been briefed to raid Seletar, while 26 Mihoro Ku G3Ms were to attack Sembawang and 18 G3Ms of the Genzan Ku had Singapore and the harbour as their target. 64th Sentai's Ki-43s provided cover for the Ki-21s, while 18 A6Ms escorted the Navy bombers, and two C5Ms accompanied the force to observe results. Brown continued:

"Then at 8.50 I saw 18 Japanese bombers in formation against the blue sky, up about 8,000 feet, going toward the Naval base. I saw six Hurricanes take off, going in the opposite direction. Then came the bombs. It was like a heavy broom sweeping the ground as stick after stick was sent into the base. The ack-ack fire seemed very good and it hit right where the bombers were, but the firing seemed to be too low. Then the second wave of 33 came over. I didn't see them, but they went right over Singapore and dropped their bombs smack in the centre of the town. They made a noise like crushing a matchbox in your hands."[24]

Despite the magnitude of the attacking force, there was a hint of optimism that morning, as at Seletar the Hurricanes were ready to go into action and great things were expected of them. Singapore's Chief Surveyor Tom Kitching, who was on roof-spotting duty, noted:

"I rushed up to the roof and soon saw 18 Japs in formation, but they were not heading in our direction. There was a lot of anti-aircraft fire – some close – but the Jap planes were over 20,000 feet up. Then six Hurricanes came right over the Fullerton Building [headquarters of the Survey Department and other Government offices]. We watched them and a little Buffalo struggling up, when, suddenly, 27 Japs came right out of the cloud overhead. We gave the alarm and beat it off the roof and, almost immediately, a salvo of bombs dropped."[25]

A Flight's Jerry Parker:

"We were in our cockpits with the engines running before the scramble order came through, and away we went in good time, Jock, of course, being the only one ahead of me. We climbed fairly slowly through intermittent cloud, which seemed to extend well above our maximum ceiling. We maintained radio silence, so it was difficult to organise our formation properly. The novices tended to fly too close, which meant that they spent too much time on checking their relative positions and not enough on looking for the enemy – particularly above and behind; when they were warned and waved further away they generally went too far and its was difficult to keep them from being cut off in cloud.

Instructions were coming through on the radio, which Jock would acknowledge and we were at 28,000 feet when the Ground Controller said: '80-plus bandits below you at Angels 15 and 20.' I understood from this that there would probably be three formations of about 27 bombers between 15,000 and 20,000 feet. Jock immediately acknowledged by shouting 'Tally-ho!' and peeled off to starboard in front of me in quite a steep but not vertical dive. I checked in order not to risk ramming him and, of course, followed him down but could get no closer than about 500 yards behind. He had left his transmitter on – which meant that he could receive no radio messages – and so did not hear the controller add: 'Navigate with caution! Other bandits believed to be fighters at Angels 22!'"

The warning was correct: the 64th Sentai pilots had seen the Hurricanes diving after the bombers and now climbed to intercept them. The Hurricanes continued to stream down through the clouds, when suddenly Parker saw a fighter appear on Landels' tail:

"It took a fraction of a moment for me to realise that this fighter with the snub nose, light brown camouflage and big red discs painted on its wings was a Jap. The enemy! Out of the steep dive I hauled back as hard as I could after the Jap, which was pulling out of a dive and climbing into the sun. I came nowhere near to getting him into my sights before I blacked out for a few moments, and I eased the pressure on the stick to straighten the Hurricane in its climb. The strain had been immense and several more moments passed until suddenly my sight came back and I found myself blinded by the sun, the stick no longer rigid and wilful, but sloppy.

The aircraft stalled, flicked over to port and spun. I closed the throttle, centred the controls and to my surprised relief, the Hurricane immediately eased itself out of the spin into an almost vertical dive. I swung it into a diving turn to check my tail and found two Japs coming down some way above, and one was firing. In a panic I turned further to the nearest cloud some thousands of feet below. At that moment a Hurricane streaked ahead from under my nose, closely pursued by a Jap, both of them streaming vapour from their wingtips. The Hurricane kept straight ahead in a slight dive, but I forgot him and the two Japs on my tail as I fell into place about 600 yards behind the pursuing Jap, and rapidly overhauled him. He evidently didn't see me and pulled up into a gentle climbing turn as I came into range, still slightly above him.

Although I had never fired more than two machine guns before and had little idea of what to expect would happen, I followed the drill I'd been taught, laid off sufficient deflection for the speeding bullets to meet the speeding aeroplane, pressed the button and followed the Jap round and up into his turn. The clatter was tremendous, even to my muffled ears and above the racket of the engine, and I found it frightening that my pressing the 'tit' should release as much malevolence. I could see my bullets in the air and was surprised when a myriad of golden flashes appeared sparkling on the nose of the enemy aircraft between the cockpit and the airscrew. The machine turned more sharply to starboard and steeply beneath me and dived away whilst I, suddenly aware of my own pursuers still firing, continued my own swoop into the nearest cloud to starboard. I came out the other side very quickly, circled round just under the cloud and waited for developments. None occurred and I realised I ought to be back up at 20,000 feet, whereas I was then down to around 7,000 feet. Thereupon, I started climbing, calling Seletar at the same time for the height and direction I should be following. Nothing came through and I saw no other aircraft, so I came down again below the cloud level to about 3,000 feet, well up the east coast of Malaya, and cruised back to Singapore."

There seems little doubt that Parker had shot down Lt Yoshio Hatta, who was seen by other Japanese pilots to crash into the sea immediately after shooting down a Hurricane himself. The crew of a Naval patrol boat also confirmed seeing a Japanese fighter dive vertically into sea in the area of the battle. Hatta's victim – the Hurricane Parker had seen diving ahead of him – was that flown by Sqn Ldr Landels. It was believed that he had been fatally wounded during the attack and his aircraft (BM906) struck the mast of a Chinese fishing vessel before crashing into the sea.

Meanwhile, the other Hurricanes were having mixed fortunes. Flt Lt Murray Taylor's section swept down on a formation of 27 Ki-21s flying in their usual three vics of nine; they claimed eight of these shot down, plus three more probably destroyed. Murray Taylor personally claimed two, as did Sgts Hardie, Hackforth and Leetham, the three sergeants also each claiming probables. Despite the assault, the bombers continued to their target – Seletar – but failed to cause much material damage on this occasion.

Following the attack on the bombers, the Hurricanes tangled with the 64th Sentai Ki-43s in numerous dogfights, during which two of the latter were claimed shot down by Sgts Nicholls and Dovell. Dovell was a 21-year-old from Willesden, North London[26]. However, two more of the Hurricanes were lost. Plt Off Marchbanks, the newly joined American, was seen to chase after the departing bombers but he was shot down in flames and killed, his aircraft (BG848) crashing some 20 miles north of Kuala Lumpur. The second Hurricane (BG818) also fell in flames, crashing into the sea after Plt Off Norman Williams had baled out, severely burned. He was pulled out of the water by native fishermen, who took him to a nearby island and sent a message to Singapore, following which an ASR launch picked him up and returned him to the Island. He was then transferred to hospital for urgent treatment to his injuries[27].

The 64th Sentai claimed five Hurricanes shot down during this fight, one of these being credited to Major Tateo Kato, the Sentai Commander (his ninth victory, seven of which had been claimed in China) and one to the missing Lt Hatta. Apart from the loss of the latter, two other Ki-43s failed to return and both Lt Takashi Takeyama and Sgt Maj Junki Saito were reported missing. Thus, honours were even in this first clash between Hurricanes and Ki-43s – three of each had been shot down. Despite the claims against the bombers, no other losses appear to have been recorded by the 7th Flying Battalion on this occasion[28]. The Genzan bombers – unhindered by attack – claimed one ship sunk in Keppel Harbour, while the Mihoro unit claimed four aircraft and a hangar destroyed at Kallang. Here, the MVAF suffered heavily, losing two aircraft, both of which were burnt out, whilst two other aircraft were damaged beyond repair. A number of C Flight Hurricanes at Kallang were damaged in a second raid half an hour later, when bombs also fell near Government House. During the course of these raids, Singapore City suffered heavily, at least 383 civilians losing their lives, with over 700 injured; there were now an estimated 150 funerals a day, although many Chinese and Malays in downtown Singapore simply disappeared without trace under the ruins of demolished buildings.

Following the loss of Sqn Ldr Landels, Flt Lt Penny Farthing assumed temporary command of the Squadron until Sqn Ldr Peter Brooker DFC[29] arrived from Air HQ to take over. Brooker, a Battle of Britain veteran, had been posted to Singapore to help set up the Operations Room, but now found himself back in action. Jerry Parker:

> "Sqn Ldr Brooker was a regular RAF officer. He was a really determined and self-assured man, humourless, and held himself under tight control. His height was less than average; his stature rather slight yet the set of his jaw and his direct stare compelled attention. I

admired him and modelled myself upon him as much as possible from the moment he took control of 232 Squadron."

To even up the sections following the losses, Plt Off Daniel was posted from B Flight to A Flight[30].

21 January

The JNAF was again over the Island in force: 25 G3Ms from the Mihoro Ku, 27 G4Ms from the Kanoya Ku, together with nine escorting A6Ms from 22nd Air Flotilla Fighter Group undertaking the raid. A single C5M accompanied them. Ki-21s and Ki-48s of the JAAF's 7th Flying Battalion also raided in strength, escorted by Ki-43s from the 64th Sentai. The Mihoro bombers struck at Keppel Harbour, claiming one merchant ship sunk and one damaged, but were then attacked by fighters identified as 'Spitfires', claiming one of these shot down. On the return journey the bomber crews reported that eight Buffaloes attacked, and one of these was also claimed. One Ki-43 failed to return with the loss of Sgt Maj HideoTatsumi, apparently the victim of the Buffaloes, whose pilots claimed two Zeros shot down and a third probably destroyed.

Meanwhile, the Kanoya Ku bombers raided Tengah, claiming 13 bombers destroyed on the ground. A Flight had only three Hurricanes serviceable at Seletar, but these scrambled – flown by Flt Lt Farthing, Plt Offs Daniel and Parker – to intercept one of the incoming bomber formations. Jerry Parker:

"Sqn Ldr Brooker was heavily engaged in taking over the Squadron and handing over his Control Room duties, so Farthing and I and the other Pilot Officer [Daniel] in A Flight set off to intercept a bomber formation in the only three aircraft the Flight had left. The Control Room was working well and we climbed as fast as possible, for Penny was a hell-for-leather type, who pushed the throttle through the gate and did not consider the quandary of a pilot with a less efficient aircraft than his own.

On this occasion, mine quickly ran up a temperature well above the safety limit and the airscrew was leaking oil. I did not like to turn back as I hoped to get amongst the bombers, but I liked straggling around the cloudless sky by myself much less, particularly when there could be many Japanese fighters about. When we'd reached about 12,000 feet and the others were a mile ahead, I reluctantly turned back to Singapore in the south. A few minutes later, as I was looking up and back to check my tail, I spotted a very large formation of Jap bombers high overhead. I hoped that Penny and his mate would get amongst them and, at that moment, spotted the two duck-egg blue Hurricanes following one another across the deep blue sky in a beam attack.

The heavy ack-ack fire was also in operation but there were so few guns and the shells exploded over such a great range of heights that their chance of hitting a bomber, or one of the fighters, was quite remote. Just before the fighters appeared to reach it, the whole formation was enveloped in an enormous and momentary flash of flame. It was as though a cubic mile of air space had been filled with petrol vapour and ignited. For a fraction of a second I could see no aircraft at all except the second Hurricane, then all appeared as before, out of an enormous cloud of black smoke, except that the first Hurricane was racing through the formation. One of the bombers had completely disappeared and two of the others were starting flaming dives. The second Hurricane also went across the formation and another bomber started streaming smoke and dropped back."

Soon after Parker landed, Farthing came in with a badly overheated engine. An inspection found a large piece of debris had been blown through his airscrew and into his radiator, apparently from the exploding bomber. Of the action, Farthing related his experience to a correspondent:

"There were about 30 of them flying a few thousand feet above us, and another lot higher still. We went in against the first batch on a beam attack, selecting a formation of three. I picked one and gave him a fairly long burst, and travelled ahead of him a few hundred yards. There was a terrific explosion behind me, and as I turned back I saw there was a big gap in the enemy formation. I actually flew through a wall of smoke and burning machine debris.

I turned on to another of the enemy and gave him a squirt of fire. He went down in a dive after a piece of the tailplane had broken away, followed by bits and pieces of engine. By then my machine was giving me trouble and I had to land. When I landed it was found that the engine intake was full of bits and pieces of Japanese aircraft, presumably from the first victim which blew up in the air."[31]

Plt Off Daniel verified his leader's report and was of the opinion that the first bomber's bomb load had exploded, which he believed destroyed two others flying close behind. Farthing was thus credited with two destroyed and one probable, whilst Daniel claimed another. There were other claimants for this success, however, the gun crew aboard the RAN sloop HMAS *Vendetta*, positioned in Keppel Harbour, was also in action against the raiders. The sloop's gunner claimed a direct hit on the leading bomber, which he reported blew up and damaged the aircraft on either side. The American reporter Cecil Brown also thought guns were responsible for the bombers' demise:

"The Japs were over again today in considerable strength, bombing indiscriminately. Five bombs were dropped on the *padang* in front of the Cricket Club and blew out the windows of the Supreme Court. Thirteen [*sic*] Jap planes were reported brought down in the raid, nine of them by ack-ack fire. I saw three of those planes destroyed over Singapore. One ack-ack shell scored a direct hit on a bomber. It immediately exploded and two planes beside it also disintegrated in the air. It was a beautiful sight. In an instant three Japanese aircraft disappeared into nothingness."[32]

Despite these reports, it seems clear from more knowledgeable witnesses that the bombers were at a level above that which the AA guns could reach. Amongst those witnessing the action from ground level was an RAAF Hudson pilot who suddenly found himself on the receiving end of the Kanoya Ku's bombing attack:

"They [the first formation of 27 bombers] had just passed us in perfect formation, as usual, and safely above the puffs of gunfire, when a lonely Hurricane made an attack, diving straight through the throng. We actually heard his guns, and then saw a flash of an explosion within the bomber group. We could see the flaming debris falling down and a hole in the middle of the formation. It seemed to me that two aircraft had been destroyed and I was standing above the slit trench trying to count the formation as they continued on towards the town..."[33]

Japanese sources reported that two fighters made a pass which caused 2/C Baijiro Kogoshi's G3M to blow up; this was the only loss recorded, although it seems probable that at least one other force-landed.

Bombs rained down on Tengah airfield. The ground shook violently as bombs exploded simultaneously, one trench taking a direct hit, where three airmen were killed and a further eight injured. The Operations Room was hit, while a powerhouse, the M/T yard, station armoury, workshops and cinema were all damaged. One Hudson was totally destroyed, a second seriously damaged and two others peppered by shrapnel and debris. Two Blenheims were also destroyed and one more damaged. At least 300 civilians were killed during the day's raids and a further 600 injured.

Sqn Ldr Brooker decided to lead the next patrol, selecting Plt Off Parker as his No.2, with Plt Off John Gorton leading a second section with Sgt Peter Lowe. Apparently unbeknown to the four Hurricane pilots, they had been spotted by patrolling Buffaloes, but were recognised before an error occurred. Parker recalled:

"Eventually I saw a Jap twin-engined aircraft pass across our flight about 1,000 feet below us and I was astonished when Brooker took no action. It transpired he had just not seen it. A few minutes later, when I was wondering if we ought not to be going back to Singapore as I turned on to my reserve petrol tank, I saw half a dozen fighters not much below us and climbing to intercept. I tried unsuccessfully to radio Brooker and then pulled alongside him and pointed to them. They were in the usual loose trailing formation used by Japanese fighters and Brooker immediately went for the leader. I was a bit astonished at this but I had allowed some distance between us so that, when as inevitably happened, the second Jap followed him, I was in position to latch on to his tail.

The first one turned smartly to port and we all four followed because I also had a Zero behind me. Gorton's section and the other Japs stayed out of this tangle and I concentrated on aiming at the one ahead of me. Brooker must have realised the mess we were in because, just as I saw my shots hitting my target's tail, he led out of the ring in a steep dive. I broke away too and Gorton's section joined us from above so the Japs were left in command of the upper air level. My radio gave me no help at all and I fervently hoped his aircraft was better equipped, as I had no idea of our whereabouts and I was determined to stay with him. I had eyes only for his cockpit a few feet away as we dived through the rain and cloud, now grey and all around us. We were still coming down at an angle of about thirty degrees when we broke clear hardly a hundred feet above the sea. Brooker pulled smartly up to the horizontal immediately and I kept with him but almost simultaneously he swung into a tight vertical turn and, as I braced myself to resist the centrifugal force, an island sloping from the sea into the clouds raced by frighteningly close past our wingtips. There was no sign of John Gorton – or his wingman.

We cruised back to Singapore a few minutes later with the cloud level still down to 200 feet and prepared to land. The bomb craters had been filled in and Brooker landed safely. I would have gone in just behind him but I was unable to move the lever into the 'undercarriage down' position. I circled the airfield twice, hitting the knob with my gloved hand and getting no response. The same lever actuated the flaps and I raised and lowered them a couple of times but still could not move the lever to put the wheels down. The red light, indicating that the reserve petrol tank was empty, was flickering on so that at any moment I would be caught at a very low altitude without any power and the Hurricane would stall straight in. Curtains! I had no option but to put the flaps down, disregard the hooting in my earphones warning me of the wheels being up and land as gently as possible. I did all my usual preparations, switched off the engine and stopped the airscrew just before I came over the airfield boundary and slid the aircraft to a stop on the grass. The damage was inconsiderable to the flaps and wings and radiator; the airscrew and engine were untouched.

Brooker was furious – not less so because, when I tried to show him and the groundcrew how the lever had stuck, it slid easily into position. He had wanted me to unstrap myself in the cockpit, stand up on the seat and kick the lever with the heel of my boot but he soon realised that that could have been suicidal at that altitude and with no petrol left. I think he was feeling guilty about the loss of Gorton's section and at not having returned to Seletar with more fuel in reserve. He appreciated that a formation leader generally used less petrol than a follower since he would not be constantly changing his throttle setting to maintain station. He cooled off finally and agreed that I'd taken the correct action. Then I asked him about the Jap aircraft I'd seen and not attacked

> and about his tactics in our small engagement. Quite evidently something was wrong with his eyesight as he'd not seen the recce plane, and until we were involved with them, most of the fighters. This was a bit alarming and I determined to be more specific in future when sighting bandits."

The Hurricanes had apparently been attacked by Ki-43s from the 64th Sentai, whose pilots claimed six victories during the day, for when Plt Off Gorton, in BE633, emerged from cloud he found himself immediately engaged in a dogfight:

> "... my aircraft came down. It probably had bullets in it or something like that, but at any rate it wouldn't work. So I saw this place where I could come down and land and when I got very, very, very close to the ground I saw that it had some walls built between the tanks, petrol tanks which were stationed up and across. It was a tank farm (on Bintan Island, about 30 miles south-east of Singapore). I saw these walls but I couldn't do anything about it. I should have pulled the wheels up but I didn't because I tried to land so we could save the aircraft and get it out. The wheels hit and it turned over and flopped. I got my face all smashed in and everything like that. I remember thinking I had to get out of the plane, and opening the canopy and putting a hand down and getting out and standing up. A fellow from some island was there with a lot of Indonesian troops. They were shooting at me and he stopped them. Then I just fell over because I had lost so much blood. They took me to a man there who had some sort of plantation. He looked after me as well as he could."[34]

Gorton had suffered appalling injuries to his face, which included a badly smashed nose, fractured cheekbones and seriously lacerated forehead, while his cut arms were bleeding profusely. A message was sent to Singapore. In the meantime a Moth of the MVAF had been despatched from Kallang to search for the missing aircraft, the pilot eventually spotting Gorton's overturned Hurricane on the beach at Bintan. Sometime later an RAF-manned launch arrived, but when the sergeant in charge saw the unconscious and severely injured Gorton, he declined to take him aboard as he considered he would be dead within a very short time. They took his wallet, watch and pay book and returned to Singapore. Within a few days, however, Gorton made a surprisingly rapid recovery from his more superficial wounds and was subsequently rescued. It was assumed that Sgt Peter Lowe's Hurricane (BE577) had been shot down into the sea; the 21-year-old from Guiseley in Yorkshire was posted missing.

Another Hurricane was damaged when Sgt Hackforth belly-landed BG864 at Seletar, having been unable to lower its undercarriage. He was not injured although the aircraft was badly damaged.

22 January

Singapore was again visited by the JNAF, when 25 Genzan Ku G3Ms and 27 Kanoya Ku G4Ms, with nine A6Ms and two C5Ms from the Fighter Group appeared overhead during the late morning. LAC Max Boyd, a New Zealand mechanic with 488 Squadron, wrote in his diary:

> "Hell on earth today. At 1130 a huge mass of bombers were seen rapidly approaching Kallang. No alarm had been sounded. Operations muffed things properly. Detectors should have picked up the Japanese marauders at 80 miles away. The 'brass hats' got tangled up in their own red tape, the dunderheads, and forgot the alarm. They admitted afterwards that it was awful blunder. Two of our own men were killed. A lot of direct hits, both large and small, were made on the aerodrome. Hangar and airport are totally wrecked, as well as several buildings on and off the drome, especially Geylong on the

> edge of the town. The Happy World Cabaret and an adjoining house of iniquity and degradation was wrecked, a dash good job, too. In places there were huge craters up to 50 feet across and very deep. There are lots of unexploded bombs around dispersal areas and we just have to take chances when going about our duty. Chaps in 232 Squadron fired revolvers at random and some of the bullets shot over our way. We soon stopped that."

The G3Ms attacked Kallang just as four Buffaloes were taxiing for take-off. Three got off, but one was destroyed by the explosion of a bomb nearby which blew it into a petrol dump. The pilot, who was picked up unconscious and seriously injured, died in hospital three days later. Two groundcrew airmen were killed instantly at their posts. A Buffalo pilot, sheltering in a trench, witnessed the whole affair, and recorded in his diary:

> "To my mind they [the groundcrews] are the heroic boys because it is bad enough – terrifying, in fact – to be in a decent sort of shelter where you are really very safe, but to be out in the open with the exceeding likelihood of bombs landing in the close vicinity, and then do your job, is deserving of very high praise."

Meanwhile, Sqn Ldr Brooker had led ten Hurricanes from Seletar into the air at 1055 in anticipation of the raid, and these were vectored onto the three streams of bombers. As the Hurricanes closed on the bombers, they were joined by more aircraft from C Flight, led by Flt Lt Cooper-Slipper, who saw one bomber spiral down in flames, apparently the victim of Murray Taylor's opening attack; NAP 1/C Tadashi Hino and his crew were killed. Closing in, Cooper-Slipper opened fire on another bomber, hitting its port engine, which caught fire, and it turned over and lost height. Throttling back, he turned into another vic of bombers, causing a second to break away in flames. He then came under heavy crossfire and his aircraft was hit many times, some bullets striking the engine and three hitting the airscrew; he broke away and despite the damage to his machine, landed safely at Kallang.

Sgt Hackforth reported that both bombers he attacked fell out of formation, one blazing furiously and the other smoking heavily, while Sgt Hardie's targets – a vic of three – were attacked from 100 yards range; he reported that the leader broke out of formation with the fuselage on fire, whilst the port aircraft was hit in the starboard engine and fell away with smoke pouring from it. Hackforth was credited with two destroyed and Hardie with one destroyed and one probable. As he turned away, Hardie noted two other bombers going down in flames. The Hurricane flown by Plt Off Mendizabal was hit almost at once by crossfire, two bullets superficially wounding him in the legs, but he continued to attack. Selecting one bomber, he saw it fall away to earth streaming smoke; he then concerned himself with getting his damaged aircraft (BM903) back to base. Apart from the loss of Hino's aircraft, one badly damaged G3M ditched off Endau on the return flight, and another force-landed south of Kuantan with two dead and one slightly wounded amongst the crew. Here it was found two days later by Japanese forces.

Others enjoyed less success, as, after the initial attack during which several bombers were claimed damaged, they not only came under heavy crossfire, but also were bounced by the escorting A6Ms with deadly effect. Sgt Holmes (BG860) attacked two bombers from the port beam, reporting that both dropped from formation and were seen heading down towards the sea trailing smoke. He then flew under the main formation and pulled up on their starboard side for a second attack but, at this moment, crossfire caught him, hitting the Hurricane repeatedly and shooting away most of the fabric covering the fuselage from behind the cockpit to the tail. As he pulled away, three fighters attacked but he managed to shake these off by diving to sea level, landing safely at Seletar despite the damage to his aircraft. During the run-in Jerry Parker spotted what he believed to be four Buffaloes coming in from above and astern of the bombers:

"I thought that this was pretty silly of the Buffs as they would be far easier targets for the rear-facing Jap gunners, who could bring every gun to bear on them, than we were but, on the other hand, they would be diverting much and perhaps all of the defensive fire from us. Good for them!

The bombers were big, twin-engined ones like Heinkel 111s but with long glasshouses on the fuselage. The polished glass flashed in the sun but I saw no machine guns firing from the one I attacked. I gave him a long burst but with insufficient deflection so I saw my shots hitting the rear of the fuselage and the tail. At the back of my mind was the consideration of Brooker to port, also pulling round in his attack, so that if I pulled too tightly I might run either into him or into his line of fire. Then I saw him quite clearly out of the corner of my eye as we naturally followed towards the stern of the bombers and I was about to correct my deflection to aim at the wing roots of my target when there was a violent thump on my armour-plate and a clang in my ears like a gong.

A quick incredulous glance in my rear-view minor showed me a Buffalo [sic] – there was no mistaking the stubby wings extending through the mid-section of the barrel-like fuselage – with his guns flashing directly behind me. I had no doubt he was aiming at me and not at the bombers and I smartly dived away. I didn't think to climb up and investigate from a superior height but wondered what was going on. I was scared silly, my radio had been shattered and I didn't know what else had been hit. The Hurricane went down in a vertical dive and the airspeed indicator passed 400mph at 15,000 feet and I could see nothing chasing me. I tried to pull out at 12,000 feet, recovering my courage, but not until I'd reached 8,000 feet did I manage to level out by straining on the almost unmoveable stick and winding back the tail trim, really designed to ease the feel of the stick in long flights and not to be abused as an aerobatic flying aid. I pulled up in a long climb, weaving and searching the sky above but I could neither see nor catch the bomber formation, so soon afterwards I returned to Seletar."

The A6Ms hit the rest of the Squadron hard: 23-year-old Flt Lt Penny Farthing from Berkhamsted (flying BG796) and his No.2, Plt Off Brian Daniel (BG804) of A Flight were shot down and killed, although it seems that another pilot reported that Farthing was seen to shoot down a fighter before his demise. Both Sgt Hardie (BG810) and Sgt Hackforth (BG720) of B Flight were hit and baled out into the sea, but the Canadian Sgt Jigs Leetham (BE579), a 23-year-old from Cobourg, was killed. Only Sgt Nicholls was able to hit back, claiming one of the fighters destroyed. Both Hackforth and Hardie survived to be picked up by ASR launches, the former with a badly bruised knee and the latter with a strained back. As a result of his enforced swim, Hardie also contracted 'Singapore ear', an infection caused by polluted water, thus he became medically unfit for further operational flying – an additional loss to the Squadron.

The 22nd Air Flotilla fighter pilots claimed eight 'Spitfires' shot down in this fight, but lost two of their number although both pilots survived (presumably the victims of Farthing and Nicholls), while the bomber gunners claimed five more – clearly an element of double-claiming against Hurricanes fired on by both. The bomber crews also claimed 20 aircraft destroyed on the ground at Kallang. The Genzan Ku G4Ms had attacked Sembawang where the crews claimed 15 more aircraft destroyed on the ground, out of about 20 seen. Actual losses were two Dutch Glenn Martins destroyed, with two others and four Hudsons damaged.

Jerry Parker subsequently reported to Sqn Ldr Brooker his belief that Buffaloes had attacked him:

"Brooker was most puzzled about the Buffaloes, which he hadn't seen, and checked whether any Buffalo squadrons from Sembawang or Tengah had been in the air. The hard core of the armour-piercing bullet, which had passed through my radio and struck my

> armour-plate, was found in the fuselage and the armament officers from HQ confirmed that no Singapore-based aircraft were using that type of ammunition. It seemed fairly conclusive that the Japs were using Buffaloes which they'd captured either from the Chinese or from the British airfields which they'd overrun up country."

This was, in fact, not the case. Clearly the head-on appearance of the A6Ms had not been familiar to him. He continued:

> "We were still only halfway through the morning and Brooker went off to Air HQ to investigate the puzzle of the Buffaloes and to receive some new orders. B Flight went off on patrol and we were stood down on reserve, although at full readiness. Although I was the youngest pilot in the Squadron – still known as Sprog – I seemed to have a talent for survival and Porter and Holmes embarrassed me by preferring my views to those of my elders and betters."

One of the Buffalo pilots wrote:

> "The RAF boys flying them [the Hurricanes] began to mix it with the Zeros which we knew was practically impossible. The Zero was just about the nippiest, most highly manoeuvrable fighter in the world. They buzzed around the Hurricanes like vicious bees. The RAF Hurricane pilots fought gallantly and courageously against overwhelming odds and during their brief period of operation in Malaya they scored several brilliant victories and shot down many Japs. But they too took the knock."

The Hurricanes had certainly 'taken the knock' in the three days they had been operational, during which a dozen Hurricanes had been lost with six pilots missing presumed killed, two badly injured, one slightly injured and another out of commission. It had been a disastrous start for the Hurricanes and their losses demoralised not only the other pilots but ground personnel and all those who were aware of the casualties. During the day's raids in excess of 200 civilian casualties were reported, of which almost 60 were fatal. LAC Max Boyd summed up the day's actions in his diary:

> "488 Squadron now has only three Buffaloes left out of the 26 it operated. Only one is still serviceable. Sqn Ldr Clouston [the CO] is being transferred to Headquarters. Flt Lt Mackenzie is to be our new CO. 488 Squadron is to be equipped with Hurricanes. 232 Squadron badly mauled and lost four Hurricanes today in action, and another sideslipped on landing and crashed. Eight Japs were shot down."

23 January

Over Singapore, C Flight Hurricanes were scrambled from Kallang to intercept the morning raid and were joined by others from A Flight from Seletar, becoming involved with the escorting fighters of the 64th Sentai. At 15,000 feet, Sgt Geoff Schaffer dogfought a Ki-43, which he believed he shot down before his own aircraft (BG846) was hit by another. With his aircraft on fire he baled out, landing near Kallang, the Hurricane crashing nearby. Schaffer was picked up and taken to Alexandra Hospital suffering from burns and shock. Another Australian pilot, Sgt Ian Fairbairn, also came under attack, nursing BE588 back to Kallang with damage to the oil cooler, tailwheel and fuselage:

> "The radiator was hit and fine spray was coming into the cockpit. I realised it wasn't petrol, so I could ride it down. As I came into Kallang with a dead motor and stopped prop, I got a red light from the control tower – and remember thinking it was a bit rude in the circumstances! Pretty soon, though, they gave me a green light – they must have realised that I didn't have a lot of options."

Some of the A Flight Hurricanes managed to intercept the bombers – 27 Ki-21s from the 12th Sentai – Sgt Swampy Marsh claiming one shot down. On this occasion the bombers' gunners optimistically claimed no fewer than eight attacking fighters shot down, with three more as probables. In the event, the interception of the bomber force did not prevent the Ki-21s from plastering Seletar, where a Walrus, a Swordfish and a Hudson were destroyed, plus seven other aircraft damaged. Chief Surveyor Tom Kitching noted in his diary:

> "My chief clerk says Geylong got it heavily today, but there were not many casualties … the Singapore Cricket Club has half a car in the billiard room and eight bomb craters in the *padang*, all within 200 yards, but the club is practically unscathed."[35]

During the afternoon Flt Lt Cooper-Slipper led two sections of Hurricanes to patrol over an incoming convoy, one section meeting Japanese fighters. Plt Off Sandy McCulloch, with Sgt Fairbairn as his No.2, became involved in a series of dogfights; McCulloch claiming one shot down and Fairbairn a probable before they managed to extricate themselves from the action. The two pilots were now beset by fuel shortage so they headed for Singapore, running into heavy cloud and rain, which split them up again. They once more came under attack, McCulloch being shot down into the sea just short of Kallang; he managed to bale out of BM898 and was picked up by some natives from a nearby island, from where an ASR launch returned him to Singapore. Fairbairn's aircraft was by now out of fuel and he force-landed BE639 on Pulau Blakang Mati, a small island off the south coast of Singapore, sustaining minor cuts and bruises. He took the ferryboat across to Singapore and was then driven back to Kallang.

24 January

During the morning five Hurricanes and six Buffaloes were ordered off to intercept enemy aircraft reported attacking troops in the Ayer Hitam area. Parker, whose rest day it was, wrote:

> "I hung around the Flight Office chatting with the clerk and the groundcrew until the scramble came through and the aircraft went off together to the south, to gain information, listen to sighting reports and to gain height before turning north to intercept. The roar of the combined engines and the speed with which the aircraft accelerated across the field together was heartening in the feeling of confidence they aroused in the breast of the onlooker. However, as they disappeared into the distance I realised only too rapidly how deceptive was the appearance of strength. I had already established for myself – and Brooker too, although he didn't mention it – that it was imperative to climb to the south to avoid any formations of Zeros before we were in a position to dive upon them. We believed that they could generally out-turn and outpace us below 20,000 feet and that the only advantages that we could claim for our Hurricanes were that they were sturdier and better protected, carried more firepower and, after the initial stages of a dive, would drop much faster."

On this occasion, however, by the time the Hurricanes had gained sufficient height, no aircraft were to be seen. Only four Hurricanes returned, Sgt Mark Porter having been obliged to force-land BG807 west of Sengarang due to a glycol leak. He eventually made his way back to Singapore by foot. Flt Lt Welch had prepared a 'Missing in Action' signal ready to send to the UK when Porter eventually turned up.

Back at Singapore, on hearing the air raid sirens wailing, some of the airmen began leaving their posts, led by a flight sergeant whose nerve had obviously broken. These men had endured much hardship under attack and there were those who had reached their limits. Jerry Parker witnessed some of the groundcrews leaving, as he recalled:

> "They clambered into a bus immediately the Hurricanes had left, shouting to those last to board to buck up, or to the driver to 'get cracking'. They were hesitating because they realised that no men would be at their posts to service any returning Hurricanes. The bus started to move away from me and the men climbed aboard, but it had to pull round in a U-turn in front of the office. I shouted to the driver to stop and, when he took no notice of my bawling and waving, I unbuttoned my holster and took out my .38 revolver, which all of us pilots wore, whether flying or not, at Singapore. I aimed to shoot into the air or at the tyres of the bus if it passed me. I was scared stiff because I knew I was far more likely to hit the bus than its tyres but I was determine to find out more of this sudden departure of the groundcrews. I had never known this to happen before.
>
> Anyhow, it was unnecessary for me to shoot as the driver hauled the bus to a stop and I called out the flight sergeant. He said they had permission to push off from the airfield during air raids (which I doubted but could not contest) and that the aircraft were nearly always away for more than an hour, which I knew to be true. I pointed out that the fitters, an armourer and a radio technician must be available to service any aircraft returning early, and he agreed hurriedly that four men should remain. He called them out and they appeared from the bus quite happily and looked rather unconcerned about remaining. I assumed that the flight sergeant had influenced the men to rush off from the field but he himself was in a panic to get away and, having agreed to let the rest go with him, I though better of arguing the toss until a better opportunity might arise. So he leapt back into the loaded bus and away they went.
>
> The four men who remained glanced around the sky before sauntering off to their workshops. Then I saw for the first time a corporal seated on top of a blast-pen in the sun, quietly enjoying a mug of tea. I asked him what he was doing there and he replied that he had too much self-respect to go chasing off every time there was an air raid, and he intended to stay there until it was obviously safer in a trench or shelter. I just grinned at him and said 'Good show!'"

It was then that Parker remembered that it was his task to go over to the mess and organise the pilots' packed lunches, and also to get some cool drinks. He borrowed a very tatty old car, which lacked a silencer, in which he drove along the airfield towards the mess. He continued:

> "For no logical reason except the complete lack of movement on the field or around the buildings, I stopped the car with the engine running, opened the door and leaned out to look up at the sky. There, almost directly above in the neatest possible formation, were 27 bombers, at about 15,000 feet. I was out of the car in a flash and down into a shallow open storm gully alongside the road. I lay stretched out on my stomach with my head on my forearms, feeling miserably unprotected and conscious that parts of me were not below ground level. Almost immediately the earth shuddered and jumped under the battering of bombs and the noise and the shaking was absolutely frightening. It didn't seem possible that the barrage of bombs falling at an uncountable rate could continue for so many seconds, without one at least blowing me apart.
>
> Soon the ground stilled and I lifted my head but could hear nothing following the blast, and could see nothing but dust and smoke. As the sky cleared above me I could see no further formations overhead, so got back into the car to carry on to the mess. The engine was still running and its vital parts undamaged, the only damage having been caused by a bomb splinter which had passed through the windscreen just off-centre of the back of the driver's seat, before going out through the rear door. If I had stayed a moment longer it would have been too late."

When the Hurricanes returned, having not made contact with the raiders, Sqn Ldr

Brooker was furious to find a lack of groundcrews. The pilots and the skeleton groundcrew began refuelling the aircraft, for they intended to take off again. Parker agreed to see if he could find the missing crews, who had exceeded their time limit. However the cause of their delay was soon evident. Some of the bombs had fallen on a nearby village outside the main gate, blocking the road. Parker was sickened by the sight and smell of burning bodies in the huts, and was glad to get back to the airfield.

Since 488 Squadron had been advised that it was to be re-equipped with Hurricanes, its two remaining Buffaloes were handed over to one of the other units. Nine Hurricanes[36] were initially allocated to the New Zealand squadron, the first two (BE632 and BE585) being collected from Seletar by the new CO Sqn Ldr Jack Mckenzie DFC, and Flt Lt Hutcheson; two more (BG800 and BG845) were collected by the same pair in the afternoon from Tengah. Mackenzie[37], a former Battle of Britain pilot, had been flying Buffaloes since his arrival at Singapore:

> "In late January I was given command of the Squadron [vice Sqn Ldr Clouston, who was posted to Ops Room]. I don't think the earlier introduction of the Hurricane would have stemmed the Japanese attacks on Singapore. I think we were well outnumbered, but certainly we would have had better results in air combat. We could at least have had firepower, which would have been adequate to get a few victories, as opposed to the pop-guns the Buffalo had."

In the afternoon Plt Off Jack Oakden collected a further Hurricane (BG723), which caused the diarist to comment:

> "This was Plt Off Oakden's first flight in a Hurricane – he is very pleased with its performance and handling qualities. He has taken over command of A Flight."

Of this day, Tom Kitching noted in his diary:

> "I went to the Singapore Cricket Club at midday. I [then] took the Perrins [friends] to the Royal Singapore Golf Club; they had never been. There were about a dozen playing golf."[38]

It was such apparent unconcern for the war by some of the civilians that so incensed war correspondents, some of whom wrote to their respective papers along these lines, as mentioned by Kitching:

> "The home papers are furious about Malaya, but the height of absurdity is reached by the *Daily Express* which says: 'Whisky-swilling planters and military birds of passage forgot that the Malay has the makings of the finest soldier in the Far East.' Ye Gods! This is the utterest of utter tripe! The Military Police have ratted all over the place; the Volunteers have refused to fight! The Governor has issued a circular! A bit late, methinks!"[39]

25 January

Two more Hurricanes were lost during the morning, together with their pilots, due to adverse weather conditions. Sqn Ldr Brooker and Sgt Swampy Marsh took off from Seletar at 0955 and encountered heavy cloud. Brooker signalled Marsh to close in but when he emerged from cloud at 300 feet, Marsh (in BE641), a 22-year-old from Montreal, had disappeared. At much the same time 28-year-old Victorian Sgt Alan Coutie (BE589) took off from Kallang with others from A Flight to patrol over the Island and, he too, disappeared in the worsening weather. He was last seen entering cloud at 5,000 feet. Neither pilot was seen again; both, it was assumed, had crashed into the sea. C Flight also lost the services of its experienced commander during the day when Flt Lt Cooper-Slipper was admitted to hospital with severe stomach pains, thought to have been caused by an ulcer, but, as he later revealed:

> "I was only in hospital for a few days with a bad stomach, caused by driving into a Chinese man carrying two cans of 'you-know-what' on a pole over his shoulder. One can came through the windshield of the station wagon, and I collected it!"

488 Squadron collected further Hurricanes during the day, including BE640, which the CO flew over from Seletar, and BG809 was ferried from Tengah by Flt Lt Hutcheson; Oakden collected a third (BM900) from Seletar. Everyone seemed delighted, as the diarist noted:

> "In the morning pilots did cockpit drill but bad weather and Jap raids prevented any first solos on Hurricanes being carried out. At 1400 we saw Plt Off Sharp and Plt Off White dash into the air for the first time in Hurricanes. Snow [White] made a good landing the first time and Noel missed on his first try but made a good homecoming on his second attempt. Sgts MacIntosh, Meharry, Clow, Kuhn and MacMillan all made fine first solos. Sgt Meaclem dropped a little but rectified OK. Plt Off Pettit pulled off a pansy pancake."

Next day, the diarist continued:

> "Sgts MacIntosh, Meharry and Kuhn did practice flying in Hurricanes until Jap planes in the vicinity forced us to remain on the ground for a while. Sgt Killick, Plt Off Greenhalgh, Plt Off Gifford, and Sgt Burton did first solos on Hurricanes today and others gained experience on type."

Sgt Jim MacIntosh was one who enjoyed the conversion to Hurricanes:

> "The move to Hurricanes was greeted very well, although I was rather disappointed in the handling qualities of the Hurricane. Nevertheless, it had far superior climb to the Zero and the Buffalo. It had greater altitude capabilities, and was faster. It would be fair to say that as soon as we went onto Hurricanes we almost stopped our pilot losses. I am quite sure it improved morale, because we knew that we were in an aircraft that offered options. When you entered combat in a Brewster Buffalo, if you couldn't use your better diving qualities, you would just have to stick it out. It was pretty hard to run away, but with the Hurricane, which had greater height, better speed and climbing ability – we could pick and choose when we went in."

An equally glowing tribute was paid by Sgt Perce Killick, another former Buffalo pilot:

> "We had to go up in a Hurricane and do flight training in them, although we didn't have much time for that. They were magnificent aircraft. If we had had a few squadrons of those out there, the Japs would never have got Singapore. They had six machine guns in each wing and were high powered. If you fired at rocks in machine-gun practice, they just carved the rock in half like a knife through cheese. They were much better than the Buffalo."

The day ended well for 488 Squadron:

> "All pilots and senior NCOs led a small impromptu farewell to Sqn Ldr Clouston in B Flight's officers' house; we finished off five bottles of champagne presented to the Squadron by the manager of the Airport Hotel and also put away a good deal of' beer. Flt Lt Hutcheson said a few words of farewell, Sqn Ldr Clouston later replied saying how sad he was to leave the Squadron but he would still keep a fatherly interest in it. Mackenzie said how proud he was to take over a squadron of his countrymen and he was lucky to have such a fine band of men under him."

Although little was seen of the Japanese air force over Singapore during the day due to the atrocious weather conditions, a few bombers did manage to penetrate the cloud, as noted by an entry in LAC Boyd's diary:

> "Two air raids today, they now seem to be just part of our existence to be taken in our stride. We also received our Hurricanes today and are busy getting them operational. They are later, long fuselage type, but have desert type air fitters to the engine air intakes, which will slow them down somewhat. In the first air raid the Japs were intercepted over Johore where they jettisoned their bombs and made for home. Here is how the second one occurred. We were working on the Hurris when unexpectedly a number of bombs started to fall. The visibility was nil owing to clouds and rain and we all made a dive for any foxhole that was handy, and huddled crowded together like frightened rabbits. The bombs kept coming closer and closer but stopped just short of the aerodrome. There is no doubt they were meant for us and our new Hurricanes. It was a miracle we escaped, but we can thank the cloud cover for saving us. Actually it is a miracle we have escaped all the bombings that have been directed at us.
>
> We are all pretty jittery. One man in our Flight won't shower unless he has his tin hat on. We wear them all day and keep them close at all times. One sergeant, when the bombs fell close, took his tin hat from his head and placed it over his behind. He seemed to think that was the highest and most vulnerable part of him that needed protection. The Japs seem determined to get the Hurricanes and I expect plenty [more bombing] soon. It was some packet they dropped today, in my estimation about 50,000lbs of high explosive. Once again the ineptness of the air raid detectors and Headquarters Operations nearly ended in tragedy for 488 Squadron. However, there are a number of high altitude ack-ack guns now in action."

Further up the east coast of Malaya, the latest Japanese strike was imminent – a planned landing at Endau, situated on the estuary of the Sungei Endau, a few miles north of Mersing. Ki-27s of the 11th Sentai from Kota Bharu, together with others of the 1st Sentai from Kuantan, provided patrols during the day over a convoy of two transports, *Kanbera Maru* and the larger *Kansai Maru*, which carried supplies to support the thrust of the Japanese Army down the east coast. As they headed southwards, a cruiser, two destroyers, five minesweepers and three submarine chasers joined them. To cover the operation from further afield were two more cruisers and two destroyers, while the aircraft carrier *Ryujo* stood by further out, escorted by a single destroyer. The force had been sighted by patrolling Hudsons, which had reported the threat to Air HQ. Overnight, a plan of attack was hurriedly devised, but any strike force that could be assembled would be pitifully weak.

26 January – Disaster at Endau

From the Singapore Straits, a motorable road ran as far north-east as Endau, also serving Mersing located on the coast a few miles to the south – and the airfields at Kluang and Kahang in Central Johore. The British, established on the line of the Mersing River, were hoping to hold a line between Mersing-Kluang-Batu Pahat. Japanese forces first made contact with the Mersing defences on 22 January.

It was obvious to the British Command that the Japanese would attempt to land supplies here to prepare the forces in the area for their part in the final push on Singapore, and to bring in supplies to allow the Kahang and Kluang airfields to be put into use as soon as they were captured. It was also believed that troops were about to be landed at Endau for the purpose of engaging the Australians down the coast at Mersing; this was not to be the case, however, since the main force of Australians had by now withdrawn further down the coast in accordance with orders. The rearguard defenders at Mersing had already been assaulted and overwhelmed.

While most RAF activity was directed towards western Johore, where severe fighting around Batu Pahat was underway, some of the Hudsons still remaining in Singapore had kept a regular watch on the approaches to Endau. At 0745, two RAAF Hudson crews spotted a convoy some miles north-east of Endau, heading southwards, just before both Hudsons came under attack by three Ki-27s from the 12th Flying Battalion. Following a short engagement, both aircraft escaped into cloud and returned to base. Next on the scene was a PR Buffalo, whose pilot reported that the Japanese had already landed at Endau. A little north of the town he had located an enemy force which he estimated to consist of two cruisers, twelve destroyers, and two transports. They were making for the estuary, and were clearly intending to land troops there.

The only striking force available on Singapore comprised 21 obsolete Vildebeest and three Albacores, plus nine RAAF Hudsons. The two RAF squadrons were thus ordered to prepare as many aircraft as possible for an attack, but most had been operating against motor transport in southern Johore during the night. Seven of the Vildebeest had later carried out a second mission to Batu Pahat. The crews were tired; the aircraft had to be prepared, refuelled and rearmed. It was clear that no early attack could be made. This was unfortunate because a torpedo attack on the vessels at sea might have achieved some success – at least against the all-important transports. However it was likely that the ships would be anchored in the shallow waters of the estuary by the time an attack could be made, and the aircraft were therefore each armed instead with three 500lb armour-piercing bombs. Meanwhile, 225 Bomber Group in Sumatra was ordered to despatch all available bombers, and ABDA Command was contacted with a request that US B-17s from Java should also be sent to Sumatra, but these arrived too late to join in the attacks. Jerry Parker recalled:

> "Brooker issued us with maps of Malaya and told us we'd be doing a couple of special patrols that afternoon, following an early lunch. We were to go up the east coast at about 10,000 feet to Mersing and there patrol west and east between the middle of the peninsula and the coast. Other aircraft would be carrying out operations near the coast and our job was to attract any enemy fighters, which were not expected, away from them. The last three days' casualties had lowered our morale considerably and we sat around for the rest of the morning in Brooker's absence but not cheered by the presence of Sergeant Hardie (of the Singapore ear) who pointed out the areas of jungle, swamp and mountain we'd be flying over until I suggested he'd be better employed at organizing our lunch."

The first attack was to be made by the Hudsons and a dozen Vildebeest. The aircraft began taking off at 1350. A dozen Buffaloes provided escort for the biplanes, and six more plus nine Hurricanes were to cover the Hudsons. The British formation approached the area at about 1500 hours. The weather was overcast, with cloud up to 4,000 feet, but the sky was then reasonably clear up to about 12,000 feet, above which was more cloud. The strike force flew up the Endau estuary through a bank of cloud, emerging from this to see the black hulks of the two Japanese transports lying a couple of miles offshore. Landing craft were seen making their way to the shore, the craft also loaded with drums of aviation fuel, bombs and stores. As the biplanes approached, flashes from the decks of the covering warships showed that the gunners had spotted them. Parker continued:

> "We duly set off with Brooker, Dizzy and myself leading sections and followed by B Flight, led by Murray Taylor. We spent some minutes forming up and then climbed off up to the north. I was not looking at the map at all since we had Malaya on our left and the sea on our right and I knew I'd have no difficulty in getting home as long as there was no cloud. I was constantly searching the skies ahead, behind and above and checking my position in relation to Brooker and Ken Holmes, my No.2.

We'd reached our operational height when I saw a fair amount of smoke above the coast a few miles ahead and a couple of steamers lying just offshore. As we came nearer – and we flew no faster – I could see several aeroplanes starting to burn in the air at a low height and go crashing in flames into the greenness of the trees below, there to look like enormous bonfires at the end of a trail of black smoke which spread and grew again from each. Brooker looked around and pointed to the fracas and went down in a fast shallow dive. I felt ill as I saw several Vildebeest and Swordfish [sic] biplanes being harried by Jap fighters and the now familiar sensations of suspense and anticipation took charge of me as I checked my cockpit for readiness and the sky for more of the enemy in the last few seconds. Apart from the aircraft already burning, I could see two other British biplanes with smoke spiralling back from their slipstreams whilst they were closely followed by the little silvery fighters with the big red discs on their wings."

The Hurricanes were soon engaged by some of the 19 K-27s from the 1st and 11th Sentais which were providing cover for the landings, together with a single Ki-44 of the 47th Independent Fighter Chutai flown by Capt Yasuhiko Kuroe. Parker continued:

"Brooker took the nearest Jap and I took on one chasing a biplane on his right but I found that owing to my high speed and the offset of the tailfin to counteract torque, the plane skidded wildly as I pulled out of my dive and I didn't have time to line up the Zero properly. I pulled up to come around again and found a fixed undercart monoplane going straight into the air and on the point of stalling. My speed had dropped considerably and I had the plane properly under control so that I was able to hit the Jap with several seconds of fire during which it remained in the same attitude before falling off under my nose. I pulled round in a sharp turn but could not see it where I anticipated and instead I found it or another similar coming at me from behind when I'd straightened out. I panicked madly, pushed the stick forward, was saved by my straps from going through the roof of the cockpit and broke down to the ground before pulling up towards the cloud several thousand feet away. However, I found I'd left the Jap behind and so I came down again in another shallow dive to take on a Zero chasing a Vildebeest almost towards me. They both turned further towards me and I turned inside them so that I was able to rake the Zero at close range with a short burst and he was unable to bring his guns to bear either on the biplane or on myself. I didn't hope to have destroyed him in such a fraction of a second but we had met only just above the trees, and when I looked back, he was burning there and the Vildebeest was still airborne. On our return to Seletar the Vildebeest pilot, who had been shot, confirmed this very lucky kill.

I swept up again towards the clouds but did not let my speed drop below 300mph. Of course I didn't glance at the air speed indicator but could tell by the engine note at what rate the speed was falling off. There were still 10/10ths of stratus clouds above so I could easily check that there were no fighters waiting to come down on me and I looked for further targets. I reckoned that I still had several seconds of unused ammunition left but, apart from the Vildebeest now moving off south, no other aircraft were in the sky. I cruised over towards the steamers lying offshore but could see no unusual activity nor did there seem to be any shooting going on and finally I turned towards Singapore and fell in behind and above a Lockheed Hudson until I reached Seletar."

All Hurricanes returned safely. While the aircraft were being refuelled and rearmed the pilots related accounts of their combats. Consequently, seven of their opponents were assessed to have been destroyed: two by Plt Off Parker, and one each by Sqn Ldr Brooker, Flt Lt Murray Taylor and Sgt Nicholls, while Plt Off Mendizabal was awarded a probable, but the 'star turn' was Sgt Ron Dovell. He claimed two destroyed and reported:

"I got over the target area and dived steeply to meet a batch of about 12 fighters spread out all over the shop. My No.1 dived in and split up two of them. One came up again, and as he was on top of a turn I gave him a short burst. Flames came from the engine, and he went down with his aircraft blazing."[40]

Dovell then climbed rapidly and came across another Ki-27:

"I must have surprised him because he made no attempt to get away. I gave him a long burst, and he went down in an absolutely vertical spin from low altitude. He couldn't have had a hope."[41]

Amidst all the confusion in amongst the scattered cloud, there had clearly been much overclaiming by both sides. While Capt Kuroe in the Ki-44 had remained above to observe and report results, the 11th Sentai Ki-27s, which had attacked first, claimed two Hudsons, two biplanes, five Buffaloes and two Hurricanes shot down, one Hudson, one biplane and one Hurricane probable, and three more biplanes crash-landed. In return only one 11th Sentai Ki-27 was reported to have been damaged. The 1st Sentai claimed six biplanes shot down and a Catalina probable – possibly a Dutch aircraft that had stumbled into the arena, although no reports of such a combat or loss have been found. Lt Mizotani of the 1st Sentai was shot down, although he managed to bale out safely. Parker continued:

"We had no time to consider the losses for we were scheduled to carry out another similar patrol immediately our aircraft were refuelled. Brooker managed to get across the airfield to the second Vildebeest squadron Flight Office and discover their flight plans before they took off. We were already too late to escort them all the way and they got off about 15 minutes before we did. Brooker was summoned to AHQ and Murray Taylor was to lead the squadron. I had a section and Dovell, who had destroyed two aircraft on the first sortie, was to lead the other and Murray Taylor, who was somewhat jealous of my luck, also insisted that Dovell was to lead A Flight, against the wishes of Dovell himself and the other sergeants. Dovell was evidently a good natural marksman but he knew he had insufficient experience in combat flying to lead a formation.

A Flight, four aircraft, took off and circled the field, waiting for B Flight, with Dovell looking anxiously over at me for encouragement. Only three aircraft came up from B Flight and I saw immediately that Murray Taylor had not got off. The radio was burbling and crackling incomprehensibly but I knew we'd not be able to meet the Vildebeest before they got to the target if we waited any longer. I waggled my wings, assuming command as the senior officer (the only one, in fact), Dovell and B Flight fell in promptly behind and I opened the throttle nearly up to the safety gate and climbed off to the north through broken cloud."

The bombers reached Endau at 1730, where ten 1st Sentai Ki-27s and two Ki-44s attacked them. Over the target area the skies were clear and devoid of cloud. Parker:

"I suppose we reached the Vildebeest about a minute after the Zeros did and they had managed to retain their formation on their way in with their bombs. We came down flat out with throttles wide open, as I'd instructed my sergeants before we left and we attacked, climbed and attacked again with aircraft all over the lower sky and the Vildebeest scattering after they'd dropped their loads. I made quarter attacks on fighters trailing the bomber formation and they generally broke off their shooting to turn towards me. I thought my shots hit one or two at longish range but was moving too fast to hit them with short, close bursts. The Zeros broke off to engage us in dogfights but for the short time of the engagement the speed remaining from our initial dives was too great for them and they could only take snap shots. One big Canadian Sergeant, Fleming, decided to fight it out with them and was shot down. The Zeros broke off soon after the Vildebeest had turned for home and we had no further trouble."

The victorious Japanese fighter pilots again overestimated the size of the bomber formation when, for the second time, they reported meeting 15-18 biplanes, and claimed 14 shot down; two victories were credited to the two Ki-44 pilots, believed to have been Capts Kuroe and Jimbo, the latter probably responsible for shooting down Sgt John Fleming's Hurricane (BG828). The Canadian reported:

"On this last trip of the day I immediately attacked three fixed-undercarriage Japs attacking a Vildebeest who was making a bomb run on one of the ships – I think a freighter. The three scattered and I saw a bomb strike at the waterline of the ship – as I broke away from this attack I was struck by fire from a Zero, I think. Oil pressure collapsed – managed to fly south for about 20 miles before the engine seized, abandoning the aircraft at low level over the beach just north of Mersing. I landed about 20 yards from where the plane landed and caught fire."

Fleming was credited with probably shooting down one of the Ki-27s before his own aircraft was attacked; his was the only Hurricane lost in this skirmish. It was probably Fleming's aircraft that the crew of one of the Vildebeest mistakenly took to be a Zero being shot down, as the Vildebeest pilot[42] later recalled:

"Ahead I saw a Vildebeest being chased by a Jap fighter and what appeared to be another one behind the first – or was it a Hurricane? Presently the two fighters started to come back. They went round one side of a hill – I went the other, still down amongst the treetops, dodging the taller ones. The shout over the intercom came from the gunner – 'It's a Hurricane chasing a Navy 0' – was delightful to hear. I swung a bit to observe how the chase was going and was just in time to see the Jap spread itself over quite a considerable area of jungle."

Sgt Nicholls claimed his second victory of the day and Sgt Dovell reported shooting down two more. The first was sighted circling a Vildebeest:

"I picked him up because of the bomber's tracers, and I swooped. He saw me coming. I chased him, firing all the way, to within ten feet of the treetops. Finally he lost control and crashed into the trees."[43]

He then chased a second:

"A short burst this time was sufficient to send it diving out of control. Another pilot verified that this Jap fighter also crashed in the jungle."[44]

In fact, although several 1st Sentai fighters were damaged in this engagement, only one seems to have been lost. Jerry Parker was reasonably pleased with his first taste of command:

"Brooker thought I'd done pretty well on this and even Murray Taylor was reconciled in the circumstances. The successful establishment of the Japanese bridgehead and the loss of eleven [sic] Vildebeest and a Hurricane were very depressing but the Hurricanes might well have come off far worse and all the bombers would have been destroyed, if the Japs had had high cover for their protecting fighters."

The Hurricane pilots were credited with ten victories and two probables, the Buffalo pilots a further four or five, although Japanese losses were minimal. At least one Ki-27 of the 1st Sentai was shot down and its pilot Lt Toshiro Kuboya seriously wounded; he died three weeks later as a result. Actual RAF losses during the two raids were ten Vildebeest, two Albacores, two Hudsons and one Hurricane, with two more Vildebeest written off and at least ten others damaged. 39 aircrew failed to return, although nine would eventually make their respective ways back to Singapore; two others were taken prisoner. One of those who managed to find his way back was Sgt Fleming, the Canadian Hurricane pilot. On his return he had quite a tale to tell:

"I saw some Japs beside bicycles on a road about 500 yards from the beach – six Jap soldiers. We looked at each other for a minute, then I proceeded along the beach and they mounted their bikes and rode off. I hid in a swamp till nightfall and then swam the Mersing to avoid the town, which had a Jap guard on the bridge. Swam from about 7 o'clock to about midnight. Clamoured through barbed wire to high ground, and slept. Awakened by a battle, which turned out to be an engagement with the Jap landing flotilla and two destroyers. These were the *Vampire* and the *Thanet*. The *Vampire* was sunk in the engagement.

At daybreak I proceeded to the beach through the barbed wire, since the jungle was impassable. Proceeded south along the beach and investigated an abandoned Aussie camp, where I was nearly blown up by a booby trap. Next day, I was still walking south. At about 3pm I ran into a whaleboat drawn up on the shore with about a dozen survivors from the *Vampire*. Proceeded south in the boat with the others, two or three of whom were badly wounded. There was a naval officer amongst the group. That evening we saw lights ashore and went in. The settlement was called Paloi, I think. Left the others with instructions to stay put, and the officer and I, with a guide, proceeded inland to a Chinese village. Heard that there was a British camp about 12 miles further on through the jungle. By the morning of 29th, the officer and I reached a second village and from there were taken upstream by native canoe, only to find the British camp had been abandoned. We returned to the first Chinese village, where we slept soundly all night.

Next morning we returned to Paloi. While digging out the beached whaleboat three more native canoes came ashore, containing more naval survivors and some Vildebeest aircrew in the same pickle as myself. Continued by water south, and all next day, and on the morning of 1 February we intercepted a freighter in the channel leading to Singapore harbour. We were taken aboard and proceeded to the harbour. We stayed on board that night and were allowed ashore next morning."

While Fleming was making his way southwards, some of his colleagues, unaware of his fate, went out that evening to relax after the day's harrowing experiences, including Jerry Parker:

"My procedure for the last few days after leaving the Flight Office in the evening had been to eat an enormous meal in the mess, have a glass of beer, shower, get on to my bed under the mosquito net and sleep exhausted until about an hour before dawn. Then I would stagger down to the Flight Office without breakfast – which I couldn't eat – and shave if I didn't take off early. Penny Farthing had left an electric shaver, which I had borrowed and which had become my property. That evening after the Mersing trips, however, Murray Taylor suggested we go along to the Tanglin Club, the really pukka club in Singapore, and relax and we wandered into this mausoleum and drank beer and played poker dice with some NZ motorboat officers. Two of them were the ones who'd reported my first victim and we drank toasts and rejoiced and sang until midnight, when I could stay awake no longer. When we got back to Seletar we found there had been a light air raid there although without material damage. One result though was that a bomb had burst outside the windows of the sergeants' mess and the Flight fitter of A Flight, formerly a very smart and ambitious young man, had completely lost his nerve although he stayed on duty for some days longer. I staggered into bed without undressing and awoke a few hours later, sick and with a dry mouth and an aching head."

27 January

The defenders now learned of the arrival of the first Hurricanes of 232 and 258 Squadron from HMS *Indomitable*, which had flown to Batavia in Java. They were desperately needed since, of the original delivery of 51 crated Hurricanes, only 21 remained available for operations, with four more that could be made ready in 24 hours. Of the rest, 19 had been lost in the air, and a further seven were at repair depots. Meanwhile, the remaining handful of pilots continued the daily defence of the island. The harassed RAF was given no respite – nor was Parker:

> "I got down to the Flight Office on time and found Brooker anxious to take me on an early patrol. I felt dreadful but didn't dare admit to a hangover in such circumstances so we took off between the bomb craters being filled in by coolies."

Accompanying Sqn Ldr Brooker and Plt Off Parker was Sgt Chris Christian from B Flight, and they took off in an attempt to intercept an approaching reconnaissance aircraft. Parker continued:

> "Deep breaths of oxygen and concentration on matters other than my hangover cleared my head considerably so after about an hour of continuously searching the bright sky and clouds I was feeling a lot better."

At this point Sgt Christian's Hurricane suddenly peeled off and swooped all over the sky, losing height rapidly. Brooker called him on the R/T and went chasing after him but could see no reason for these antics, nor did he receive any reply. The chase was called off when the Hurricane disappeared through the low cloud blanket, and Brooker and Parker made their way back to Seletar. On landing they learned that an aircraft had been observed to crash at great speed into a small rubber plantation near Kranji W/T Station, where it exploded.

Flt Lt Norman Welch, 232 Squadron's Adjutant, was in charge of a small party which went to the scene of the crash, where they had to dig to a depth of 13 feet just to reach the tail of the aircraft, on which the serial number was painted. After confirming that it was the missing Hurricane BE590, the hole was filled in and a funeral service was held on the site since no trace of the 29-year-old married pilot was found. It was assumed that he was entombed in the aircraft. Flt Lt Welch noted:

> "It is not known what happened but he was probably in action, and the machine dived vertically with the engine roaring at terrific speed."

Later in the morning two-dozen G4Ms from the Kanoya Ku, escorted by A6Ms and accompanied by two C5Ms, attacked Kallang, where 488 Squadron's new Hurricanes were being refuelled. Once again LAC Boyd's diary recorded the terror and destruction being experienced:

> "Three air raid alarms went this morning. The first, a reconnaissance, but we sensed that they have our drome in view as target area No.2. Second raid was on Seletar, a wave of 27. They come in 27s, waves of 27. The third raid got Kallang; two waves of 27. How I have learnt to dread that number. Another run about 30 minutes later with another 27 from a different direction. The second wave we did not expect, as we had no warning, as usual a total shambles at Command HQ. None of our planes took off and we just had time to dive for our foxholes. I was terrified the whole time; the foxhole shook like a ship in a storm, and the blast from a bomb at the back of the foxhole lifted the roof clean off and put it back almost in the same place again. The suction effect following the blast is also very unpleasant. Big and small bombs were dropped right across the drome. Ten large bombs landed within 50 yards of our foxhole. Three large and innumerable small craters within ten yards and one within ten feet.

We got a terrible shaking up, but our foxhole did not collapse as most of it was built up above ground level with sand bags, owing to the water level at high tide being near the surface. It was built to hold only two but in this case three squeezed into it. Two Blenheims, four Buffaloes, four Hurricanes, and one Tiger Moth were completely destroyed or burnt. Nine Hurricanes were written off as unserviceable along with one Blenheim, and two de Havilland biplanes. Also three petrol tankers, one Bofors anti-aircraft gun, and several cars, trucks and buses were destroyed. One of the tankers was near our foxhole and the burning fuel came within two feet of the edge. The sloping build up of earth and sandbags saved us. None of our boys were killed but other squadrons had heavy casualties, including the adjacent 232. The drome is badly knocked about. Being built on the sea level it is on an old reclaimed salt-water swamp, the ground is all bulging and sinking in different spots. Nerves very bad. Japs bomb with uncanny accuracy, even scoring direct hits on the planes from 20,000 feet and over. We can put up no fighters tomorrow as we have none left serviceable. The Japs have knocked us out as soon as the Hurricanes arrived. Spies must be everywhere."

He added, disconcertedly:

"It is only a matter of days now before Singapore must fall. I am now only waiting for the Jap troops to advance over Johore and our troops will then cross back over the causeway to Singapore Island. The Japs will sever the water pipeline, and then it will only be a matter of time. This place is like Dunkirk, Greece, and Crete, only there is no place to go. It will be terrible. In a week we shall be besieged, I am sure. I am told I am a defeatist but I reply that I am a realist. How can a hundred thousand poorly armed and badly led men hold up the march of a nation? We might have held out if Singapore was not such a myth, a bluff. Our equipment is outdated, poor, scarce, and the heads are a lot of fools."

Of the battering 488 Squadron was subjected to, the Squadron diarist wrote:

"Never before have we seen such terrific bombing as this morning when Kallang was raided twice in the morning. The first raid (27 heavy bombers) came in from the North and dropped everything they had on us. Everybody was underground having learnt their lesson from previous raids and therefore injuries were very slight. However our aircraft suffered rather badly and everyone sustained some degree of damage although they were widely dispersed. The aerodrome literally rocked for about 25 seconds, the noise was terrific. Sqn Ldr Mackenzie, Sgts Kuhn, Clow, MacMillan and Meaclem, Plt Offs Pettit and Greenhalgh were sheltering in a sandbagged gun emplacement when one dropped against the sandbags and buried most of the boys. However they were all dragged out safely covered in dust and sand."

Sqn Ldr Mackenzie recalled:

"I was in a Lewis gun emplacement right on the edge of the aerodrome. The next thing we knew, we were all buried and had to be dug out. As a result of the bomb blasts my eardrums were damaged and I was effectively stone deaf. I couldn't even hear the engine when I was flying. It did heal a bit but it was never the same again and I was off operations for about a fortnight."

The diarist continued:

"A party hurried down to the hangar to put out a fire there and did yeoman service. They removed a quantity of ammunition although there were other rounds exploding nearby. Another party rushed up to give aid to our sister squadron, 243. The second raid was about 40 minutes later (27 heavy bombers again) and dropped another packet. The aerodrome literally shook but again everyone had gone well to ground and no casualties resulted.

Aircraft and tankers blazed furiously around the drome. The CO's car was blown to bits. Also Hutch's van is u/s. Hardly had the bombs stopped dropping when parties again rushed to give aid. Our boys behaved magnificently throughout both bombings, there was no sign of panic and all worked like niggers to get the fires out, help others who had urgent work to do and get undamaged planes to safety. Those who read this diary in later years would have difficulty in imagining what it was like on Kallang this morning and the scene of desolation after tons of high explosive had been dropped. Also the seconds waiting for the bombs to drop and the feelings and thoughts one has when they are falling all around. The troops are working like slaves getting aircraft serviceable and we hope to be operational in two days time."

488 Squadron had six of its Hurricanes destroyed or damaged beyond repair; these are believed to have been BE585, BE632, BE640, BG723, BG800, and BG845. During the second raid, while personnel were attempting to salvage aircraft and stores, two more Hurricanes, BM902 and BG588 of 232 Squadron's C Flight, which were awaiting repair after earlier damage, were destroyed as were two Buffaloes. Of these latest raids, Tom Kitching wrote:

"There was a short alert at 8.30am, then another at 9.15am and another at 10am. The Japs unloaded a lot on Seletar. We saw 27 Japs clearly from the roof of the Fullerton Building, flying in formation apparently too high for the anti-aircraft guns. At 11.30 I sounded the 'imminent danger' signal. Lots of bombs dropped and the building shook, but, on emerging onto the roof, I saw that the nearest damage appeared to be on Kallang airport; one plane was blazing on the ground. The next excitement was a tanker blazing away a few miles out at sea; there was a terrific column of smoke and flames. Whether it was bombed or not, no one knows – it may have hit a mine. There I was – just sallied forth into Battery Road, when I saw 27 Jap planes coming straight at us from the south-west. I ran for it to the Fullerton Building and the Japs dropped a lot more, probably in the sea, and a number in the Kallang area again. The all clear sounded at 12.30."[45]

Shortly after these raids on Kallang, a Blenheim of 27 Squadron with defective brakes approached to land. Its New Zealand pilot, Plt Off Brian Stringer, recalled the moment:

"There were three parked Hurricanes – it was all they had left – and, as I couldn't stop my aircraft, I ground-looped between the first two and the third, which was staggered a little, and got through all of them. From what I was told later from either MacIntosh or one of the others who was there, Sqn Ldr Clouston had said: 'Here comes a bloody idiot – he's going to wipe out the rest of the fighters we've got!' And with that, he drew his revolver and said he was going to shoot me on the spot if I touched them! But I didn't touch any of them and, in fact, was blissfully unaware of the whole damn thing as I taxied away round the corner.

They had cut down all the trees alongside the airfield at Kallang and were using the road as a runway. There was a wrecked Hurricane and, as I had never examined one, I went across and had a look. In the map case was a photograph of the prettiest woman I have ever seen in my life; she was obviously the wife or friend of the pilot. I don't know what had happened to him but the wrecked Hurricane was on its belly on the edge of the roadside – he'd probably crashed on the road."

28 January

Early morning saw the arrival of another convoy in Keppel Harbour; this, together with the two preceding arrivals, had between them brought the rest of the 18th Division, a Brigade Group from India, troops from Australia and some more anti-aircraft units. Of this period, Jerry Parker wrote:

"By this time duty pilots sat in their aircraft awaiting the call to scramble, instead of lounging about the flight office. It could be very fatiguing to spend an hour and a half in a state of nervous tension searching the skies on patrol after already having sat in one's cockpit for up to an hour in the tropical sunshine. The discomfort was materially increased by our having replaced the cushions on our parachutes with dinghies packed between them and our bottoms and the addition also in the same place of a *parang* or heavy jungle knife for hacking one's way to civilisation in the event of a crash-landing in that largely uninhabited territory. Nevertheless, we considered the discomfort and fatigue of waiting in the cockpits necessary when weighed against the probability of being caught on take-off by the Zeros."

During the morning Sqn Ldr Brooker led all available Hurricanes to strafe Japanese-occupied Kluang airfield in Johore, but on arrival no aircraft were to be seen on the ground. AA positions around the airfield were strafed instead. Plt Off Sandy McCulloch had been obliged to return early when a fuel line broke. He managed to reach Sembawang by flying slowly to conserve his fuel, but then had to crash-land when only one wheel came down. He was not hurt. Two Hurricanes from 488 Squadron also ventured over the mainland, Flt Lt Hutcheson (BM900) and Sgt MacIntosh undertaking a reconnaissance up central Malaya towards Kuala Lumpur. No opposition was encountered.

Meanwhile at Kallang, the hard-working ground personnel striving to get Hurricanes serviceable were performing many minor miracles. 488 Squadron's Max Boyd noted:

"We were up early working on the planes. Maintenance section led by Flt Sgt Andy Chandler is doing a magnificent job repairing the damaged Hurricanes, using bits and pieces from one to make up another good one. Even joining the wings from one to the fuselage of another and a motor from a third. Flight riggers are doing smaller repairs to the less damaged airframes and the Flight mechanics and other tradesmen are checking out everything else for bomb splinter damage. Also bomb holes had to be filled in on the dispersal access ways. When the air raid siren sounded they evacuated us from the drome out to Katong, but the Japs were after a different target. They wanted the ammunition dump and Air Headquarters at Katong. As it was, we just passed through the township out of range of the bombs when they started to fall. There is nothing so nerve-wracking as the swish, swish of them falling. The string of bombs fell across the township of Katong but missed the ammunition dumps. They apologised later over the radio for bombing Katong as an accident – they hit the township due to miscalculation. Many natives were killed in the raid."

29 January

Singapore again came under attack, 26 Genzan Ku G3Ms – with 18 escorting A6Ms and a C5M – attacking Seletar during the morning. The escort reported eight intercepting fighters, but no victories were claimed. JAAF units also raided Sembawang and this airfield was heavily bombed. 64th Sentai Ki-43s provided an escort to the island, but Sgt Maj Shokichi Ohmori was delayed taking off and arrived alone, meeting some unescorted Ki-21s and accompanying them to the target. On return, he reported seeing five Hurricanes and Buffaloes above and, when these dived to the attack, he claimed two shot down with ease, driving the others off.

A section of Hurricanes and a pair of Buffaloes were involved in the interception, Plt Off Mendizabal returning to claim a bomber shot down, plus another probably destroyed and a third damaged, but crashed his Hurricane (BG808) on landing at Seletar due to undercarriage trouble, possibly as a result of combat damage. One of the Buffalo pilots also claimed a bomber probably destroyed but was then attacked by a fighter and was obliged to crash-land on returning to Sembawang. Meanwhile, the other Buffalo pilot pursued the departing bombers, believing that his fire damaged one before they outpaced his Buffalo. Two of the bombers were indeed hit and damaged, one force-landing at Kuala Lumpur on return. During an afternoon patrol, a Buffalo was attacked in error by a Hurricane and crash-landed at Tengah. The New Zealand Buffalo pilot was shaken but otherwise unhurt. At the end of the day Max Boyd wrote:

> "Three air raid alerts today, we collected no bombs but Seletar got another large packet from two waves of 27 with fighter escorts of about 40 each. We are to be issued with rifles, bayonets, Tommy guns, and machine guns to defend our drome. 20,000 troops arrived today, poor devils. Just suicide to land them, too. The troopship *Empress of Asia* carrying troops was dive-bombed and hit. It caught fire and was beached. The soldiers lost all their gear and a tremendous amount of vehicles; Bren carriers and anti-aircraft guns also went down with it. It is most unfortunate at a time like this. I saw the fastest plane today that I have ever seen [obviously a Ki-46]. It left great streaks of condensation behind it, and it was a great sight to see the ack-ack having pot shots at it as the shells leave great long streaks on a clear day such as today. The sky was criss-crossed with the streaks, but the plane got away, flying at a great height."

The situation at Singapore was rapidly going from bad to worse,, the Hurricane numbers dwindling to almost single figures. The Buffalo force had also practically ceased to exist.

CHAPTER III

MORE HURRICANES ARRIVE – THE FALL OF SINGAPORE

30 January – 15 February 1942

> "As for the Japanese with their feeble wooden biplanes, they seemed as the scent of a drag hunt or a drogue in firing practice. It was almost as if someone had arranged their presence as an excuse for this splendid jamboree."
>
> Sgt Terence Kelly, 258 Squadron

Help was on the way for the besieged, outnumbered and dwindling band of fighter pilots defending Singapore, in the form of 48 Hurricanes and their pilots, currently aboard the carrier *Indomitable*. Of conditions aboard the carrier and the journey from Port Sudan, Sgt Terry Kelly of 258 Squadron wrote:

> "*Indomitable* was quite a different kettle of fish from *Athene*. There was naturally a degree of segregation between sergeants and officers, but the gulf in quality of sleeping quarters much diminished. One could sling a hammock anywhere and in fact after a day or two I abandoned mine altogether and took to sleeping on a kind of shelf I discovered on the port side of the edge of the *Indomitable*, and being able to lie and hear the gentle hiss of a quiet sea a hundred feet below and watch the stars swinging in the sky I envied no one. I was cool and fresh in my cubby-hole, afloat it seemed in the air itself, with salt in my nostrils instead of oil and the light by which my thoughts were lit, the phosphorescence and the stars. These were the nights.
>
> The days were pleasant too. I played a lot of bridge and poker but mostly the days were spent on deck, pacing with others, disbelievingly, the flight deck, refusing mentally to accept it was possible to unstick in so ridiculously short a length. But best of all there were many hours we spent sitting on the very front edge of the *Indomitable*. This was cambered in the most restful and convenient manner and there was a little fence which provided a footrest all the way along. One was suspended over the sea and could feel the prow cut the glorious blue of the Indian Ocean and watch the flying fish leap and scatter and fly like Spitfires by the hour. And again we would comment as we had in Khartoum that really it was the most wonderful of wars."

At least one pilot became ill during the voyage, the Canadian Sgt Rod Lawrence:

> "In the week that we were at Port Sudan, I had been quite sick with nausea and diarrhoea and felt generally pretty rotten. However, after a day or so at sea I started to feel better, but noticed that my eyeballs were turning yellow, as was my skin. This was later diagnosed by the carrier's doctor as jaundice. In any case, I was not allowed to fly off the carrier a week later when the two squadrons were launched."

The journey north-eastwards to their ultimate and as yet unknown destination was thus peaceful for the pilots and without major incident, although the aircraft assemblers were required to work flat out. Sub Lt(A) Popham wrote:

> "The hundred RAF men turned out to have worked only on Blenheims and Lysanders and did not know one end of a Hurricane from another; the mainplanes had all got mixed up and had to be sorted out; and the squadron ratings and officers were in the hangar, almost without a break, for 72 hours, staggering round, twelve or fifteen to a wing, juggling them

till the right ones were found, and juggling with them again until the bolt holes on wing-root and mainplane could be made to correspond and the bolts fitted. Then fillets had to be put on, guns loaded and checked, ailerons connected up; then fuelling, ranging, engine-testing, lashing down, and back on to the lift for the next one, with eyes blurred with sweat and bodies raw with prickly heat."[46]

Sgt Kelly's narrative continued:

"There were a few odd incidents but not too many – just one of note. *Indomitable* carried its own Sea Hurricanes for defence, which were catapulted off. Under their bellies were great hooks which when the pilot landed caught in the arrester wire, it being accepted that it was impossible to land and stop a Hurricane in the length of the flight deck otherwise. On this occasion 'Bats' [the batsman] so instructed, but the pilot either misreading the signal or preferring his own judgment, continued his approach until by the time he decided perhaps he had better go round again he had left it fractionally too late and his hook caught in the arrester wire at the precise moment he opened up his throttle. And there, for fascinating moments, the matter rested doubtfully. The Hurricane stayed where it was, motionless, ten feet above the deck, pointing to the sky like some huge bird straining at a leash, its engine roaring and its propeller creating a tremendous gale. The wire on the other hand, taut as a V-shaped iron bar, resisted. It was clear neither would give way and the expression on the poor pilot's face was a study in consternation. In the end it was propeller torque which settled things, slowly turning the Hurricane to the port side of the ship to deposit it, as the pilot throttled back and the hook was slipped, in the most undignified of positions athwart a gun turret."

Snowy Newlands enjoyed the restful time aboard the carrier:

"Halfway across the ocean they told us we were going to Singapore, but we didn't need to worry as all the Japanese would have were obsolete biplanes! We were wondering how we would get enough stickers to put on the sides of our Hurricanes for every one we shot down! I hadn't shot down anything by then.

The voyage was incredible – you could just sleep anywhere round the ship you wanted to. About three of us went up and slept in the anchor well, up in the bow. It was just below the flight deck where there was a bit of fresh air. One night the water came up the anchor shoot and went all under our beds without us getting wet. I remember having bacon and eggs and things and learning how to pack parachutes, and the Navy put on quite a display with their own planes on board. They used to do practice runs, towing drogues and shooting them down with the Bofors guns and ack-ack, and flying and entering patrols, landing and take-offs. We found it very interesting. Our Hurricanes were stacked below with their wings off. There was only room on the deck for 16 at a time to take off, so they assembled them in three batches and there were three flights to Batavia."

Indomitable continued unrelentingly towards the general direction of Java, to where the Hurricanes were to be flown. Kelly:

"On 27 January, having seen no land apart from the incomparably beautiful green and white foaming surf and the yellow green palm studded horseshoe of the Chagos Archipelago, the two squadrons were summoned to a flight deck brief delivered by the ship's commander. It had of course been accepted by now that it was Japanese we were booked to fight and here, on a blackboard erected on an easel, the commander chalked their advances so far as known."

Plt Off Tom Watson, one of the seven Canadian pilots aboard, remembered:

"The commander told us that it depended as to how far the Japanese had advanced down the Malayan peninsula as to where we were to land – Singapore, Palembang in Sumatra or Batavia in Java. Of course, it was to be Batavia."

Terry Kelly continued:

"I suppose it would have been proper for the 48 young men ranged in a semi-circle, in their khaki and shorts, with their detachable brevets pinned over their left breasts and their motley peaked or forage caps or pith helmets on their heads, to have been, if not alarmed, at least sobered by these revelations. But they were not. The sun was hot, the sea was sparkling blue, the breeze soft and steady – and there was excitement and adventure in the air. The map drawn on the blackboard meant nothing to most of them and they had heard of few of the places spoken of before. They didn't know with any sense of certainty quite where in the world they were, their geography being in most cases abysmal. As for the Japanese with their feeble wooden biplanes, they seemed as the scent of a drag hunt or a drogue in firing practice. It was almost as if someone had arranged their presence as an excuse for this splendid jamboree. But the commander's voice was grave and he spoke stirringly of the deeds of derring-do they would no doubt soon perform, assured them he was sure the world would hear of them and wished them luck. They listened with due politeness, a trifle embarrassed by these eulogies and having in spite of all his efforts conceived no real grip on the proposition, broke away with some relief to have a drink or two and talk it over."

Many of the pilots showed natural concern for what faced them but of more immediate importance were their first carrier deck take-offs. To allay these fears, the CO of the Sea Hurricane unit, Lt Cdr Butch Judd – at over six feet tall, a fearsome-looking, red-bearded, volatile but highly respected character – had long-range tanks fitted to his aircraft, took on a full load of fuel, and effortlessly took off. He completed a couple of circuits and landed, albeit with the aid of the arrester-hook. Plt Off Watson commented:

"He was quite a guy. He and all the Navy pilots talked to us and encouraged us – they were all nice guys."

At dawn on 28 January, with the carrier some 50 miles south of Christmas Island in the Indian Ocean, she prepared to fly off the Hurricanes to Batavia's civil airfield at Kemajoran, but there was a delay of several hours before the first aircraft could depart due to the late arrival of Blenheim escorts from Java, much to the annoyance of Wg Cdr J.D. Urie, RAF officer in charge of the operation, codenamed 'Opponent'. Pairs of Sea Hurricanes provided CAP in case Japanese aircraft approached, one pair flown by Lt(A) Brian Fiddes and Sub Lt(A) Popham being vectored onto an aircraft plotted on the ship's radar, which turned out to be an unannounced Catalina from Java and had been despatched to act as 'lifeboat' in the event of any of the Hurricanes being forced to ditch en route to Batavia. Popham noted:

"Brian and I were sent off on our first operational interception with our stomachs doing somersaults and our thumbs on the gun buttons – and that was one Catalina flying boat that nearly didn't get home."[47]

The 48 Hurricane pilots preparing for their first carrier take-offs were:

232 Squadron
Sqn Ldr A.J.A. Llewellin
Flt Lt E.W. Wright DFM
(attached from 605 Sqn)
Flt Lt I. Julian RNZAF
Plt Off J.C. Hutton

258 Squadron
Sqn Ldr J.A. Thomson
Flt Lt D.J.T. Sharp RNZAF
Flt Lt V.B. de la Perrelle (NZ)
Flg Off A.G. Donahue (US)
Flg Off H.A. Dobbyn RNZAF

232 Squadron
(attached from 605 Sqn)
Plt Off M.C. Fitzherbert
Plt Off R.T. Bainbridge
Plt Off L.A. Emmerton (Rhod)
Plt Off J.K. McKechnie RCAF
Plt Off T.W. Watson RCAF
Plt Off W.McG. Lockwood RCAF
(attached from 605 Sqn)
Plt Off E.C. Gartrell RNZAF
2/Lt J. Stewart SAAF
2/Lt N.R. Dummett SAAF
2/Lt N. Anderson SAAF
Sgt J.A. Sandeman Allen
Sgt G.J. King
Sgt R.W. Parr (South African)
Sgt F. Margarson
Sgt D. Kynman
Sgt A.W. May
Sgt G.J. Dunn RCAF
Sgt T.W. Young RAAF
Sgt I.D. Newlands RNZAF
Sgt W.A. Moodie RNZAF

258 Squadron
Plt Off B.A. McAlister RNZAF
Plt Off C. Campbell-White RNZAF
Plt Off A.H. Milnes
Plt Off J.A. Campbell (US)
Plt Off C. Kleckner RCAF (US)
Plt Off G.C.S. Macnamara (Rhod)
Plt Off A.D.M. Nash
Plt Off A. Brown (Can)
(attached from 242 Sqn)
Plt Off E.M.T. Tremlett
Plt Off D.B.F. Nicholls
Plt Off N.L. McCulloch
Sgt C.T.R. Kelly
Sgt P.T.M. Healey
Sgt H. Lambert
Sgt K.A. Glynn
Sgt N.H. Scott RCAF
Sgt A. Sheerin RAAF
Sgt R.B. Keedwell RCAF
Sgt L.A. Miller RCAF

In fact, due to the lateness of the day, only 16 Hurricanes – eight aircraft from each squadron – took off during the afternoon of the 28th, the remaining 32 following the next day. Plt Off Campbell-White recalled:

> "The big day arrived. All the gun positions and well decks to the side of the flight deck were boarded over – rather insulting – in case we swung on take-off. Then one by one we took off. A Naval control officer waved us into position. My turn came at last. Full rich mixture. Fine pitch. Trim adjusted. I put on 28 degrees of flap and was ready to go. At the signal to go, I stood on the brakes and opened up the engine to full throttle. As the plane began shuddering and straining on the brakes, I let it go. I shot down the very short runway keeping my eyes on the white line running down the middle, shot past the bridge island, ever the show off, waved to all the Navy and Air force crowding into the available space to see the take-off. The take-off was much quicker and easier than I expected, although most of the required take-off speed was reduced by the carrier steaming in the wind. In no time I was airborne and looking down on a very small aircraft carrier with its escorting destroyers. We had long-range tanks. I tested that fuel could be obtained from the tanks, as we all did according to our instructions. Then set course for Batavia. The journey was without incident."

Sgt Kelly again takes up the story, describing the occasion in greater detail:

> "...the first 16 Hurricanes were raised by the lift and packed herringbone fashion at the stern of the *Indomitable* and by the time the day had broken bright and clear and the sea had lost its greyness we had run up our engines, checked our instruments, made sure our kit bags were secure in the bellies of the fuselage and had stowed away the few odd pieces such as razors and revolvers in side pockets and camera gun mountings. There was nothing left to do but wait. We climbed from the cockpits, paced the now shortened deck, checked and rechecked our maps trying to grasp locations, harried the meteorological officer, chatted and smoked – and tried to ignore our beating hearts. It was not until

midday that we were ordered back into the cockpits and even then there was a long tense wait for the escorting Blenheims; for an hour perhaps we sat, helmets on gunsights or hung loose around our necks.

The Blenheims came and Squadron Leader Thomson was the first to go ... off he went ambling, it seemed, along the deck and was gone steadily, smoothly upwards. Junior [Sgt Ken Glynn] was his No.2. He taxied out and throttled back; down came the nose, up came the tailplane, along the pitiful length of flight deck roared the Hurricane and at the end, dropped out of sight and disappeared. It was very disconcerting. Third off was Flight Lieutenant Denny Sharp. I followed [in BE212]. Gingerly. There was a shade more room now that three aircraft had gone, that much longer runway, but Bats caught my eye and grinned, signalling me forward, remorselessly. It seemed very unreasonable – to waste those few precious yards, which might make all the difference to what happened to me. But Bats was implacable – right to the very mark I was directed. Go!

I opened the throttle with the greatest care, sliding my left hand very consciously along the box, keeping the brakes on for the last fleeting fraction of a second, then letting them go as I thrust the throttle fully forward. I remember the moment with extraordinary clarity even after all these years, the sudden surge of power, the touch of rudder to check the slight swing to port, the exaggerated tightness of the cockpit straps, the closeness of my helmet all dangling wires and tubes. I saw the control tower hurtle past on my right hand and the sea of faces with the entire ship's complement except those on essential duty watching, felt a bump and a sickening downward sink and saw with horror the sea rushing up to meet me.

Then the Hurricane was settling in the air as if it were a cushion against disaster and lifting me up and up and up. I raised the undercarriage lever, the green light went off obediently and by the time the red replaced it I was turning anti-clockwise and the huge *Indomitable* was only a tilted postage stamp a long way below. Ahead and above was Denny and higher still Thomson and, miraculously, Junior already tucked in neatly on his left. I closed in on Denny, who grinned his wicked grin and stuck a thumb up. And looking down I could see, like so many fluttering butterflies, aircraft streaming upwards from the speck below, and the otherwise empty sea was not empty after all for there was Christmas Island. We circled twice to form formation then fell in behind the Blenheim heading north for Java with the sun on our left, high and burning hot. With the unaccustomed long-range tanks the Hurricane felt sluggish and resentful yet still willing. It was an aircraft that engendered tremendous confidence, easy and even to fly, tough, with a fabric fuselage but powerful riveted wings. I could feel it objecting to the load of those tanks slung like bombs beneath the mainplanes, much as a runner would object to a pack upon his back.

We flew in comparatively loose formation, rising and falling in the air currents, glad to be sharing after all this time that curious intimacy of the air again. We had to keep radio silence so all we could do was grin and make small signs at each other. There was no land anywhere and we were land birds, this vast expanse of cloudless sky and endless sea was faintly disturbing. The sun blazed on us as our bodies grew stiff and cramped, so the left side of our faces were burned red and sore, something not considered. After two and a half hours flying when I was just beginning to wonder, we saw the faint blur of Java. We lost height steadily so that by the time we crossed the coast we were low enough to fly over the vivid red and emerald landscape, lower than a ridge of hills, on the starboard side before we roared over Batavia, with its red roofs and parks, its fine buildings, its busy streets and its canal flowing through the very centre of the city."

All landed safely.

"There was a welcoming committee and a marvellous light meal set out on a long thin

> table. There were Malays to serve us, dressed in sarongs and tunics and wearing curious hats like washerwomen. There was copious light beer. Outside on the tarmac, seen through the glass wall of the dining room, were our sixteen Hurricanes, safe and sound."

Next morning, 15 Hurricanes (the other had developed a fault) led by Sqn Ldr Thomson flew on to the secret Palembang 2 airfield (known to the RAF as P2) in Sumatra, a two-and-a-quarter hour flight over sea and jungle. The main airfield in Sumatra was sited at Pangkalanbenteng (known to the RAF as P1), about five miles north of Palembang township. It had been developed for civil use and was well known to the Japanese. In the early days of the war three squadrons of Dutch Glenn Martins had been based there. P2 airfield had been created some 50 miles south of Palembang, in a natural clearing within the jungle at Praboemoelih; to this airfield the RAF's bombers had been diverted, while the fighters remained at P1. Two smaller airfields were located at Djambi, about 120 miles north-west of P1, and at Lahat, about 50 miles south-west of P2. Terence Kelly continued:

> "We landed not without mishap, two more aircraft being temporarily put out of commission through their wheels catching the deep ruts left by Flying Fortresses which had used the place [it is believed that one of the damaged Hurricanes was that flown by Sgt Lloyd Miller]. And everywhere the disorganization of a hastily put-together piecemeal resistance showed. When we landed the airfield was deserted, our Hurricanes with their long-range tanks slung like bombs under the wings having been presumed a raiding force. The air raid sirens had sounded and with curt unanimity the waiting ground staff, their nerves tattered by the events of Singapore, had taken to the jungle.
>
> It was here, at P2, within two-and-a-half hours' flying time of Singapore, we learnt for the first time the capabilities of the Japanese fighter now called a Zero, but to us and the pilots of Singapore, a Navy 0. We were warned of a speed, which matched our own, and difficult to believe, in fact hardly believed, a superior manoeuvrability. No one told us where the Navy 0 was inferior, which in many ways it was, because no one was in a mood to talk of cheerful things or even imagine there could be cheerful things to talk about. When we flew off the *Indomitable* it was to clear the Jap wooden biplanes from the skies. This was unfortunate. We were going to learn the hard way and in the process fritter away a golden opportunity. No one thought to tell us we had better fire power, a better ceiling and that a Hurricane could take punishment which reduced a Navy 0 to shreds; no one imagined there was a tactic which in the end four of us would use time and time again against equally large numbers, as those met with in Singapore, with negligible personal risk."

An immediate task was to remove the guns, which were coated in anti-corrosion grease, and have them cleaned and reloaded – not a quick nor simple undertaking, but one that had to be done with all haste. Campbell-White later reflected:

> "It was at Palembang that we first heard the Japs were not the pushover that we believed and they had a very good fighter aircraft called the Zero which was extremely manoeuvrable, particularly so as they did not have protective armoured plating. Why British intelligence hadn't discovered this important fact, I don't know, but then the Singapore campaign was a disaster from start to finish. Many good lives were lost unnecessarily. Good planning and leadership would have made a lot of difference to the final outcome, but even that would not have helped much without a knowledge of the Japanese military resources and strategy."

With guns thus operative and with full tanks, the Hurricanes departed during the afternoon on the last leg of the journey to Singapore, guided and led by two Blenheims. Plt Off Ting Macnamara recalled:

"We soon left Sumatra behind us and flying low over the water crossed many islands dotted about the sea and were more than pleased to see Singapore materialise way ahead of us. Lowering our wheels we flew in slowly over the river and soon landed and parked our aircraft on what appeared to be the deserted aerodrome of Seletar.

After some delay we contacted someone from Ops only to learn that our coming had been unheralded, the sirens had sounded and everyone had scuttled. Had we not lowered our wheels we would have been fired on by naval units and anti-aircraft guns. Hurricanes, it appeared, were not two a penny out here and to have as many as 18 British aircraft approaching the island in formation was extremely rare and, had it not been for the two Blenheims that led us in, we would have in all probability have been fired on anyway! We were learning slowly."

Watching their arrival were a number of Buffalo pilots who were expecting to be posted to the new Hurricane unit – which, in the event, did not happen. One of the Buffalo pilots recalled:

"We reached the drome about 15 minutes before about 50 Japanese bombers. When the bombs started to fall we found a couple of slit trenches, and kept our heads down. On looking around, we saw the place was a shambles – the stores, hangars and lots of buildings were on fire. Trucks and planes were burning, and the drome was full of craters. While we were surveying the scene, into the circuit came a Hurricane, which made a copybook approach and landing. The RAF used to issue ferry pilots a sun helmet – a real Livingstone job, known as a 'Bombay Bowler', converted to fly in and equipped with ear phones, microphones, etc. One can imagine how these looked in the cockpit of a fighter plane! The Hurricane taxied up to us and stopped. The pilot, complete with Bombay Bowler, slid the canopy back and in a very English voice, enquired: 'I say, what is going on around here?'"[48]

The first task was to get the underwing, long-range fuel tanks removed to enable the Hurricanes to be prepared for combat. Among those called upon to assist was the Engineer Officer of one of the Buffalo squadrons, Plt Off John David:

"Our major effort was to remove the external tanks and lighten the airframe as far as possible, so as to raise the rate of climb and give them some hope in turning combat with the Japanese Zero fighters. Amongst other things we removed the outer two pairs of Brownings, reducing the armament to eight guns. As usual, no provision had been made for the supply of ethylene glycol, and since cooling was marginal in that climate, coolant leaks became a continual nightmare."[49]

Meanwhile, Sqn Ldr Thomson and Flt Lt Denny Sharp were soon to be shocked by their first impressions of Singapore's Command, as the latter recalled:

"As courtesy and duty calls, I accompanied the CO on a search for the Station Commander. It was the middle of the day when you would think that he would be at Station HQ, on the airfield, so we went there. The Station HQ was deserted; rather, there were people there but nobody could tell us where the Station Commander was. So we went searching various places around the airfield to see if we could find him, but we couldn't. Somebody then suggested trying his quarters – one of the houses on the edge of the airfield. The two of us went round there- about 4 o'clock in the afternoon now – because we wanted our orders and needed to organise the servicing of the aircraft. We knocked on his door and he answered – in his pyjamas! This was typical of the state that Singapore was in. It was a waste of time asking him for orders. So we said our goodbyes and found another officer whom he had left in charge."

With the first contingent to arrive at Seletar was Plt Off Campbell-White, who later reflected:

> "There were banner headlines in the Singapore papers 'Hurricanes come to save Singapore.' How disillusioned the people of Singapore were soon to be. What should have been done, and the Japanese would have suffered a major defeat in the air, if it had been carried out, was to keep all the Hurricanes on the ground until they were in top fighting condition – all 30 of them – then have their outing at about 25,000 feet, at least, above the Japanese attack. The Japanese held the British Air Force in such contempt that they made no attempt to hide their intentions. Early in the morning a lone reconnaissance plane would circle the intended target, followed some time later, always at the same time, by a wave of bombers, 27 I think, in perfect formation. They were quite predictable so it would have been easy to lie in wait with a formidable force of Hurricanes. British losses would have been small but Japanese losses would have been heavy."

Also at Seletar, among those watching groundcrews working on their aircraft were Plt Off Bruce McAlister and Sgt Kelly, the latter writing:

> "The groundcrews were busy and working under difficulties. They had never worked on Hurricanes before, their spanners didn't fit and the removal of the long-range tanks was proving to be a stubborn mystery. They possessed no spares and they had no supplies of glycol, which was the coolant fluid for the Merlin engines. Above all, the guns, six in either wing, were presenting them with an unconsidered problem. Presumably to protect them from salt at sea, they were thickly caked with sticky grease of which, incidentally, we knew nothing – had we met Japanese, or even tried trial bursts, we would probably have blown the wings off! Or so they said. Anyway there was nothing to do but strip them down to each tiny part and clean these in hot thin oil and reassemble … and there were a lot of parts and a lot of guns.
>
> We hung around, Bruce and me – not because there was anything we could do but because there was not much else to do anyway and I suppose we felt that hanging around was the right thing to do. We chatted, smoked, remembered the odd bits and pieces, including our revolvers stowed away in the ciné gun camera mountings and retrieved them. At about half past nine the attention of the groundcrew began to wander and their eyes to turn with growing frequency to the sky. Not that there was any sound of aircraft – there was only the sound of birds and of the gentle shift of the morning breeze in the nearby rubber trees. The sun had begun to gather heat, the damp ground begun to shimmer – voices drifted, insects hummed. And the war seemed far away.
>
> And then, quite suddenly, one man called something to his mates and the man working on my guns dropped the sear pin, or whatever it was he happened to be wiping at the time, back into the bath of amber oil and set off with the rest with one accord towards the rubber. I never knew till then that Bruce McAlister could be angry. 'What the hell', he shouted, in his twangy, nasal voice, 'do you think you're doing? Where the hell do you think you're going?' They stopped, momentarily, and one man pointed to the sky. I looked up and there in an otherwise unmarked blue sky was drawn a white circle, a vapour trail which even as I looked at it was thickening lazily and leaving behind the white sparkling diamond of the reconnaissance aircraft which had made it. 'So?' said Bruce, puzzled. 'Means it's us this morning, sir.' That made no sense – that circle must have encompassed the whole of Singapore. So I asked him what he meant. 'It's what they do, Sarge. They send a kite ahead and draw a circle where they're going to bomb. They'll be here in half an hour.' And he set off towards the rubber, with no more ado, with the rest of them after a momentary hesitation straggling after him."

McAlister, being the only officer present, spontaneously made the same decision as Plt Off Jerry Parker had reached a few days earlier, when faced with a similar problem:

"'Get your gun out', I heard Bruce say and to my surprise I saw that he already had his revolver in his hand. I fumbled for my own with a feeling that the situation was extra unreal. 'Stop!' shouted Bruce to the back of the departing men. They stopped, turning their heads. 'Come back,' he ordered them. They came slowly back. When they were near enough, Bruce said: 'Anyone who heads back that way again until I've said he can is going to be shot.' There was a pause. I think we both felt the same as we stood there pointing our revolvers at that knot of unhappy men – uncomfortable and embarrassed. 'It may not be very pleasant,' he said, 'but there does happen to be a war on and we've got to be able to get these Hurricanes in the sky and you're going to stay and clean our guns until we say you can go and that's all there is to it. Now get on with it.' We didn't have any more trouble."

In the meantime, the second batch of Hurricanes had taken off from *Indomitable*, Sgt Sandy Allen of 232 Squadron being the first off in BG687:

"I was a little bit worried because I was the first to go. I just sat there, at the front, and wondered if I would get airborne but, in the event, I reckon I was in the air as I passed the bridge. We circled around until all were up safely and then sailed on in."

Sgt Snowy Newlands was about halfway down the line:

"They were pretty jittery on the carrier and that's why they made us fly off at that stage. Apparently they had word that the Japanese were flying around in that area, and had shipping there too. There was a dotted line down the middle of the deck and you put your nose on that and you held it there, because the carrier was rising and falling and rolling sideways a bit. Because the leading plane was about a third of the way up the deck, the forward pilots were going crook having less deck-space in which to take off so they made everybody go up and start from that forward point.

We had big, heavy, long-range tanks on and all our own personal kit stored behind the radio sets. It was a nice, beautiful sunny day and we didn't fly very high. We were just strung out flying in coarse pitch at the most economical speed – 180mph I recall. On the flight I kept checking my brake pressure, which wasn't increasing, as it should have. So I knew I didn't have any brakes. By the time I got there the petrol was getting well down, and I thought I didn't have enough to do another circuit, so I came in over the jungle pretty low. I was about halfway in the flight I suppose – quite a few had landed before me and I could see one plane had come down on the runway and was standing on its nose at the far end. I guessed he didn't have any brakes either and, as I didn't want to bang into him, I kept down fairly low and I actually cut my motor, before I got on the ground. But, with the heat coming off the concrete runway, I just kept floating and floating. Kemajoran had quite a long runway and I was getting down towards the end of it and could see these Hurricanes – obviously ones that had got there before me, including some from the day before – parked on the grass either side. My speed got down to about 20mph and by kicking the rudder hard a few times, I just managed to get myself off the runway without banging into the chap at the end. As I came off I tried to go between a couple of parked planes but it had been raining heavily and I skidded sideways and actually ended up bashing into another plane with my prop. He was a South African named Anderson. He was just getting his head out of the cockpit and my propeller slid his cockpit cover back over his skull, so he ended up in hospital. The CO was furious! So I had to wait a few days until my plane got fixed up."

A third Hurricane had also been slightly damaged when the port oleo leg of the aircraft collapsed on touching down, its pilot 2/Lt John Stewart escaping unhurt[50]. Of Kemajoran and the subsequent flight to P2, Flg Off Donahue wrote:

"This airport was a stopping-point in peacetime for the big Dutch airline KLM and they had a passenger terminal, complete with restaurant, waiting-room, and bar where I got the first 'Coca Cola' I'd tasted since leaving America. We had lunch, and then took off on the next leg, a flight of three hundred miles or so north-west to a jungle airdrome in Sumatra. It was a beautiful trip, for the sun was out and the fertile, well-cultivated farmlands of Java appeared rich and green as we cruised over them. There were scattered fluffy clouds under us at low altitude that glistened softly in the sunlight and set off the beauty of the landscape underneath. Then the coast, the sea, a beautiful blue-green, and the white-capped waves gleaming in long lines of snowy crest as they collapsed majestically along the beaches far below us, in all the splendour of colour that you see in technicolor pictures of South Sea islands.

On out across the sea for half-an-hour or so – and then Sumatra, a far different kind of country from Java. No cultivated farmlands here. No sign of any kind of civilization. Just endless dark jungle stretching off into the steamy horizon in all directions, broken only at great intervals by some silvery stream winding its way across our course and off into the distance. Many, many miles of this, until at last a broken patch appeared ahead of us, and as we neared this it took shape as an airdrome cleared out of the jungle – our stopping-point. As we circled the field before landing, I noticed a strange type of four-engined bomber parked on the ground. It looked like pictures I'd seen of the American Flying Fortress bombers, and I wondered if it could really be an American plane out here in the war zone. I knew America was in the war now, but somehow I just couldn't connect the Stars and Stripes and American uniform with the awfulness of real fighting.

But when I landed and taxied past the bomber, I saw that it really was so. There were the American insignia of white star over red and blue circles on the sides of the fuselage, seeming very strange to me now after having seen only British and German insignia for so long. There were the strange, light-tan uniforms and caps of US Army officers and men around the machine, and they gave me a queer thrill. The men were starting their engines then, and before I had time to park my machine and climb out, they were already taxiing down the field to take off, so I didn't get to talk to them. I was told they didn't belong here and had only landed for gas."

The B-17 was in fact conveying General Sir Archibald Wavell (Allied Commander-in-Chief SE Asia) to his headquarters in Java following another brief visit to Singapore. The General took the opportunity to stretch his legs and soon found himself in conversation with another of 258 Squadron's American pilots, Plt Off Cardell Kleckner, as Kelly recalled:

"Kleckner was a husky Texan who was not in the least overawed and pre-empting any higher ranking officers hastily polishing their buttons, he strode out and met the General halfway between his aircraft and the terminal building. And there they stood for the time it took the refuelling to be completed – perhaps 20 minutes – chatting. And the subject of their conversation, as Kleckner was to relay once Wavell was on his way, was the situation at P1, our problems and our shortages. And for good measure Kleckner had thrown in his own opinions as to why it had all gone wrong so far and what should be done to make sure it didn't go so wrong in the future. I often wondered what Wavell thought of Kleckner's views."

It was now too late for the Hurricanes to go any further that day, so after getting their aircraft serviced and put away, the pilots prepared to stay for the night. Donahue:

"This airdrome was simply a couple of enormous runways cleared in the jungle, which grew thickly right up to the edge of the field on all sides. Little bays for parking airplanes were cut back into the trees, so that when a machine was parked and branches thrown over the top it was effectively concealed from the air. The RAF was just getting established here, and the officers' mess was a large wooden shed with concrete floor, and wooden benches and tables for us to eat at. We lined up at mealtime and drew tea in tin cups from a big boiler, and dipped stew from another boiler into tin plates. Bread, margarine, canned strawberry jam, fresh bananas, and pineapples completed our fare. We slept in camp cots and learned the intricacies of enclosing ourselves in overhung mosquito-netting affairs, which all beds have in tropical places.

The air had been very hot and muggy when we landed, but during the night there were little rains accompanied by some thunder and lightning every hour or so, and it became comfortably cool. However, by the time we got up next morning it was hot and steamy just as before. The weather was too questionable for us to continue to Singapore, so we lay over, and most of us spent the day working on our airplanes. Our machines were brand new, having just been shipped out from England, and there were numerous things to take care of before they would be in fighting condition.

Among other things, all the machine guns were heavily coated inside and out with a special grease to resist corrosion on the long sea journey. I spent most of the day working with some armourers on my airplane, removing and disassembling its twelve guns, carefully cleaning all the parts in gasoline, greasing, and oiling the parts properly for service, and then reassembling, installing, and loading them. We worked beside the airplane, sitting on empty gasoline cans, retreating under the wings to work during the frequent showers that swept across. And while we worked, by chatting with these armourers who had all been in the fighting zone in Malaya until recently, I gradually assimilated some of the picture of what lay ahead for us."

Sgt Gordie Dunn of 232 Squadron similarly recalled cleaning the grease out of the gun barrels, but by using a very different and much quicker method:

"Once I had removed the gun barrels, I suggested to Tom Young that we lay them on the embers of a nearby fire so that the grease would slowly melt. As we were doing this, the CO came over and angrily enquired what the hell we thought we were playing at! Didn't we realise we would warp the barrels? I told him that my grandfather had been a gunsmith in Canada and had imported fowling pieces from England. These were always heavily coated in grease to avoid corrosion during the long sea crossings, and he would clean the grease away in this manner. I added that if delicate and expensive shotgun barrels could stand the heat, I was sure that the heavy-duty machine-gun barrels would not be adversely affected – anyway, the barrels heated to a greater temperature when they were fired! He quietly accepted my argument and walked away. The method worked."

Another problem was lack of harmonisation of the guns. Sgt Fred Margarson devised a method of harmonising his own:

"The procedure for harmonising was to jack up the aircraft in a flying position, drop a plumb-line from the propeller base and the tailwheel, lining this up with a target at an appropriate distance – as far as I can remember, it was about 300 feet. All the guns were sighted by means of this prism eyesight, which converted a vertical line of sight to sight along and through the barrel of the gun, the gun then being adjusted to point directly at the target marker, this giving concentrated fire at this point. I personally stripped the prism viewfinder from my camera, fitted this to an empty .303 shell case, in an attempt to make a harmonising instrument. It worked, but due to the time involved and the vast amount of work that had to be carried out by the pilots, I was only able to synchronise the guns of three aircraft."

With the various tasks completed, a few of the pilots decided to do a bit of hunting, including Sandy Allen: "We went hunting wild boar with revolvers – not a very wise thing to do as it was very dangerous."

The CO of the NZ Buffalo Squadron at Singapore, Sqn Ldr Wilf Clouston DFC – former CO of 258 Squadron in the UK – was full of praise for the efforts of all concerned in getting the Hurricanes operational:

> "The most outstanding event from the fighter angle after the outbreak of the war was the arrival of Hurricane reinforcements, both crated and by air. It was soon apparent, however, that owing to the lack of personnel for assembly and maintenance, they were not quite the asset that was first imagined. The aircraft that flew in were without groundcrews; they had been transhipped by carrier and their guns were packed with grease. This all had to be removed before the aircraft were operational. The pilots showed great initiative and the squadrons were operational within 24 hours of arrival. With the assistance of the groundcrews of 488 and 243 Squadrons, a comparatively high degree of serviceability was maintained."

30 January

Early in the morning Flt Lt Ricky Wright led 2/Lt Neil Dummett and Plt Off Joe Hutton – the advanced echelon of the second batch of 16 Hurricanes – from P2 to Seletar, arriving shortly before an air raid commenced. The new arrivals at Singapore soon had a taste of war at first-hand when 27 bombers with fighter escort raided various targets, including the docks, during which one of the new Hurricanes was damaged. Ting Macnamara and his colleagues – with no aircraft ready to fly – passed the time watching the Japanese air raid:

> "We lay down on our backs behind some mounds of earth and watched this lovely armada of bright silver planes slowly turn to do their bombing run. Their escorting fighters played around high above. We saw the bombs released and they crashed down on us with a whine and with sickening thuds. Their bombs dropped, they all turned again and flew off home leaving one with the impression that they had all been out on a routine practice run. The drome was a mess. Some of our own planes, a Blenheim and one or two Brewsters, were wrecked or burning. The hangars situated – thank God – on the other side of the drome were a blazing mass. I doubt if a bomb had been wasted."

A number of 232 (Provisional) Squadron's Hurricanes managed to intercept the raid and Flt Lt Murray Taylor claimed a Ki-27 destroyed and a bomber probably so, while Plt Off Sandy McCulloch claimed another bomber as probably destroyed and Sgt Henry Nicholls a Ki-27 probably shot down. One of the Hurricanes (recorded erroneously as BE728) was flown by ace Buffalo pilot Sgt Geoff Fisken of 243 Squadron, who had soloed on the type a few days earlier. He failed to make contact with the raiders, however. Flt Lt Hutcheson (BG722) and Sgts MacIntosh and Meharry of 488 Squadron also flew a sortie with 232 but similarly failed to make contact. There were no losses on this occasion.

The three 488 Squadron Hurricanes landed at Tengah, where the one flown by Sgt Meharry collided with a pile of rubble and was slightly damaged. Their arrival did not please Grp Capt Frank Watts, the Station Commander, as later related by Flt Lt John Hutcheson:

> "I was leading a flight of three Hurricanes and, when we came to land at Kallang, found the drome was out of action so we landed at Tengah. It was absolutely deserted and an air raid warning was still on. I took my two pilots into the deserted officers' mess. We had a couple of drinks to soothe our nerves after being in action and then the all clear sounded. Well, out of the rubber trees and surrounding shelter all of the Station personnel came out from hiding. The Station Commander demanded to know why we had landed on his

drome of all places possible. He said: 'If they know you are here they will bomb us', and he told us to take off immediately. As he was doing his scone two more Hurricanes came in. They were from 232 Squadron and were led by Sqn Ldr Brooker. Like us, they had been ordered to land at Tengah by Ops.

The Station Commander finally gave permission for us to go and have some food – our first that day – but said that we must get our machines off the drome asap. Brooker and I then went to the officers' mess and the others to the sergeants' mess. In the middle of the meal I was called to the phone and was told by the Station Commander to get our machines off the drome at once as a raid was coming in. We raced down to the field but could not find any airmen to help us start up. We could only get two machines started so Brooker and I took off. We called Control as soon as airborne and advised we were on patrol. They were very surprised and said that they had not given any instructions for a scramble. However, they kept us up and finally ordered me to land back at Tengah, while Brooker was able to get down at Seletar. Such was the depth to which morale and confidence had sunk in some areas."

A little later, Flt Lt Jack Oakden (BM900) and Plt Off Bunt Pettit (BG722) took off from Kallang in the two serviceable 488 Squadron Hurricanes and carried out a patrol over the Dutch islands. Nothing was seen but on return, the two pilots did a formation approach and landing, as the latter's air speed indicator was unserviceable. Both got down safely.

Later still, in bad weather, three Buffaloes patrolled off Singapore when one became separated and subsequently lost; the Australian pilot belly-landed his aircraft in a swamp on Bintan island, about 50 miles south of Singapore, the impact rendering him unconscious. The Buffalo had in fact come down within a few hundred yards of where 232(P) Squadron's Plt Off John Gorton – who had crash-landed nine days earlier – was being cared for; the same natives lifted the Buffalo pilot from the wreck and carried him to Gorton's hut. On recovery, the Buffalo pilot put a call through to Singapore, following which Air Sea Rescue pinnace *No. 53* skippered by Sgt W.A. Bullock RAF, was sent to convey them back to the Island. While the two pilots waited on the beach, three A6Ms flew low over the island, obviously attracted by the crash-landed Buffalo, but did not open fire.

During one of the raids, three of 258 Squadron's pilots – Plt Offs Micky Nash, Ambrose Milnes and Campbell-White – narrowly missed injury when they were caught in the open during a bombing raid. They just managed to reach a drainage ditch and were showered with dirt from a bomb that landed close by, but were unhurt. The remainder of the second batch of 16 Hurricanes arrived at Seletar from P1 that evening, including that flown by Donahue:

"After I was down I taxied to a spot as far as possible from any other plane (for dispersal in case of bombing), and hopped out gratefully. As I was stretching to get rid of my cramps, I happened to think that by rights I should have made a ceremony of climbing down from my machine, for it meant that I was setting foot on the continent of Asia for the first time. I borrowed a screwdriver to remove the panels in the sides and bottom of the fuselage of my airplane, and hurried to untie and unload my baggage, which I had fastened in various nooks and crannies of the framework. A lorry came around to collect some of us, and we were driven to the officers' mess, a great beautiful building of dark-grey stone at the top of a gentle grassy incline overlooking the airdrome. I was anxious to get word of my American friend from Waxahachie, Texas, Tex Marchbanks, whom I'd said good-bye to in the American Eagle Club just before I left England, when he told me he was going to Singapore. He should have arrived here ahead of us, because we had been delayed and re-routed on the way. Red Campbell, who was also a friend of Tex, gave me the bad news. Having arrived here ahead of me in the first group, Ted had already enquired, and learned that Tex had been killed a couple of weeks before."

That night a section of the concrete causeway joining Singapore to the mainland across the mile-wide Johore Straits was blown up, effectively sealing the fate of the Island. The only escape now was by air or sea.

31 January

More violent action returned to the skies over Singapore on the last day of the month, when the siege of the island began. A JAAF bombing force approached, again escorted by the 64th Sentai. A Flight of 258 Squadron scrambled, seven Hurricanes taking off led by Flt Lt Sharp, together with some from 232(P) Squadron, Donahue observed:

"Pilots were bolting from the dispersal huts and racing towards their airplanes, groundcrews running to help. Nearest to us, we could see Red [Campbell] take the bottom wing of his machine in a leap and then disappear into his cockpit. A moment of tense quiet followed, while the boys were getting settled in their machines with helmets, parachutes, and seat-straps buckled; then, down the line, the first engine came to life, its note rising to a surprised bellow almost as soon as it started, when the pilot slammed his throttle ahead rudely to get going. Other engines joined the chorus one after another, and clouds of dust billowed up as the Hurricanes left their parking spaces, coolies running in all directions to get out of the way. The field became alive with planes, all heading for the end of the runway, the pilots taxiing jerkily, as fast as they dared, dodging bomb craters, racing in clear stretches, slowing down again, stopping to avoid collisions or let others by, speeding up again, all in a bedlam of noise from the dozen Rolls-Royce engines, each roaring fiercely in spurts, quieting momentarily, bellowing out again, and slowing once more, in response to the hurried manipulations of throttles as the pilots made their way by fits and starts across the drome.

The two leading machines arrived and turned in the end of the runway, pausing momentarily, their mighty engines trumpeting at idling speed. Then their idling propellers became invisible and a great stentorian roar swept across the field to us, drowning all the other din, as these two machines gathered speed down the runway and were off, skimming up over the boundary, wheels rising upward and inward to their recesses in the fuselages after taking off, like pigeons folding up their legs. Others followed, one pair after another. They made a gentle left-hand climbing sweep around the airdrome, while the last ones to take off caught up and took their places in the formation; then they disappeared into the blue, climbing steeply, and peace and quiet came back to the airdrome. A few minutes later the air-raid sirens sounded."

Flt Lt Sharp's flight ran into a large formation of bombers over Johore and immediately attacked:

"We had some radar up the Malayan peninsular and they were able to forewarn us when a Jap raid was approaching Singapore. So initially, on the first raid we actually did get above the bombers, and I am unsure at this point of time, whether I was leading the Squadron or leading my flight. Anyway we divided the Squadron into two flights; one flight to go to the left of the bomber formation and attack the fighters, and the other flight to go to the right of the bombers and attack them. We were over Singapore when it all happened. So one flight [from 232 Squadron] attacked the fighters and I was leading the flight that attacked the bombers.

We made a quarter attack. The bombers, 27 in vic formation, each carried machine guns in the upper fuselage and any attack from behind ensured you ran into a concentration of machine-gun fire. I made a quarter attack from right angles and I came in underneath the leading aircraft, firing about a three-second burst. As I was diving smoke came into the cockpit and I knew that I had been hit, so I just kept on diving down and levelled out around about 15,000 feet. I wasn't on fire, but had been hit in the oil and glycol tank and the radiator. I was losing oil and glycol and knew the engine was going to seize, so I decided to land at Seletar, which was full of bomb holes, but I was able to dodge them. I never saw what happened to the aircraft I had attacked – but the pilots coming behind me saw it blow up and go down in flames. I don't know whether it was the leader or the one next to the leader, because it was a close formation of three aircraft – and it could have been either one of those three. I wasn't wounded."

Plt Off Red Campbell recalled:

"The Singapore warning system was bad. We would take off, heading south, away from the Malay peninsula to get altitude. 'Tally-ho!' on the bombers came just north of Singapore, and our squadron – all seven of us – dived into them. The lead bomber in the right-hand section attracted my attention. My first burst hit in the upper rear gunner's position, putting him out of action. I could see him lying back over the gun, which was pointing straight up. I continued my attack all the way in until I was dead astern. From this position I took several short bursts with no effect. I then realised that since I was holding my gun-sight square on his tail cone, my guns were about six feet below and about eight feet out from my line of sight, so most of my bullets were passing below him.

I pulled up to correct this, and his two wingmen, whom I had been ignoring, opened fire on me. They had not been able to depress their guns sufficiently to do this before, without hitting their own tail surfaces. I got the hell out of there and then pulled up and made a quick belly shot. By this time there seemed to be fighters and tracer bullets all over the place. As I dove away I saw one bomber drop out of formation and blow up. I could not tell if it was mine or the one Denny Sharp destroyed."[51]

Two elements of Ki-43s led by Lts Shogo Takeuchi and Yohei Hinoki then attacked the Hurricanes. Campbell continued:

"In the next moment I noticed two Zeros chasing a Hurricane. They had him boxed in, and I started to dive to help. The Hurricane pilot, probably Bruce McAlister, turned as if he was going to attack me. In the confusion he must have thought I was an enemy aircraft. I turned away so he could see my lower surfaces, where the markings were easier to read, and he turned back. The two Zeros closed in on him and he dove away, appearing to be out of control and trailing white smoke. I continued my dive and observed hits on the Zero on the left side, who appeared to be the section leader. I continued firing from about 50 yards when he pulled up vertically, engulfed in flames. I had to do a very violent snap roll to avoid hitting him. I was doing about 400mph when I snapped it. Something must have bent; that Hurricane never did fly straight again.

When my eyes came back into focus, I noticed that the other Zero was flying alongside of me, parallel, and we were just looking at each other. I turned into him, and for some reason he turned right in front of me. I opened fire and saw some hits. I fired only a few shots and suddenly had a feeling that there was something behind me. By the time I had cleared my tail, he was long gone. I dove for the deck to make myself a more difficult target. On the way back I used the little ammunition I had left on some troops along the road. For this engagement I claimed one destroyed, two damaged."

At about the same time Sgt Ron Dovell of 232(P) Squadron saw a fighter diving on his tail; he put his Hurricane into a steep dive and saw the fighter pull away. He followed and gave it a long burst:

"When I saw the enemy there seemed to be dozens of fighters weaving about and

> covering the bombers. I saw a Navy 0 fighter diving on my tail, and I went into a steep dive. Looking in my mirror, I saw him pull out and do a steep turn. I went round in an even steeper turn, and gave him a fairly long burst. Flames and black smoke poured from the aircraft, and my flight commander saw the Jap 'go for a Burton.'"

It would seem that Campbell and Dovell attacked the same aircraft, for the 64th Sentai reported only one loss, Sgt Maj Tsutomu Goto baling out over Johore, later returning safely to his unit on foot. The victory credited to Dovell raised his personal score to six and two probables. Donahue later wrote in his journal:

> "After some time a lone Hurricane appeared from the north-east, losing height until it was near the airdrome, when its pilot opened his engine and roared low and fast across the field, rocking his wings in the victory signal. We finished our drinks and hurried down to meet him as he taxied in. It was Red [Campbell], and we saw at once that his guns had been used because the fabric patches were shot away from the holes in the wings in front of them. He was grinning from ear to ear as he climbed out of his cockpit. 'I got a fighter, Art!' were his first words when he saw me. Boy, did we have a party!
>
> More Hurricanes were stringing back in at intervals now [including Plt Off Milnes in BE365], until all except four of the boys had landed safely. When these four didn't show up after a reasonable time we began to get worried. Finally we got a call from Sembawang airdrome, a few miles to the east, informing us that three of the four missing boys had force-landed there with their airplanes shot-up, and were unhurt. They were Kleck, Denny, and Micky [Nash]. The CO drove over to get them, returning about mid-afternoon, and after razzing them for 'forgetting to duck' we listened to their stories. Denny had shot down a bomber in flames, making the morning's score two definitely destroyed, in addition to several damaged. He had got some bullets in his engine and radiator from return fire from the bombers, so that his oil-tank and radiator went dry and his engine overheated and seized on the way back. He just made Sembawang, which was the nearest airdrome.
>
> Kleck also had an exciting time. He damaged a couple of bombers in the initial attack and then turned around to chase after one that was lagging behind the rest. He was almost within range when a Navy Zero fighter jumped him from behind. The first thing he knew, showers of tracers were going by him and there were several loud explosions in his airplane from cannon shells. Then he was blinded by steam and glycol and oil spray in his cockpit, so he rolled over and dived to get away. Flames were coming from his engine and he thought he would have to jump; but the fire went out after a moment and being over enemy territory he chose to try to make it home. His engine ran intermittently, giving him a little power, although catching fire a couple of times more for short periods. He finally made it to the Straits and across them to Sembawang. The field was badly bombed, with many unfilled craters. As he didn't have enough height to glide in on the runway, he had to land right among some craters. He bounced over most of them and then rolled to a stop at the edge of one, miraculously avoiding a crack-up.
>
> Micky said he had a go at one bomber and was attacking another when he suddenly noticed 'funny little holes', as he described them, appearing around him in his machine, whereupon he dived away. His engine and radiator were hit so that he, too, was blinded by steam, glycol, and oil. Once he thought he was on fire and unfastened his straps with the intention of baling out, but the fire didn't materialise. Then he saw Sembawang ahead so he stayed with his machine, trying to make it. When he got there his windshield was so covered with oil and glycol that he couldn't see enough to tell whether he was landing on the runway or not, and like Kleck he landed among the bomb craters. This was very bad because he hadn't had a chance to fasten his straps again. When Micky saw the bomb craters going past his wings he retracted his wheels so that his machine dropped down on its belly and slid to

a quick stop – a very wise move. By thus deliberately doing a minor crash he avoided the probability of a serious one, for if left on its wheels his plane would probably have rolled on until it hit a bomb crater. Not expecting to see anyone there whom he knew, he was quite astounded, on climbing out of his wrecked machine, to see Denny and Kleck approaching, laughing at him; and to learn that he was the third to force-land there!

Only one pilot now remained missing. That was Bruce, a New Zealand boy, one of the finest chaps I've known and the best-liked boy in the Squadron. Though we knew we had to expect casualties now, we felt it was too bad that he, of all of us, had to be the first. There was a Chinese businessman in Singapore who had a standing offer of a bottle of champagne for every Jap plane destroyed, so that evening Red and Denny, accompanied by some of the others, drove into town to collect the two bottles they had earned by their victories."

It was later learned that Plt Off Bruce McAlister, a 24-year-old from Invercargill, was shot down in flames over Johore, and had not been seen to bale out. He was one of the Squadron's more experienced pilots and had shared in the unit's first victory over Europe during the previous summer[52]; his loss was keenly felt. Thus, 258 Squadron had effectively lost four Hurricanes and one pilot in its first engagement with the Japanese. Pilots of the 64th Sentai reported seeing 15 Hurricanes after their charges had bombed. Attacking these, they claimed eight shot down, Lt Takeuchi claiming three in quick succession and thereby 'amazing' his CO, Major Kato, who witnessed the action, while Lt Hinoki claimed two more and another was credited to Sgt Maj Goto, despite him being shot down.

Later, during the afternoon, two sections of Buffaloes were ordered to patrol south of Singapore, there to rendezvous with three Hurricanes. On running low on fuel, one section returned early – and was promptly pursued by the Hurricanes who thought they were enemy fighters. One Buffalo was hit and crash-landed at Tengah, where the pilot managed to put the damaged aircraft down between two tree stumps, and it was not badly damaged. Art Donahue witnessed the crash:

"A Buffalo came gliding out of the distance, its engine dead. When about 300 feet up, the pilot apparently saw that he couldn't make the drome. He turned and disappeared behind a wood nearby, and the crash truck and ambulance went off in that direction. Later we learned that the pilot wasn't seriously hurt. His engine had been damaged in combat and he'd glided all the way back, trying to make the aerodrome, falling only a few hundred yards short."

488 Squadron was now ordered to leave. At the last moment, however, the ground party was ordered to remain and service the Hurricanes still on the island, 232(P) Squadron's ground personnel being shipped out to Palembang instead. Next day Sqn Ldr Brooker was ordered to evacuate the majority of his squadron, only he and five other pilots remaining. Consequently, Flt Lt Cooper-Slipper, now recovered, Plt Off Mendizabal and five sergeant pilots – Hackforth, Holmes, Porter, Dovell and Fairbairn made their way to Keppel Harbour, as Cooper-Slipper recalled:

"During the final days in Singapore I took most of the remaining airmen and pilots to the docks where we managed to secure passage to Palembang in the [old coaster] *Whang Po*."

They were accompanied by Sgt Dave Kynman, who had arrived at Seletar as a reinforcement only the previous day, and were also joined by Sgt John Fleming, just back from his adventures at Endau. The *Whang Po* eventually sailed at 0730 on 2 February, reaching Palembang at 1730 the next day. The 232(P) Squadron contingent made their way to P1 airfield, where they were absorbed in Sqn Ldr Llewellin's 232 Squadron.

During their brief period in action – 11 days – the pilots of 232(P) Squadron had been credited with 37 confirmed, 18 probables and 14 damaged for the loss of 18 Hurricanes. At least seven more had been badly damaged in combat, while two were destroyed on the ground. Nine pilots had been killed and four seriously wounded. Claims submitted during this period were as follows[53]:

Sgt R.L. Dovell	6:2:0	Plt Off R. Mendizabal	1:2:2
Flt Lt E. Murray Taylor	5:0:0	Plt Off W.N. McCulloch	1:1:0
Sgt H.T. Nicholls	4:1:3	Sgt C.F. Marsh (killed)	1:0:1
Sgt S.N. Hackforth	4:1:2	Sqn Ldr R.E.P. Brooker	1:0:0
Plt Off B.J. Parker	3:4:4	Sgt G.W. Schaffer (wounded)	1:0:0
Sgt G. Hardie	3:2:0 (injured)	Plt Off B.P. Daniel (killed)	1:0:0
Flt Lt H.A. Farthing	2:1:0 (killed)	Sgt I.S. Fairbairn	0:2:0
Sgt J.H. Leetham	2:1:0 (killed)	Sgt J.P. Fleming (missing-returned)	0:1:0
Flt Lt T.P.M. Cooper-Slipper	2:0:0 (ill)	Sgt K.H. Holmes	0:0:2

With most of Singapore's airfields coming under shellfire, a re-appraisal of the position was made and some change in dispositions followed. Two senior officers, Air Commodores S.F. Vincent DFC AFC and H.J.F. Hunter MC, had reached Singapore from the UK on 29 January, Hunter immediately being sent back to Palembang to command 225 (Bomber) Group, while Vincent took over 226 (Fighter) Group. It was decided to maintain only the six surviving Buffaloes and a force of about eight Hurricanes on the Island, which were to operate from Tengah, although Vincent and his Group Headquarters also left for Palembang (see Chapter IV).

1-4 February

The Japanese were back before midday on the first day of February, 60th Sentai Ki-21s escorted by 64th Sentai Ki-43s, attacking Sembawang. The latter engaged four Buffaloes and were credited with one possible victory. One Buffalo was indeed shot down and one Ki-43 claimed in return. There were no Hurricanes available to assist the handful of Buffaloes, since eight or nine of 258 Squadron's Hurricanes had earlier left Tengah for Palembang, six unserviceable or damaged aircraft remaining to follow as soon as possible. At the same time four 488 Squadron pilots – Plt Offs Noel Sharp, Snow White, Wally Greenhalgh (BE587) and Sgt Eddie Kuhn flew the remaining NZ Hurricanes to Palembang. The exodus had begun. One of those left behind was Art Donahue:

> "I didn't get to fly today either. My high hopes of seeing my first action against the Japs were frustrated by a new and most disappointing order, which we received early in the morning. Our squadron was to leave Singapore and move to Palembang. We were to go there because of the prospect of enemy raids on Palembang and on shipping in the Banka Straits. We were all terribly disappointed. None of us wanted to go, for here in Singapore we were right in the middle of things, while it would be comparatively quiet, so we thought, in Sumatra. And so it was that I felt anything but sorry when the CO told me I was to remain here temporarily, at least, in charge of a group of boys who had been left behind. It was necessary to leave six because there were that many aeroplanes not serviceable for the trip. The only order the CO gave me was to do what I could toward

getting these machines into flying condition. The boys took off for Palembang after lunch, leaving the airdrome strangely quiet and silent after the roar of their engines had died away in the distance. The only sign of war was the silent, sullen black smoke-column brooding above the horizon east and south of us."

Next day (2 February), following dawn reconnaissances by Ki-46s, Japanese bombers attacked Seletar airfield, Singapore City and the harbour, while escorting fighters patrolled overhead in strength, but no opposition was encountered. For the handful of fighter aircraft remaining at Tengah it was a day of respite and repair, for the pilots a day of enforced rest from flying and fighting.

By the morning of the 3rd, the Japanese air force continued its softening up of the defences; there remained an absence of defending fighters over Singapore, where large pails of black smoke now stretched across the sky from oil tanks ablaze at the Naval base. Japanese bombers continued pounding the harbour area, where the former P&O liner *Talthybius* (10,254 tons) – on war duty as a troopship and in the process of being unloaded with the help of RNZAF personnel owing to the disappearance of native labour – was disabled by one or two direct hits and a salvo of near misses. Fires broke out and the Chinese crew deserted, leaving the British crews to fight the fires. Plans originally intended for 488 Squadron were now changed. Instead of Sumatra, all pilots were ordered to proceed to Batavia at once, while the ground personnel were to remain with 232 Squadron. Although Jack Mackenzie had assumed command on 23 January, it was only now that he was promoted Acting Squadron Leader, whilst Plt Off Jack Oakden was promoted Acting Flight Lieutenant at the same time. The New Zealand pilots withdrew to Keppel Harbour that evening where they went aboard the cruiser HMS *Danae* and the troopship *City of Canterbury*, sailing at 2300. The troopship had been diverted to Singapore from the main convoy making for Batavia, but the situation now called for her to leave the area with her human cargo intact.

On the ground, work continued to raise unserviceable aircraft to a level of repair which would allow them at least to be flown to Palembang. At Tengah, 258 Squadron's three Hurricanes were almost ready, although Donahue's party would need to work well into the early hours of the following morning to complete the task. One of these was probably BE163 that had incurred minor damage when it overshot and ended up on its nose in a drainage ditch. At Kallang meanwhile, many 488 Squadron groundcrews – still awaiting the order to evacuate – were engaged in repairs to the airfield while others managed to make sufficient repairs to two of the Buffaloes left behind for them to flown to Sembawang before the end of the day.

Towards the end of the afternoon, a dozen of 258 Squadron's Hurricanes re-appeared over Singapore, led back to Tengah from Sumatra by Sqn Ldr Thomson. They were under orders to undertake a bomber escort mission at dawn the next day, when Hudsons and Blenheims were to attack Kluang airfield. At first light on 4 February, therefore, the Hurricane pilots duly arrived at dispersal – only to find no sign of any groundcrews, and their aircraft unprepared. The groundcrews were dispersed in tents all around the airfield, so there was no question of rousing them swiftly, and as gun panels were not fixed and no screwdrivers could be located anywhere, the operation had to be cancelled. Consequently, when the Hudsons reached the rendezvous point from Sembawang, no escort was waiting. The Blenheim flight also failed to rendezvous with the Hudsons, and finding no escort, they continued alone and bombed a railway line instead. Meanwhile the Hudsons made their way to Kluang where they bombed from 6,000 feet but were then intercepted by three of 59th Sentai's Ki-43s, which shot down one and damaged a second[54].

About an hour after the cancellation of the Hudson escort operation, Sqn Ldr Thomson was ordered to take all non-operational but airworthy Hurricanes to

Palembang, joined by the three repaired Hurricanes. This time however, two aircraft refused to start (Flt Lt Sharp's and Sgt Healey's) and these had to be left behind. Donahue was ordered to stay on in Singapore with Plt Offs Brown and Tremlett; they were to attempt to get three more Hurricanes airworthy, including the two that had failed to start. Ting Macnamara wrote:

> "The morning we were due to fly out we had a champagne breakfast at about 5am. It was not the happy affair it sounds for as we only had some eight aircraft that were not fit for operational flying, we tossed to see who would fly them away. There was no favouritism – whether officers or sergeant pilots we always endeavoured to give everyone the same equal chance."

There followed a tragic sequel to this disastrous episode. Grp Capt Frank Watts, Station Commander at Tengah for two years, had seen the morale and efficiency of his station deteriorate steadily. His squadrons had been cut to pieces and scores of airmen who had been attached to Tengah at short notice after the retreat from Malaya, now wandered around aimlessly. The Chinese, employed as labourers, would only carry out repairs to the runways under guard, and indeed a dozen had already been shot in an effort to stop the others fleeing. After the Hurricanes' mission had been called off, Grp Capt Watts was in the mess when a signal was received from Command Headquarters requiring him to report on why the fighters had not been ready. He finished his drink, excused himself, and went quietly to his room where he shot himself. One pilot[55] reflected:

> "By his suicide Poppa Watts solved nobody's problems but his own, as everyone else had to keep going and manage as best they could. Actually, I am sure Group Captain Watts had a death wish on him for some time before the event, because of some irrational behaviour on his part. Frequently, during daylight high level bombing attacks on Tengah, he would be seen walking about the airfield, out in the open, refusing to take cover at all while everybody else jumped into the nearest slit trenches available. If his behaviour was meant to be an inspiration it had the opposite effect, and we thought him out of his mind. When the Japanese came over for a high level attack in their formations of 27 or 45 aircraft at a time, they let everything go at once. However, paradoxically, I suppose he was right, as some men did get caught by direct hits on slit trenches while he went scot-free, but nobody would have accepted his logic at the time."

5-9 February

By the morning of 5 February, ships of the latest convoy to reach Singapore, loaded with troops and equipment, were now rapidly approaching and were being harassed on the way by Ki-48s of the 3rd Flying Battalion. At 1115 the largest of the vessels, the 16,909-ton liner-cum-troopship *Empress of Asia*, was attacked off the Sultan Shoal lighthouse about nine miles from Keppel Harbour, and was severely damaged, fires breaking out. She was loaded with the automatic weapons and heavy guns of the 18th Division and although these were destroyed there was only small loss of life.

Shelling of Sembawang became so intense that the airfield had now become untenable and, at last, Air HQ ordered all flyable aircraft to proceed to Tengah. Flt Lt Doug Vanderfield, a Buffalo pilot, flew a Hurricane (BG695) to safety, as did Flt Lt Jack Oakden with BD891. Several aircraft were destroyed on the aerodrome before they could get away; a shell passed right through the fuselage of a Buffalo just as it was about to start up but fortunately did not explode! The pilot, having escaped injury, leapt out, dashed to another aircraft and took off amidst a shower of explosions. Nonetheless, five Buffaloes and two Hurricanes managed to get away but, as they approached Tengah, the Japanese opened fire on that airfield also, damaging two of the Buffaloes as they came in to land.

As the shelling of Tengah intensified, orders came through to evacuate that airfield also. Before flying to Kallang, however, the pilots were briefed to patrol the area of the *Empress of Asia*. By now the troopship was burning steadily although rescue and salvage operations continued. The patrol was uneventful and, on reaching Kallang, two of the aircraft were damaged by taxiing into water-filled bomb craters, the whole surface of the airfield being under several inches of water following a torrential rainstorm. Even at this late stage, more Hurricanes were on their way from Palembang, a dozen 232 Squadron aircraft led by Sqn Ldr Llewellin (BE208/O) with orders to land at Tengah. The aircraft flown by Plt Off Bill Lockwood was not the one he had flown from the carrier but a veteran of the Singapore fighting:

"I was allotted a Hurricane that had come down from Singapore somewhat the worse for wear, having a few bullet holes in the canopy. We went into Singapore at 200 feet and saw plenty of black oil fires. I had to fly all the way with considerable pressure on the right rudder to keep the aircraft straight. We landed singly at Seletar. No sooner had I rolled to a stop than I was waved off by someone in a slit trench. An arm from the trench was pointed in the direction of another aerodrome, which I was to go to. I took off and taking the signal as an indicator, flew to Tengah. Immediately I fixed the trim tab by bending it in the appropriate direction, and then went to a building nearby for a cup of tea and a bite to eat. While sitting at a table looking out on the airstrip, the Japs started dropping shells close to and on the airstrip."

One of the Hurricanes had suffered engine trouble en route and had turned back, while the others were led to Singapore by two RAAF Hudsons, on board one of which were six additional Hurricane pilots, including Sgts Gordie Dunn, Tom Young, Fred Margarson, Bill Moodie and Snowy Newlands, who recalled:

"I had only a day or two at Palembang before they asked six of us to go to Singapore to pick up and bring back a few repaired Hurricanes, that had previously been damaged. So we went up in two Australian Hudsons. We were told to leave our kit at Palembang, and just to take an overnight bag, with toothbrush, razor and incidental stuff. I didn't even take a jacket and went just with shorts and shirt, although I had my parachute. Approaching Singapore the future did not look bright. Thick palls of smoke hung in the air fed by burning oil tanks and various ships. It looked like pictures we had seen of Dunkirk.

We landed on the first aerodrome, Sembawang, to find it deserted, but there was a hot roast dinner in the oven in the cookhouse, to which we helped ourselves. We were halfway through when Jap shells started landing all around, from guns only half a mile away, over the Johore Straits. Departing hurriedly we made for Tengah but it was also under shellfire so we didn't even bother landing. We might have barely touched the ground – that would be all. So we decided that was enough of that and we went and landed at Kallang airport, on the south side of the island. The airport had been extensively bombed before our arrival and was just a mass of bomb craters and we actually had to steer between them. The craters were about five metres wide and about two metres deep."

The Hurricanes landed at Tengah, three of A Flight being ordered off, once refuelled, to patrol the *Empress of Asia*, as Flt Lt Julian later wrote in his report:

"Three aircraft were quickly refuelled and took off, piloted by Sqn Ldr Llewellin, Flt Lt Julian and Sgt Pilot King. By that time the runway was under heavy shellfire. About 20 enemy fighters attacked the section from above as it tried to manoeuvre into position. Flt Lt Julian's aircraft was badly shot-up and he landed with his undercarriage u/s. Sgt King claimed one damaged and Sqn Ldr Llewellin managed to land slightly damaged. Upon the arrival of the British fighters the enemy abandoned the bombing of the *Empress of Asia*. Meanwhile, the balance of the Squadron under Flt Lt Wright was patrolling at 20,000 feet. R/T was useless and nothing was seen."

He added, in greater detail:

> "On the first day I got what could have been a probable. We didn't go off as a squadron but took off individually just as we were refuelled. You just couldn't wait. I got a lovely burst into one and he sort of fell away, so I didn't see the result. All I could see were Jap planes around me. I was in a tight turn and they were capable of turning inside me, so I quickly realised that if I stayed there I'd be dead. They were queued up waiting their turn and I could feel the bullets hitting the aircraft and bits and pieces started to disintegrate in the cockpit. I recall that the chain on the tail trim was shot off. So I just flicked straight over and went down. I remember having a hell of a job pulling out, because you used to take the slack up when you got it back on the stick, and the tail unit had just about been wiped off. But I was alive and that was my first real taste of action."

When returning to Tengah the Hurricanes were again met by heavy shellfire, two shells exploding on either side of Plt Off Joe Hutton's aircraft as he levelled out to land, causing him almost to lose control and crash. He was not injured. While the pilots were having lunch, a Buffalo came in to land just as a shell hit the ground beside it. The fighter turned over and caught fire, the Australian pilot being rescued by Plt Off Tom Watson amongst others. The pilot was badly burned on the face and head, and was driven to a nearby Army hospital by Watson. As a result of the constant shelling, all aircraft were now ordered to Kallang, including the two 258 Squadron machines, spare pilots following by car. When Watson returned from his trip to the hospital it was to find the squadron gone, his own aircraft included. This had been taken by a pilot whose unserviceable machine had been left behind, examination of which revealed that it lacked only a wheel. With the aid of Plt Off Pop Wright, the unit's Engineering Officer, Watson was able to obtain a replacement, subsequently taking off to rejoin the others, who had been ordered to Kallang. This latter airfield was also heavily bomb-pitted, which had caused Plt Off John McKechnie – at 30 probably the oldest pilot on the squadron – to crash when landing; he emerged from his damaged Hurricane shaken but unhurt. LAC Boyd was still keeping a record of events:

> "This morning, before any of the Hurricanes landed, we had a terrific bombing raid. It ran right down the aerodrome extension; straight past the Dutch dispersal foxholes where we are now sheltering. Once again it was all so sudden and without warning. We all crowded and grovelled in the foxholes like frightened rabbits. We were all fearful. I now know what stark fear is, when suddenly faced with the unexpected. You sweat terrifically, shiver all over involuntarily. They seem to be aiming at the centre of your back, and there are the hammer blows of the bombs that seem to start a long way away, and then they gradually go away again. And what relief when it is all over. You feel so helpless, being unable to hit back. You just sit there, and your mind whirls, and you hope for the best all the time, dreading a terrible shattering, blinding hammer blow of extreme terror and agony if the bomb should hit your puny, miserable, little foxhole in which you are sheltering like a scared kitten. If only we could fight back, to be given a sporting chance. But when there is no opposition to the Japs and they can pick the exact spot they wish to hit, it is just hell on earth. One is stricken with a terrible fear as well as anger. When it is all over one crawls out of the foxhole, joins one's comrades, and laugh and joke a little idiotically to try and cover up one's nervousness. When bombs are falling all men are equal, they have to take cover and grovel into the earth, the whole lot of them from the Air Marshal down to the lowliest erk. Some amazingly can hide their feelings and can appear unmoved. (This written minutes after a raid.)"

He added:

> "Today a section of 488/B Flight was sent to Sembawang but it was being shelled for about an hour so they had to withdraw to Tengah, where they were heavily shelled, their transport took off without them and they had to crawl along ditches and make their own way back under shellfire. They arrived back at Kallang in a murderous mood and if they could have caught those responsible for their abandonment dire retribution would have taken place. The word 'shooting' was spoken."

At Kallang, the pilots of 232 Squadron were warmly welcomed by Sqn Ldr Brooker and the remaining five pilots of his 232 (P) Squadron, several of whom renewed old friendships; but the reunion was brief as Brooker and the others were about to fly to Palembang for a well-earned rest. There was no time or labour available to fit long-range tanks to the Hurricanes which were to depart, but the pilots were advised that a Blenheim would meet and lead them to Sumatra. Jerry Parker wrote:

> "Provided therefore that we navigated directly to Palembang and did not have to fight against either Japanese or strong headwinds, we should be able to reach P1 with fuel to spare. The course to be flown was 168 degrees magnetic and the distance 301 miles. We were able to take only the personal gear that could be stowed in our aircraft, which resolved itself into little more than underwear, distributed in parachute bags above the guns in the wings, although I did manage to include a 120-volt battery to operate my electric shaver. The rest of our uniforms, log-books, etc were left behind."

As they taxied for take-off, Brooker ran his aircraft into a bomb crater and was forced to remain behind. The other five were led off by Flt Lt Murray Taylor and, in addition to Parker, included Plt Off Sandy McCulloch and Sgts Nicholls and Hardie. They rendezvoused with the Blenheim guide south of Singapore and completed the flight without mishap. Parker continued:

> "The islands in the south, quietly bathing in the sunshine, seemed remote and peaceful in comparison with Singapore which was now assuming the aspect of an island under siege – which of course it was. Ships were burning in the harbour, areas of broken buildings could be seen where bomb carpets had been laid and the island was partly covered by a layer of thick black smoke from burning oil tanks. When we reached the marshy jungle of Sumatra, it showed yet another vista. The flat dark green foliage with water reflecting brightly between the trees had an aspect not at all reassuring, in fact most threatening. I could well visualise the plight of the pilot forced down over this enormous expanse and imagine the perils from snakes, lizards and animals with which the area would abound. So it was with great relief that at last we sighted the glistening silvery oil tanks and the neat roofs of Palembang and one by one came in to land on the short runways."

In the event however, their hoped-for rest from operations did not materialise, and they would soon be in action again over their new base.

During the afternoon B Flight Hurricanes were scrambled from Kallang to meet an incoming raid, which comprised a formation of bombers and fighters heading for the still burning *Empress of Asia*. These were intercepted and in the ensuing combat Plt Off Ernie Gartrell and Sgt Jimmy King each claimed a Ki-21 shot down, and several others were damaged. Of his first combat, Gartrell recalled:

> "Two of us, Sgt King and I, came across these nine bombers – Army 97s in a vic formation, like a gaggle of geese, just north of the causeway, north of Singapore. We were slightly above them – an ideal situation – and slightly behind, so we could get a decent dive and just go straight down. I thought I'd go for the outside one – the right – and King could take the left one. So we just came down as a pair and we took the two outside aircraft. It was a straightforward, no deflection shot and I was able to give mine a good

squirt. The rest of them just broke formation, jettisoning their bombs. They were all over the place. So that broke that nine up, rendering them completely useless in fact. Unless bombers were escorted they were dead ducks. I didn't see my one go into the ground but when we got back to the squadron we said we think we got two – one each. We were told one was reported crashed in the jungle and one went into the sea. I certainly fired at another couple of them before they vanished but what the damage was I wouldn't like to say. You couldn't follow an aircraft down to the ground and say you know exactly where that went in – once you got up to height you stayed there. That was my first success in Singapore."

By evening only 232 Squadron remained at Kallang with 14 serviceable Hurricanes including the two from 258 Squadron; most other flyable aircraft had got away from Singapore, as ordered. Five Buffaloes, two Hudsons and 13 Hurricanes had gone, to be followed later by 453 Squadron's last four Buffaloes, which escorted two more Hudsons. Soon after landing at Palembang, two of the RAAF Buffaloes were destroyed on the ground during an attack on the airfield by high-flying bombers. Since arrangements had already been made in situ for the damaged and repaired Hurricanes to be flown to Palembang, the six pilots who had arrived aboard the Hudsons volunteered to remain at Kallang. Newlands commented:

"The airport terminal had already been bombed – it was just a shell – and we operated out of a bungalow-type building on the edge of the drome. We only had a telephone and an Aldis lamp – that was about everything. Perfect formations of 27 twin-engined Japanese bombers came over several times each morning, and dropped all their bombs at the same time from heights between 10,000 ft and 20,000 ft. How they ever got so accurate I never knew but the bombs used to land right around the perimeter of the aerodrome, and anything parked there was liable to get hit."

Many of the groundcrews remaining at Singapore were now issued with rifles and Browning machine guns, in anticipation of a paratroop attack on Kallang, which in the event did not occur. LAC Boyd wrote:

"We knew the Japs were on the island but were not aware how little of the island was left in our possession. We went back to the school, passed on our information and before long were issued with ancient American five shot rifles and bayonets. As there were not enough to go around we had to draw straws for them. I drew a rifle and Wally [Murray] said to me he would like the bayonet, which I gave to him as he missed out. We were divided up into sections and under an NCO were sent out to be deployed to meet the Japanese, who were just on the other side of a canal in the adjacent rubber plantation. Wally and I were separated at this point. My NCO was Sgt Yanovich, a fiery man who took us up to within sight of the canal on the other side of which were the Japs. He set out our positions and I well remember Dusty Rhodes settling down beside me in a favourable position behind a rubber tree. By this time we had lost all touch with reality and failed to recognise the gravity of the situation except that we would probably be killed. Here we were, totally untrained as soldiers, some were holding rifles for the first time in their lives, and we were facing seasoned troops fresh from war in China and who had fought their way down the Malayan peninsular. My thoughts were what a place to die, in this stinking hole, and those in the High Command; those who had brought this about were treasonable. Fear was overshadowed by rage and hate of British incompetency. As said before we were totally in a never-never state of mind."

Fortunately, during the early afternoon, the airmen received word that they were to withdraw and to make their way to the docks to be evacuated to Java.

While these men feared for their lives, others were sampling the good life, albeit for a brief period. Of the many buildings that had been destroyed at Kallang, one was the officers' mess. Sqn Ldr Llewellin acted fast, arranging for his pilots to be accommodated at the exclusive Sea View Hotel, where they were at least able to enjoy a brief taste of luxurious living. Donahue wrote:

> "I found myself ensconced in a room which was like a movie star's boudoir in its furnishings – elaborate wardrobes, tables, dressers, cabinets – all in beautiful hardwood; expensive-looking chairs, settees, stools, footstools, and perhaps as many as half-a-dozen mirrors. I had little trouble in finding room for my wardrobe of shirt and shorts when I climbed into the huge, luxurious bed. A couple of days later I learned that a small but nicely furnished sitting room adjacent belonged with my room. Altogether, it was a strange lair from which to go forth to battle."

Hurricanes of A Flight/232 Squadron were off at dawn on 6 February, although nothing untoward was seen. Sgt Fred Margarson was leading a section when he experienced loss of fuel pressure, and found that he could only fly the aircraft by constantly changing from gravity tank to main tank. After half an hour he left the flight and returned to base, where it was found that the Hurricane had been sabotaged – the fuel tanks had had latex rubber poured into them. This had apparently also happened to other aircraft.

Throughout the morning, sections of two or three Hurricanes continued to carry out patrols and, at approximately 1045, Plt Off Mike Fitzherbert and Sgt Snowy Newlands spotted a lone Ki-27 while flying at 25,000 feet. As Fitzherbert closed rapidly on the Japanese fighter, Newlands' aircraft suffered an overheated engine and fell back a few hundred yards. The Ki-27 was apparently acting as a decoy for a second fighter, which promptly jumped Newlands' Hurricane (Z5481), gaining strikes on the engine. He later recalled:

> "I rolled over and dived for the deck smartly, calling up No.1 at the same time to let him know he had lost his escort. The Japanese were known to have fired at blokes under parachutes so I kept diving. The engine cut out after a short time, so I feathered the blades and tried to pull out at about 6,000 feet, but was going so fast that I couldn't pull the nose up. As a last resort I had to use the trimming wheel and with an effort managed to level out around 1,000 feet. I did a few circuits of the drome. The airspeed had jumped hard over on the dial; the cockpit was full of smoke and glycol fumes; the wheels would not go down; I had no flaps, obviously no hydraulics and no engine! I decided on a belly landing, clearing the boundary fence by a few feet and waited for the crash. By some miracle the wheels had dropped and locked. I made a smooth landing, zig-zagging the bomb craters and pulled up 50 yards from the far boundary, by which time the smoke had cleared."

Newlands' aircraft was in fact claimed shot down by the Japanese pilot. Shortly after he landed, Fitzherbert followed to report that he had destroyed the first Ki-27 that they had seen – his first victory. During the subsequent patrol led by Plt Off Tom Watson, several hostile aircraft were seen heading for Kallang and, in the engagement which followed, Sgt Margarson gained strikes on one fighter which he claimed damaged, although a second got on the tail of Watson's Hurricane. Sgt Sandy Allen at once attacked this, forcing it to break away. The 12th Flying Battalion pilots claimed one more Hurricane probably shot down during the day's combats, while two Ki-27s of the 1st Sentai were reported missing over Singapore. Both Capt Goro Okazake, leader of the 1st Chutai, and Lt Tadanao Tomizawa were killed.

A Flight of 232 Squadron flew two patrols during the early hours of 7 February – the first at 0200 – over ships leaving Singapore, which included those carrying the 488 Squadron personnel. Following breakfast, Flt Lt Sharp offered the services of his 258

Squadron detachment and their two Hurricanes to Sqn Ldr Llewellin and, after a swift telephone call to Air HQ to obtain permission, the five pilots were officially attached to the unit. Just after 0930, A Flight landed from a patrol to be relieved by B Flight, but almost at once (at 0945) they were ordered to scramble. In his haste to get airborne, Llewellin failed to fasten his seat harness or, it would seem, to set his propeller to fine pitch. With the blades apparently clawing ineffectively at the air in coarse pitch, the Hurricane (Z5482) struck the mast of a junk in the harbour as it struggled sluggishly into the air and crashed into the sea, carrying Llewellin to his death. Later, back in the dispersal hut other pilots found his lucky charm – a little black rag cat – something he would normally never have flown without; he had not been flying his own aircraft. LAC Boyd wrote:

> "Unfortunately, one of the carrier-supplied Hurricanes, while taking off, struck the mast of a junk passing up the main canal at the side of the drome. It somersaulted to earth, killing the pilot, who had been a crack long distance flying ace before the war. A sad loss. Most of the raiders today were repulsed, only two waves reaching the City. We still shelter in the rubber trees while the planes are airborne. To stay on the drome is not healthy, with a great danger of lead poisoning."

The rest of the Hurricanes, led by Flt Lt Julian, climbed to 23,000 feet where a mass of bombers were spotted way below. These aircraft – estimated as 80-plus in strength – were bombing and strafing over the Johore Straits at altitudes of 6,000-8,000 feet, and were obviously 3rd Flying Battalion light bombers. With a good advantage for once, Julian led the Hurricanes down:

> "The enemy – who numbered 80-plus – were patrolling, bombing and strafing over the Johore Straits at 6,000 feet. The enemy was taken by surprise and the Hurricane attack was successful. One Hurricane was lost but the pilot was safe. The remaining seven aircraft landed, refuelled and re-armed quickly, then climbed to 20,000 feet from which they repeated the attack."

Plt Off Joe Hutton was the pilot shot down during the first attack, although he survived the crash. It is probable that he was shot down by a 59th Sentai pilot, one of whom claimed a Hurricane from a reported dozen encountered; this was possibly Sgt Maj Hiroshi Onozaki. Hutton later reported that he had attacked a Ki-27 and followed it down to observe its crash, whereupon his own aircraft came under fire, several bullets striking the engine and radiator. He dived to sea level, pursued by two fighters, but suddenly the engine seized and he was forced to crash-land on the shore of one of the many small islands near Singapore. Although the aircraft was torn to pieces by rocks beneath the surface, Hutton was unhurt and was able to climb out of the wreck, making his way back to Kallang on foot after a motor launch had delivered him to Keppel Harbour. He had learned one of the fighter pilot's premier rules the hard way – never follow a victim down!

Plt Off John McKechnie experienced trouble due to a faulty gun panel on his starboard wing, his Hurricane falling into a spin from 23,000 feet. Unable to rectify this, he prepared to bale out at 4,000 feet, but the aircraft levelled out of its own accord, and he was able to land safely at Kallang. Another of the Squadron's Canadians, Plt Off Bill Lockwood, had become separated during the climb:

> "We climbed to 25,000 feet and there I lost my buddies, but I found 27 Jap bombers in tight formation. I made one pass through this formation, spraying all and sundry, with nothing definite in mind. This was my first attempt at aerial gunnery since my four or five passes at a drogue behind a Fairey Battle at OTU."

Two bombers were claimed damaged by Plt Off Mike Fitzherbert. The main raiding force had comprised Ki-21s of the 12th Sentai, gunners in these claiming two of three attacking Hurricanes shot down; the 12th Flying Battalion Ki-27 pilots submitted no claims on this occasion. On the way back to Kallang a number of aircraft identified as Zeros attacked the Hurricanes, Flt Lt Wright's aircraft having its flaps shot away; he crash-landed BE208/O (the CO's aircraft) on arrival, as remembered by Plt Off Lockwood:

> "Ricky Wright came in with a shot-up engine and landed dead stick through the fence and almost out onto the highway beside the aerodrome."

Wright was shaken but unhurt[56].

Further aircraft flew out to Palembang during the day, as they were rendered airworthy, including a Hurricane flown by Sqn Ldr Brooker. Following Sqn Ldr Llewellin's death, Flt Lt Wright was promoted to command 232 Squadron, with Flt Lt Sharp, the 258 Squadron attaché, taking over A Flight. Donahue noted:

> "That night Ricky threw a little party to celebrate his promotion to squadron leader. He was able to get hold of some champagne, and a boisterous time was had by all. I've forgotten most of what went on, but remember that about halfway through the party someone remarked that he heard the Japs had landed on the island of Bali. We were all for taking off at once and going down there to make sure Dorothy Lamour escaped."

With the loss of two further Hurricanes and with the addition of the 258 contingent, the unit now had twice as many pilots as aircraft, therefore to enable some of the men to enjoy longer rest periods, Wright's first action was to introduce a system whereby one flight would undertake the majority of the flying for a full day whilst the other rested. Duty was to be from dawn until 0900, and then from 1300 until dark. The second flight would thus be on readiness only from 0900 to 1300 on alternate days. On the state of the airfield, Flt Lt Julian commented:

> "By this time the aerodrome was in a shocking state, only one main strip about 700 yards long being serviceable and even then the aircraft had to be bounced over bomb craters during take-off. Coolies refused to fill the bomb craters."

He added:

> "The liaison between Army, Air HQ and squadron level was pitiful. In Singapore they had blokes who had been there mainly during peacetime and their pastime, apart from playing the officer part to death, usually was having swimming parties, drinking parties, sex with anything that was around, gorging, and afternoon siestas. I remember having a furious argument with a wing commander at HQ. He was having his afternoon siesta and I wanted some information. His batman or somebody said: 'He's having his siesta.' I said: 'For God's sake drag him out of bed, get him to the phone.' Eventually he came to the phone, muttering and performing and carrying on. I was only a young kid, a flight lieutenant, and he said, 'Well, I'm a wing commander and I'm not accustomed to such disrespect.' I just let fly. 'Hell! I can picture you from here – you're a bloody, pasty-faced, over-fed, fat slug! Don't you realise that the Japanese are on the island? We're working our guts out and need this information and we want it now, otherwise I'll report you to the Air Vice-Marshal."

Without realising at the time, although he must have anticipated it, Julian was reported for his insolence; however, he obtained the information he required and went back to fighting the war.

Large numbers of Japanese aircraft operated over Singapore throughout Sunday, 8

February, 75 Ki-27s of the 12th Flying Battalion being joined by six Ki-44s of the 47th Independent Chutai. Bombers from three battalions were active, including 102 sorties by aircraft from the 7th Flying Battalion alone; JNAF aircraft were also out in numbers over the sea-lanes south of Singapore. War correspondent Ian Morrison and friends decided to visit the Naval base and nearby evacuated Seletar airfield:

> "The aerial base at Seletar was supposed to be equivalent to, and complementary to, the Naval base. It had indeed taken a tremendous hammering. Day after day, huge formations of Japanese bombers had come over and bombed it. The craters there were the biggest that I saw on Singapore. Hardly a building stood intact. Most were blackened skeletons. The field itself was pitted with bomb-holes. It was littered with some half-dozen burnt-out Hurricanes and Buffaloes and Blenheims. In some of the less-badly damaged hangars near the shore were aeroplane engines still in crates and much miscellaneous aeronautical equipment. The place was deserted except for some English soldiers down on the foreshore. They had three or four machine guns, not many, which had been emplaced amongst some rocks. There were coils of barbed wire down by the water's edge. It seemed that there were ludicrously few men in that particular sector, and those that were there, we thought, might have been very much more active than they were in preparing positions."[57]

B Flight of 232 Squadron carried out the main shift on this date, the first operation involving a patrol over the Johore Straits, during which barges were seen operating and were effectively strafed. Sgt Gordie Dunn flew on this mission, his only operation while at Singapore and the first time he had fired his guns in anger:

> "We went out on patrol around Singapore to wipe out some Japs and I ended up shooting at a hut because that's what the other guy was doing. We blew the roof off it."

Sgt Snowy Newlands (BG667/C) similarly failed to see any Japanese troops:

> "We strafed some invasion barges on the edge of the Straits between Singapore and Malaya. They were tied along the northern shore, getting ready for the invasion across, but I don't think there was anyone in them. We tried to disable them. There was a bit of ground fire, but nothing too serious. It was just a quick dash and then we were off on our way home. I was up four times on the 8th, but no Nip insignias to my credit. On one scramble [in BE160/E] we sighted 27 bombers, but they were about 10,000 feet above us."

At 0900, A Flight had just taken over when a scramble was ordered, eight Hurricanes taking off, four led by Sharp to tackle any bombers sighted, while Donahue's quartet was to engage escorting fighters. He wrote:

> "For the first time in more than three months I began to experience the familiar tension and nervousness, with the sickish pain in the pit of the stomach unusually strong. After we'd been at readiness for some time we heard the orderly taking a call and this time, after listening a moment, he replied to the voice at the other end, 'Twenty thousand? Yes, sir.' Someone said 'That's it!' and there was a shuffling and scraping of chairs as we started getting to our feet. I found myself sprinting towards my machine. The alert groundcrew were already starting our engines. Mine was running and the mechanic climbing out of the cockpit when I got there, and I scrambled in. There was the old feverish fumbling at parachute and seat straps, helmet and gloves – and glancing around to see if I was later and whether the others were taxiing out. All tucked in and ready to go at last, I found my tenseness relaxing its hold a little. A moment's wait with engine idling, for Denny's four machines to taxi out ahead, and then I was following after them onto the rain-soaked field, fast but carefully, dodging the newly-filled bomb craters in which the earth would still be soft. It wasn't safe to take off in formation, because of the condition of the field, but

Denny's four followed one another off quickly and I timed my taxiing to arrive in position just after them, with the rest of my section coming along behind me.

Denny was already a distant little silhouette up ahead, climbing and turning over the harbour; the other three of his section following, with the last one just leaving the ground, when I opened my throttle. There was the raucous full-throated bellowing of my own thousand horse-power engine, the Hurricane's windstream forming a wall around the cockpit, tugging at my helmet and blasting my face when I peered out to watch for bad spots in the field; then came the surge of the airplane picking up speed fast, the growing tightness and responsiveness of the controls, and I was off and skimming up over the boundary."

As the two sections formed up, Sharp was informed by Control that 30-plus bandits were some 30 miles north-west of Singapore at 20,000 feet. He later recalled:

"By this time the ground radar had been abandoned up the Malayan coast and the only radar we had was now in Singapore. It could only give us about half-an-hour's warning of e/a approaching and it would take about that time before we got to 20,000 feet and generally they flew above that height. Only once were we above them and that was because the bomber formation that had raided Palembang had overflown Singapore on their way back to their base up in Malaya. We managed to get above them, but without bombs they were surprisingly fast and we were unable to catch them. The Hurricane just wasn't fast enough."

The Hurricanes climbed furiously but by the time they had reached the required altitude the bombers were heading for home, having dropped their bombs on and around Kallang, their own airfield. Despite the damage, the Hurricanes were ordered to land. Donahue continued:

"Now we were faced with the ticklish problem of getting our Hurricanes down safely in the middle of all the bomb craters and debris, for there was of course no other field for us to land on. Reaching the drome a little ahead of the rest, I circled for several minutes, trying to figure out a way to land, 'shooting' the field in fake approaches at low altitude from various directions just as I had often done over pastures and stubble-fields back in America in barnstorming days – trying now to work out an imaginary runway between these craters. Finally I made my choice, a short narrow stretch between the paths of several sticks of bombs, with water standing in the low area at one end and a cracked-up Hurricane which appeared to have just landed, lying on its belly near the other end. By this time I was leading a procession of all the rest of our Hurricanes around the field, all the pilots likewise trying to figure out how to get down. I made a try at 'my' runway – and made it all right, with room to spare, and then the rest followed."

A Buffalo was blazing furiously near a hangar, the runway was again heavily cratered and, as they came in to land, the pilots were able to see a Hurricane on its belly near the boundary fence. This was Stewart's aircraft (BE195), which had broken away during the climb due to engine trouble. On flying back he had run straight into the bombers, attacking one and hitting both engines and the rear gunner. As he broke away, his own aircraft was hit, as he later related:

"I knew my leg was hit, because there was blood all over it but it didn't hurt and I felt all right. However, I was still in an awful pickle when I tried to land, because there was so much oil and glycol and stuff all over my windshield that I couldn't see ahead. I decided to try and make it wheels up. I could see the field when I was circling by looking out of the side of my cockpit, but when I was making my approach to land, coming straight towards it I couldn't see the field at all because of the stuff all over my windshield. I could tell by the buildings and high trees on each side where it should be, and I just steered in between them and hoped. I came in real fast, trusting to luck that I'd miss the bomb craters, touched down at well over 100mph and slid to a nice stop in the middle of the field. I got out and looked at my aeroplane. By luck I'd landed in the one place on the whole field that wasn't full of fresh bomb craters. I sat down in front of my machine, and after a couple of minutes a car drove up with a wing commander and some other officer in it. I said: 'Sorry boys, they got me!' which must have sounded awfully silly. They laughed and told me to get in, and drove me off to the hospital."

Stewart was operated on that afternoon, a piece of cannon shell being extracted from his hip. Other pilots on the ground had a narrow escape during the raid, including Plt Offs Hutton, Fitzherbert, Lockwood and Watson. Bill Lockwood commented:

"I, along with Joe Hutton and a couple of the other pilots, was caught on the perimeter of the airfield. It was then I realised that it was safer in the air. Joe and I were on the ground beside a large tree. He was holding on to my right leg for moral support and every time a bomb landed nearby, Joe pulled on my leg! It was then I knew of a tingling spine."

Again, Donahue provided another account of the incident, related to him by Joe Hutton:

"Three [four] of the boys from the other flight, who were on the ground, had a narrow escape during this raid. These were Joe, Fitz, [Bill] and Tom, who had been loafing in the hotel after they went off duty when we relieved their flight. They heard us take off and heard the air raid sirens a little later. Having nothing better to do they thought they'd take a drive to the airdrome to see what was going on. They took one of the cars, drove down East Coast Road, and were just turning in at the gate of the airdrome when the sentry there shouted to them and pointed upward. Stopping the car, they climbed out just in time to actually see the bombs coming down in a great cluster. They only had time to throw themselves flat and cover their ears before the bombs were striking. Two big five-hundred-pounders landed, each about a hundred feet from them, one demolishing a house directly across the road. Their car was holed in places by shrapnel, and one door was wrecked, while the boys themselves were bruised and blackened with dirt, their clothes torn, and they were badly shaken up. Fitz had to be taken to the hospital for treatment for shock, but was released the same day; Joe was told to stay off flying for a couple of days. Poor Joe! It was he who had had two shells crash beside him at Tengah two days before. Then yesterday he'd been shot down and had crashed in the sea. So he was shelled one day, shot down the next, and bombed on the third."

Flt Lt Sharp summed up this frustrating and confused period:

"We were annoyed with our controllers. I am unsure whether it was the air force or the army – but they wouldn't let us take off on occasions, when we were quite capable of interfering with Japanese bombers that happened to be operating at low level. In particular I am mindful of the occasion when they started bombing the airfield over at Tengah. That is where the Japanese landed on the island – on the far side of Tengah. Bombers were operating over there, softening up the airfield prior to the landing that they were going to attempt in that vicinity. They had some lone bombers over there, milling around and we wanted to take off from Kallang, but weren't allowed to."

The Hurricanes were off again just after midday, Sqn Ldr Wright leading ten on a patrol during which they encountered another escorted bomber formation. On this occasion Sgt Jimmy King claimed damage to a Ki-21, while Sgt Sandy Allen (in Z5667/T) opened his account when he attacked a trio of bombers:

"I jumped three Army 97s [Ki-21s]; the first went into cloud on fire with a dead gunner;

the other two I was able to hit but I was forced away by Zeros before I could complete the job or estimate the damage. One had glycol leaking and probably did not get back; the other I don't know."

Three Hurricanes were also damaged, Plt Off Tom Watson making a dead-stick landing at Kallang after being hit by fire from both fighters and bombers. Plt Off John McKechnie again had his aircraft badly damaged when pursued over Singapore by several Japanese fighters, escaping further punishment by flying into the thick smoke over the harbour; he later landed safely at Kallang. It was a poor day's return, with four aircraft badly damaged for negligible results. The airfield was pitted like a moonscape and only one strip about 700 yards long was usable. The Chinese and Malay labourers refused to fill the craters any more and, on occasions, Hurricanes had to be manhandled over bomb holes before they could take off. Construction of an alternative strip for the Hurricanes at Grove Road was begun, but the end was clearly not far off. Gartrell commented:

"Alongside Kallang was a road, lined with trees, and they got the Ministry of Works to remove them and this was used as a runway. We used this concrete road, which was very effective, until we flew out to Palembang."

Despite the desperate situation, it was not all work and no play, as Donahue describes:

"At the Sea View the management were keeping a score-board of our successes, so when we came to lunch that noon we told them they could put down another enemy plane destroyed, as the result of Stewie's victory. We were quite popular with most of the guests there in those days, in spite of our rough everyday working dress, which must have seemed out of place in such an exclusive hotel. Of course there were a few, the more blue-blooded, I suppose, who didn't take to us so well. Probably they thought the only legitimate officers were those they saw in peace-time at their exclusive dances, dressed in band-masters' uniforms; so our usually boisterous return from work, in sweaty shorts and shirts (open-necked) with revolvers slung in rough service webbing, was quite beyond them.

One grumpy old codger in particular appeared to have nothing to do but sit around all day drinking pink gins and looking liverish and important. He was waiting for a boat to evacuate him, so that in addition to fighting to keep the Japs off his head now, we would quite likely have to patrol and perhaps fight over his ship later, to keep him from being sunk. His dislike for us was made obvious quite often. Some of the boys went for a dip in the hotel swimming pool on this afternoon, and he came snooping around and tried to chase them out, saying they couldn't swim there because they hadn't been 'introduced'. Among these boys was Brownie, and he rose nobly to the situation. 'Well, my name's Brown. I guess that introduces me!' he replied. The others introduced themselves likewise and went on with their swimming. The poor fellow retired quite perplexed, which, whether he knew it or not, was a good thing for him. The boys were trying to have enough fun to loose themselves from the strain they were under and would have thrown him in if he'd bothered them any more."

Across the Johore Straits, Japanese forces were massing for the invasion. To ensure secrecy and in a bluff to deceive the defenders, they had cleared civilians from a 12-mile strip along the Straits while the troops assembled under cover of jungle. As a feint, mobile guns fired into the north-east corner of Singapore and troops drove their empty trucks, with headlights blazing, to simulate movement in the area opposite the Naval base. Australian reconnaissance patrols had been sent across the water hoping to discover what was happening, but to no avail, although 400 Japanese troops had already landed on Ubin Island. At 2030 that evening, however, all was revealed when the first Japanese forces crossed over from Johore. Australian defenders opened fire with heavy machine guns on the small craft, several of which caught fire but although heavy casualties were inflicted, others succeeded in getting ashore; red, then blue rockets were fired into the night sky by the invaders to signify successful crossings.

By dawn on 9 February, some 13,000 Japanese troops had reached Singapore Island with a further 10,000 following on their heels. Japanese fighter and dive-bomber attacks on the Australian forward positions were incessant, whilst some aircraft scattered anti-personnel bombs and others strafed. B Flight Hurricanes were off at dawn. An hour later all returned safely, landing in ones and twos, most pilots visibly exhausted but generally jubilant, nearly everyone having made a claim of some sort. Sgt Sandy Allen, flying Z5667/T, recalled:

> "I was sent up to annoy the fighters and I was lucky enough to get up sun and catch two before I had to run for cover in the clouds. I bumped into them at about 20,000 feet and one set himself up as a decoy for the other. I dived at a great speed and shot him down, then carried on diving. The other tried to follow but couldn't catch me, but I managed to get on his tail and shoot him down also.
>
> At about 1150 we came in at low level, about 50 feet up, and landed. While the Hurricanes were being refuelled and re-armed, we lounged around. Suddenly the phone went and I answered it. It was a Wing Commander Somebody-or-other from HQ, who asked for the CO. He wasn't around so I asked what could I do for him and he told me to kindly stop the pilots from flying low over the family area during the siesta! I replied that I thought it was very decent of him and that if he would like to come over to the aerodrome personally, I would have him shot as he came through the gate! We heard no more."

When claims were sorted out, the Squadron was credited with three destroyed, three probably destroyed and 13 damaged in the two fights. Flt Lt Julian was credited with one bomber destroyed and three damaged, while Plt Off Gartrell claimed one bomber destroyed, one probable and three damaged, and returned with his aircraft's tailplane damaged by gunfire:

> "We had ceased flying as pairs, and were operating on staggered time, so that we weren't all airborne at once. There were however three of us airborne on this occasion, east of Singapore, waiting for the bombers to come in. They would always come in like a procession – like railway trains. I think I had Bill Lockwood and a sergeant [probably Sgt King] and while we went to attack the formation, we were jumped from behind by Zeros. The bombers in the meantime didn't break at all, and just kept on going, leaving the Zeros to do their job. I admired their flying discipline."

Sgt Pip Healey (one of the attached 258 Squadron pilots) also claimed a bomber, which he sighted over the mainland; after a quick firing pass he reported that this had gone into a spin and crashed into the jungle. Although Sandy Allen believed he had shot down two Zeros, it would seem that he was credited with two probables only. Meanwhile Plt Off John McKechnie, whose Hurricane had twice been shot-up recently, evened the balance when he reported damaging two bombers. Fellow Canadian Plt Off Tom Watson claimed damage to two more and Sgt Snowy Newlands (Hurricane 'L') believed he damaged a further three:

> "I did two trips and on the first one failed to catch 27 bombers. They just kept coming over, higher and higher, with their bombers and then they got the idea of circumnavigating Singapore, turning round and coming back from the south in a dive from height. We couldn't catch the damn things. On the second trip they were at 30,000 feet and I got a long burst at them but didn't see anything conclusive. They were going too fast and the windscreen was a bit fogged up with the condensation, but I believe I damaged several."

Although credited with only one, Julian thought he probably brought down two of the bombers:

> "I was up there with my flight and there was something like about 120 bombers, could have been Bettys, at that stage over Singapore. We came down on them and oh did we have a merry old time because everything within our sights was enemy. I think I got a couple that morning and a couple of damaged. When we broke off we re-assembled, climbed straight up and repeated the dose again. There were so many of them and so few of us. They weren't even looking out for us. They just thought that they had the whole bloody sky to themselves. We got a large number."

No sooner were the fighters refuelled and re-armed than the pilots of B Flight, who had just taken over, were scrambled. Flg Off Donahue had taken Sandy Allen's aircraft (Z5667/T), the last to be serviced, so was off a little later than the others as it had not been quite ready. This time the Hurricanes failed to intercept, but Donahue, unable to catch the others, stalked two fighters alone, only to find that they were Hurricanes just as he was about to attack! He then chased a pair of bombers but lost them in cloud and, then finding himself over Johore, attacked and destroyed a parked lorry on a road below.

For a fourth time on this hectic day the Hurricanes were off again as soon as they had been serviced, Flt Lt Sharp having been ordered by Control to detach one section to deal with low-flying aircraft attacking British troops in the north-west of Singapore. Donahue (Z5667/T) and Sgt Bill Moodie (BG797) were allocated this duty, but on arrival initially saw nothing:

> "We were travelling north just then, toward the section of the Straits where the Johore causeway crossed into the enemy-occupied city of Johore Bharu, and I caught sight of an airplane in the distance straight ahead, low down and travelling north. I fumbled excitedly for the transmitter switch. 'Tally-ho! Straight ahead of us, Blue Two!' I called. Crossing the Straits we streaked low across the rooftops of Johore Bharu, chasing our quarry who was now following along the main highway, which leads north-west from the city up into Malaya. I remember noticing that the road was packed with military traffic. The enemy plane had a good start on us, and at first we hardly seemed to gain on it. We started getting flak – the first Japanese flak I'd seen. There was just an occasional black puff near us at first; then soon a regular hail of it, following us right along.
>
> At last we were gaining noticeably on the other machine, and soon I could discern its shape as that of a single-engined plane with fixed landing gear. It alternately flew at about five hundred feet for a minute or so and then dived to treetop height for a way, where we could scarcely see it against the jungle. We stayed at about five hundred feet ourselves. Behind me a couple of hundred yards Sergeant Moodie's plane, guarding my tail, appeared as a vicious silhouette against a background of angry anti-aircraft puffs sprinkled pepper-like against the sky. I think I was perhaps four or five hundred yards behind our quarry, for I remember that I already had my thumb on the firing button ready to press it in a few more seconds, when the beginning occurred of one of those nightmare experiences that last actually but a moment but live for ever after in inescapable memory.
>
> First a bright flash of colour caught my eye. I was staring down fascinated at a green Navy Zero wheeling across below and ahead of me, turning steep left just above the treetops, while seemingly without any conscious decision I was twisting over viciously in a diving turn after him. I closed in, still diving, pulling my nose around until my sights lined up with him and a little ahead, leading him. Then I let him have it, the quick, shattering roar from my guns startling me, and my long white tracers reaching out to caress the graceful little green wings ahead of me with their strange red discs painted near each tip. Only for two or three seconds, and then I had to break off to straighten out of

my dive before hitting the trees. Just as I was breaking off I heard a bang and felt a jolt, and saw that one of the smaller gun panels was gone from my right wing. I thought it had been shot off; but I forgot about it in what I saw a moment later.

I zoomed up hard, nearly blacking out and just missing the trees. My runaway gun was chattering away on its own irritatingly and spewing its tracers aimlessly out over the jungle. I turned left to get around at any new enemies that might be behind. And there, amid the confusion of anti-aircraft fire bursting all around, I saw Sergeant Moodie's Hurricane diving steeply, obviously hit! I was right over him as he struck, in the corner of a little field, at close to three hundred miles an hour, in a terrible ghastly eruption of splintered wings and flying pieces and then steam and dust and smoke that swirled out to obscure the awful sight. I recall circling cautiously for a moment, dazed and shocked by this and trying to take in the whole situation and see how many new enemies I had. In doing so I apparently lost sight of both the one we'd been chasing and the Navy Zero. There were no new ones to be seen either.

Thinking back on the event, I believe the Navy Zero pilot must have been above us when he saw us chasing the other Jap, so he dived on us from behind, firing and hitting Sergeant Moodie. Then his speed carried him on down and ahead as he levelled out from his dive, until he was below and in front of me where I first saw him. Sergeant Moodie must either have been killed by the bullets or had his controls disabled, and went into the fatal dive that I saw. A pathetic little wisp of smoke and dust rising above the trees was the last I saw of him, as escorted by the storm of anti-aircraft fire I made my way alone back to Singapore."

However, it seems likely that 22-year-old Moodie's aircraft had been hit by the AA guns of the Japanese 25th Army, their gunners claiming four out of a dozen attacking aircraft shot down during the day[58]. On return to Kallang, Donahue discovered that the rest of the flight had again encountered bombers and had chased them over Johore, three being claimed damaged by Sharp and Plt Offs Brown and Tremlett. The Hurricane pilots received a visit from war correspondent Ian Morrison, among others, who wrote of his meeting with the pilots:

"That afternoon I went out to the civil airport at Kallang from which our few remaining Hurricanes were operating. There were six machines in commission. A seventh was having its wheels repaired and might be available for service later. Never have I admired people more than I admired those boys. They were tired out. They had been flying infinitely longer hours than fighter pilots are supposed to fly. The strain was all too evident. But they stuck grimly to their task. They were doing what they could to harry the dive-bombers who were giving our ground troops such hell in the western part of the island. They had had a good bag that morning and had shot down three certainties, three probables, and several possibles. A young squadron leader was in charge. He cannot have been more than twenty-three. The others were lolling in easy chairs. They knew that they would have to go up in another half-hour or so. They were finding it difficult to relax. The most phlegmatic was a Canadian pilot who sucked philosophically at his pipe [this was obviously Tom Watson]. One of their number had not returned from that morning's operations. There was an atmosphere of tremendous tension amongst that little group. But I came away feeling that I had been amongst true heroes. The airfield itself was pitted with craters. The planes often took off from the long asphalt road that ran alongside. There were two Hurricanes that had crash-landed by the side of the road. Other burnt-out hulks were littered about the field. The big hangars at the far end were charred ruins."

Plt Off Gartrell had a narrow escape when he was later instructed to collect a new Hurricane from Seletar:

"Behind Seletar was a very large rubber plantation with roads through it, all beautifully kept because they had plenty of native labour to look after them. The Hurricane I picked up this day was about a mile from the main hangars and Flt Lt John Hutcheson brought me in from Kallang on the utility, then went ahead shooing off any vehicles to let me through. I really felt quite proud of myself in this brand new Hurricane, just sedately taxiing down these winding roads. So when I arrived at the main hangars on the side and out onto the airfield, I sat there for some minutes feeling in no desperate hurry. In fact I had all the time in the world for running the aircraft up, testing the boost control and air pressure, guns, brakes, elevators, trim, rudder bars etc. But anyway, eventually I opened up and was taking off down the runway towards the Johore Straits – and was about sixty miles an hour – when all of a sudden, whoomph! wham! It was just like if you're travelling in a car and you jam the brakes on and let them off again. I instinctively hauled the stick back, brought the aircraft level and thought 'God Almighty, the brakes are seizing on.' And, I'd no sooner levelled the aircraft off than the same thing happened again and the whole aircraft juddered and it tipped right up with the prop more or less chewing into the ground. Again, instinctively, I hauled the stick again, violently, and as I'd almost reached flying speed, clawed off the ground and proceeded to test the aircraft.

I was quite apprehensive about landing so I came in on powered approach, with nose up and engine on and more or less stalled on to the ground. But it was all right, nothing happened, so I taxied up to the dispersal hut, and told the groundstaff blokes there was something wrong with the brakes and that they were slamming on, that they were dangerous. About twenty minutes later Hutch came screaming up in the utility demanding to know if I was all right. I said, 'Yes, I'm all right but there's something desperately wrong with the brakes on that aircraft.' He said: 'Brakes be damned! You had two howitzer shells explode behind you up the runway as you were taking off. I thought you'd had it! The first one tipped you and your tail right up in the air and I thought your propeller must have been dug into the ground. I couldn't see you for a moment and another one landed right under your tail and up went your tail again.' And he went on to tell me the Japs had heavy howitzers across the Straits and they'd been shelling fuel dumps and that they must have spotted me sitting on the runway running up the engine and testing, and tossed a couple across to speed me on my way."

The Hurricanes were scrambled again at 1430, this time to intercept raiders over the south-west coast of Johore, which were heading for the docks. As they reached 2,000 feet, the Hurricanes were pounced upon by Ki-43s and Sgt Fred Margarson was shot down in BE158, probably a victim of the 64th Sentai (the unit's last victory over Singapore). Yorkshireman Margarson recalled:

"During the action we were flying at approximately 22,000 feet with six aircraft, when I sighted a formation of enemy aircraft about 500 feet below and to the starboard. The flight was positioned for an attack when I heard bullets hitting the armour plate behind the seating; I broke off and dived through the formation and attacked a twin-engined bomber, scoring hits on the port wing. I broke off again and was looking round to rejoin the formation when I was attacked by several Zero [sic] fighters. In the fight that followed I fired at and hit enemy aircraft on two or three occasions, eventually being attacked from two directions at once; I half rolled and attempted to execute a half loop. I must have misjudged the height and the aircraft did a high compression stall into the sea.

My next recollection was regaining consciousness underwater. During the latter part of the fight explosive bullets had hit the engine cowling, and one hit me in the right wrist, necessitating the flying of the aircraft left-handed. On reflection I feel I could not have reached Kallang, and as it was generally agreed that single-engine fighter aircraft could not be force-landed on the sea due to the weight of the engine carrying the aircraft into

> deep water too quickly to enable the pilot to abandon. I feel fairly certain that the force at which I hit the sea tore the engine from its mountings and therefore the fuselage sunk comparatively slowly, giving me time to unplug the oxygen, radio, undo the straps and open the hood and then escape. I then lost consciousness again and have no recollection of getting out of the aircraft, but regained consciousness and pulled up the inflatable dinghy and managed to climb into same. Rifle fire from the shore punctured the boat on either side of me and I then fell into the water and with great difficulty detached the dinghy which had almost deflated and kicked this away as I realised that this was what was being shot at.
>
> I understood from the Australians [Privates Nash and Hulbert] who, after some considerable time, about two hours, came out in a boat to pick me up, that the firing did not come from the Japanese as I had thought, but from the gunners of an Indian battery who said they had seen a Japanese fighter aircraft shot down. I understood they were some distance from the shore and when they arrived on the beach, I was presumably the only thing in sight and this is the reason they mistook me for a Japanese, and the reason they opened fire. I was taken to City and General Hospital with severe concussion, three broken ribs and a lacerated wrist."

Sgt Tom Young had managed to climb to 20,000 feet where he attacked a formation of a dozen bombers – most likely 7th Flying Battalion Ki-21s – claiming one probably destroyed. His own aircraft came under fire, the hydraulic system being hit, and he headed back to Kallang to find the airfield under attack. Rather than risk putting down on the runway, he force-landed instead at Sembawang between the opposing lines. Hurriedly evacuating his aircraft when he realised Japanese shells were exploding nearby, he jumped into a nearby trench. It soon dawned on him that the aerodrome had been abandoned, and he was startled by the sudden ringing of a telephone beside him in the trench. He picked it up, not knowing what to expect:

> "A cultivated British voice asked me if I knew where I was. I said no, and he advised me the aerodrome had been evacuated and was now the British front-line, told me how to get back to where the British troops were and wished me luck. I decided to go back to the aircraft to pick up my 'chute, ran back, put it over my shoulder and drew my Smith and Wesson .38, which we had been issued with. One huge hangar door was swinging half off and the grating noise was quite eerie. My imagination took over and I was expecting to be confronted by Japanese infantry any moment. It was an unusual feeling to be alone on an aerodrome, which was completely bombed out. Anyway I got past the perimeter and followed this fellow's directions. I remember going down what I would now call a jungle track.
>
> Can't remember what time it was and under those circumstances when you're under a bit of stress, time can be a bit distorted. I can remember not being so concerned once I got away from that aerodrome. Somehow that aerodrome with its bombed-out atmosphere and fires, and the abandonment of buildings that had been occupied by personnel so recently, made me feel strange; but once I got into the jungle, I felt less apprehensive. I strolled down and was very relieved to see British troops – they would have been the forward elements of the British infantry. There were certainly no Australians amongst them. I remember being greeted by these troops and they had some sort of Tommy guns and they thought it was all quite a huge joke, an RAF bloke being stuck up in front of them. I was taken back to their headquarters and then driven back in style to Kallang. I was back on the job next day and strangely enough didn't feel all that apprehensive."

Tom Young's colleagues meanwhile skirmished with the raiders but were unable to prevent the bombing taking place. Of the latest action, LAC Boyd recorded:

> "Six kills were claimed this morning, so we are still getting successes although we still find we have to leave the drome. Hand-starting the Hurricanes with a winding handle is extremely hard and the safety margin between warning and attack is very small. Our tradesmen have no trouble servicing the Hurricanes thanks to our excellent training in New Zealand. It is not so much the air combat that wipes off our planes as the bomb holes in the runway. The planes just pile up in them and wipe off the landing gear and propeller. Hardly any runway is left and even if the holes are filled they sink about a foot overnight and catch the unwary. Some planes overshoot.
>
> Earlier on we had an Indian Works Company to fill in the bomb holes and keep the runways in operation. They worked all night plugging the holes with sandbags and then resurfacing with earth. However they decided to do it during the day instead. We told the English officers in charge to get them off the runways when the air raid warning sounded, because if any personnel were caught above ground when the raiders struck, they would be wiped out by the daisy-cutter type anti-personnel bombs which destroyed everything at ground level. We told them of the small margin of safety between the warning and an attack. The officers said that would not be necessary as in the event of a raid they would just lie down flat and accept that possibly one or two of them would become casualties (the old military theory that men are expendable). We were ignored, almost sneered at. When a raid did come the whole Works Company lay down on the ground as they were instructed, and were wiped out almost to a man."

In the late afternoon of this seemingly endless day of action, the Army requested fighter cover from ceaseless air attack. Dive-bombers were constantly attacking two the 6-inch gun batteries at Pasir Laba on the west coast, which had put them out of action. In response to this request Sqn Ldr Wright led off four aircraft during a rainstorm. The low cloud, combined with smoke from the oil fires, provided cover for the Hurricane pilots to surprise a number of single-engine, fixed-undercarriage bombers (probably Ki-30s), Flt Lt Julian claiming one probably shot down while Wright damaged another. Sgt Sandy Allen (Z5667/T) engaged three more:

> "We went up the peninsula to help out because dive-bombers were being a nuisance. I could claim only three damaged because there were no witnesses but, in fact, I saw two go into the ground and the third went into cloud with a few parts missing."

Plt Off John McKechnie's aircraft (Hurricane 'A') was again hit and, with an overheating engine, made a deadstick landing on return to Kallang. Sgt Gordie Dunn, 232 Squadron's Duty Pilot for the day, ran over and asked McKechnie to move the Hurricane from the middle of the runway where it was causing an obstruction, but the latter explained that he thought the engine was about to blow up. In the event it did not, and the Hurricane was later removed safely. This brought to an end the operations of 232 Squadron over Singapore for, at 2200, Sqn Ldr Wright was ordered by Air Vice-Marshal Paul Maltby to evacuate the unit at dawn next day. Despite their successes on the 9th, the position of the fighters was now hopeless. With the Japanese so near there was now no real warning available, and the bombs were frequently falling before the Hurricanes even left the ground.

Under cover of darkness a Dutch Catalina conveyed General Sir Archibald Wavell to Singapore (from Java), his arrival on the island coinciding with that of General Yamashita, who crossed over from Johore about the same time! Wavell brought with him a cable he had just received from the Prime Minister, which read:

> "I think you ought to realise the way we view the situation in Singapore. It was reported to the Cabinet by the Chiefs of the Imperial General Staff that Percival has over 100,000 men. It is doubtful whether the Japanese have as many in the whole Malay peninsula. In

the circumstances, the defenders must greatly outnumber Japanese forces that have crossed the Straits, and in a well-contested battle they should destroy them. There must at this stage be no thought of saving the troops or sparing the civilian population. The battle must be fought to the bitter end at all costs. Commanders and senior officers should die with their troops. The honour of the British Empire and of the British Army is at stake. With the Russians fighting as they are and the Americans so stubborn at Luzon. The whole reputation of our country and our race is involved."

Whatever Wavell thought of this he issued the following 'Special Order of the Day' to General Percival:

"It is certain that our troops on Singapore heavily outnumber any Japanese troops who have crossed the Straits. We must destroy them. Our whole fighting reputation is at stake, and the honour of the British Empire. The Americans have held out on the Bataan peninsula against far heavier odds; the Russians are turning back the picked strength of the Germans; the Chinese, with almost a complete lack of modern equipment, have held back the Japanese for four and a half years. It will be disgraceful if we yield our boasted fortress of Singapore to inferior enemy forces."

To which Percival added:

"In some units the troops have not shown the fighting spirit which is to be expected of men of the British Empire. It will be a lasting disgrace if we are defeated by an army of clever gangsters, many times inferior in numbers to our own."

During the meeting a bomb scored a direct hit on the HQ building but it failed to explode, and all present escaped unscathed! With his meeting with Percival concluded, Wavell was driven to Seletar, there to be ferried to the waiting Dutch Catalina. As he stepped out of the car in the dark, he fell several feet down from the sea wall onto the rocks and barbed wire entanglement below. He was obviously in great pain as his aides extricated him, and gently got him out to the Catalina. On arrival at Tandjong Priok he was taken to hospital but refused to stay.

10-15 February – the final days

Having received the order to evacuate Kallang, eight Hurricanes departed for P1 at first light on 10 February. Groundcrews had worked tirelessly throughout the night to get the aircraft ready, which brought forth a comment of gratitude from Flt Lt Julian in his subsequent report:

"The Hurricanes were in a poor state. They were tied together with wire and widely patched. Only quick daily inspections had been possible. Groundcrews had performed magnificently, particularly in view of the absence of spare parts, the scarcity of Hurricane tools and the fact that they had no previous experience of work on Hurricanes. As a result of their tireless efforts, the Squadron was able to show a daily serviceability sheet of 100 per cent."

On recollection, he added:

"They transferred our groundcrew away and we were left with the New Zealand groundcrew of 488 Squadron. God, they were magnificent! I recall we had an sergeant armourer by the name of Yanovich[59]. He was the toughest bloke you could meet. Discipline was everything and the men weren't allowed breaks or allowed to rest or anything. Everybody wanted to lynch him. If anyone knew his job though, he did. Then you saw the result of training and discipline. He was wonderful. They were the ones who kept us going. They never had any prior experience with Hurricanes but boy they were quick."

Not all seemed to fully appreciate the emergency and that proper procedures had to be ignored. LAC Boyd was a witness to one ridiculous exchange:

> "Today a Headquarters RAF officer wallah saw Flt Sgt Stan Guiniven [RNZAF] refuelling a Hurricane by standing on the wing and pouring from a can. He said it was risking the aircraft. Stan told him to bugger off as he was holding him up as the plane was needed. At that moment a reconnaissance Jap plane came over. The sky was criss-crossed with trails from both the plane and the anti-aircraft fire. The RAF officer wallah disappeared, not to be seen again, and through all the commotion Stan just kept pouring petrol."

The Hurricane allocated to Sgt Gordie Dunn for the flight to Palembang was aircraft 'A', which McKechnie had force-landed with engine trouble the previous day. Dunn's close friend, Sgt Tom Young, had not been allocated an aircraft but had been promised a place in one of the Hudsons due to fly out. They discussed the possibility of the two of them squeezing into Dunn's Hurricane. By discarding their parachutes it would have been possible for Dunn to sit on Young's lap and still control the aircraft, but they eventually decided against it. However, as the departing Hurricanes started to taxi to the runway, Young discovered that there was not room aboard the Hudson after all, and he hurriedly returned to the strip, only to find that Dunn's aircraft was in the process of taking off. Once airborne the Hurricanes formated with the Hudson, which was to guide them to P1, but before long Dunn's engine began to overheat:

> "Soon after we were airborne my temperature gauge started to rise. The engine finally seized over the jungle and I jettisoned my port side panel, jettisoned my helmet with the radio wires and oxygen hose, released my safety strap and forced myself out, right elbow on the windshield, and flopped onto the wing, The action pulled my ripcord. My flying boots shot off and I was brought to an abrupt halt. I floated down. I landed in a bit of a grassy clearing. I had been yelling over the radio transmitter that I had to bale out. I spread open my chute so I could be seen and sat down for a smoke, but I had no matches. I could hear the bullets exploding in the wreckage of my aircraft, but I couldn't see it. I went to climb a dead tree to get a vantage point, but I was immediately covered in red ants. I brushed them off and went back to my chute. I went back to my parachute and sat down. I took a long, hard look at my revolver but then figured 'what the hell – if there are any Nips around I'll get some of them before they finish me off.'"

Before long however, Dunn heard someone approaching:

> "As the figure approached, a voice enquired 'Japanese? Japanese?' to which I replied 'No! English! English!' The figure turned out to be a native boy, who then asked 'London, England?' When the boy noticed that I only had one boot he set about making a shoe for me out of leaves. As we walked along the paddy dykes, everyone we passed fell in behind us – kids, men, women and dogs! I was presented with a beer bottle full of lukewarm, sweet coffee and, although a bit apprehensive about drinking it, I eventually shared it with my new friends. The headman, a Javanese native who worked for the Dutch, explained that although they had not seen my aircraft crash, they had seen my parachute. He then offered to drive me, in his 1937 Oldsmobile, to Palembang, some 20 miles away."

Dunn's arrival at Palembang was welcomed by his surprised colleagues. Due to poor radio contact only two of the pilots on the ferry flight had heard his radio call and, as they looked back, they thought they saw his aircraft explode, and reported this on their arrival at P1. The alleged "white puff of smoke" they had seen was no doubt Dunn's blossoming parachute. Sometime later, the native boy arrived at Palembang:

> "He had ridden a very old bicycle all the way just to collect my autograph, so I gave him

a parcel of food to take back to his family and friends, which seemed to make him very happy."

With the departure of the Hurricanes, Singapore was practically devoid of an air force – but not quite. Indeed, on this very day a watching journalist wrote:

"The Japanese are not completely alone in the skies this morning, for I have just seen two biplanes [Tiger Moths from the MVAF[60]] fly low over the enemy positions where they unloaded their bombs. It makes me ashamed of myself sitting here, with my heart beating faster than their old motors, when I think what chance those lads have of getting back in their antiquated machines. If ever brave men earned undying glory, those pilots have this tragic morning. There are many other brave men in Singapore today. Not far away are AA batteries in open spaces – they must be to have a clear field of fire. But those gun crews are keeping on fighting, their guns peppering the smoke-limited ceiling every time Japanese planes come near, and that is almost constantly."

Due to the Herculean efforts of the groundcrews at Seletar and Kallang, working under constant shelling and bombing, three battered Hurricanes were brought to a flyable state by dawn on 11th. At 0500, Plt Off Teddy Tremlett and Sgt Snowy Newlands set off from Kallang in a chauffeured car to collect two of the repaired Hurricanes from Seletar.

"Plt Off Tremlett and I were told to get up early and collect two Hurricanes over on Seletar. They had repaired them up a strip in the jungle and we had to pick them up before daylight, to avoid being shelled. So they put us in either a taxi or a staff car. It was about half past 4 or 5 in the morning, and we kept checking with Gurkhas, who were on guard at different road blocks, whether the road was OK for the next mile or two. We had our revolvers at the ready out the window and it was a bit scary because the Japs were landing on the island and, in the darkness, you didn't know where they were. Finally, we got there and found the groundcrew standing by these two planes. They were hidden up little cuttings in the jungle, off the runway, and were camouflaged under branches to make them invisible from the air. I hopped into one [BG830] and waited a few minutes, then cranked it up and it started right away. It was no good hanging round, with the engine running, so I taxied onto the aerodrome and took off. As I circled I strafed right around the perimeter, just firing into the jungle. It was just on daylight. We got the planes back to Kallang, by which time I was getting pretty damned hungry so I went up to the hotel [the Sea View] for breakfast. By the time I returned to the drome again the planes had gone. I understand the bloke who took mine [Flt Lt Denny Sharp] crashed into a swamp en route to Palembang. We found out afterwards that Tom Watson had flown one of the Buffaloes that was at Kallang. So we were left a message just to get out the best way we could. I wasn't too happy about it."

Flt Lt Sharp had been ordered to take the three flyable Hurricanes to Palembang forthwith, selecting Donahue and Brown to accompany him. Searching the airfield for likely means of escaping the doomed island, Plt Off Tom Watson – another of those left behind – found an abandoned and battered Buffalo, the engine of which, nonetheless, started when fired. Having gained permission to attempt to fly it out, he taxied it to the runway, following closely on the tails of the three departing Hurricanes. Sharp took off first, followed by Donahue, who wrote:

"We taxied out, picking our way carefully among the bomb craters and soft spots until we reached the end the runway, where Tom already waited for us in his idling Brewster. Brownie followed in his Hurricane. Pausing to let Denny start off first, I looked back furtively, half expecting to see Jap soldiers entering the drome and getting ready to pot at us; but all I saw were Ted [Tremlett] and two or three other pilots and some groundcrew

> chaps in little knot around the car, probably discussing what to do. As Denny's machine rocketed down the runway I turned and opened my throttle, following him."

Watson recalled:

> "I had never been in a Buffalo before and had some trouble with the throttle controls, particularly as the pitch was controlled from the dashboard. Also it took me a bit of time to figure out how to raise the wheels. We had no maps and I had no parachute. As the parachute was also your seat, I was sitting pretty low in the cockpit. The three Hurricanes had taken off. I pointed the nose of the Buffalo south, pushed the throttle forward, and the thing took off. We were an odd looking lot, three Hurricanes and a Buffalo leaving a smoking Singapore behind us."

Donahue added, obviously entranced by the scene below:

> "We made one circuit of the airdrome after we took off and were followed by Japanese anti-aircraft fire – the first time I was ever shot at by enemy anti-aircraft fire over my own drome! I had my camera in my pocket, and while we were making this circuit I took a snap of the north part of the city, where a huge ugly fire was raging among a lot of buildings. We turned and headed southward out over the sea. When we were out two or three miles I took another snap over the tail of my machine – presumably the last air picture of Singapore, outside of any taken by the enemy. My final memory of Singapore, as it appeared to me looking back for the last time, is of a bright-green little country, resting on the edge of the bluest sea I'd ever seen, lovely in the morning sunlight except where the dark tragic mantle of smoke ran across its middle and beyond, covering and darkening the city on the seashore. The city itself, with huge leaping red fires in its north and south parts, appeared to rest on the floor of a vast cavern formed by the sinister curtains of black smoke, which rose from beyond and towered over it, prophetically, like a great overhanging cloak of doom."

After about 45 minutes flying, Sharp – who was leading the formation in BG830 – discovered that one of the main fuel tanks was not emptying. This meant that he would not have sufficient fuel to reach P1 and decided he would have to force-land on one of the many islands dotted along the route (see Chapter IV). Meanwhile, Donahue and Brown both eventually arrived at P2 without mishap, though more by good fortune than skilful flying, as recorded by the former:

> "We'd been warned that our airplanes were in very ropy condition, having been patched up and put together so hastily; and I found this was no exaggeration concerning mine. One of my wheels wouldn't lock in its retracted position and kept dropping down. I had to raise it every couple of minutes. The position indicator light for my wheels wasn't working, so at first I could never tell for sure when this wheel was clear up. Then noticing a hole in the bottom of my fuselage right by the place where the wheel came up, I found I could tell by the amount of daylight coming through the hole whether it was clear up or not. My air-speed indicator registered zero at all times, and the airplane was out of trim so that I had to keep holding the stick to one side to keep it level. However, the engine purred nicely and the oil pressure and radiator temperature were normal, so I didn't mind the other faults. And Tom, in his Brewster, flew for the first ten or fifteen minutes with both his wheels clear down. His trouble was just that he couldn't find the right gadget to raise them with, not having flown a Brewster before. Brownie seemed to be getting along all right in his Hurricane, although afterwards he said his propeller pitch control wasn't working, so that his engine just ran at any speed it felt like."

Following Denny Sharp's departure, Donahue had taken over the lead:

"I took over the lead of the remaining three. Denny was obviously planning to force-land on this island, so followed after him with my three, to see where he landed and whether he made it safely. We circled around above him while he made a couple of passes at a small field in one part of the island; but this seemed to worry him. He came back up alongside me, motioning me to go on, so, regretfully, the three of us headed on southward. In a few minutes we struck the coast of Sumatra. We had to follow it southward now, until we came to the River Moesi leading inland to Palembang, all of which had seemed very simple so far. But I had only followed the coast a short distance before I realised that I might soon be in difficulties. The crude map which I had picked up in the dispersal hut for an emergency was a absolute menace – it showed only the one river going inland, with hardly any details by which I could identify it, whereas there seemed to be fully a dozen rivers leading in from this section of the coast. Picking the right one was going to be a most delicate matter. To make matters worse the weather was getting bad, with the ceiling down to a thousand feet and thunderstorms and rain scattered all around, so I didn't have the visibility I needed to discern the course of each river. We didn't have enough gas to allow for errors in navigation; if I picked the wrong one we'd be sunk.

One after another I passed up these rivers, each one because it didn't seem to check with the one on my map from what I could see of it, until I had gone by several and it seemed I surely must have gone far enough. I began to wonder helplessly if one of those I'd passed up had been the right one, and if so how I'd ever be able to find which it was if I went back now. Then out of the rain and mist ahead another appeared which seemed to take the right direction in from the coast, curving like the one on my map, so I turned inland on it, praying I wasn't making a mistake. Within a few minutes I saw a couple of steamers on it, so I thought I must be right. And a little farther on we came in sight of Palembang itself. I gave one of my biggest sighs of relief! There was a large storm raging to the north of town where the airdrome was located, but in view of our limited gasoline supply I decided not to wait for the storm to pass over. The jungle airdrome [P2] where I had landed before on the way from Java up to Singapore was only about 50 miles south-west from Palembang, and as the weather looked good in that direction I led on towards it. I wanted to get my three machines down as safely and quickly as possible, and I didn't care where! A few minutes more, following the little old-fashioned railway that twisted and curved roughly south-west from Palembang, and we were circling to land. As I was taxiing towards the watch office, I thought how much had happened in the two weeks since I had landed here before, when the American Army Flying Fortress [B-17] was here. It seemed a much longer time."

Watson, in the Buffalo, had by now become separated from the two Hurricanes:

"More by good luck than anything else I found Palembang, but it was socked in, so I went on to P2 and landed there. Personally, I was rather pleased but the commanding officer [Grp Capt McCauley] did not share my pleasure and reprimanded me for flying an aeroplane on which I had not been officially checked out. My interest was to get to P1 where the Squadron was located and this presented a problem, as I did not know how to start the motor. However, an Australian pilot got it going for me and I flew to P1. I was a bit concerned, as the radial-engined Buffalo could be taken for a Japanese plane, but there were no problems. The pilots in the Squadron were as glad to see me, as I was them. I put the Buffalo away at Palembang, in the trees alongside the aerodrome, and I suppose the Japanese took it when they captured the aerodrome."

* * *

Black Friday

Many hundreds of service personnel joined civilians in a quest to escape Singapore, including numbers of aircrew who were still trapped on the island. An exodus of small shipping poured southwards, to face a relentless Japanese pursuit by sea and air, as Tokyo Radio announced:

> "There will be no Dunkirk at Singapore. The British are not going to he allowed to get away with it this time. All ships leaving will be destroyed."

True to their word, Japanese air and naval forces hunted down the fleeing vessels. By the evening of 13 February, it was estimated that about 3,000 people had officially been ordered away from Singapore during the preceding few days, whilst as many as 5,000 more had departed by whatever means they could find – gunboats, motor launches, coasters, tugs, harbour launches, yachts, dinghies, tongkans (sailing barges) and sampans – many of these vessels not even seaworthy. Japanese Naval aircraft – G3Ms and G4Ms from the Mihoro, Genzan and Kanoya Kokutais, together with F1M floatplanes operating from Muntock and B5Ns from the aircraft carrier *Ryujo* – were now very active against the shipping leaving Singapore, though little effort was made to interfere with vessels carrying supplies towards the island, presumably as it was considered these would be of immense use to the occupying forces. The smaller vessels headed for Sumatra, the larger ones making for Batavia. Most of those that left Singapore in this period failed to reach their intended destination – many of the would-be escapees were shipwrecked amongst the numerous islands south of Singapore, where hundreds perished: some were rescued and others were captured. Exact figures will never be known but in excess of 70 steamers and smaller craft were believed to have been sunk, wrecked, abandoned or beached, with civilian and service personnel losses put at between 2,000 and 5,000.

With the last of Singapore's aircraft gone, 488 Squadron's groundcrew went aboard the 12,656-ton *Empire Star* which sailed at 0630 with 2,500 evacuees on board, including many stranded aircrew, amongst whom were a number of 232 Squadron personnel. Two hours later the ship was dive-bombed by several waves of aircraft, and received three direct hits. Among those on this vessel were 258 Squadron's Sgt Pip Healey and 232 Squadron's Sgts Tom Young and Snowy Newlands, who later wrote:

> "Everybody had been evacuating Singapore and abandoned motor cars, complete with the keys, were lined up about a mile out from the dock. We went up to the hospital to see one of the blokes, Margie Margarson. He had been shot down and landed in the Straits, in his parachute and dinghy, and had been machine-gunned. Somehow he got rescued and we knew he was in the main military hospital. We heard we could get out on the *Empire Star* and thought we might be able to take him. He looked pretty crook and was heavily bandaged, lying near the corpses and the dying spread around the hospital corridors. He wanted to come with us but it was impossible because we thought we'd get bombed getting out ourselves, so we left him there in the end. That night we went aboard the *Empire Star*, which didn't sail till almost daylight.
>
> At about 8 o'clock in the morning, we'd just got out a few miles, when we got bombed to hell. About six or eight dive-bombers came over and got three direct hits on us. They didn't sink us, but nearly all the ships in that convoy were sunk and there were some terrible stories told by the survivors. They got machine-gunned and God knows what when the Japs caught up with them. I was on deck at the time of the attack and was firing at them with my revolver. They were machine-gunning the boat at the same time as dive-bombing. It was like a hailstorm, and the bullets were hitting the deck and bouncing up. There were only a few of us who survived on that deck. We lost at least 18 airforce men. I took a chap, who had lost his eyesight, down the ladder and then went back up again.

One bomb had gone through the deck and into a cabin where there were eight air force officers. Bodies were laying everywhere. Some could have been blasted straight over the side. You would pick up a uniform and there would just be a mass of pulp in it, just like a bundle of rags."

Everyone with access to a Lewis gun, a Thompson machine gun or a rifle, returned fire, one aircraft being claimed shot down by a Lewis-gunner, and another damaged. Newlands continued:

"After that numerous waves of 27 bombers came over. The captain waited until the bombs left the planes and then took strong evasive action – this went on nearly all day without a further hit. At one stage two formations of 27 bombers attacked at different levels and directions, dropping all bombs! I think the skipper just put the engines 'astern'. I can't remember much except the whole boat seemed to jump ten feet in the air as the bombs landed all around us. We arrived in Batavia that night."[61]

Less fortunate was the 4,799-ton freighter *Derrymore*. Crowded with servicemen and loaded with ammunition, she also carried six crated Hurricanes amongst her deck cargo. She had departed Keppel Harbour the previous evening and during the hours of daylight had escaped damage when attacked by bombers but, at 2102, she was hit by two torpedoes fired by the Japanese submarine *I-55*. Only nine of the 200 airmen embarked were lost, and the old vessel sank about 90 minutes later, allowing time for the majority to take to life rafts. One party reached a small nearby island, from where they were rescued three days later by the Dutch minesweeper *Cheribon*. The day following the sinking, the Australian minesweeper HMAS *Ballarat* picked up about 20 others from a small raft, half of who had clung to its sides throughout the ordeal, including 232 Squadron's injured Plt Off John Gorton:

"At the time I was lying outside the pilot house when the torpedo hit. We sort of bounced up and down and then there was another roaring rush and the captain came out of the bridge, grabbed the steward who was looking after him and they jumped into the only lifeboat on board, dropped it and cleared out. So we were all on board without a lifeboat. We had time to cut the hatches off and to get some stuff and floating wood and anything else that would float. We got our survival equipment afloat and jumped overboard to take pot luck. I found myself close to one of the ship's life rafts and clambered aboard. It was designed to carry about seven people. It was quite desperate. We could see all around there were things like aircraft tyres that were still floating there, and they'd have somebody lying on them. Many survivors were swimming or floating on improvised lifebuoys and wreckage. They drifted up to us and our passenger list increased through the night until there were about 20 of us crowded on to the raft. The raft barely floated with its deck at sea level and often under the wave tops. So we were floating around on a sort of a raft thing that you could sit on, but there were so many people on it that you were in water. As we floated, a submarine came through us. We couldn't see it but we could hear it. It didn't open fire on us and it went away.

We had few clothes on but some of us had lifebelts we picked up before the ship sank. There were no stores or other supplies on the raft. Before the *Derrymore* went down I raided the store room and pinched a tin of carrots, the only thing that could be found that looked as though it might come in handy later. I also filled a flask with fresh water from the ship and remember getting an open tin of fresh water on to the raft before she went down. It didn't help much. The washing seas that flowed over the raft to the level of our waists soon spoiled it as drinking water.

During the night the *Derrymore*'s second officer, a very good young fellow who had been swimming in the sea, came up with us and came aboard. I found myself glad of his

> company before it was all over. It was a long night and it was very quiet on the raft. We just seemed to float and wallow motionless on the sea, squatting on the raft, wondering how we would make out. We didn't talk much, just seemed to drift and wonder. When it became daylight we could see relics of the *Derrymore* floating on the sea about us. Low islands stood out on the horizon. We didn't quite know what they were or who might be on them. Some of the fellows became a bit despondent as the day wore on. They speculated uneasily about whether there were sharks about us and whether they might attempt to attack the overloaded raft. There were signs that morale might drop. It was then I was glad of the company of the second officer. We had no oars but used bits of wood and even shoes to try to propel us along. I don't know whether this actually made any impression on the progress of the heavy, clumsy, waterlogged raft but at least it was something to do. It helped pass the hours, which a lot of us found to be very long ones, and we just kept at it. We were still a quiet crowd, being drenched by the waves and pretty uncomfortable. Then, about 5pm on the Saturday, we saw smoke and the *Ballarat* emerged from it. She did not know of our plight and was not looking for us. It was an accidental meeting. She was glad to find us. We were a lot happier to be found by her. We were picked up smartly."[62]

The *Ballarat* picked up 63 RAAF men and about 20 members of the ship's crew.

During the afternoon of 15 February, *HSL 105* – one of the Air Sea Rescue launches that had departed Singapore with AHQ staff on board, including Grp Capt E.B. Rice, former AOC 224 (Fighter) Group, Wg Cdr Robert Chignell (former OC Kallang) and Sqn Ldrs Wilf Clouston DFC and Frank Howell DFC, former commanders of 488 and 243 Squadrons respectively – was attacked seven times in the Banka Straits. A direct bomb hit after about 20 minutes severely damaged the craft, a splinter instantly killing the popular and respected Chignell: his body was put over the side. One other passenger was wounded and the craft caught fire. The crew and passengers were picked up by two the small steamers *Renrau* and *Relau* – but both were intercepted and captured at dawn, all aboard becoming prisoners (Grp Capt Rice died in a prison camp in 1943). Another launch, *ML310*, carrying amongst others Air Vice-Marshal Conway Pulford[63] (AOC Far East Command) and Rear-Admiral Edward Spooner (Rear-Admiral Malaya), was attacked firstly by a Japanese floatplane and then a destroyer, the craft being forced ashore on Tjebia Island, where 17 of the survivors died from malaria and starvation, including both senior officers.

Another of 232 Squadron's wounded pilots, the South African 2/Lt Stewie Stewart, also had quite a tale to tell when he eventually reached Batavia. He was in Alexandra Hospital when the Japanese landed on Singapore:

> "You can imagine how I felt lying there in the hospital, with them coming! Then Tuesday night and Wednesday morning I could tell by the artillery fire that they were getting close. I never felt so helpless. There was a big gun only a little way from the hospital. It started working early Wednesday morning, making a terrific racket, shaking the building every time it went off. Then, what was much worse, the bombers started coming after this gun, some of their bombs just missing the hospital. It was terrifying. About mid-morning on Wednesday we heard rifle and machine-gun fire just outside the hospital. I figured this was the finish. I had an orderly bring my revolver, because I was going to shoot myself when the Japs came in."

At that moment a doctor came running into the ward and enquired if anyone was able to walk and, if so, would they be prepared to take a chance and hope to be evacuated by ship? Stewart answered in the affirmative but when he jumped out of bed to show that he could walk, he promptly collapsed on the floor. His wounded leg would not support him but then saw a broom in a corner and, using it as a crutch, managed to hobble around the room a little. Although not convinced, the doctor finally agreed to take him, the only one in the ward able to accept the challenge:

> "The other fellows in my ward were all too badly off to be moved. I'll never forget the look of utter despair in their eyes when I last saw them as I was going out. There were five of us that the doc had collected. We all got into an ambulance that was full of shrapnel holes and had its windows smashed, and we drove off. On the way into town we had to stop because of a bombing raid. The doc, who had been riding in front, came around in back to encourage us, but he seemed more scared than we were. We could see his teeth chattering. One stick of bombs dropped in a line right across us. I could see the first three explosions coming towards us, the third one real close. Then the fourth landed the other side of us. After that was over we drove on as near as we could get to the docks. The doc was taking a chance on being able to squeeze us onto a medium-sized merchant ship that was getting ready to leave. We had to walk about half a mile to the dock. I was using that broom for a crutch; and I was just sweating with agony when I got there. We were in luck. There was still room for us. I got put in the fourth assistant engineer's cabin, along with an RAF engineer officer who had lost one eye, so we called him 'One-Eyed Ike'. There were more than two thousand people on board, mostly European civilians, men, women, and children. It was a refrigerator ship, and they turned off the refrigerating machinery so that some of the people could stay down in the hold. The rest had to stay on deck, except for a few of the wounded, who were given the ship's officers' cabins.
>
> About six o'clock that evening the ship pulled away from the dock and anchored outside the harbour. Then about seven o'clock next morning we sailed, in convoy with another merchant ship, with a light cruiser for escort. We got our first attack about ten o'clock that morning. Several of us were chatting together, talking about how lucky we were to get away, when the call was passed along, 'Enemy aircraft approaching.' After that there was pandemonium. A big bunch of planes, mostly dive-bombers, came over and most of them made for our ship because it was biggest. We were in narrow waters, so the ship couldn't manoeuvre to avoid the bombs, and they fell all around us, shaking the ship and almost lifting it out of the water sometimes. Each time after a close one we listened for the sound of the ship's engines. We knew as long as they kept running we weren't hit seriously, and boy, they were running so hard they sounded as though they were coming right up through the deck. I heard afterwards that during this attack they got three knots more out of the ship than she had ever been able to do before!
>
> The gun crews on deck were wonderful. They let off with everything they had at every plane as it came over – pom-poms, Lewis guns, Tommy guns. There were even chaps firing with rifles and revolvers. They got two bombers definitely destroyed and three probables out of some thirty planes that attacked us. One small bomb came through the roof of a cabin about ten yards from ours and exploded, killing the fellows in there. The concussion knocked an electric fan off the wall in our cabin. It fell on 'One-Eyed Ike', who was lying face down on the floor, and I had to laugh because it lay there on top of him, still running, as if it was getting electricity from him! The bomb started a fire, but they called for volunteers and got it out in a little while. Two chaps were brought into our cabin to die – they had been on a gun-post that got hit by another small bomb. They were so mangled that they had to be carried in blankets. The blood was soaking through the blankets and running all over, and the nurses gave the men morphia to ease them out.
>
> The nurses were wonderful and shielded the patients with their bodies each time the bombs fell. Most of the bombers machine-gunned us as they passed over, but they didn't cause many casualties. One fellow got a bullet that went right through his chest from front to back without hitting any vital spot. They just covered up the two holes and he was all right. After this attack we had a two-hour respite, and by the time the next one started we were out in open water, where the ship could manoeuvre. I had been moved down then to

the bottom of the hold, so I couldn't tell what was going on myself, but the others told me what happened. It was a high-level attack by 67 planes, and it lasted for more than two hours. We received most of the attention, just as before. Each plane dropped its bombs in a stick after a careful run. The captain was credited by all with saving the ship, for he kept watching the bombers through his binoculars, and each time one came up on its bombing run, and he saw its bomb doors swing open, he'd call out 'Hard a-port!' or 'Hard a-starboard!' and the ship would turn as sharply as it could which was just enough to mess up the aim. One stick of them went off so close to us that the bombs lifted the ship way up, almost clear out of the water, and damaged it some. Another lot were much closer yet, just grazing the ship's side, and would have blown in the whole side of the ship and sunk us, but they all failed to go off. Either it was a miracle or the pilot forgot to fuse his bombs. There were many more near misses, too. It was tough on us down below, because we didn't know what was happening or when the next ones were coming. We could hear and feel the explosions. Each time we'd listen for the sound of the engines afterwards and when we heard them we knew we were still all right.

Finally it was over and we were still going strong. Most of the passengers had been on the top deck all the time, and had spent the time singing hymns and songs to keep from going nuts. Now that it was over they all had a communal prayer of thanksgiving, and then took up a collection to buy a plaque for the ship in commemoration of all this. They raised about twenty-five hundred Singapore dollars and gave it to the captain, who made a little speech of thanks."

Of the two remaining hospitalised Hurricane pilots at Singapore when the Japanese landed, only Sgt Geoff Schaffer was able to evacuate, his burns not unduly hindering his escape from Alexandra Hospital; he reached Batavia safely, from where he was evacuated by sea to New Zealand before returning to his native Australia. The other wounded pilot, Sgt Fred Margarson, was not so lucky:

"At the time of surrendering I was still in the City and General Hospital, the conditions being extremely crowded, with patients on the beds and in between the beds. Two days prior to this there was a severe shortage of drinking water. I was suffering from three broken ribs, concussion and a bullet wound in the right wrist caused by an explosive shell. On the two days prior to the surrender the hospital was under artillery bombardment but the portion in which I was housed was not seriously damaged. On the 16th we heard of atrocities committed in various parts of the hospital but the inmates of the ward in which I was housed were fortunate in that the front-line troops did not go through it and, when the Japanese came in, they were administrative staff rather than fighting troops. We were, however, all made to walk, with very few exceptions, to the Changi prison camp and were housed in some empty Chinese shops. The entire RAF continent along with survivors of the *Prince of Wales* and *Repulse*, which included Marines, were attached to the Argyll and Sutherland Highlanders, for prison camp administration. During the period that I was in Changi I attended the hospital which was administered by the RAMC and was admitted for an operation to my wrist to restore the use of my fingers."

* * *

In the meantime, a lone reconnaissance aircraft had flown over British positions around Singapore City during the morning of 11 February, where it released 29 small wooden tubes, decorated with red and white streamers, each of which contained a copy of a document addressed to the 'High Command of the British Army, Singapore', which called for immediate surrender. Time was rapidly running out for the defenders, and when General Percival learned that the advancing Japanese had captured the Kranji ammunition magazine, where the island's reserves were stored, he ordered the reserve fuel depot, located east of Bukit Timah, to be set on fire to avoid it similarly falling to the enemy. Percival now felt that the position was fast becoming hopeless and he held another emergency meeting with his commanders. Whilst he had well over 125,000 men on Singapore, many thousands were non-combatants from the mainland who had withdrawn to the island during the preceding weeks to join the thousands of others engaged in supply duties. These included ordnance, vehicle repair, fuel, hospital and HO formations, as well as the sick and wounded. Amongst all of these, the actual number of 'fighting soldiers' was no more than 22,000! Worse still, Percival believed that the Japanese had available in excess of 100,000 front-line soldiers in Southern Malaya, and had already employed 68,000 in the attack on Singapore. This was a gross overestimate for General Yamashita subsequently insisted that the number was far lower, recording in his diary:

> "My attack on Singapore was a bluff – a bluff that worked. I had 30,000 men and was outnumbered more than three to one. I knew that if I had to fight long for Singapore, I would be beaten. That is why the surrender had to be at once. I was very frightened all the time that the British would discover our numerical weakness and lack of supplies and force me into disastrous street fighting."

This huge non-operational administrative tail was something that was to provoke Prime Minister Churchill throughout the war. He could never accept that every soldier and airman could not be a "rifle-and-bayonet fighting man" with an alternate duty to perform, who could resume his main function at times such as this. Be that as it may, Percival was well aware that the greater part of his force was not combat-worthy. He was also aware that with the loss of Johore, much of the island's water supplies had been lost, and much of the rest was now under threat to the invaders. He advised the Governor, Sir Shenton Thomas, accordingly, and the latter cabled the Colonial Office in London:

> "General Officer Commanding informs me that Singapore City now closely invested. There are now one million people within radius of three miles. Water supplies very badly damaged and unlikely to last more than 24 hours. Many dead lying in the streets and burial impossible. We are faced with total deprivation of water, which must result in pestilence. I have felt that it is my duty to bring this to the notice of General Officer Commanding."

The Governor had already ordered the destruction of Singapore's liquor stocks and before the surrender one and a half million bottles of spirits and 60,000 gallons of *Samsu* (a Chinese spirit) were destroyed. At the same time the Acting Federal Secretary had arranged for the burning of five million Singapore dollars of State money, to deny its access to the invaders. Meanwhile, bombs and shells continued to fall on the island. It was conservatively estimated that at least 500 civilians died on this date alone (14 February); raging fires could not be fought and corpses littered the streets, many of which were blocked by collapsed buildings and other debris. Although the Hurricanes had long gone, the island's gunners continued to put up a token resistance and probably one of the last Japanese aircraft to fall – incorrectly identified as a Zero – crashed in Singapore's red-light district on Lavender Street. An Army officer who drove the scene remarked:

> "The plane was scattered over a very wide area as though it had hit a building as it crashed. It looked small on the ground. There were sections of wings and fuselage and a crater where the engine had buried itself. At my feet I saw the forearm and hand of the dead pilot. My gunner driver turned the limb over with his boot and looked at it. 'Bloody dirty fingernails, sir', was his only comment."[64]

General Yamashita's bluff was extended at first light when a reconnaissance aircraft of the 71st Independent Chutai dropped a cardboard tube attached to red and white streamers, containing a message inviting Percival to surrender his forces since further resistance appeared pointless. Percival called a meeting of his remaining military and civilian officers at 0930 to consider Yamashita's message, and also a telegram that had just arrived from General Wavell in Java. The latter required:

> "So long as you are in a position to inflict losses and damage to enemy and your troops are physically capable of doing so, you must fight on. Time gained and damage to the enemy are of vital importance at this juncture. When you are fully satisfied that this is no longer possible I give you discretion to cease resistance. Before doing so all arms, equipment and transport of value to the enemy must, of course, be rendered useless. Also, just before final cessation of fighting, opportunity should be given to any determined bodies of men or individuals to try and affect escape by any means possible. They must be armed. Inform me of intentions. Whatever happens, I thank you and all troops for your gallant efforts of the last few days."

Following consideration of the facts as they appeared, Percival decided to accept Yamashita's invitation to meet and, with a small party of officers, departed under a flag of truce to attend a rendezvous near Bukit Timah. What followed was an uncompromising demand for virtual immediate unconditional surrender, which a humiliated Percival acceded to. He nevertheless sought to secure the safety of all male and female civilian personnel on the island, to which Yamashita gave his word to uphold. Returning to his HQ at Fort Canning, Percival despatched a final message to Wavell:

> "Owing to losses from enemy action, water, petrol, food and ammunition practically finished. Unable therefore to continue the fight any longer. All ranks have done their best and are grateful for your help."

At 2000 on 15 February therefore, resistance officially ended, the British Empire suffering probably the worst and most humiliating defeat in its history. As with all 'ceasefires' however, not all combatants would lay down their arms immediately. Some, from choice, continued fighting, whilst others were unaware of the order to cease.

Although the figure of 85,000 British and Empire troops is generally quoted as having surrendered on Singapore, totals in fact amounted to no fewer than 138,708 men: 38,496 British, 18,490 Australian, 67,340 Indian and 14,382 local troops; approximately 25,000 of the Indians would later be coerced into joining the anti-British India National Army, some of them later fighting in Burma. It must be remembered that during the final week the Japanese had complete and undisputed mastery of the skies; not one British fighter was available for the defence of Singapore. When losses could be tallied and claims assessed, it was revealed that 45 Hurricanes had been lost to date (plus 122 Buffaloes), including those destroyed in accidents, or by bombing/shelling on the ground. The Hurricane pilots were credited with about 100 victories including probables, the Buffaloes a further 30, while Percival reported that over 100 more had been claimed shot down by Singapore's AA defences. After weighing up all these claims, it was thought that total losses of Japanese aircraft in the campaign so far had been around 183 but this was undoubtedly a substantial overestimate. Tokyo, however, estimated that the RAF had lost about 390 aircraft including bombers and miscellaneous other types, whilst admitting a Japanese loss of 92. In fact the 3rd Composite Air Division reported the loss of 331 aircraft to all causes since the outbreak of war, and about 500 personnel. The total losses of the JNAF's 22nd Air Flotilla during the fighting for Singapore are not known, but included five A6Ms, four G3Ms and one C5M. Several abandoned Hurricanes were captured by the Japanese including BE208/O of 232 Squadron.

British and Commonwealth casualties during the defence of Singapore had amounted to about 8,000 servicemen killed, together with many thousands of civilians. The Japanese suffered 1,700 killed and 3,400 wounded during these actions. Thus, with the surrender, the defenders and up to a million civilians commenced a harsh and brutal occupation, which many were not to survive. Although a brilliant commander and brave soldier, General Yamashita (thereafter known to his troops as the 'Tiger of Malaya') clearly did not keep his word to Percival – a transgression amongst others for which he would suffer execution when tried for war crimes after the war ended.

CHAPTER IV

PALEMBANG

February 1942

"The din was fierce as the machine guns mounted around the field opened up on the Jap but they couldn't save the Hurricane which continued its steep turn into the trees on the far side of the field. It didn't burn and the Jap pulled back up into the cloud unscathed."

Plt Off Jerry Parker's eyewitness account of the death of Flt Lt Murray Taylor

Sumatra's position, partially to the west of Malaya, saved it from air attack during the opening weeks of the war. Not until the Japanese advance down the Malayan peninsula brought their forces into closer proximity with the northern tip of the island, across the Malacca Straits, did any air activity of note commence. While the main airfields, P1 and P2, were situated in the south around the major town and oil refinery at Palembang, there were others in this inhospitable country, too, which was clad mainly in thick and impenetrable jungle. One was situated at Pakan Baroe, well inland from the Malacca Straits, opposite Malacca itself, but latitudinally slightly to the south of Singapore. The landing ground and its general facilities were not very modern, although the Dutch worked hard to extend the runways and improve conditions. Further north, on the east coast, was Medan, while in the far north at Lho'nga, there was a small landing strip and – just off the coast – the island of Sabang, used in peacetime by both British Overseas Airways and Qantas as a refuelling stop for their flying boats.

P1 airfield was still guarded only by a few Dutch troops with four Bofors guns. There was one Dutch-manned Operations Room with an unreliable telephone line, and few other facilities except for a relatively efficient chain of observer posts. Wg Cdr George Darley DSO[65] was posted there as Wing Commander Fighter Operations:

"In Singapore I had to set up an Ops Room from scratch, so I called upon the Dutch army garrison for help. Having found me a suitable house, they connected it by telephone to P1 where there were a few ex-Singapore Hurricanes. I was supplied with R/T receivers commandeered from shops but transmitting was a problem until I realised that oil tankers on the Moesi connecting Palembang oil refinery with Banka Straits, some 40 miles north, were controlled into single lane traffic by R/T transmitted by the refinery. I found that it could transmit on our fighter frequencies, so I was then connected to it by telephone, and when I wished to transmit, I asked the operator to switch me over to 'transmit'. Such were the ad hoc arrangements, but our 'shop' worked and we were able to maintain a 24 hour shift by living and eating over the shop."

Air Commodore Vincent was not enamoured with what he found at P1:

"There was no R/D/F (Radio Direction Finding) and no D/F (Direction Finding) for homing aircraft in bad weather. This deficiency was a serious handicap, particularly in view of the daily tropical storms, which made flying extremely unpleasant and homing very difficult. Hurricane tool kits were almost non-existent and it was necessary to service aircraft with any tools, which could be locally purchased or made. Aircraft spares were similarly almost non-existent and supplies of ammunition, particularly AP (armour-piercing) and de Wilde (incendiary) were extremely low, as were glycol (cooling fluid) and oxygen supplies. There were no battery-charging facilities at the aerodrome and no battery starters for the aircraft.

> 258 Squadron aircraft were serviced by Buffalo groundcrews and all these factors contributed to a low state of serviceability. It was considered that eight Browning guns per Hurricane were sufficient for the unarmoured Japanese aircraft; the removal of four from the twelve-gun aircraft would give additional manoeuvrability and more rapid climbing ability. The four outside Brownings were therefore removed and 50 per cent of these were used for spares and 50 per cent for ground defence. Arrangements were made with a local firm to make mountings for these guns, but unfortunately the attack on the aerodrome took place before the mountings were completed."[66]

Early in the month 232 Squadron and the part of 258 Squadron still in Sumatra moved from P2 to P1 to undertake convoy patrols over the Banka Straits. 232 Squadron's first patrols were made on the morning of 3 February, over incoming Convoy *BM12*, which was attacked by 18 bombers. They were opposed only by the ships' anti-aircraft defences, the Hurricanes failing to make contact. On this occasion only minor damage resulted from a number of near misses, but the 16,909-ton *Empress of Asia* did not escape the next raid and was seriously damaged.

The Japanese bombers enjoyed further success when they attacked the 4,958-ton *Loch Ranza* off Palembang during the day. The master managed to beach his burning vessel, following which it blew up; five of his crew were killed and two others died later in hospital. A British tanker, the 6,121-ton *Pinna* was also bombed while in convoy but she did not sink and drifted helplessly. Next morning she was again bombed and set on fire, running aground in a minefield off Lingga Island, with the loss of 20 of her crew. Two small Dutch coasters were also caught by Japanese bombers during the day – the 1,937-ton *Van Lansberge* sustained heavy damage by bombing, and was then torpedoed and sunk by the Japanese submarine *I-55*. Twenty of her crew perished. Further north the smaller *Togian* (979-tons) was sunk with the loss of all aboard. The Hurricanes at P1 had not been able to prevent these attacks.

Meanwhile, at Batavia, the latest convoy had safely arrived including the *Warwick Castle* and the *Empress of Australia*, aboard which were the personnel of 266 (Fighter) Wing, and the *Athene* carrying 39 crated Hurricanes, while a similar number of fighter pilot reinforcements arrived aboard the troopships including, it is believed, the following[67]:

Wg Cdr H.J. Maguire (Wing Commander Flying)

Plt Off R.L. Cicurel (US)
Plt Off A.M. Morris RCAF
Sgt F. Bidewell
Sgt P. Browne
Sgt J. Hamilton
Sgt A.D. Jack
Sgt D.A. Poland
Sgt W.J. Belford RAAF
Sgt K. Collins RAAF
Sgt G. Gratton RAAF
Sgt H.V. Hobbs RAAF
Sgt A.B. Martin RAAF
Sgt J.M. Souter RAAF
Sgt W.H.J. Williams RAAF
Sgt F.N. Hood RNZAF
Sgt D.L. Jones RNZAF
Sgt C.E. Sharp RNZAF
Plt Off K.D. Dawson-Scott
Plt Off G.K Palin RCAF
Sgt G.D. Binsted
Sgt W.E. Collins
Sgt D.J.B. Isdale
Sgt A.R. Payne
Sgt P.S. Ambrose RAAF
Sgt K. Boyd RAAF
Sgt R.A. Dickson RAAF
Sgt H.L. Hargreaves RAAF
Sgt A.K. Lawrence RAAF
Sgt S. Munroe RAAF
Sgt F. Williams RAAF
Sgt K.J. Wylie RAAF
Sgt H.P. Jenson RNZAF
Sgt N.G. Packard RNZAF
Sgt J.G. Vibert RNZAF

Sgt E.R. Worts RNZAF	Sgt E.F. Horton RCAF
Sgt W.H. James RCAF	Sgt H.P. Low RCAF
Sgt W.H. Monsell RCAF	Sgt R.C. Smith RCAF

Plt Off Leon Cicurel, an American of Egyptian extraction, and Plt Off Keith Dawson-Scott were both members of 258 Squadron, while Sgt Don Isdale, Sgt Fred Bidewell and Sgt Bill Collins were on the strength of 242 Squadron; Sgts Albert Jack, Frank Hood, Collis Sharp, Harley Monsell and Keith Collins were attached to 605 Squadron. Sgts Howard Low and Russell Smith were Canadian friends who had both briefly served with 122 and 611 Squadrons before joining 266 (Fighter) Wing; similarly, Sgts Ewen Worts and Neil Packard were New Zealander friends who had served together with 131 Squadron; another New Zealander, Sgt John Vibert, was a former member of 79 Squadron. It had been intended that these pilots would replace losses within the existing units, but the rapid deterioration in the fortunes of the Allies would prevent this happening. Wg Cdr Maguire noted that the replacement pilots included "15 or so Pool pilots, not officially attached." He added:

> "The crated aircraft were originally Far East reserves. After arrival in Java as Wing Leader, I spent a fair amount of time testing erected aircraft at Batavia, refreshing aircrew, and trying to get HQ to use us as a full Wing, and not in penny packets. Regretfully, I didn't succeed."

* * *

Following their arrival at P1, the Hurricane pilots from Singapore found Palembang and its surroundings a relatively peaceful haven compared to the daily bombings they had been accustomed to. Jerry Parker wrote:

> "During the next week we stayed in a hotel except some of the sergeants, who were billeted with families. We envied Hackforth – a handsome young man nicknamed 'Dean', that being his father's vocation – whose landlady had three delightful golden-haired daughters of his own age. We were comfortable and not dissatisfied with our lot. We spent the greater part of each day patrolling over the Banka Straits, just to the east of Palembang, through which many vessels and some convoys were passing in an attempt to escape capture at Singapore.
>
> In this period I had a chance to relax and recover my nerve. I decided that, although I had stilled my fears of death or injury in aerial combat, what had reduced my morale to a very low level was the suspense. I had observed so many of my comrades fail to return from sorties that as the survivor, with Murray Taylor, of the ten officer pilots I had lost my assurance that 'it couldn't happen to me'. The end of the war seemed a long way away and surely I should soon be clobbered if in only three weeks so many others had gone. So every night, exhausted from constant weariness and nervousness at Singapore, I would retire to bed thankful at having survived another day's operations. Immediately on waking in the morning I would remember that more action and patrols lay ahead and I would wonder, 'Will this be the day?' Breakfast would choke my dry mouth and throat and the cry of 'The car's here!' would send me instantly to the toilet to empty my bowels. Upon arrival at the Flight office I would sit and wait, trying to read and dashing to the latrine every time the telephone rang. Yet in the air I would regain my composure and fighting spirit, prepared to think and act in self-preservation and ready to have a go if the odds looked fair. So, at Palembang, I managed to rationalise my behaviour and realised that I need have no fear of losing my nerve whilst I was in the air but must take care to control myself between flights. Action took my mind off consequences which were, after all, not entirely avoidable and were likely to occur any day."

By the evening of 5 February, following the various moves to and from Singapore, P1 housed 18 Hurricanes of 258 Squadron, 11 of 232(P) Squadron, plus four more attached to this unit from 488 Squadron, and a few unserviceable Buffaloes. The presence of so many Hurricanes at P1 did not escape the attention of the crew of a reconnaissance Ki-46, who reported six large and up to 50 medium-sized aircraft on the airfield. The Ki-46 had been sighted by a Hurricane patrol led by Sgt Bertie Lambert:

> "We sighted an enemy recce aircraft heading north, with good height advantage. We pursued it but having made only a slight impression on the considerable distance separating the enemy aircraft from us, we had to return to base due to fuel shortage."

On receipt of this information, the JAAF immediately planned an attack for the morrow. Consequently, at first light on the morning of 6 February, 23 Ki-48 bombers of the 75th and 90th Sentais, together with 18 Ki-43s of the 64th and 14 of the 59th, began taking off from Ipoh and Kahang, but heavy cloud and adverse weather conditions prevented a rendezvous. The 75th and 64th Sentais did manage to join up, but the other units made their way towards the target area individually. The former units arrived first at about 1100, but found low cloud obscuring the area, the Ki-48s diverting their attack to Banka Island instead. The 64th's fighters were, however, able to penetrate the cloud over the airfield. On the airfield the pilots were awaiting reinforcements and replacement aircraft from Java, as Sgt Kelly recalled:

> "I suppose we were talking about how it would be after a few days to get ourselves organised and when the expected reinforcements of Hurricanes, still in Java, had arrived. Whatever our conversation might have been, it was to the last subject that conversation switched when we heard the note of aircraft engines. There were sounds of satisfaction; some of those in their chairs stood and strolled out to the airfield, others again, including me, decided it was too hot, too hot and too sticky, and stayed where we were. I remember being quite impressed that with miles of cloud above, the Hurricanes had found P1 and thinking how lucky it was there was that one break or they could never have landed and might have been very pushed to make it back to Java. And it was then that we saw the first of the Hurricanes break into view in the small blue gap to the north in the mass of sullen cloud like overlapping slates which otherwise roofed the sky. Only, of course, it wasn't a Hurricane but a Navy 0. We watched the first and then, one by one, the others, still tiny specks, pouring through the gap, diving on us in the traditional beat up. It was the expected thing on arriving at a new station, to beat it up. It told everyone you were arriving; it made everyone stop whatever they were doing to look at you; it brought people inside buildings outside or at least to the window; it drowned all conversation.
>
> It was only when the fighters were comparatively near we realised they had radial engines, that they weren't Hurricanes. It took only moments to realise what they were – Navy 0s. And by then it was too late! The air was filled with the whine of bullets and cannon shells and the roar of engines. The first Navy 0 pulled out of its dive and climbed away from its first attack not twenty feet above my head, the blood red circles on its wings mocking us. Behind me was the sound of shattering glass and yards to my left a man was screaming and clutching at his stomach. The second Navy 0 was already into its attack seeming to be aiming directly at me and was not a hundred yards away, its machine guns and cannon blazing. I dropped, and, as it pulled up, ran. P1 was filled with running men: pilots on readiness running to their aircraft, ground staff running out to help them in and start them up, others, with no purpose in remaining, running for the jungle. I began to run – and then I had to stop, if briefly, because few yards away I saw something that seemed to me quite incredible. Red Campbell was standing calmly, revolver in hand, aiming at the next Navy 0. It was useless of course, but not simply a gesture. One does read of men who

have no fear but they are very rare. Campbell was one of them. When the fracas had died down I went back to the verandah and picking up my chair, which had fallen over, saw there was a neat bullet hole through one of its chromium legs. The Bofors guns had fallen silent and the sky was fast clearing of clouds. I went out again and now there were no aircraft to be seen, only the more distant sounds of them and men were fast emerging from the jungle."

The Japanese pilots were not to achieve much on this occasion, claiming only one aircraft burned, five probably destroyed and five damaged – all on the ground – before they were forced to break off the attack due to cloud. Maj Tateo Kato, the 64th Sentai's leader, reported:

"Steering to the north below cloud layers. I spotted a runway. Started firing at once. Although there were many planes on the ground, I could not pierce through the clouds, which were hanging low. Accordingly, after smashing two enemy planes, I decided to return."

Fifteen minutes later the other units arrived but, like the 75th, the light bombers of the 90th turned away to Banka. The 59th Sentai pilots had meanwhile encountered a pair of Blenheims, part of a flight of six such machines acting as escort to the convoy heading for Singapore and these were swiftly despatched to watery graves. Although only the two Blenheims were lost, the jubilant Japanese pilots claimed three shot down, and the probable destruction of another. One of the bombers was almost certainly credited to Sgt Maj Hiroshi Onozaki. The 59th Sentai formation continued to Palembang, where they found the clouds already clearing, and as they went into the attack, met a number of British aircraft in the air. Six Hurricanes of 258 Squadron were just returning from a patrol and engaged the raiders, while other Hurricanes of both units had scrambled following the initial attack. While some of the Ki-43s swooped down to strafe, others took on the Hurricanes. Pilots on the ground sheltered where they could, again some firing their revolvers at the low-flying raiders. Plt Off Ting Macnamara later recorded:

"I witnessed one of the greatest fights that has ever taken place. Our flight was on the midday to dusk shift and on our way out to relieve the other flight, the Japs came over. As their fighters were ground strafing the road to the drome, we were obliged to skip very smartly out of the cars and make for cover, standing in the bushes alongside the road, when we had all but reached the drome. Red Campbell, the great big six foot two American, and I made our way to the drome. Six Hurricanes and a Blenheim were returning from a patrol and lost no time in mixing it with 18 Zeros that attacked them, while nine more hovered high above, doing aerobatics! The fight took place at less than 1,500 feet, just off the aerodrome. How the aircraft whirled and twisted, their engines now snarling, now wailing, guns blazing – they looked for all the world like a pack of dogs all fighting each other!"

It was over swiftly, the Japanese pilots claiming five Hurricanes shot down and three more probably destroyed. They also claimed to have destroyed three more Blenheims and a Hudson on the ground. Amongst the casualties suffered on the ground during the attack was Plt Off Keith Dawson-Scott, a 21-year-old replacement pilot posted to 258 Squadron from 266 (Fighter) Wing, who was killed. He had only just arrived at Palembang from Tjililitan, probably aboard a Blenheim or Hudson. In return only a single confirmed claim was submitted by Plt Off Reg Bainbridge of 232 Squadron, while a second was damaged by the combined fire of Plt Offs Ambrose Milnes, Doug Nicholls and Jock McCulloch of 258 Squadron. Amidst the burning aircraft – including two Buffaloes – and debris littering the airfield, the remaining Hurricanes came in to land, one at a time. Sgt Parr's aircraft (BG678) had been hit in the cockpit area, an explosive shell striking the throttle and severing the little finger of his left hand. Sgt Kelly witnessed his return:

> "...he made a most remarkably efficient job of landing, switching off his engine and landing very fast with wheels up – usually a much easier operation than might be imagined, as all that normally happens is that the radiator is torn off and the propeller shatters to small pieces and the Hurricane slides along on its belly until it stops. But that is at the recommended landing speed and Parr was probably travelling twice as fast. So in his case instead of sliding on its belly the Hurricane mounted on its nose and slid along on that, a most extraordinary and alarming sight. Had it toppled that would probably have been the end of Parr. But it didn't, it went on sliding until it was conveniently far enough along the runway not to prevent taking off and landing and there it stopped. Bertie Lambert and I tore out in a Bedford. Parr had climbed out of his machine and was waiting, watching us arrive. When we did so he put his right hand into his shirt pocket and handed something to us. 'I guess I won't be needing that any more,' he said. It was his left hand little finger taken off by the explosive bullet, which jammed his throttle open."

Parr was rushed to Palembang Emergency Hospital. A second Hurricane crash-landed on the airfield, a total write-off, although the Canadian pilot, Sgt Nelson Scott, was unhurt. Two Hurricanes failed to return. Of the two missing 258 Squadron Hurricanes, the wreckage of Plt Off Cardell Kleckner's aircraft was later found in the jungle; the body of the American pilot was recovered and buried in Palembang Cemetery. Kleckner had only arrived from Singapore the previous day, having fitted a propeller to his own aircraft from a badly damaged machine. The other Hurricane, piloted by Plt Off Campbell-White, crashed deep in the jungle and he returned several days later, to recall:

> "I was only at treetop height when I noticed six to eight Zeros just above me. Three peeled off and although I took urgent, evasive action, I was hit. The engine stopped and I crashed through the trees into a swamp."

The Hurricane ended upside down in the swamp. He had been knocked out and fortunately the aircraft did not catch fire. He later related his experiences to Art Donahue, who recorded:

> "Cam had been shot down and had crashed in heavy jungle a long way from Palembang, but managed to extricate himself from the wreck quite unhurt, though shaken. Some natives came around soon, appearing reasonably friendly, and they indicated that they'd take him to civilization in return for the gasoline in his tanks. Considering this quite a bargain, he wrote out a slip of paper, saying they could have all the gasoline they found, and gave it to them. None of them could read, but they seemed to trust him all right.
>
> They were very interested in the wrecked Hurricane, climbing all over it and inspecting it carefully. Cam was afraid that sooner or later one of them might accidentally fire the guns. He spent quite a while trying to show them by signs that they mustn't meddle with the firing button. He says he gathered them all around and then acted as though he were going to press the button, then shook his head and waved his hands, saying, 'Bad! Very bad! Mustn't do!' He repeated the performance until he was sure they had the idea. Then he started off with those who were to take him to safety. They made their way to a river where they got into canoes and paddled off, but their progress was very slow and constantly interrupted. About every half-hour the natives would meet some friends in other canoes, whereupon they'd stop and all pile into each other's boats and sit cross-legged, jabbering to each other, for an hour or so. His rescuers would point at him and jabber to their friends and laugh, saying what sounded to him, 'Look what we've got!

Isn't he funny?' And he would beam back at them. He said he felt called upon to sit cross-legged, too. He said, 'I'd make signs that I was thirsty, and one of them would say, 'Thirsty? All right – have a drink'- or what sounded like it. Then he'd take a gourd and scoop up some filthy muddy water out of the river and give it to me!' Frequently they'd stop at some native village along the river and go ashore for a visit, all sitting cross-legged and jabbering by the hour, while Cam smiled at everyone and tried to look interested. Meals were gourds of rice, so filthy it made him sick to his stomach.

After four days of this kind of travel they arrived at a village where he was able to get in touch with the outside world by a radio set. He was told to stay where he was, and soon a Dutch army car arrived – the village was connected with the outside world by a road of sorts – and he was driven back to Palembang. He was still quite weak and shaken from his ordeal when we met him."

On his return, Cam White asked Sqn Ldr Thomson to take him off flying as he did not believe his nerves could stand any more of it.

Early during the morning of 7 February, one of the ubiquitous Ki-46s was over Palembang again, the crew confirming many aircraft on the airfield, resulting in a further attack being launched during the late afternoon. Before the raid materialised however, three transit B-17s from the Middle East safely departed P1 for Bandoeng and would therefore luckily escape the onslaught. A total of 31 Ki-43s from both fighter sentais accompanied six 90th Sentai light bombers to P1, where insufficient warning of the impending raid was received. Consequently the last Hurricanes were still moving down the runway when the first bombs began to explode, although all the fighters escaped damage at this stage. It seems that the 90th Sentai formation may have included some of the unit's Ki-30s as well as Ki-48s, for single-engined aircraft with fixed undercarriages were identified, incorrectly recognised by the defenders as fighters.

As the Hurricane pilots struggled to gain altitude, the Japanese fighters tore into them, claiming no less than ten shot down, plus five probables; Sgt Maj Hiroshi Onozaki of the 59th Sentai almost certainly claimed at least one of the four credited to his unit, while pilots of the 64th Sentai claimed a further six, including one each by Lt Yohei Hinoki and Sgt Akeshi Yokoi, while another was shared by Capt Katsumi Anma, Lt Takeshi Endo and Sgt Maj Yoshito Yasuda. The unit's 3rd Chutai strafed the airfield, claiming ten aircraft destroyed and six damaged, while 59th Sentai pilots also claimed a 'Lockheed' shot down, and a second probably destroyed. The 'Lockheed' was in fact a Blenheim, which was attacked as it approached to land. Meanwhile, the 90th Sentai crews released their bombs over an estimated 14 aircraft on the airfield, reporting that four of these were set on fire. Losses to the RAF during the attack were indeed heavy, with six Blenheims plus three Hurricanes burnt out on the ground, and a further 11 Hurricanes, a Buffalo and a Hudson damaged. Air Commodore Vincent and his SASO, Wg Cdr Ron Barclay, found themselves caught in the open:

"P1 was a very easy target and I remember Air Commodore Vincent and myself flattening ourselves in the sticky orange-coloured mud in the middle of the airstrip, while a Japanese rear-gunner casually sprayed the field."

The Hurricanes that had been scrambled also suffered serious losses, as implied by Vincent:

"Once again the warning came late, and once again the inexperienced pilots found the Japanese more than a match. The Hurricanes were unable to gain height in time and were attacked in ones and twos immediately after taking off."

Plt Off Doug Nicholls of 258 Squadron was among those who managed to get airborne:

"We were not scrambled until the bombers and escorting fighters were in view and I remember taking off with bombs exploding around me. I did a steep turn soon after take-off and climbed up beneath the rear formation of bombers, which was only about 1,000 feet high. The bomber I attacked started to smoke and shed a few bits, but I had to break off to avoid the fighter escort coming down. Once clear of the airfield I climbed up to about 6,000 feet and became involved in a hide-and-seek dogfight in among the clouds. Eventually my cockpit filled with smoke and coolant and, as I was over thick jungle, I had to bale out about 30 miles west of P1. I landed in a swamp, injuring my leg as I fell through the trees. I could hardly walk and I tried to find a place to sleep. I found an old rubber drying hut, but the mosquitoes became so bad that I set off again and eventually found a kind of log walk across part of the swamp and I came to some more dry land, still in thick jungle, with very thick undergrowth and old neglected rubber trees.

Occasionally I fired my pistol and, after a long time, there was an answering shot from a distance. With paratroops all around the place I then wondered if I'd been rather unwise and I thought even more so when eventually, out of the trees, came these little brown fellows with their funny hats and their tightly putteed uniformed legs, all of them pointing rifles at me. And I thought, I have made a mistake here! But fortunately they were Dutch troops and they had a white officer in charge and he took my revolver and dressed the wound on my leg and they carted me, half hopping, half walking, to a truck about seven miles away and eventually we got back [after seven days] nearly to Palembang only to find that we couldn't get back to the aerodrome because it was cut off."

Two more 258 Squadron Hurricanes had been badly shot-up, both pilots being obliged to crash-land on the airfield, Plt Off Mick Nash surviving his second such landing in a week, albeit suffering from shock afterwards. The other pilot, Canadian Sgt Roy Keedwell, was not so lucky. Again, Donahue recorded a moving account in his journal:

"Not all the stories were pleasant. The saddest was that of Roy Keedwell, a very young Canadian sergeant pilot, from Toronto. Vic [de la Perrelle], who was Roy's flight commander, told me about it that evening after dinner in the hotel where we boarded, while we sat toying with our coffee and watching the funny little wall lizards on the high ceiling of the dining-room go about their trade of keeping the mosquitoes and other insects cleaned up. I wish I could reproduce Vic's words the way he told it, speaking slowly and haltingly, his voice starting to quaver once or twice, pausing occasionally to get control, his eyes blinking and watching the ceiling, avoiding mine. For Roy was a wonderful kid and Vic had been his very close friend.

He told me that Roy was wounded in the leg during a battle. His airplane was shot-up badly, but he managed to get back and land all right. Then while he was taxiing across the field his damaged machine caught fire. The gas-tanks must have been holed, for it was all ablaze in an instant; and because of his wounded leg Roy had trouble getting out. By the time he got clear he was badly burned about the face, legs, and arms [Sgt Art Sheerin was among those who helped pull him out]. He was taken to the Dutch hospital at Palembang, where he seemed to do all right for the first twenty-four hours. Then shock set in and he started weakening. Vic went to see him as often as he could get time. He visited him about eight o'clock in the morning on the third day, promising to be back again at four in the afternoon. Something told him that morning that all was not well, for the doctors were letting Roy have morphia to ease the pain, something they had refused him before.

Vic was very busy that day and was delayed slightly in the afternoon, so he didn't arrive at the hospital until a few minutes past four. There he found, to his grief, that Roy had just passed away. The sisters told him that Roy held on desperately until four, waiting for him to come, because he wanted so badly for Vic to be with him when he died. But when Vic didn't arrive on time his strength gave out. Just before he passed away he looked around at the sisters and begged, 'Someone please hold my hand and call me Roy before I die.' One of the sisters took his hand and called him 'Roy', and that was how he died, halfway around the world from his home in Toronto."

Some measure of success was obtained by Plt Off Red Campbell, who claimed a Zero (sic) shot down:

"We scrambled, and the meeting broke up into a general dogfight. Three of them came after me. The Hurricane, climbing full power at 220 miles an hour, would simply leave a Zero behind. The Zero could never catch up. This time we did not have altitude and were just off the deck. I started to lose one of the Zeros in my rear-view mirror, and began weaving to see where he was. All three were closing on me, and as one opened fire I did a 180-degree turn – during which he scored several hits on me – and fired head on. As I came on top I could see one-fourth of his engine cowling ripping away. I went over him and back up in the clouds and had no idea where he was. Luckily for me he crashed right off the airfield – rolled and went right into the deck. The groundcrew confirmed that it was a definite, not just a probably destroyed."

The Ki-43 crashed on the perimeter of the airfield, as witnessed by 232 Squadron's Plt Off Bill Lockwood, who had just returned from Singapore:

"I had to take off in the face of strafing Navy 0s, lying on the ground beside my Hurricane until I had a reasonable opportunity of getting off. As I lined up on the runway to take off, an 0 fell in flames at the end of the runway."

Another Navy 0 was claimed by Plt Off Milnes, who reported watching his victim catch fire and dive in a graceful arc into the jungle. He also claimed a 'Type 97' fighter damaged, while Sgt Scott reported damaging another; these were possibly Ki-30 light bombers since no Ki-27s were involved. The Japanese admitted the loss of two of their aircraft including a Ki-43 of the 64th Sentai – obviously Campbell's victim; the other loss was almost certainly a Ki-30 of the 90th Sentai.

Whilst the fighting was raging over Palembang, two more of 258 Squadron's Hurricanes returned from a convoy patrol and were at once set upon by a dozen Ki-43s; 20-year-old Sgt Ken Glynn[68] failed to return, while Plt Off Jock McCulloch was chased into the clouds and became lost. He subsequently ran out of fuel and crash-landed in a swamp near a river. On his return to Palembang, he told his story to his colleagues. Red Campbell remembered:

"He'd got quite a story. Seems he'd been shot down and when he landed it was actually beside another Hurricane that was on its back beside a riverbank and I believe that was Glynn's crash. He couldn't do anything for Junior, who was dead, but there were these natives and he tried to get them to give him a hand but they just stayed at a distance, so he inflated his dinghy and got in the river. And these natives were just standing at a distance so he took his pistol and fired a couple of shots over their heads and they ran off. And when I asked him why he'd done that, he said: 'Well if the buggers weren't going to help me, I certainly didn't want them standing there and staring at me.'"

Donahue added:

"These dinghies aren't built for speed, and Mac found his progress very slow. Presently he saw a canoe tied to the shore with no one in attendance and paddled over to it. He couldn't find anyone around, so he pinned a ten-guilder note to a nearby tree in payment and paddled off in his new purchase. After a time he met up with some natives in canoes, who escorted him to a village nearby, where he was shown to the chief's house. There to his amazement, right in the heart of the jungle, he was treated to ice-cold beer from a refrigerator and put up in a huge room with the biggest and most luxurious bed he'd ever seen! He stayed there for a couple of days, living elegantly on imported European foods, which the progressive-minded chief kept in stock, until he was rescued."

For the third day in succession (8 February) the JAAF attacked Palembang, although on this occasion the 25 Ki-43s and 17 K-30 light bombers of the 90th Sentai arrived in the morning; the bomber crews claimed nine aircraft burned on the ground, many of them aircraft already damaged during previous raids, although at least one operational Blenheim was destroyed. Air Commodore Vincent wrote:

"I was with a group of officers trying to move a Hudson which had had both tyres punctured by splinters while being refuelled from a tanker. The tanker was ablaze and we were endeavouring to save the aeroplane. We succeeded in this, but a Blenheim fully 500 yards away was also on fire. I had driven past the Blenheim in my car shortly before, and having noticed it was bombed up, ordered everyone away. The bombs exploded with a tremendous roar, and an airman standing beside me gave a cry of pain, for a bomb splinter had come that great distance and pierced his wrist, and was protruding on both sides."

The Japanese fighter pilots reported meeting four Hurricanes, each sentai claiming one shot down, but only two were airborne, flown by Flt Lt Murray Taylor and Sgt Hackforth, who unhesitatingly engaged in combat; it was believed that each probably gained a victory before they were overwhelmed. Murray Taylor's aircraft (BE115) was seen approaching the airfield, low and fast, pursued by a Ki-43. Jerry Parker was among the witnesses:

"I heard cannon fire and multiple machine guns above the droning, whining and screaming of the aircraft. Suddenly the sound of diving aircraft increased to a shriek as they approached the airfield and a Hurricane hurtled through the cloud just above my head, pulled level and whirled across the airfield. It was almost accompanied by a Zero at a slight angle but, as soon as the Jap spotted the Hurricane, he pulled around behind him and opened fire. The Hurricane came around in a tight turn with the Zero almost on top of him, letting go with short bursts. Although the Jap looked as though he'd overshoot and pass him at first, he easily turned back and stayed with the Hurricane, which completed one and a half full circles. As it turned towards me I could only stand as straight as I could behind a very narrow rubber tree and pray that the British pilot would turn away and not subject me to the cannon shells which were bursting in the trees all around. The din was fierce as the machine guns mounted around the field opened up on the Jap but they couldn't save the Hurricane which continued its steep turn into the trees on the far side of the field. It didn't burn and the Jap pulled back up into the cloud unscathed."

Murray Taylor, who had been mortally wounded, crashed into some trees on the edge of the airfield. Meanwhile, 19-year-old Hackforth's aircraft (BE219) was under attack by five Ki-43s and he was last seen being chased away from the airfield with two fighters on either side and one on his tail. He too was killed when his aircraft crashed into the jungle. When some of the pilots accompanied ground staff to retrieve Murray Taylor's body from the wreck, they discovered that although the aircraft had been hit many times, his death had resulted from the fact that he had been out-turned in vertically-banked turns, so that bullets had come over the top of the armour plating into his back and head. Their conclusion was that if he had flown straight, or had made only slight turns, he would doubtless have been shot down, but the armour would have kept his body protected and he would, probably, have survived. The loss of the two 232 Squadron pilots was a severe blow, for they were both among the more successful. Dean Hackforth, from Weston-super-Mare, had been credited with at least four victories;

within a day or so of his death, the squadron received notification of his commission. Edwin Murray Taylor, a Buckinghamshire man, although relatively inexperienced in combat on arrival in Singapore, had nonetheless led his flight with conspicuous success and was personally credited with at least six victories; the award of a DFC would be promulgated the following August.

During these raids, many brave deeds were witnessed – in the air and on the ground. Plt Off Gartrell praised the groundcrews for their steadfastness while under fire and in particular two flight sergeants:

> "I particularly remember an action of two New Zealand flight sergeants at Palembang. We had Flt Sgts Rees and Chandler. Flt Sgt Andy Chandler was first class. I recall him standing on the wing of a Hurricane when the Nips were machine-gunning the aircraft on the ground. We had just finished a sortie, and they were flying to get us. There was Andy Chandler, standing on the wing cursing and swearing, saying what the Nips were and telling the troops to get on with it and arm and refuel the Hurricanes. This was while the bullets were flying."[69]

This was to be the last attack on the Palembang area for several days, but the defences were now very short of fighters. An opportune visit to P1 by Air Vice-Marshal Sir Richard Peirse, Commander-in-Chief Allied Air Forces, ABDA Command, permitted Air Commodore Vincent to plead his case for more fighters, spares, AA guns and ammunition. A promise was made to hasten the despatch of new Hurricanes being erected at Batavia and, during the day, eight pilots were flown from P1 to Tjililitan by Dutch Lodestar to collect the first of these. Flg Off Harry Dobbyn was in charge of the party of four officers and four sergeant pilots and Ting Macanama was one of those selected to go:

> "We were to fly back Hurricanes which, we were told, were ready and waiting for us. We were to have lunch there and fly back the same evening, so off we went, clad only in flying boots, shirt and pants, flying helmet and parachute. On our arrival we found that the planes had not even been uncrated! We were then told to wait in Batavia for them and were billeted at the Flat Hotel, where we duly pitched up – dirty and unshaven – looking anything but commissioned officers of His Majesty's Air Force!
>
> To our great delight we learnt that these planes had been brought out by the same ship [the *Athene*] on which we left England and had last seen at Takoradi. We lost no time in going aboard where we were warmly received and sympathetically allowed to purchase such clothes and odds and ends we needed from the 'Slops'. While aboard her, the Japs raided Batavia Airport but left the ships alone with the exception of one lone fighter, which swooped down and machine-gunned a merchant vessel as the raiders flew home. This performance was left unchallenged by anything. The airport had no fighter protection nor, at the time, anti-aircraft guns, and the naval vessels in the harbour did not open fire until the raid was over and, as the enemy disappeared well out of effective range, a cruiser – the famous *Exeter* – let off two or three solitary rounds!
>
> Our four days in Batavia were spent working on the Hurricanes, assembling them with the aid of Dutch Airways' personnel who were doing the job. Our evenings were spent in doing shows and dancing, as we were fortunate in soon making friends at the hotel. Before we left, another nine pilots arrived to take delivery of more 'phantom' Hurricanes! The mix-up was unbelievable. Among this batch was Jock McCulloch who had been shot down two days before we left Palembang, and had more or less been considered dead by us. Harry Dobbyn, who was in charge of our party, came to see me with a blank expression on his face, saying that he had seen a ghost. Harry's face had to be seen to be appreciated. I set off with him to see the ghost and, as we looked through the window of the restaurant at Batavia Airport, Mac turned round and greeted us."

Further reinforcement fighter pilots – these from 266 (Fighter) Wing – arrived at P1 on 9 February, having travelled from Batavia by boat to Oosthaven, then by rail and lorry to the airfield. One of the new arrivals, Sgt Frank Hood, a New Zealander, commented:

> "Very wild country. City rambling and very Eastern. Very little money and issue grub lousy. Lots of air activity. No kites for us."

Despite the losses, the command infrastructure for the defences continued to flow in to Palembang. Headquarters staff and ground personnel of 258 and 605 Squadrons reached 266 (Fighter) Group from Java on 10 February, their good morale having a rejuvenating effect on the ex-Singapore men, some of whom were failing to stand up to the bombing. Other new arrivals at P1 included seven of 232(P) Squadron's Hurricanes from Singapore, led by Sqn Ldr Brooker, while next day Air Vice-Marshal Paul Maltby arrived from Singapore to assume control. Unable, however, to find a suitable headquarters location on the island, he and his SASO Air Commodore Bill Staton would move on to Java a few days later.

Sqn Ldr Brooker was briefed to lead off all available Hurricanes at midday on the 10th, but one taxied into a MVAF Dragon Rapide and was damaged. The remaining Hurricanes, meanwhile, saw nothing of note during the patrol and were soon recalled, two pilots having returned early, sick and dizzy due to a lack of oxygen bottles in their aircraft; owing to this serious shortage, one flight was not able to climb above 18,000 feet. Throughout this period, Hurricanes continued to patrol over shipping in the Banka Straits, which were evacuating personnel from Singapore. During one such mission on 12 February, the luckless Plt Off John McKechnie of 232 Squadron was obliged to crash-land BG768 in the jungle due to a violent storm. He later wrote in a letter to his uncle:

> "I crashed in the Sumatran jungle, suffering rather a bad concussion and a fractured wrist, and damaging one eye. However, when I eventually got out of my plane, which was upside down, I managed to make my way through swamps to a river, and then got picked up by a Dutch minelayer and taken to the Palembang hospital."[70]

That evening, newly arrived Air Vice-Marshal Maltby paid P2 a visit, and gave assembled Blenheim aircrews a lecture about the "pernicious habit of looking over one's shoulder". He vowed that there would be no evacuation and that everyone, from pilots to cooks would fight to the last, emphasising that "this was to be an effort to retrieve the good name of the Air Force, which had been lost in Singapore." One of those on the receiving end of the lecture was the CO[71] of 84 Squadron, who recalled:

> "A talk of this nature was an excellent thing as the morale of the personnel who had come from Malaya and Singapore was extremely low, but it must be confessed that a lot of the effect was lost as the AVM had only just arrived from Singapore, and had no conception of the conditions under which we were operating, which precluded shaving every day and keeping our buttons polished."

Others noted that, with the lecture over, the Air Vice-Marshal then evacuated himself and his staff to a relatively safer and more comfortable haven in Java:

> "By the end of the day we were a pretty dirty, scruffy lot. The Air Vice-Marshal did nothing but carry on about what a disgrace we looked and how it was necessary to maintain a high degree of smartness, with well-polished shoes and buttons. My only thoughts were that his knife-edge creases and spotless uniform would have looked a sorry mess if he had to do the jobs that I had done that day. He certainly did nothing at all to boost the morale of what was a gathering of very experienced aircrew, many of whom had operational experience in Europe, Greece and North Africa. Having had his say, our great leader flew off, never to be seen (by me) again."[72]

The Hurricane pilots at P1 had been given a similar lecture. They were none too impressed, either, as Macnamara recalled:

> "We had been addressed by the AOC and were told we were the thin red line, that there was no retreat and that we simply had to stop the Japs at any price. Beer was then issued all round, and that was the last we saw of him. What the hell he thought we were going to do with it, nobody knew!"

By Friday 13 February – unlucky for some – some of the erected Hurricanes at Tjililitan were ready, the eight pilots of 258 and 232 Squadrons being ordered to prepare for the flight to Palembang. Joined by Wg Cdr Maguire, who was to lead the formation to P1, they took off at dawn. At about the same time, a dozen Hurricanes had taken off from P1, seeking six Japanese 'flying boats' reported by the Dutch HQ to have alighted near the north-east coast of Banka Island; these were in fact F1M floatplanes from the seaplane tenders *Kamikawa Maru* and *Sagara Maru*, which had been detached to operate from Muntok. Despite a careful search by the Hurricanes nothing was to be seen and Sqn Ldr Brooker led them back to Palembang, low on fuel. They had just landed when the JAAF returned to the attack, 29 Ki-43s from the 59th and 64th Sentais, with seven Ki-48s. At that moment, the seven reinforcement Hurricanes from Java arrived overhead; almost out of fuel, some were forced to land at once, but Wg Cdr Maguire and Sgt Henry Nicholls remained above to try and give some protection, and these two at once attacked the incoming raiders. Maguire became involved with two Ki-43s, and in the confusion, one of these opened fire on the other. He later commented:

> "I claimed one Zero, although I am pretty sure he was damaged by his own No.2 first – possibly over-excited."

Nicholls also fired at this machine, which he saw crash at the end of the runway, probably the aircraft flown by Sgt Maj Choichi Okuyama, who was killed. Nicholls then engaged another, which he believed also crashed into the jungle. He was attacked by a third fighter, and his engine was hit, obliging him to bale out at 600 feet, a few miles to the south of the airfield. Suffering from shock, he was picked up by a group of natives, who took him down river to a Dutch missionary, from where he eventually made his way to Oosthaven; in the meantime he was posted missing.

Another of the reinforcement Hurricanes, flown by Sgt Nelson Scott, was on its landing approach with flaps and undercarriage down, when two Ki-43s dived onto its tail. Red Campbell witnessed what happened next:

> "… two Zeros were sitting about 2,000 feet above him. One of them was weaving and the other was starting to drop his nose and come down and the silly thing was that if he had just done that, if he'd have dropped his nose and come down, I guess Scotty would have bought it right then and there. But what he did was to pull up into one of those beautiful stall turns they liked to do in an attack; he pulled it up and stood it on its tail and kicked it over at the top and came straight down. And he gained a lot of speed and I think the problem was that he didn't realise Scotty had his wheels and flaps down and was going so damn slow. So he just had time to open fire when he was starting to overshoot, so he pulled back very hard on the stick and the next thing I saw was that the two aircraft seemed to merge together and one of them came out with his wings folded and the other one was still stooging along with his wheels and flaps down. What happened was that he'd apparently hauled back the Zero so violently he'd had a structural failure because he went on ahead, looked like a goose, folded his wings and crashed and his No.2 dropped his nose and actually flamed Scotty.

The last thing we saw was this Hurricane, smoking badly, which looked like it was on fire, turn and go below the trees. We thought he'd bought it. We had the air raid and a lot of things happened about that time but at the end of all of this – a good half hour, or an hour – there comes Scotty walking down the dirt road, and he had his chute under his arm and he was nothing but brassed off with us because we hadn't come to get him. But of course nobody thought he had the slightest chance, seeing the aircraft go down in flames that low they figured he'd bought it. But what happened, he said, he'd jettisoned his canopy, jumped, pulled his chute, it blossomed, the aircraft crashed, he landed. I really think if records were taken Scotty probably held the record for the lowest survivable parachute jump in history!"

Lt Masabumi Kunii of the 64th Sentai was the unfortunate pilot of the Ki-43 that crashed and burst into a ball of flames (Kunii may have been Nicholl's second victim). Watching Japanese pilots believed Kunii had shot down the Hurricane before his crash, but in fact Macnamara was able to land his undamaged aircraft safely, as did the other four ferry pilots, although one aircraft had suffered slight damage. Of Scott's predicament, Donahue – who had just arrived at the airfield – wrote:

"The ground chaps were very concerned about a Hurricane they had seen shot down. They didn't know who the pilot was. It had been approaching to land, they said, with its wheels and flaps down, when two Navy Zeros dived on it. The first one, in pulling out of its dive, snapped its wings and crashed, but the second one shot the Hurricane. Some thought they'd seen the pilot bale out, but no one knew yet. At present some low clouds over the airdrome obscured all view of what was going on above, but we could hear no noise. Just then Scotty, a big husky chap from Alberta, walked into the dispersal building – and what a Scotty! It was he who had been piloting the Hurricane that was shot down. He had escaped by a miracle, baling out at less than 500 feet, and landing in the jungle a mile or so away. He was dirtied and dishevelled and still very dazed, wearing an expression on his face as if he'd just fallen out of bed! He had just arrived from Java, ferrying a new Hurricane for the squadron. Quite a reception! It was too bad that his machine was lost so quickly, but it cost the enemy an airplane and pilot both, so we couldn't call it a bad trade."

The wreck of Sgt Maj Okuyama's Ki-43, which had crashed at the end of the runway, was later inspected by amongst others Wg Cdr Ron Barclay, who noted that the lack of armour plate had been mainly responsible for the pilot's death; he was riddled with bullets from head to seat. With the Hurricanes so engaged, the Japanese bomber crews were able to gain a number of successes when they attacked shipping on the river. Of these new Hurricanes, only five were immediately serviceable and three pilots were placed on readiness, including Macnamara:

"The three of us sat at readiness knowing only too well our fate if the Japs returned. We did not talk much but smoked a good deal in heavy silence, except for fake bravado utterances such as 'Well, if it comes we'll chat about it afterwards, upstairs!' or 'Hang on Kleck, here we come!' Suddenly the alarm blew. The CO, Harry Dobbyn and I raced for our machines. The CO's machine apparently wouldn't start so Harry and I got off, racing like mad low over the trees. We got well away and climbed rapidly as was our custom and turned to face three bombers we had seen breaking cloud as we took off. We searched high and low, but after patrolling for an hour or more we returned to base, only to find it had been a false alarm! They were Hudsons returning to their own base at P2. No one had thought of telling us sooner. I don't know what Harry's feelings were as we climbed out of our planes, but I know what mine were!"

Soon after, three more Hurricanes – these from 232 Squadron – scrambled on the approach of further raiders, and climbed into cloud. They were followed a few minutes later by Sqn Ldr Brooker at the head of several more Hurricanes, which began a hide-and-seek fight with Japanese fighters and bombers amongst the low clouds. Plt Off Gartrell engaged a fighter he believed was a Zero and claimed it probably destroyed:

> "In the general mêlée we were jumped and it became a matter of trying to out-turn the Nips. I got a couple of bullets, as I found out afterwards, through the tailplane. As I was turning round, another Zero came from the other side, and I think he got in the road of the first bloke, and they almost collided trying to get at me. As he peeled away I managed to get a shot in and there was just a cloud of smoke and down he went. I didn't see it crash, because we were too high, although I reported to the Intelligence Officer that I thought I had shot one down. He said he had heard that one crashed about the same time and that the other two hadn't claimed one."

Of this action Sgt Sandy Allen (Z5667/T) reported:

> "I was separated, and attacked, in error, 24 Navy 0s guarding the bombers. I was credited with two Zeros, and one bomber probable."

Sqn Ldr Brooker claimed a second bomber for his sixth personal victory of the war (four of which had been credited prior to his arrival at Singapore). Several other Japanese aircraft were claimed damaged, including a Ki-21 by Sgt Ken Holmes who reported seeing his victim fall away with one engine stopped before he was forced to break away. One of the Hurricanes (BG693) failed to return, the Rhodesian Plt Off Leslie Emmerton, a 25-year-old married man, last being seen at low level over the treetops, being pursued by several Ki-43s. He was killed. When the raid began, one unserviceable Hurricane had been taken into the air by Plt Off Tom Watson to prevent it being strafed:

> "It had no air pressure so I had no brakes and my guns would not fire. I was several miles from P1 when I was attacked by six or seven Zeros and all I could do was run for it. My whole plane was shot-up – wings, fuselage, engine and instrument panel – and I had the uncomfortable feeling of hearing or feeling the Japanese machine gun bullets hitting my armour plate. With engine smoking, I headed for P1 and the cover of our own anti-aircraft fire. My engine conked out but I was able to land: fortunately the undercarriage came down OK. I had no brakes and rambled on past the end of the runway, the plane a complete write-off."

Flt Lt Mike Cooper-Slipper, who was acting in the capacity of OC Flying at P1, also managed to get airborne and reported meeting several bombers, two of which he claimed probably destroyed. During this attack the Japanese pilots claimed three Hurricanes shot down, plus two more probables and four large aircraft on the ground. In return they reported the loss of three aircraft during the raid. At least two Ki-43s are known to have failed to return, the other loss may therefore have been a Ki-21, possibly the victim of several pilots.

The rest of the day would see sections of Hurricanes kept at readiness at P1, from where there were scrambles although no further attacks developed. During the afternoon, two sections again went out to look for flying boats, but nothing was seen; a violent storm was encountered over Banka, which broke up the formation although all returned safely. That evening the defenders witnessed 14 Hurricanes take to the air together. The 258 Squadron Engineer Officer, Flg Off Tudor Jones, assisted by Plt Off John David, his 243 Squadron counterpart, and their groundcrews had performed Herculean tasks in makeshift hangars on the boundary of the airfield, to make so many fighters serviceable. Much cannibalisation of badly damaged aircraft had taken place to enable others to be made good. Wg Cdr Maguire led this formation out to look for a Japanese convoy reported approaching Sumatra. Again the aircraft flew into a severe storm, and although navigation lights were switched on, some aircraft became separated. One flight from 232 Squadron, led by Sgt Sandy Allen, was severely buffeted and forced away from the airfield, with the result that two of the Hurricanes eventually crash-landed. Both pilots survived, although both 2/Lt Neil Dummett and Sgt Fred Bidewell, one of the new arrivals, suffered shock and injury[73]. Sgt Bertie Lambert was another involved in this flight:

> "As we approached Banka with the leading section probably 2,000 feet or so below us the weather worsened and, as the leading section lost height to look for the reported target, Dobbyn and I saw them for a time in very poor visibility and then lost contact with them. After searching for some time, the two sections returned to base separately having seen nothing of the flying boats. On our return to base Dobbyn and I had to pass through the centre of a vicious electrical storm. We were thrown about like corks on a rough sea to such an extent that for me to try to keep in formation was simply too dangerous. Two things stick in my mind following this operation: first was a fork of lightning which appeared to go down vertically in front of me right in line with the centre of the airscrew and second, on appearing over base the intense pall of black smoke hanging over P1 under very heavy clouds."

Valentine's Day Massacre at Palembang

Dawn on 14 February found the Palembang area in a high state of tension as word of an approaching invasion fleet began to spread. At P1 the Hurricane pilots were in good spirits however, following the successes of the previous day; the number of aircraft available had also improved considerably with the arrival of the reinforcements from Java. 232 Squadron had about a dozen fighters on hand and 258 Squadron eight more. Of these, 15 had been made serviceable and were ready to take to the air.

Early reconnaissance revealed that the Japanese vessels had entered the Banka Straits and, as soon as it was light enough, all 15 Hurricanes were ordered off, led by Sqn Ldr Thomson, to escort nine Blenheims of 84 Squadron and six more of 211 Squadron (from P2), the bomber crews having been briefed to attack an aircraft carrier which was reportedly accompanying the convoy. Meanwhile, shortly before first light, five RAAF Hudsons had taken off from P2. More Hudsons followed, and soon all were in action against the invasion fleet. Not only did they have to face intense AA fire from the ships but also determined attacks by A6Ms, five Hudsons being shot down. While the Hudsons were being so savagely mauled, the Hurricanes wasted an invaluable 15 minutes at the rendezvous before the 211 Squadron Blenheims arrived, but not those from 84 Squadron, which followed a few minutes later. Unable to delay further, the formation at last set course for the target area, the Blenheim crews claiming several hits on various transport vessels, one of which was sunk and several others damaged. With the bombers on their way home, Sqn Ldr Thomson ordered all Hurricanes to return to base. As they approached the Palembang area, they entered dense cloud, the two squadrons becoming separated. Several of the aircraft were plagued with faulty radios and communications became extremely difficult. Sgt Kelly remembered:

> "As we neared P1 on the return from our pointless and wasted flight, the squadron was instructed not to land at P1 but to fly on to P2. Having no R/T (by no means an unusual situation) neither Lambert nor I received this instruction which was given at the same time that I noticed a number of what I took to be Zeros above. Being unable either by hand signals or frantic wing-waggling to convey this information successfully to Thomson, accompanied by Lambert I set about engaging them, while the balance of the squadron

gracefully departed.

At all events after a good deal of diving, climbing, and turning and all of us spraying the sky with bullets and cannon shells, I found myself with one of them firmly on my tail. The only thing to do was get down low and quickly – after all, if I pulled out sharply, the damn thing's wings might fall off. So down I went using rudder more than aileron to skid, weaving as ragged a course as I could make it and one of the nine lives the war undoubtedly granted me was doled out then because, by the time I had pulled out at treetop level – although the Navy 0 hadn't lost its wings and was still firmly on my tail – I, in turn was still intact. From then on I felt very much as I imagine a fox does when chased by hounds. There was no possible way of attacking the Navy 0; if I had tried to climb or turn to attempt to do so, I should have been shot down at once. The only hope was in ignominious flight.

Anyway, although occasionally I saw tracer making lines ahead of me and whenever I looked in my mirror I could see this chap somewhere behind, and although in fact he chased me over Palembang itself (as I was informed by others of the squadron not flying that day) he didn't manage to hit me. I just hung on to the principle of flying flat out, skidding with my rudder and, whenever I saw a couple of trees fairly close, turning between them. Why, I thought, who knows, I might bring him down that way. Well perhaps I did. I don't know. One moment he was there and the next I was using petrol and nervous energy to no purpose because he wasn't. In pieces in the jungle, short of petrol or just plain bored and homeward bound, he was gone.

I felt much better and reviewed the situation. I wasn't quite sure where I was and calculated I was probably nearer P2 than P1 and it was tempting to go there. But there was no good reason. I had no idea the rest of the squadron was already there; I had ample petrol still to make P1 and plenty of ammunition left. So I flew around until I spotted the town and made my way back to P1. I couldn't land at once because there were still one or two Navy 0s about, of which I managed to shoot down one, and finally I got in to discover it queerly deserted. A few minutes later Lambert joined me."

Meanwhile, through gaps in the clouds, several pilots had spotted groups of Japanese aircraft milling around over the airfield. Calling out warnings, individual pilots – although short of fuel – broke formation and dived to the attack. What they were seeing was much more than just another bombing attack. The Japanese had recently moved 460 paratroops of the 2nd Parachute Regiment to Southern Malaya and, at dawn, 270 of these had embarked in 34 Ki-56s (licence-built Lockheed 14s) and Ki-57 (similar in configuration to the DC-3) transport aircraft of the 1st, 2nd and 3rd Chutais of the Parachute Flying Unit. Accompanied by seven more transports of the 12th Transport Chutai, the force had taken off for Palembang, led by Maj Niihara. Taking up station behind a formation of 18 Ki-21 bombers of the 98th Sentai, which were to drop anti-personnel bombs ahead of the paratroop landings, and nine other Ki-21s loaded with supplies, the whole formation was escorted by a strong force of Ki-43s from the 59th and 64th Sentais.

Earlier, as the force of Hurricanes and Blenheims had been heading out towards the Banka Straits, 226 Group HQ had received a warning from an observer post 100 miles north of Palembang, that a large formation of big, low-flying aircraft was approaching. Wg Cdr Maguire, who was manning the Ops Room, recalled:

"We got the Hurricanes off fairly early in the morning and about twenty minutes later we saw the first Japanese parachute-carrying aircraft heading towards Palembang town. A series of them headed over the airfield. They were engaged by the two British anti-aircraft batteries, one heavy and one 20mm light ack-ack as far as I could see with the usual thing of fuses going off at the wrong altitude. I saw no casualties as a result of anti-aircraft fire although some of them did swing about a bit and as a result the parachutists were dropped rather irregularly mostly to the south of the airfield. Some were dropped to the east and there were some overshoots to the west. Later on these gave a certain amount of trouble from their habit of hiding themselves in trees and sniping with a good field of fire. There was, as you can imagine, a certain amount of confusion."

By chance Air Commodore Vincent had not gone out to P1 that morning, and at once arranged for the airfield defence officer to be warned to expect a paratroop assault, ordering that rifles and ammunition be issued forthwith. These were scarce, however, and about 100 of the airmen at P1 remained unarmed – to their considerable peril, as it was to transpire. There were no British Army units based in Sumatra other than the crews of the anti-aircraft guns around Palembang and P1, although some Dutch troops – mainly native levies – were available: two infantry platoons were stationed at each of the main oil refineries at Pladjoe and Soengi Gerong, while three companies were in reserve at P2, and others were at P1 and in Palembang town itself. Shortly after Vincent's warning had been received, the Japanese attack developed, the Ki-21s dropping anti-personnel bombs that caused a number of casualties, while the 64th Sentai's Ki-43s strafed the airfield and buildings. Thirteen Ki-48 light bombers of the 90th Sentai, which had flown to the area independently, then attacked barracks as the paratroopers began to leap from their transports. Some 180 landed in the scrub between the airfield and the town, while another 90 came down to the west of the oil refineries at Pladjoe, on the south bank of the Moesi, the second major target for their attack.

By now the Blenheims and Hurricanes were approaching the area, the bombers actually flying through the falling paratroops as they headed for their airfield at P2. At 226 Group HQ, Wg Cdr Darley broadcast an urgent message to the Hurricane pilots, warning of the landings and ordering them to head instead for P2. Due to the trouble with their radio receivers, several of the pilots failed to receive the message. It was at this stage that they approached the airfield and first saw the hostile aircraft ahead of them. Plt Off Bill Lockwood and his No.2, Sgt Ian Fairbairn, observed three formations of 27 bombers and transports, together with 15-20 Ki-43s. Lockwood recalled:

"I was flying arse-end Charlie with Fairbairn arse-end Charlie to me. With a considerable distance between myself and the rest of the Hurricanes, I noticed below to port, through a cloud opening, a large number of Jap aircraft. I immediately called Sqn Ldr Brooker but received no reply. I proceeded in a wide turn above and in the same direction as the Jap, back out to sea, with Fairbairn beside me. I observed two formations of bombers, 27 in each, in vics of nine, another formation of transports, also 27, and approximately 15-20 Navy 0s as cover, quite close above the bombers and transports. Having a height advantage, my intention was to get to a point slightly ahead and dive on the leader of one of the bomber formations. As I neared my position, Fairbairn couldn't wait and dropped down to make a pass at the rear, with no effect that I could see. The 0s started to become fidgety and as I gained a position of interception, I chose the leader of the starboard formation of nine bombers and made a diving attack on it. I think I may have holed its fuel tanks. I could see my ammunition flashing on its wings. I did not stay around long enough to climb and have another go.

As I levelled out at fairly low altitude, I ran into a torrential rainstorm. I followed the Moesi to Palembang and P1. On coming out of the rain over P1, I could see a lot of white objects on the aerodrome. Someone gave me a red Very light and I suspected the Japs had dropped paratroops. I flew on to P2 and landed there. I went to the native *kampong*, got some native coffee and a few pineapples, went back to the airfield, sat in the shade of a wing of a Hurricane and sliced up a pineapple."

Lockwood's victim may possibly have been Lt Naohiko Sudoh's Ki-21, which was shot down during this operation, although Japanese records suggest it was a victim of AA fire.

Although low on fuel, Sgt Gordie Dunn and others flew around the airfield, the Canadian strafing the paratroops where he could, having heard the warning that the base was under attack. After using most of his ammunition, Dunn saw several aircraft he thought were Hudsons, dropping bombs at the far end of the runway. He assumed that they were attacking the paratroops, only discovering later that they were, in fact, Japanese bombers. Some of the pilots – including Flg Off Art Donahue – attempted to engage the Ki-43s:

> "I looked back to see a Navy Zero diving down on me, his big stubby round nose and silver-coloured propeller-spinner identifying him as enemy even at quite a distance. Another was following him. I opened my throttle and swung round hard to face him. I was facing him before he could get into firing range and I thought it was going to be a head-on show, both of us coming straight at each other, shooting, seeing who would give way first before we collided; but he didn't seem to want that now that he'd lost his chance for surprise. Before we were in firing range of each other, he zoomed up away. His partner behind did likewise. They had all the advantage of height and speed, so there was nothing I could do about it and I lost track of them."

After delivering attacks on various groups of bombers, during which his own aircraft was damaged, Plt Off Macnamara headed back towards Palembang. There he caught sight of, high above, another group of aircraft, which he thought were Hurricanes, and endeavoured to reach them. Before he could gain altitude however, he was jumped by three Ki-43s of the 64th Sentai, the pilots of which reported intercepting a lone Hurricane. The Rhodesian remembered:

> "I found the Japs and had a good scrap. Mixing in fiercely, I was severely shot-up. I was limping home, disgusted with everything in general, still ignorant of the state of affairs at my base when, high above me, I caught sight of a formation of aircraft, so pulling the 'tit' I opened her out to try and catch them, making the fatal mistake of climbing steadily and straight. I never caught them! Three Zeros swooped down on me. I had seen these three well above, but they had appeared to be making for the formation ahead of them, so much so that when they dived down in the form of the 'Prince of Wales' Feathers', I actually called on my radio warning the formation I was trying to catch up, that they were being attacked! For some unknown reason, as I fell away with oil and glycol streaming from my bleeding and stricken aircraft, they left me alone.
>
> Now a very strange thing happened to me. I lost no time in undoing the Sutton harness, pulled off my helmet and was all ready to bale out when some warning came to me – call it what you may – I maintain it was from the Good Lord, for it was so urgent and so life-like that I abandoned the idea of jumping, and glided down, force-landing on the edge of our own aerodrome. The warning was in the form of two words – 'don't jump' – loud and clear, and not to be denied. On my glide down I thought plenty. The aircraft might have burst into flames at any moment: my body had the peculiar feeling one gets when warm blood trickles over one's skin – this was due to a goodly burst on the armour plating protecting my back – feeling inside my shirt and trousers I was amazed to find no trace of blood at all! I felt better now and concentrated on getting down safely, and getting down quick!
>
> As I climbed out and started to make my way across the drome, Mick Nash came running over and his first greeting was, 'What the hell have you made your way back here for, you fool!' I was, not unreasonably, annoyed and lost no time in telling him so. He then told me about the bombing and strafing all around the drome soon after we had left, and of the dropping of paratroops, who were then busily engaged in closing in on the

aerodrome, and how all the pilots had been warned through their radios, while still in the air, to make their way to P2. I then realised that had I jumped out of my aircraft, as was my intention, I would have ended up with the paratroops who had, evidently, landed on three sides of the aerodrome. Because of my faulty wireless I had heard nothing of these events. My bullet-ridden tub being out of the question, I scouted around to try and get another aircraft, but there was nothing serviceable."[74]

Macnamara's damaged Hurricane was only the first of several that landed at P1, Sgts Lambert and Kelly being the next to arrive. Just as he switched off his engine, Bertie Lambert taxied in and parked next to him. The latter recalled:

"We saw Mick Nash running out to meet us and he gave us the news of the paratroop attack, saying the base was surrounded and telling us of the instructions to land at P2. Nash put himself at great personal risk to give us this information, as he was completely exposed on the aerodrome to any fire which the paratroopers may have been able to direct towards him. A check on fuel indicated virtually empty tanks, but as the lesser of two evils, I taxied out and prepared to take-off for P2, which was only a short distance away. Kelly did the same. Fortunately we were not attacked by ground fire as we took off."

Within a few minutes of their departure four more Hurricanes arrived over the airfield and came in to land. These were not from the returning bomber escorts however, but were the survivors of nine replacement aircraft being ferried up from Batavia. These nine aircraft, led by Flt Lt John Hutcheson of 488 Squadron in BD892, had set out from Tjililitan airfield at 0700 and, in addition to the six pilots from 232 and 258 Squadrons, there were two more 488 Squadron pilots, Plt Off Noel Sharp and Sgt Jack Meharry. It had been the intention to take off at 0600, in an attempt to avoid being caught by the regular Japanese raiders, but the departure had been delayed due to transport problems in Batavia. Hutcheson had only a pencil tracing of the route to be taken owing to a lack of maps:

"Because of the lack of detail on the chart, I decided that the safest thing would be to make for the Moesi. Had been airborne best part of two hours and everyone was getting low on fuel. Some of the boys started to flap after a bit and kept flying up alongside, where I could see from their hand signs that they were almost out of fuel. The aircraft radios were not functioning, but they made their meaning clear. Things were getting desperate. Below was a solid mat of jungle and I had no means of checking my position. The country was featureless and the chart showed only coastal checking points. The fear grew and grew that I had made a mistake. Then, just as I was about to search for some clear area in which it might be possible for us to make forced-landings with some degree of safety, I sighted the Palembang river, then Palembang township, and then the aerodrome. The relief was terrific.

I signalled the other pilots to echelon starboard so that we could land quickly and then, just as the machines on the port side were sliding across under me, it happened. The Zeros were amongst us! There was no warning – one moment nine Hurricanes almost out of fuel were getting ready for a quick landing at what they expected to be a friendly drome, and the next they were scattered as the Zeros dived on them and the pilots took what evasive action they could and tried to get into position to fight back. As I broke clear of the Zeros I noticed a large formation of what I took to be bombers sweeping towards the aerodrome, in the usual perfect formation. The ground about the drome was sprinkled with white patches and the air below and stern of the bombers was filled with white puffs. Suddenly the meaning of it all dawned on us. The Japs were dropping parachutists!"

One of Hutcheson's pilots, Sgt Art Sheerin, recalled a slightly different version of events:

"Hutch got lost and decided to descend and have a look – you can imagine our surprise when he lobbed us fair in the middle of a formation of Zeros and bombers dropping paratroops. Hutch said: 'God, go like bloody hell' as we had no ammo or fuel – there was a scurry of Hurricanes headed for the trees. I thought I was good at low flying but some guy passed underneath me going in the opposite direction. I was hightailing it through the trees, 'nil' fuel on the gauge when three Zeros pounced on me. Having slipped them, the engine stopped and it was then the jungle or the river. I took the latter and, according to the manual on ditching, the flaps should have come off on impact. Well they didn't. I did three beautiful take-offs and on the final landing I sank like a stone.

After drinking half the river I surfaced, got into the dinghy and made the bank, found a native fire going but no bods. After a while they did emerge – I told them in some stupid lingo I wanted to get to the 'Big Town' or village, and fast, as the place by this time was full of paratroops. They in turn took me to another village that had a boat. We then set off down the river for Palembang. After some time, out of the vines on the bank came a speedboat with Dutch Naval blokes all taking a bead on me with their guns thinking, I suppose, I was a Jap paratroop. Standing up, shouting, I tipped our boat over and was picked up by the Dutch and taken back to the bank whence they had come from and was surprised to see hidden under the bushes quite a large ship, which was stuck. Further surprise when the captain took me to his mess for a Scotch and there was Campbell-White, who had also been shot down. The Dutch then agreed to take us as near to Palembang as was possibly safe. When we got there it was a shambles – panic, everyone trying to get away. I got across the river on a punt and having spotted a staff car with a very frightened LAC driver at the wheel asked him what he was waiting for. His reply: 'My CO.' My reply: 'You stupid bugger, let's get out of here', and jumped in. We then drove to P2."

Meanwhile, the other ferry Hurricanes, down to about 15 minutes' fuel, scattered as the escorting Ki-43s converged on them. Plt Off Sandy McCulloch's aircraft was hit almost immediately by fire from two of the fighters, the first burst wounding him in the left leg, the second in the right leg and arm and also shooting the tail assembly off his aircraft. As the Hurricane was only a few feet above the jungle, the Australian had no time to bale out:

"I went into the jungle and hit very hard. Luckily mud and two feet of water took the engine and I lost one wing coming through the trees and ended upside down. All I noticed was left of the aircraft was one wing, the cockpit and a bit of fuselage. I pulled my harness pin and just fell out into the water and slush. I found I was in very dense jungle both high and low, and after a rest set out on a compass course. [He had cut out the compass from the wreck of his inverted aircraft.] After travelling for an hour and making very little progress, I had to give up, as the jungle then was practically impassable. I then returned to my machine and gathered my dinghy and case to use as a battering ram. This was most useful in flattening the seven-foot scrub and I started on another course. I was unable to call for help or fire my revolver as I knew Jap paratroops were somewhere in the vicinity. After travelling four hours and again making very little progress, perhaps two miles, I heard a cock crowing and immediately set my compass by it. I finally reached a small area of water deep enough to inflate my dinghy, mainly to get a rest free from ants, bugs and millions of mosquitoes. This led me to a large river, which I paddled across reaching two native huts. The natives housed themselves as soon as they saw me, but came out willingly when told I was English. They rowed me down the river to a native village. The natives were exceptionally good, supplying me with beer and cigarettes. After a wait of about two hours, a Dutch truck arrived and took me in to Palembang, 12 miles away, and then to hospital."[75]

Another of the Hurricanes, that flown by Plt Off Noel Sharp, was also forced to crash-land in the jungle; he too survived shaken but otherwise unhurt. The 64th Sentai was undoubtedly involved in the attack on the reinforcement Hurricanes, the unit recording that after the initial success against Macnamara's aircraft, ten Hurricanes were attacked and two claimed shot down, one by Major Tateo Kato.

Meanwhile, Flt Lt Hutcheson was also fighting for survival:

"The whole formation had been scattered by this time and, with no radio, it was not possible to find out how the others were making out or to get any instructions from the local controller. In desperation and feeling that I was finished, I barged into the formation of troop carriers and sat there and fired at everything I could see as long as my ammo lasted. There was nothing good or calculated about my attack. It was just a case of fighting back pretty much as a cornered rat must do. The guns stopped firing. The ammo was finished. I broke away. A look at the petrol gauge showed the needle reading on zero, but the motor still ran. I turned south, for my thoughts now were all of escape. More troop carriers swung in over the township and one flared up as it was hit by ack-ack, but it never left its place in the formation until it was a mass of flames and then it swung away to port and dived in. The river was just behind me when the motor faltered and quit.

Below and to one side was a smooth green patch I took to be a swamp and so I made a gliding turn towards it, locked the canopy open, jerked my harness tight and set myself to make as good a landing as I could. There was a terrific jolt and I arrived base over apex in a swamp. A wall of water surged into the cockpit and then I was out and clinging to the tail of the machine, which projected above the water. With visions of crocodiles in my mind, I scrambled up onto the tail. Ashore I saw some native houses and remembering that Cam White had had some success by calling the name of the Dutch Queen, I tried a similar approach. Natives appeared, glanced in my direction, and then beat it. The approach was apparently wrong. There was nothing else for it but to swim ashore. I blew up my Mae West, eased myself into the water, and with my revolver held as clear of the water as possible, I floundered through the weeds and muck. As I approached the huts some natives came towards me and the leader spoke to me in what I took to be Malay.

However, English is the only language I can cope with so after much jabbering and waving of hands on both sides we finally found a word that had a common meaning – British. The spokesman would say 'British' and point and me. I would say 'British' and point at myself. After quite a bit of this pantomime everyone seemed pretty happy and they led me to a small creek that ran out from the swamp, pulled out a canoe and made signs that I was to get in. I thought that they must be going to take me to Palembang, for the stream turned in that direction and the sounds of battle that could be heard gave me no joy. I said: 'Palembang – Japanese!' and shook my head but they only laughed and again made signs that I was to enter the canoe. I climbed aboard and the native paddlers followed and off we went. Ahead was the sound of sporadic firing and my hopes sank as we progressed. After some time we came to a little village and, having helped me ashore, the natives gathered round and gazed at me. I was quite a curiosity and apparently an amusing one at that.

Then a young Chinese thrust his way through the crowd and addressed me in halting English. I told him what had happened as best I could and asked that I should be taken to some Dutch controller, but stressed that I did not want to go towards Palembang for quite obvious reasons. He understood and said that I must wait for a time but asked if in the meantime there was anything I wanted. There was. I had a raging thirst. My water bottle, and such jungle kit as we were issued with, was still in the machine and I had had nothing to drink since take off time. I asked for water and he brought me some from the creek – dark muddy water. I would not drink it. He smiled went away and returned with a bottle of beer complete with a crown top. I drank that."

After further trials and tribulations, Hutcheson eventually reached safety and embarked aboard a vessel bound for Batavia, from where he was soon evacuated[76]. Meanwhile, Plt Off Parker, whose aircraft had an unserviceable compressor, avoided a similar fate by using cloud cover:

> "We must have been a mile or two away when I saw, converging to meet us over the airfield, a number of twin-engined aircraft like DC-3s accompanied by fighters. I needed only a moment to register this but, before I could decipher the aircraft markings or the familiar aspect of the Zeros, lines of parachutes appeared below the transports. The Japs were attacking P1. I have heard of mixed emotions before but then a whole sequence flashed through my head in an instant – frustration that we'd not been able to get among the troop-carriers, soft targets, before they'd unloaded; disgust as I remembered my guns wouldn't fire; fear of the Zeros almost on top of us and particularly regards defenceless me; relief as I realised that I had no option but to pull out of the attack which the others must make on the transports regardless of the accompanying fighters. I eased back on the stick and lost sight of the action in the cloud.
>
> I only nipped out of sight for a moment before turning away from P1, until I was sure I could not be involved with the Zeros. Had I climbed, I might well have gone through the cloud layer to be silhouetted there as a target for any top cover the Japs may have posted. I circled near the town, which was covered in a pall of black smoke from burning oil tanks, until I thought the aerial battle had moved away and I could see neither parachutes nor planes. Then, keeping a very sharp eye out all around me for other aircraft, I whistled over to the airfield, dropped my wheels and flaps and flew downwind just above the runway, stall-turning at the far end when I received no red flare and landing upwind. I had thought the groundcrew would have shot off a 'red' [flare] if there had been any danger but, as the Hurricane rolled to a stop – without brakes – near the end of the runway, a Dutch NCO in a sandbagged machine gun post waved me frantically over to him. I kicked the rudder bar hard over and opened the throttle for enough power to take the plane off the runway, undid my helmet and straps and was out of the plane in a flash.
>
> There wasn't room for me in the machine gun post and anyway I wanted to get to the control tower to find out what was happening. I certainly wasn't going to taxi the Hurricane up the runway at that time so I ran for the plantation a couple of hundred yards away across the perimeter track. I wasn't very easy about it because I couldn't see where the Jap paratroops were and only had my pistol but the Dutchman said they were on the other side of the field. Once I'd reached the trees I was at least safe from view from above and I starting picking my way along the half mile or so separating me from the main gate, worrying because, by the time I reached the control tower, the raid was over but there was still fighting going on in the surrounding plantations. Some more Hurricanes came in to land."

By this time Plt Off Nash, in his capacity as Duty Pilot, was becoming frantic and, as the last Hurricane rolled in, he jumped into a car and rushed over to warn the pilots. All four aircraft were in need of fuel and it was necessary to arrange for a petrol tanker to come out. The pilots and groundcrews felt conspicuous and exposed, expecting the paratroops to burst onto the airfield at any moment, but the aircraft were refuelled safely – in all probability in record time. As the four pilots prepared to take off again, they were advised that Flt Lt Julian was on his way to guide them to P2. Immediately his aircraft arrived, he circled the airfield and waited for the others to join him; all five aircraft reached P2 without further event, where Parker indicated to the others that he would land last since he could not steer his aircraft on the ground. He flew an extra circuit as he watched the others land:

> "To my horror, two of them bounced violently as they touched down on the bumpy

surface. The undercart of one failed and it leant over on one wing; the other stood on its nose. I did another circuit to look at the field and chose what looked like a virgin piece of land further away from the most used area and the airfield buildings. I got down, although with a fierce shaking, and then taxied as far and as slowly as I could go to the edge of the airfield well out of the way."

Parker spent most of the remainder of the day, with the aid of two mechanics, removing the compressor from one of the damaged aircraft and fitting it to his own Hurricane. He now found himself temporarily attached to 258 Squadron and under the command of Sqn Ldr Thomson.

On the airfield Wg Cdr Maguire had positioned those men who were armed, including the defence sections of 242, 258 and 605 Squadrons. Ground personnel stripped Browning machine guns from unserviceable aircraft and mounted these on mounds of earth, while the Bofors anti-aircraft crews prepared to fire their guns horizontally, over open sights. In all, about 200 men were dispersed in groups, mainly on the road from Palembang, which bounded the airfield and continued to Djambi. Maguire recalled:

"I went down the road to see if it was still open about an hour after the parachutists had dropped and it was at that time, although people had been fired on travelling up and down. I then went back and found that we had no means of communication at that stage with P2, for what reason I'm not sure and we did reconnect after a bit until about twelve o'clock when communications were broken again. We tried to recall the aircraft that were airborne to deal with the raiders but I think they didn't have fuel or didn't get back in time. And about this time we learnt that all aircraft airborne were to return to P2. On learning this I decided that the groups of airmen trying to repair aircraft in exposed positions on the edge of the jungle at P1 should be withdrawn. Most of them were unarmed and I thought they could be much more usefully employed at P2.

I formed up the troops we thought we could spare, told them (those without transport) to try to walk to the town and keep in the rubber on the right-hand side of the road and not go aimlessly down the road itself. We sent some armed parties with them down the road to act as some form of protection. I gather that some of these parties got through and some were ambushed and quite a few were lost as a result or wounded. One of the New Zealand pilots did magnificent work going up and down the road, giving information from the town, picking up wounded and troops who'd missed their way. At this point I decided that all outlying aircraft, which were badly damaged and could not be easily repaired, should be destroyed. And this was done by a party of volunteers and done effectively. We dragged in all those aircraft we thought there was hope for nearer the protected zone. We got all transport that we could gather – it wasn't very much, I think it was about three lorries – and parked that also in the protected area."

After the various Hurricanes had landed, refuelled and been despatched to P2, a number of Army officers arrived to inspect the positions and give advice. They had their own headquarters about a mile down the road to Palembang, but reported that after firing at the parachutists as they descended they also had had no further contact with the enemy. For the airfield defenders the waiting seemed to go on for ever; the telephone lines to Palembang had been cut by the Japanese, so there was no contact with the town. Finally, more Army officers appeared and advised the defenders that orders had been given to retire to Palembang. For Maguire it seemed a good opportunity to get his pilots and unarmed personnel out of the trap, and consequently a number of cars and lorries were prepared ready to leave for the town. Much confused action then ensued. The Japanese had concentrated their forces between Palembang and the airfield, one section having thrown a block across the road about a mile or so from the latter. Subsequent reports indicated that this was cleared at least once, but re-established later. Some vehicles managed to get through but others did not. Certainly much of the main action for the rest of the day centred on this location. For example, Ting Macnamara of 258 Squadron was offered a lift into Palembang with two other officers and a warrant officer; they drove at top speed, the doors of the car slightly open and their revolvers drawn, and managed to get through unscathed. They arrived at 226 Group HQ to find the place deserted and the telephone lines ripped out.

After broadcasting his warning to the Hurricanes not to land at P1, Wg Cdr Darley had joined a party from HQ to drive out to the airfield to assess the situation, since the telephone line to P1 had been cut. Approaching the area, they came under fire from an ambush and, as they had only a couple of revolvers between them, retired to organise a properly armed relief party:

> "I was ambushed as I tried to reach them by road. The Dutch garrison then took over. Eventually, after supervising the transfer of all our hospital patients by ferry across the river dividing Palembang, having commandeered the ferry by arms, I was able to ensure their eventual arrival at P2. Few ambulances were available and so I had many service vans unloaded of kit and detailed fit airmen to act as medical assistants. When all airmen were safely across I then left myself, withdrew the armed guard from the ferry and thanked the captain for his valuable help. I reached P2 late afternoon and found a quiet corner for Fighter Operations in the Bomber Operations room and briefed the pilots."

From P1 meanwhile, Sqn Ldr Brooker, together with several other pilots and non-flying personnel, had evacuated by road. The vehicles following were ambushed however, and a petrol bowser overturned by grenade explosions. One airman was trapped under the bowser, whilst another sustained a broken leg and jaw; he was helped to one side of the road while Plt Off Pop Wright, 232 Squadron's Engineer Officer, led a party to administer help to the trapped airman. Just then the Japanese attacked and Wright was killed. The trapped airman could not be released and later an orderly crawled up under covering fire and injected him with a double dose of morphine. Flt Lt Julian was on the airfield when the paratroops landed:

> "They landed all around us. Our Bofors were just firing over open sights at them as they were coming down. And they closed the road. So we had to wait there till our aircraft returned, in order to get them off again. We were under fire while that was going on – naturally the Japs weren't going to give us a free passport. They were on the edge of the aerodrome but we got our aircraft off. There were four of us pilots and we had a Humber, and we were told by the Dutch that they thought they'd temporarily cleared the road, so we got through. The Japs may have been lurking in the trees alongside us, for all I know. Anyway, we got through to Palembang town, and then across the river to P2."

In the township Air Commodore Vincent had contacted the local Dutch commander with a view to going to the aid of Maguire and his men on the airfield. A convoy comprising three lorry loads of Dutch troops, together with an RAF van full of food, was hastily organised, Vincent and his driver leading the way in his own commandeered car. Four miles short of P1 they found the road blocked by the overturned petrol tanker and a lorry, and as they approached this obstruction, they were fired upon from the undergrowth alongside the road. Vincent later wrote:

> "The only one hit was the RAF van driver who swerved across the road and got ditched. The Dutch lorry loads fired not a shot, and their drivers turned round and drove off leaving us to bring the two from the van, one hit in the arm, and return with ignominy after the supposed escort, leaving the supplies to the Japs. I was disgusted and ashamed."[77]

Some of the newly arrived reinforcement fighter pilots (from 266 Wing) at P1 found themselves involved – ill equipped and untrained as they were – in close-quarter fighting with the paratroopers, as noted in his diary by Sgt Frank Hood:

> "Paratroopers! Great panic! Lost all kit. Pete Browne wounded. Lost track of Packard and Worts. Both believed killed. Went to P2."

In fact, Sgt Neil Packard was taken prisoner while fellow-countryman Sgt Ewen Worts managed to evade capture and reached P2 safely. Two of the Canadians, Sgts Howard Low and Bill James, were captured: both had been placed in charge of parties made up of RAF airmen, AA gunners and Dutch troops, and had put up spirited resistance before being captured. A friend of the pilots, Corporal Charlie Cooper, later provided a statement of events:

> "I was in company with Sgt Low and Sgt James in Palembang at 1030 when we saw Japanese paratroops attacking Palembang aerodrome. We reported back to headquarters and picked up arms and ammunition and set out for the drome in two single files, one either side of the road. There were 30 men. One column was led by Sgt James and the other by Sgt Low. When we were a mile off the drome, I saw Sgt James being taken prisoner. Sgt Low and myself then charged over the road to try and release him. There was a burst of automatic fire and Sgt Low, who was approximately six yards ahead of me, threw up his arms and fell. I ran to him and saw that he was still breathing but was very badly wounded on the chest and throat. At this time I was taken prisoner and forced into a ditch approximately 15 yards from Sgt Low, I never saw him again. I am fairly certain that Sgt Low was killed [sic], as the nature of his wounds were such as to make it impossible for him to live."

The injury to Sgt Low, although bloody and painful, was superficial rather than life threatening, and he was amongst those rescued and recovered when Dutch forces arrived to force the Japanese to flee. However, Low's reprieve was to be brief; a few weeks later he was executed by the Japanese following an attempt to steal a Japanese aircraft (see Chapter VI). Meanwhile, Sgt James and Corporal Cooper also managed to escape their captors and reported back to headquarters. Cooper volunteered to take a truck of provisions to the aerodrome, where he saw two more of the replacement pilots, Sgts Harry Jenson[78] and Alan Lawrence:[79]

> "They were arguing with Flt Lt Welch [now attached to 266 (Fighter) Wing], trying to obtain permission to fly against the Japs in any serviceable aircraft. They stated that should they be refused permission, they would go off anyway! They left Flt Lt Welch, running towards the drome."

Despite their keenness to get into the air, no serviceable aircraft were found and they made good their escape to P2. Another to be captured was Flt Lt Cooper-Slipper but, during the night, he escaped:

> "I was treated well by the officer in charge of the unit, who spoke very good English. Just before dark I saw the road to town and when it got dark I ran away and walked into Palembang. At first light I crossed the river, and after an argument with a Dutch officer, I led about 20 officers and airmen and three nurses to the south. After several days a few of us made it to the southern tip of Sumatra where a coaling ship took us across to Java, from where we eventually made our way to Batavia."

Another member of the RAF caught up in these traumatic experiences was one of 258 Squadron's drivers, LAC Johnny Johnson. He had been ordered to drive to Palembang from the airfield immediately after the bombing attack, but did not realise that paratroops had landed. About two and a half miles from the airfield, he found his way blocked by a six-wheel Scammel truck and, as he approached, was attacked by about 20 Japanese soldiers, who threw grenades and opened fire. Leaping from his vehicle, Johnson took cover in one of the deep ditches which flanked the road and returned fire with his .38 Webley revolver, claiming later to have hit at least two of his attackers. When he had emptied his gun, Johnson was captured while attempting to reload. The paratroop commander then relieved him of the revolver and proceeded to shoot him through the thigh with it – presumably to prevent him from being able to escape. The soldiers then apparently decided to kill him, for he was stood against the lorry and several lined up and levelled their pistols at him. At that very moment, however, another vehicle came round the bend in the road and the troops scattered into the ditches, forcing Johnson to go with them.

The latest arrival was full of 258 Squadron personnel and, on reaching the road block, the vehicle was overturned by the explosion of hand grenades. Those not killed were taken prisoner, joining Johnson in the ditch, where at least four of the wounded were then killed by the soldiers. After that, Johnson lost count of the number of times vehicles were overturned and wrecked, but finally Dutch troops and armed RAF personnel approached the area and began sniping, while a low-flying Hurricane strafed the roadblock. Steadily the Japanese were picked off, while others drifted off in the direction of the airfield. Johnson's ordeal was not yet over however, for suddenly he felt a violent blow on his back. He had been struck by a burst of machine-gun fire aimed by a Dutch soldier, who had mistaken him for a Japanese. At last the battle passed them by, Johnson's companions were able to bind up his wounds and put him on a lorry with about eight other wounded who were then rushed to Palembang hospital for treatment.

258 Squadron's Plt Off Micky Nash, the Duty Pilot on Aerodrome Control at P1, suffered a similar harrowing experience. When Wg Cdr Maguire decided to evacuate all possible personnel, Nash obtained a lift from an army doctor. Their vehicle rounded the bend to find the area in front of the roadblock littered with wrecked cars, so they halted, but before the driver could reverse, a hand grenade was hurled at the car. Nash later told Donahue:

> "... just then there was a terrific explosion in front of the wind-shield and I felt something stab into my neck. Next thing I knew I was lying face down in the road, coughing and gagging on blood in my throat and mouth, with blood all over my clothes, too. I thought for sure I was dying. I couldn't talk or breathe or do anything except gag on blood that kept flowing into my throat as well as outside, and I expected that if I didn't die the Japs would be along in a minute and shoot me anyway. But nothing happened right away, and after a bit my ears stopped ringing so much and I was conscious of a voice calling me in a loud whisper. 'Hey! Come on and get down in this ditch – quick!' It was the doc calling me. I opened my eyes and saw I was a few feet from a ditch at the side of the road. I gathered all my strength and half leaped and half fell over into it and huddled down by the doc. The ditch was about three feet deep.
>
> I still thought I was dying. The blood in my throat made a rattling sound when I breathed, and I remembered the phrase about death rattling in one's throat, and thought that was it. The doc must have thought so, too, for he kept reaching over and feeling my pulse. In a few minutes we heard another car coming. It stopped a few yards up the road from ours and we heard the occupants scrambling out and making for the ditch. Then pretty soon we heard the Japs coming out of the jungle and onto the road, and I thought: 'Now it's coming!' We heard them talking and heard their footsteps on the road, and then they came up to our car, which was only three feet from the edge of the ditch we were in. They walked all around it, jabbering to each other, opening and shutting the doors, and

left: Sqn Ldr John Llewellin, CO 232 Squadron, d in action 7/2/42.

right: Sqn Ldr James Thomson, CO 258 Squadron.

dle left: Plt Off Tom Watson RCAF, 232 Squadron.

dle right: Sqn Ldr Leslie Landels, CO 232 visional) Squadron, killed in action 20/1/42.

om: Sgt Bill Moodie RNZAF, 232 Squadron, killed tion 9/2/42.

Top: Sgt Ken Holmes of 232 Squadron survived a near-fatal attack by a Ki-43 of the 64th Sentai on 21 January 1942, his Hurricane (BG860) returning severely damaged.

Bottom: Sgt John Fleming RCAF, (left), Sgt Sam Hackforth (centre) and Sgt Jigs Leetham RCAF of 232 Squadron were all shot down during the fighting, with only Fleming surviving, although he was later taken prisoner.

Left: Hurricane in improvised blast pen at Kallang.

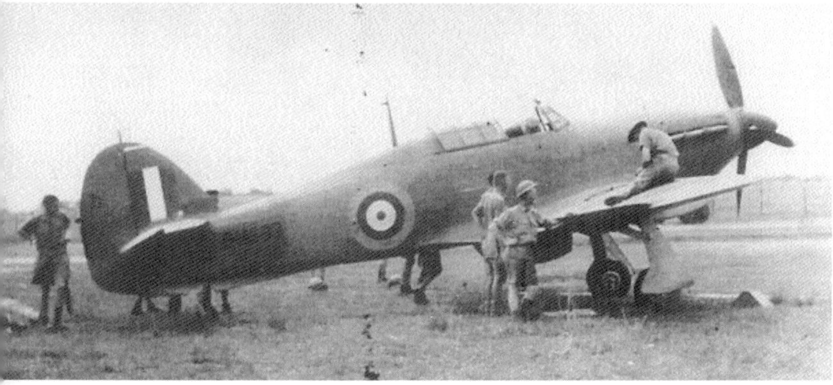

Left: BM899 was issued to 488 Squadron.

Left: BE332 being 'rebuilt' at Kallang.

Below: BE332 later at P1. This aircraft was shot down on 25 February.

Top: Pilots of the 'main' 232 Squadron aboard HMS *Indomitable* on their way to the East Indies. Standing, left to right: Plt Off W.McG. Lockwood RCAF, Plt Off M.C. Fitzherbert, Plt Off T.W. Watson RCAF, 2/Lt J. Stewart SAAF, Flt Lt I. Julian RNZAF, Sqn Ldr A.J.A. Llewellin, Flt Lt E.W. Wright DFM, Plt Off J.C. Hutton, Plt Off E.C. Gartrell RNZAF, 2/Lt N.R. Dummett SAAF, Plt Off J.K. McKechnie RCAF, and 2/Lt N. Anderson SAAF. Seated, left to right: Sgt G.J. King, Sgt R.W. Parr, Sgt J.A. Sandeman Allen, Sgt T.W. Young RAAF, Sgt G.J. Dunn RCAF, Sgt A.W. May, Sgt F. Margarson, Sgt D. Kynman, Sgt I.D. Newlands RNZAF, and Sgt W.A. Moodie RNZAF.

Bottom: Pilots of 258 Squadron aboard HMS *Indomitab* Standing, left to right: Plt Off J.A. Campbell, Plt Off A. Milnes, Flg Off H.A. Dobbyn RNZAF, Flt Lt D.J.T. Sha RNZAF, Sqn Ldr J.A. Thomson, Flt Lt V.B. de la Perrel Flg Off A.G. Donahue, Plt Off A.D.M. Nash, Plt Off B.A. McAlister RNZAF. Centre, left to right: Plt Off D.B.F. Nicholls, u/k (spare pilot), Plt Off C. Kleckner RCAF, Plt Off C. Campbell-White RNZAF, Plt Off G.C.S. Macnamara, Plt Off N.L. McCulloch, Plt Off E.M.T. Tremlett, Plt Off A. Brown. Seated, left t right: Sgt C.T.R. Kelly, Sgt L.A. Miller RCAF, Sgt K.A Glynn, Sgt R.B. Keedwell, Sgt A. Sheerin RAAF, Sgt A. Lambert, Sgt P.H.T. Healey, Sgt N.M. Scott RCA Sgt D. Caldwell (spare pilot).

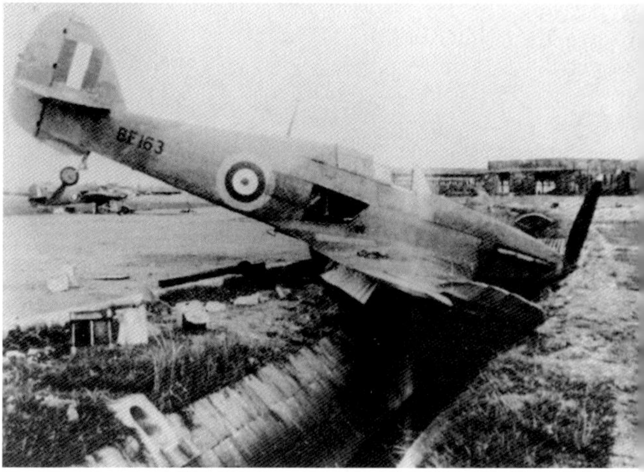

Top left: Flt Lt Ricky Wright DFM, with Flt Lt Vic de la Perrelle, Plt Off Joe Hutton and Plt Off Art Brown.

Top right: Hurricane BE163 of 258 Squadron at Kallang following emergency landing.

Middle: Newly promoted Sqn Ldr Ricky Wright DFM following his crash-landing in BE208/O at Kallang.

Bottom: New Zealand contingent of 258 Squadron prior to leaving the UK:
Plt Off Bruce McAlister,
Flt Lt Vic de la Perrelle,
Flt Lt Denny Sharp,
Flg Off Harry Dobbyn,
Plt Off Cam Campbell-White.

Top: Plt Off John Gorton RAAF (also seen on right) of 232 Squadron was shot down and badly injured on 21 January 1942; he later survived the sinking of the MV *Derrymore* on 13 February, and is pictured here immediately before rescue.

Bottom left: Plt Off Bruce McAlister RNZAF was the first 258 Squadron pilot to be lost at Singapore.

Bottom right: Flg Off Art Donahue, an American serving with 258 Squadron, wrote graphically of his experiences, published as *Last Flight from Singapore* shortly before his death in 1943.

: Hurricane of 232 Squadron under the trees at Kallang.
'dle: Unserviceable Hurricane at Kallang after being ;ured by the Japanese.

Bottom: Hurricane at readiness; note pilot's parachute on wing.

Top: BE584/P of 232 Squadron, possibly at Palembang.

Middle: Sgts Eddie Kuhn and Jim MacIntosh, two New Zealanders.

Bottom: Sgt Perce Killick RNZAF with a Hurricane at Tjililitan.

op left: Air Commodore Stanley Vincent, AOC 226 ighter Group.

op right: Flt Lt John Hutcheson RNZAF, former uffalo pilot, crash-landed his Hurricane at Palembang.

Bottom left: Plt Off Micky Nash of 258 Squadron survived being shot in the throat at Palembang.

Bottom right: Another who was shot down at Palembang, Plt Off Ting Macnamara of 258 Squadron.

Top: Sgt Jim MacIntosh, another New Zealander.

Middle: Sgt Eddie Kuhn received a DFM but by then was a PoW.

Bottom left: Plt Off Noel Sharp's DFC was announced after his loss on 1 March 1942.

Bottom right: Copy of illustration from a Japanese magazine purporting to depict Hurricanes strafing Japanese invasion craft on 1 March 1942. The original had been torn from the magazine by Jim MacIntosh during his early days of captivity and he managed to conceal it for his 3½ years as a prisoner.

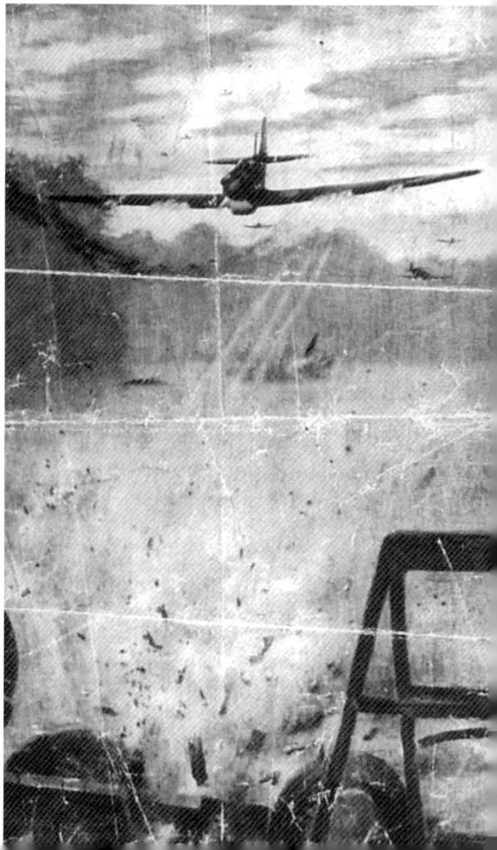

›p: The surviving pilots of 258 Squadron pose
ı the steps of the Hotel des Indies before drawing
ırds to establish who would remain to man one
ght of 605 Squadron. Back row, left to right:
arry Dobbyn (remained), Ambrose Milnes,
ng Macnamara, Sqn Ldr Thomson, Sgt Terry
elly (remained), Plt Off Teddy Tremlett,
gt Dusty Miller, Sgt Bertie Lambert (remained),
t Off Micky Nash (wounded), Plt Off Cam
ampbell-White.

Front row, left to right: Plt Off Red Campbell (volunteered), Sgt Pip Healey (remained), Plt Off Jock McCulloch, Plt Off Leon Cicurel (remained), Sgt Art Sheerin, Sgt John Vibert (volunteered), Plt Off Artie Brown.

Bottom: Sqn Ldr Boy Brooker flanked by Plt Off Mike Fitzherbert (left) and Plt Off Ernie Gartrell RNZAF, while another pilot (possibly Sgt Ron Dovell) leans against the partition wall.

THE HURRICANE ACES

Top left: Sgt Sandy Allen DFM, 7 victories.

Top centre: Sgt Jimmy King DFC, 6½ victories.

Top right: Sgt Ron Dovell DFM, 6 victories.

Middle right: Sgt Henry Nicholls, 5½ victories.

Bottom left: Sqn Ldr Taffy Julian DFC, 5 victories.

Bottom right: Flt Lt Jerry Parker DFC, 5 victories.

NB: No photographs of Flt Lt Edwin Murray Taylor DFC have been located; he was credited with 6 victories.

p: Ki-43s of the 64th Sentai – the main opponent.

me of the successful and formidable Japanese pilots:

ddle left: Sgt Major Hiroshi Onozaki of the th Sentai, whose claims during the fighting over ngapore and NEI included eight Hurricanes; he rvived the war with his total score having reached 14.

ddle centre: Major Tateo Kato, CO of the 64th ntai, had scored 10 victories in China and increased s to 18 before he was killed in action in May 1942.

ddle right: Lt Yohei Hinoki of the 64th Sentai rvived the war with 12 victories, including two rricanes over Singapore.

Bottom left: Lt Shogo Takeuchi of the 64th Sentai had 19 victories when killed in action in December 1943. He claimed three Hurricanes in quick succession over Singapore on 31 January 1942.

Bottom centre: Sgt Major Yoshito Yasuda of the 64th Sentai survived the war with at least 10 victories, including three Hurricanes over Singapore and the NEI.

Bottom right: Capt Yasuhiko Kuroe of the 47th Independent Chutai survived the war with 30 victories. Three of his victories were claimed while flying a Ki-44 over Singapore and Malaya.

Top left and right: Two photographs of Sgt David Kynman of 232/242 Squadron while a PoW. He was selected for severe mistreatment by the Japanese interrogator when first taken prisoner.

Bottom left: A happy Fred Margarson of 232 Squadron, resplendent in new shirt and wings, following his release from prison camp.

Bottom right: A gaunt-looking Plt Off Red Campbell following his release. On reaching the UK, before returning to his hometown in the USA, he learned that he had been awarded a DFC.

HAPPY TO HAVE SURVIVED…

·p left: Wt Off Ian Fairbairn RAAF, 232/242 ¡uadron, on the way home.

·p centre and right: Newly commissioned Tom ›ung RAAF (left), and Snowy Newlands RNZAF; e latter commented, "still a bit swollen from the fects of beri-beri after 3½ years as a PoW."

Bottom: Newly commissioned Gordie Dunn RCAF (left), (232/242 Squadron) and Ed Horton RCAF (266 Fighter Wing), enjoying a cuppa on returning to Canada; they had gained much weight during a two-week stopover in the Philippines, courtesy of the Americans, and therefore look well and healthy after their 3½-year sojourn in PoW camps.

Top: Brian Cull with a trio of Canadian veterans of 232 Squadron, at Alton near Toronto in 1993: from left, Gordie Dunn, Brian Cull, Tom Watson DFC a Bill Lockwood.

Middle: Brian Cull with Jerry Parker DFC, Exmouth, Devon, 2002.

Bottom: Sandy Alle MBE DFM with Brian Cull, Paignto Devon, 2002.

apparently giving it a general once-over. I knew it would come now, because it could only be a matter of seconds before one of them glanced down and saw us, and I was trying my best to look like I was dead, lying with my mouth open and the wound in my neck showing. Once one of them jumped right across the ditch without noticing us. I just couldn't believe it when I heard them walk away after a little while. However, they didn't go far, and they kept coming back.

It was evident they were taking up stations around here for the time being, for they kept walking up and down the road and in and out of the jungle and all around, jabbering back and forth to each other. Then one of them standing near us in the road called out excitedly and several others came running, and my blood froze! 'Now they have found us,' I thought. But it wasn't us. It was two other fellows a few yards up along the ditch from where we were – the ones who'd scrambled out of the car that came after us. They put two bullets into each of them, and after each report there was a sickening 'oof!' from the one who was hit. Then at the last report the doc himself moaned and jerked, and I thought they were shooting us now, but he'd just done it involuntarily. Pretty soon we heard a lorry coming. It stopped a little way up the road. We heard the door open and the driver getting out, and then his voice, pleading: 'Don't shoot me, you *******! Don't shoot me!' Then a shot, and silence. It began to rain, and all I thought was, 'Thank God! A little concealment!' But it stopped again soon. After a time some Japs came along in a Dutch armoured car they'd captured. It stopped near us and there was lots of jabbering and running about, and then we heard it drive up and start pushing against our car. It was pushing it sideways, towards us, and we thought they were pushing it into the ditch, which would mean it would fall right on us. But they stopped pushing it when the wheels were just on the edge of the ditch. Apparently they just wanted room enough to get by. Another three inches and it would have toppled in on us.

Finally, after we'd lain there for over two hours, we heard machine-gun and rifle fire from up the road and bullets whining overhead, and striking around. The Japs withdrew from around us down the road a way. For a time we were in a no-man's-land between the two fires, but finally our forces got to where we were, and we were able to come out of our cover."

A small group of 258 Squadron pilots, who had been off-duty in the town, now found themselves isolated from their flying echelon. Two of these, Plt Offs Milnes and Nicholls – the latter having just returned to Palembang after being missing for seven days following his bale-out – joined forces with some 232 Squadron pilots, commandeered a car, and drove to the railway station, from where they boarded a train to Oosthaven. 232 Squadron's injured Canadian pilot, Plt Off John McKechnie, was in Palembang hospital when the fighting started and he and other moveable patients were loaded into ambulances and driven to the south coast, where they boarded a ship for Batavia. Others, including Plt Off Red Campbell and Sgt Nelson Scott, had been met by Plt Off Jock McCulloch, who had also just arrived back at Palembang.They were joined by another of the reinforcement pilots, Plt Off Leon Cicurel, and Flg Off Tudor Jones, the unit's Engineer Officer. When Ting Macnamara arrived from P1 and excitedly related what was happening along the road, they decided to round up all the RAF men and arms they could find. Some ancient Italian rifles were discovered at the Dutch Home Guard HQ, together with a few sub-machine guns, and these were issued. However, when permission was sought to take a relief party back to the airfield with arms and ammunition, they were ordered to head for P2 instead.

After patrolling around the town for a while, unhappy to leave their colleagues to their fate, Macnamara's group decided to ignore the order to evacuate and, commandeering an RAF lorry and its driver, the party of about 18 volunteers set off in this and a car, picking up such information as they could en route from Dutch barricades. They were finally halted about three or four miles short of P1 by a Dutch officer, who advised that it was not safe to proceed any further by road. British and Dutch troops were moving up each side of the road, and after guarding the barricade for about 45 minutes, it was agreed that the RAF men be allowed to move forward. Dividing into three parties, each led by a Dutch officer – one a colourful character carrying a sabre in one hand and a pistol in the other – they edged their way through the jungle under mortar and machine-gun fire. Macnamara later wrote:

> "I am no soldier or woodsman, and pushing through those woods, not knowing whether I would bump into friend or foe, hearing all sorts of noises, was not, to say the least, a very pleasant job. However, finally my turn came to get back and I made my way round to the river below the roadblock. We had many casualties but the Japanese had more. One of our squadron warrant officers accounted for 17 of them before receiving a bullet clean through his forehead."

Plt Off Red Campbell was with Macnamara and his group, and his account is more graphic:

> "Ting and I ran into some Dutch native troops. They were showing us the way through and there was some gunfire and we all took cover. We saw these soldiers – looked like Japanese – and Ting, who it turned out was a dead shot, drew a bead on one of them. I drew a bead on the other one, and fortunately missed. Ting didn't. He hit one and it turned out they were Dutch troops. But about this time the Japanese did arrive – about four or five of them. Ting took off in one direction and I took off running away from them. They ran after me and for some reason they were going to stick me with a bayonet. They didn't fire their rifles. I had a pistol and was trying to shoot over my shoulder. Fortunately some native soldiers came along and waded in, and just wiped those Japanese out."

Meanwhile, Macnamara reached the stretch of road leading up to the roadblock, which was cluttered with parked, abandoned and overturned vehicles, where he joined others who were working their way along the ditches on the side of the road. However, they were soon pinned down by machine-gun fire:

> "There were a small number of army types around with rifles and they did all they could. I even saw an RAF lad attempt to fire a Bofors gun from over the cab of a lorry – he was severely wounded by return fire from a machine gun, but a pal of his lost no time in jumping out of the ditch and carrying him back to what safety they could find. With some other members of my squadron, we left the ditch and again made for the woods and pushed forward until, with the suddenness of a bolt from the blue, a machine gun rattled out its song of death. That left us with four men and myself. The slightest movement was recorded with a burst of machine-gun fire and looking at each other lying deep down in mud, dirt and water, full length, hardly daring to move a limb, we could not help but laugh. We looked so utterly miserable and helpless. We finally wiggled our way to better protection. From the position we were in, not more than 20 yards from the spurts of flame from the Japanese machine gun, one of our number crawled forward under the very noses of the Nippon overlords, to drag a wounded comrade back to us, and from there, after many tricky interludes, he was carried safely back to a makeshift Red Cross clearing. After nightfall we finally made our way into the outskirts of Palembang, where we hitch-hiked a ride into the town itself.
>
> We saw paratroopers hanging in trees, strangled by their own cords, and others who had struck terra firma without their parachutes opening. I like to recall the three who came driving down the road in a Dutch armoured car. We naturally thought that the Dutch had at last broken through to our relief, but after many had revealed themselves from the side of the road, they were greeted with hand grenades. They shot smartly back into hiding and

when the Japanese, knowing their game was up, and having crashed the armoured car into our stranded vehicles, tried to make a break – a volley of fire from small arms – rifles and revolvers – greeted their exit from the turret."

There now remained on the airfield Wg Cdr Maguire's small party of about 60 RAF men and a few Dutch colonial troops, with very little ammunition left. At one stage, Maguire and 258 Squadron's Ground Defence Officer, Flg Off Matthys Taute[80], found themselves in a slit trench, facing a number of Japanese soldiers similarly entrenched. These suddenly climbed out of their cover and started running for the jungle, whereupon three or four were promptly shot by Maguire and Taute, using rifles they had acquired. Believing that Dutch troops had come to their aid, Maguire and Plt Off Paddy Creegan (232 Squadron's Ground Defence Officer), walked to the main gate of the aerodrome, expecting to meet Dutch soldiers, but instead encountered the remaining 60 or 70 paratroops who had concentrated on the road about half a mile from P1. Maguire recalled:

"As we reached the top of a slight incline, we saw a Japanese soldier bending over a machine gun. He stood up and saw us at a range of about 50 yards. Although we were both armed – we had Thompson sub-machine guns – I had no confidence in the ability of these weapons to reach him in time. So, telling Creegan we would have to bluff it out, I laid down my unwieldy weapon and marched briskly up to him. He looked very surprised but did nothing. So, sounding as confident as I could, I demanded to see his officer and, to my amazement, he shambled off and produced an officer. This officer had some command of English, and I immediately demanded surrender, saying that I had a large force behind me. He replied that he had a large force and that he would give us safe conduct if we marched out."

Maguire explained that he would have to go and discuss the whole matter with his non-existent senior officer! Their departure was not challenged and they walked back to where they had laid their guns, then briskly back to the airfield where, on arrival, they learned that the remaining unserviceable aircraft an the fuel dump had already been fired. With fuel dump and abandoned aircraft blazing satisfactorily, Maguire ordered his men to turn their lorries round and prepare to escape in the opposite direction; they beat a hasty retreat up the road towards Djambi. Maguire continued:

"Our general plan on that first evening was to do a wide left-hand circuit and cut back to P2 by crossing the river at a more western area. About seven or eight miles to the west of the airfield there was a large rubber plantation and we pulled up to see if we could get some local knowledge from the manager. We told them about the landings and that they should move out and they said they would be delighted to use us as an escort. We were also told that there was a major petrol dump in the rubber some distance from their plantation house. There was a problem in that there was a native kampong quite close to this petrol dump but we tracked down the head man, explained the situation and eventually put a match to a couple of million gallons of aircraft fuel which we reckoned there was no sensible reason to leave the Japanese to find.

We reached a palm oil estate whose factory manager was extremely on the ball. He had prepared his people for a pull out if necessary and paid all of his staff and his workers and he was all set to put a match to the assets. He also told us that some of the ferries had been destroyed in panic and that we would have to stay on the northern bank of the Moesi for some considerable time. In fact on departure we found a ferry that was working and had a fairly uneventful day's trekking west. We pulled in to another *kampong* where the natives were extremely hostile to the point where we kept a very sharp eye on their doings. We left early and as it had been wet in the night I purchased one of these oiled paper umbrellas, dark green in colour, which I think then cost about twenty cents. I then thought that they would make good camouflage so we bought the whole stock at the shop and these sunshades, or umbrellas, were issued to each truck with orders to put them up if any aircraft was sighted or sound should occur. I don't know how effective this ploy was, but we certainly did use them two or three times in this rôle and were not attacked. This may have just been good fortune.

We reached the north/south road junction about a day later. We were told at a local police post that shipping had ceased at Padang and that their information was that the road south was cut. Afterwards I had reason to believe that both these statements were wrong. But there was a considerable amount of confusion and rumour. After some discussion we decided that we would head west to Bencoelen, which was apparently still receiving shipping, and was fairly well away from any Japanese advance. On this part of the journey, I remember vividly the beauty of the mountains, the savannahs and a general air of peace and although the area was very thinly populated, it struck me at the time that it would sooner or later become a great asset in eventual development.

Three or four miles from Bencoelen, we set up a rearguard to delay or stop any Japanese who might appear. We were quite well armed, the road was a ravine and our people were of high morale. When I went into the town and sought out the authority, I believe a High Commissioner, he was aghast that we proposed to oppose the Japanese and was all for the quiet life. He told me that he was sure the Japanese would leave the Dutch administration in place and he didn't want them upset. I said my ambition was to get out of Bencoelen as fast as possible and could ships be summoned? He told me that all radio sets had been destroyed. However after a while, with help from the local police and our own people, who had several radio experts, we found and operated a set, which got through to Tjilatjap. At any rate we found a coaster, a small coaster, was due in twenty-four hours and we waited. By this time several of the local Dutch had changed their minds about waiting for the Japanese and had decided to come with us."

By the time they were evacuated, Maguire's party had been joined by various other escapees and survivors from Singapore and elsewhere, including Flt Lt Denny Sharp of 258 Squadron who had force-landed his Hurricane on the island of Singkep some two weeks earlier while evacuating from Singapore. He also had quite a story to tell:

"... the likelihood of landing in the mangrove swamp, that stretched from the sea practically all the way up to Palembang, didn't appeal to me so I force-landed at Pulau Singkep[81]. There was an airfield there but the Dutch had dug trenches across it so I couldn't land and I had to crash-land in a field. I wrecked the Hurricane and had a little blood on my forehead, and on my elbow, but that's all – the forehead because I cannoned into the gunsight. Singkep was in the hands of the Dutch who had tin mines there. The miners were in their Territorial Army and had been ordered to go up to another Dutch island, which was about ten miles south of Singapore. It was just across the water and visible from Singapore, so I warned them that they would be foolish to go because the Japs were virtually there. They had a motorboat and I asked them to let me have it so that I could go over to Sumatra and get down to Palembang. They did, and I agreed to take an English mining engineer with me. After a good lunch, which included two bottles of the only beer within a hundred miles, we set off.

The boat was manned by a native skipper and two deck hands and they did all the work. We went over to Sumatra, up a river called the Djambi to the little town of the same name, where I organised some money from the Dutch governor there and engaged a taxi to take me down to Palembang. The Englishman came with me because he thought it would easy to get to Java from there. So we set off by taxi next morning. Palembang was about 150 miles down the road and we were hardly five miles out of Djambi when we were stopped by Dutch troops, who had blown up the oil pipelines on the side of the road, and advised us that Jap paratroopers had landed in the vicinity of Palembang airport. So I decided that we should go inland from Djambi and then down the central road and over the hills to Bencoelen, on the south-west coast of Sumatra. We got to Bencoelen, where we stayed for a couple of nights, and made telephone communication with a wing commander [Maguire], in charge of irregulars from the RAF, in another town up in the north of Sumatra. He arranged for a steamer to pick us up and take us to Java. There were about 200 RAF troops with me and we all got aboard this tramp steamer, and we went through the Sunda Straits, and the next day landed in Batavia."

* * *

Now assembled at P2 was almost the whole RAF strength in the East Indies – 35 Blenheims, many of which were unserviceable, 20 Hudsons and 22 Hurricanes. Towards noon 258 Squadron's Flg Off Donahue volunteered to carry out a reconnaissance over the Palembang area:

"I scouted the road all the way, flying just above the treetops and getting lost once or twice by taking the wrong turns while flying in the rain, but didn't see anything that looked like military traffic coming. There were dozens of motorcars streaming down the road. Apparently all the civilians were getting out at high speed. I could see white shorts and coloured dresses in the cars, so I knew they couldn't be Japs. At Palembang the only indication I could see of how the fighting was going was that the Dutch had set fire some of their big oil storage tanks, which seemed a bad sign. There was the familiar sight of frightening red flames, with angry black smoke pumping skyward and drifting over the city, nearly hiding it. It would have awed me if I hadn't come so recently from Singapore. I returned and gave in my report, which relieved everyone because they had feared that the Japs might be attacking here right away, and we spent the rest of the day at readiness."

For those still on the run from P1, to get to P2 it was necessary to cross the Moesi by ferry, and here at first chaos reigned. The river was a quarter of a mile wide, and there was only one ferryboat in which only four vehicles at a time could be carried. Pladjoe was still in allied hands however, and a mixed force was positioned on the road between the town and the airfield at P1. Indeed, the Dutch commander was quite confident that he could retake the airfield, so much so that Wg Cdr Darley was ordered to re-open the Operations Room. However, it was too badly damaged and the idea was dropped. It was accepted therefore that a new Ops Room would have to be established, as planned, at P2 on the morrow. Further orders from Group HQ, received during the evening, stated that the squadrons at P2 were to prepare to destroy unserviceable aircraft.

Meanwhile, as darkness approached, the leading Japanese vessels in the Banka Straits anchored off Muntok (Banka Island), opposite the Moesi delta. Two companies of troops went ashore on the island in the face of only token resistance, and secured it; one company remained ashore as garrison. As this was happening, an allied naval force headed towards the area from a rendezvous in the Sunda Straits, in an attempt to attack the covering warships by approaching from the north of Banka Island. The weather was not favourable, heavy rain and poor visibility hampering progress. Almost at once, a Dutch destroyer struck a reef in the Gaspar Straits and was abandoned.

At dawn on 15 February, Japanese troops aboard the ships off Muntok began to disembark into landing craft (barges) and head up the three main rivers towards Palembang; the small transport accompanied them, as did a destroyer, eight patrol boats and four sampans. Soon afterwards, the commander of the invasion force ordered the remaining transports to raise anchor and follow them into the delta for their own protection. The second convoy was ordered to turn back, and the covering force to prepare for a surface battle. At first light a reconnaissance aircraft pinpointed the position of the multitude of transports and landing barges, many of which were seen in the estuaries of the Moesi and adjacent rivers.

First off, at 0630, to attack the invasion force were three Hudsons and three Blenheims. Escort was to be provided by half a dozen Hurricanes led by Flg Off Donahue but as these became airborne, the pilots encountered heavy fog and were forced to try and land again in the very poor conditions. Donahue went down first, and landed safely; he then fired a Very light up through the fog to indicate the whereabouts of the airfield to the others of his flight. Sgt Kelly was one of those who now had to find his way down again:

> "Once through the layer all that could be seen was a sheet of smooth white cloud stretching to the horizon while the airfield, the only one to which we had the range to return, had disappeared. It was somewhere there below and a little behind us. We had no means of ever finding it again for there were no sophisticated systems, such as radio direction-finding, such as were available to fighter pilots in the UK. Indeed had it not been for the quick thinking of one of our American pilots there is no doubt almost the last few Hurricanes available in Sumatra would have been lost in a single mission. Donahue, who was leading the strike force, appreciated the danger the moment he entered the mist, immediately banged down his undercarriage lever and, because of P2's enormous size, was able to land safely on his take-off run. Hurriedly finding a Very pistol, he raced to the middle of the field firing cartridges through the mist which, exploding like roman candles above it, gave the unhappy pilots now mislaid in a void a point around which to circle while trying to decide what they should do next."

Sgt Lambert had also shoved the nose and undercarriage down in time and landed safely:

> "Having brought my aircraft to a standstill, I saw another Hurricane coming in to land on a similar path to myself and about to pass me before coming to rest, and still with a fair burst of speed on, when the undercarriage simply went into a lot of soft muddy ground we had all experienced before and went straight over on its back. That pilot, I think, was named Fleming. I immediately left my aircraft and by that time Donahue and one or two more on the ground had managed to get a truck out to Fleming's aircraft and we lifted one of the main planes up and wedged the truck underneath it in order to release a somewhat shaken but, I believe, not badly injured Fleming."

Donahue had also seen Fleming's aircraft come down:

> "… another Hurricane broke through into sight. It landed on the cross runway at the far side of the field, disappeared behind a slight rise in the ground; then its tail appeared above the rise, poised vertically for an instant, and went on over, and the next minute the fire-truck and ambulance went flying across the field in that direction. Two safe, one crashed. Another got down safely a couple of minutes later but the last one spent a good fifteen minutes more milling around and making approaches that weren't quite right to bring him in, until finally he made it, too, and I sighed thankfully to see him roll to a stop, undamaged. We lost one machine in the whole affair. For a time I was afraid we were going to lose five. The ambulance came back from the far side of the field, bringing the pilot of the wrecked airplane, Sergeant Fleming. He was sitting in front with the driver, bruised and dirtied, but uninjured. He said he had struck a bad soft spot in the field, which made his machine go over on its back."

As pilots who had either escaped from P1 or been off duty in Palembang streamed into

P2, the two Hurricane squadrons had many more than there were aircraft for them to fly, and it was agreed that the available fighters should be pooled. At 0900 the fog cleared, and Hurricanes manned by 232 Squadron pilots went off to continue the attack on the landing craft. Plt Off Lockwood:

> "I dived from a near-vertical position. As the cone of fire hit the water, I centred it on a sampan and bodies went over the side. I only just pulled out of the dive and recall looking up at the trees on the river bank!"

Amongst the strafers was Sgt Sandy Allen, flying No.2 to Flt Lt Julian, who recalled:

> "I seem to remember that we were helped by a large number of alligators, which prevented any escape from the barges by swimming!"

Julian added:

> "We sent out some Blenheims to bomb their ships, off the entrance of the river. We escorted them, and used the operation as a bit of a decoy, for out of the corner of our eyes we could see all these little estuaries running off the river, and the Japs hiding there. The barges bringing the troops up had gone into these little estuaries, so we peeled off and, brother, did we get our own back. They couldn't move as they were packed in so tightly and we roared right down an estuary and just tore them up, backwards and forwards and back again until we ran out of ammunition. But they were game and fired at us from their barges. They sent up as much as they could. We repeated the dose and went back again and I've got no idea how many we would have killed."

Sqn Ldr Thomson independently led off a small force of four Hurricanes, including that flown by Plt Off Parker:

> "I had no idea what a landing craft might look like but supposed it would be some sort of self-propelled barge. I was therefore a bit surprised when Thomson waggled his wings and peeled off in an attacking dive on what looked like a couple of sampans under sail, about a hundred yards apart. I let him gain as much of a lead as I could in the short time before he opened fire and I watched the pattern of his bullets striking the first sampan and then as, still firing, he pulled up his sights on to the other. Then I was almost on top of the first and opened fire, only to see as I flashed towards it that it was indeed a very small native boat and no enemy target at all. Quite impersonally and astonishingly, I was furious at this identification error and chased off after Thomson who was climbing back to regain height while still going downriver. However, as I caught up with him, he pointed down to some other craft a mile or so away on which other aircraft were diving.
>
> These turned out to be Hurricanes attacking about eight genuine landing craft, which were putting up a barrage of light anti-aircraft fire. There were no larger vessels about nor, as far as I could see, any defending fighters. Thomson didn't wait to assess the situation but tore straight in at one of the landing craft near the centre, which seemed to he a sort of flak ship. As we went down, the guns aboard it didn't aim at us but I could tell from the blue smoke jetting upwards in the bright sunshine against the brown-green of the river that the guns were laid in a sort of fan-like shield over the group of vessels through which we'd have to fly. They seemed to be shooting at a fixed angle and Thomson went straight through the fan and out again. I had a little more time to consider the position and came in at right angles to it in a very shallow dive and then pulled up between the pumping lines of smoke from the guns. I looked for Thomson ahead but he was returning to P2 at a low level. I assumed he'd run out of ammunition but his aircraft had in fact been hit. My own seemed all right and with the other two following I turned and came down again on the gunship out of the sun. This time there was less fire to go through but before I got really close my guns stopped firing and I pulled up and over towards the smoke pall to await the

> others. They joined me almost immediately having also run out of ammunition and there being no other aircraft in the sky, we returned without problem to P2. There I found Brooker with the other 232 pilots."

Blenheims, escorted by Hurricanes, continued to bomb and strafe the hapless troops while others went after the troop transport, which was set on fire. The Hurricanes, their escort task completed, swept down to strafe numerous small troop-filled craft, which were seen moving up the river. During the early sorties there had been considerable, though inaccurate, anti-aircraft fire from the special 'flak-ships', which were covering the barges and sampans, but by now return fire was mainly limited to what the troops themselves could throw up from their vulnerable and open vessels. Flg Off Donahue led one attack, accompanied by Sgt Kelly, who recalled:

> "The oil wells had now been fired and a great column of intense black smoke rose high into the sky to level off and drift in a very broad swathe in, as I recall, a north-easterly direction. Under cover of this shield for at least part of the way, we set off for the Moesi. I do not know how many of the others found the barges but at least Donahue and I, split off from the rest, did so. I flew behind Donahue as he made his first attack, which he executed brilliantly. The barges at the point where we came upon them were, unluckily for their occupants, on a straight piece of the river so that they were in line astern. They were packed with infantry like sardines in a tin and their sole defence was a machine gun mounted at the back. I watched the bullets from Donahue's guns forming a pincushion behind the rearmost barge, moving along both sides of it, and then plopping the water between it and the barge ahead. And so along the line. The casualties he caused must have been ferocious. I could see the both the flicker of the defenders' machine guns and the path and flash of the tracer bullets. Donahue made only a single run having been (unknown to me) hit by a machine-gun bullet. Somewhat mystified by his departure, I made three attacks before returning to P2."

Of his injury, Donahue later wrote:

> "I was conscious of having been hit, harder than I have ever been hit in my life – a quick, cruel blow in the calf of my left leg – I had a momentary glimpse through a big rent in my trousers of two holes in the side of my leg, one small and round, the other a gaping sort of thing an inch wide by a couple of inches long, with raw red and blue flesh and muscle laid open, before the blood welled up and started streaming out."

Bleeding profusely and in a near-fainting condition, he managed to get back to P2 where, under extremely difficult circumstances, he carried out a successful if somewhat bumpy landing:

> "I did not mind, though. The feeling of triumph at having made it safely, made the bad landing seem inconsequential! I felt almost boisterous as I taxied up to the Watch Office. Some of the boys lifted me out . . . and put a field dressing on my leg. Then I was packed off in an ambulance to the dressing station."

Plt Off Jerry Parker, now back with 232 Squadron, made a second strafing attack on the barges along with others:

> "As soon as we were refuelled and re-armed, away we went again. The landing craft were only 20 minutes flying time away from P2, but there were only two in the middle of the channel that I could see. There were no other aircraft in sight and we came down on the two barges from the south-east, out of the sun. I opened fire at quite a steep angle, a long way off, and saw the pattern of my bullets striking the water near them. As I approached and corrected my aim, the pattern grew more concentrated, and then the de Wilde was

bursting all over the first one. It seemed that dozens of men dressed in light brown uniforms jumped over the side to escape the hundreds of rounds pumping into the barges, but they had no chance. The bullets were still striking the water all round it. Then I was over and up, and the other Hurricanes were following and treating the barges similarly. We went down the river and saw no more landing craft, so turned and came back up to Palembang again, but still nothing moved. I reckoned that we were in any event short of ammunition now, so went back to P2."

During the afternoon orders were received at P2 for all remaining aircraft to proceed to Java on completion of allotted tasks. Only three Hudsons now remained. As regards the Blenheims, the respective squadron commanders decided that their commitment precluded despatching aircraft immediately to Java and, by the time all aircraft and crews had completed their tasks and refuelled, it would be impossible to reach Batavia before dusk. Hence, their departure would be delayed until the morrow. Both Blenheims and Hudsons continued the onslaught, the last operation for the day being flown by two Hudsons. Eight Hurricanes from 232 Squadron provided cover over the target area, and four of these strafed the decks of two destroyers from mast height. However, eight Ki-27s of the 11th Sentai had arrived to operate from P1, and three attempted to intercept the bombers, but two of these were claimed down by the Hurricanes, Plt Offs Tom Watson (BE130) and Reg Bainbridge getting one apiece, the Canadian claiming a second as damaged; two of the Japanese fighters did indeed sustain damage and crash-landed on return to base. In return, the three 11th Sentai pilots claimed two 'Buffaloes' shot down out of four they reported engaging! None of the Hurricanes were lost however. Two F1M floatplanes from the detachment at Muntok patrolled over the ships during the late afternoon, one being shot down by the gunners aboard one of the Hudsons as it attempted to intercept.

Throughout the day evacuation of Palembang continued. In the morning, Wg Cdr Darley had collected 30 armed men, setting up guards each side of the river and actually on the ferry boat, their presence persuading the local crew to keep working. Gradually, everyone got across and, by evening, the evacuation was all but complete. Darley carried out a last swift tour of the town to make sure all were gone and then withdrawing the guards, crossed on the last ferry with Air Commodore Vincent, following the others to P2. The town was left blazing and under a great pall of smoke from the burning refineries. No sooner had P2 been reached than the order was given to begin evacuating this base, all personnel not involved in operating and maintaining the aircraft being ordered to the port of Oosthaven, 300 miles away on the south-eastern tip of Sumatra, for trans-shipment to Java. With Vincent and Darley was Wg Cdr Ron Barclay:

"I travelled by car, with Air Commodore Vincent and others, from P1 to Oosthaven via P2 but, armed as we were, sighted no Jap paratroopers. We reached Oosthaven at 0300 and, at dawn, jettisoned our Buick in the harbour and embarked for Java."

Fortunately for the evacuees, two trains were located in the station close to P2 and the reluctant crews were forced at gunpoint to drive them to Oosthaven, loaded with supplies, wounded and other personnel. Meanwhile, a large convoy of overcrowded vehicles began the long and arduous journey to the port, other personnel making such arrangements as they could for their escape. The route to Oosthaven included a lot of bridges, over small rivers and streams, many of which featured relatively low roof structures; as a result a number of high-sided vehicles and 3.7mm anti-aircraft guns which could not be got under them had to be abandoned. Many of these bridges were demolished after the convoy had passed over them, in order to slow down the Japanese pursuit. RAF personnel at the airfields in Northern Sumatra were ordered to make their way to the west coast, from where they would be evacuated by destroyers.

When not providing escort for the bombers, the Hurricanes continuously landed, re-armed, refuelled and returned to make strafing attacks against the troop-carrying barges. The last operation was against a number of aircraft sighted on the beach on the south-west of Banka Island. Flt Lt Julian led his flight down to strafe what were believed, at the time, to be A6Ms but were most probably F1Ms from the seaplane tenders; one was claimed destroyed by Julian. The number of casualties suffered by the Japanese troops during the series of strafing attacks has never been accurately ascertained, but is believed to have run into hundreds. Certainly the programme for the invasion was seriously upset and by mid-afternoon all movement on the rivers up to Palembang had ceased. Ironically, it was at this point that the Hurricanes were ordered to withdraw to Java, all flyable aircraft departing without delay, manned in the main by 232 Squadron pilots.

There were not sufficient aircraft for all pilots but, as the majority of 258 Squadron's pilots were still in or around Palembang town, only three of the unit's NCO pilots were left at P2 to make their own way to Java, together with a number of the replacement pilots who had arrived earlier at the airfield, including Sgt John Vibert, a New Zealander:

> "I walked to P2 aerodrome where 258 Squadron was stationed and, after informing one of the officers that I was a replacement pilot newly arrived from England, I was invited to join this squadron. However, later in the day the order arrived to evacuate and as there was a shortage of serviceable aircraft I was again back with a walking party trying to reach the railhead before the Japs captured it. Eventually we caught a freight train to the southern port of Sumatra where we embarked on the ships waiting to pick us up."

Another of the replacement pilots, fellow New Zealander Frank Hood, wrote in his diary:

> "Morning: by car to Oosthaven. Lost way. Got to Lahat. Retraced steps. Nearly ran into advanced Nips. Arrived port Monday night. Oil dumps ablaze all way down. Weird night. Left on small boat. Very crowded that night. Arrived Batavia. Very tired. Been wet through for hours. No apparent ill effects. Things look bad."

Also at P1 were the three stranded 258 Squadron pilots, Sgts Terry Kelly, Bertie Lambert and Art Sheerin, the latter just back from his adventures. Kelly wrote in his diary:

> "We sat around watching, rather gloomily, an impressive oil fire somewhere near at hand. There was a terrible atmosphere of depression and defeat; much the same as in Singapore and yet in a way more tangible. One almost expected Japanese suddenly to rush us from the jungle. We ate tinned sausages and wondered what was going to happen next – we hadn't any Hurricanes. Others had taken them. I don't know whom. Then came the casual, weary order that we were on our own. We walked down the lane, which led to the airfield. A rutted sort of track with low thick bushes on either hand. We knew quite well that there weren't any enemy in miles but we still felt uneasy. The track came to a T-junction. To the left it led to the railway station and the road to Palembang, to the right to the airfield. We held a council of war – which way to go?"

The trio decided to return to the airfield, where several unserviceable Hurricanes remained. One of these was Z5481, which Kelly had flown during the past few days, so he decided to start the engine. It made a terrible grinding noise while taxiing, and pulled savagely to port when he began his take-off run but, by giving the engine full boost, he obtained sufficient power to get into the air, where the aircraft flew perfectly. Lambert also found a flyable Hurricane, but Sheerin experienced greater difficulty. Having not found a suitable machine, he was then approached to fly a Blenheim full of ground personnel, who were awaiting a pilot. Initially agreeing to give this a try, he then spotted a Hurricane concealed in the undergrowth. On inspection, he noticed it was minus its tailwheel but, notwithstanding this, he jumped in:

> "So in I got, started up, popping and smoking and commenced to taxi on the rudder when a flight lieutenant Duty Pilot jumped on the wing and shouted, 'That's mine. I hid it there.' I thought there is only one thing to do – blow him off – which I did. As I commenced my take-off run Japs were on the end of the drome and firing at me. I lost no time heading very low for Batavia with my popping Hurricane and a map on a cigarette case to navigate by. Later to land in safety."

One small group of airmen, who had been sent to P1 to remove the propeller from a severely damaged Hurricane with orders to convey it to P2, arrived at the jungle airfield aboard a truck during the morning. They had quite an experience to relate including brief capture at P1 by a Japanese paratroop officer who, in turn, surrendered to Dutch forces that came to their rescue. One of the men, LAC Geoffrey Rex Collis, recalled:

> "Having fixed our sleeping accommodation the first job was to find the place where the crippled Hurricane was dispersed in the jungle. The airfield itself consisted of no more than a grassed area, of no particular shape, but seemed to stretch for miles in the jungle that was all around us. Although it was situated along the top of a ridge, the heavy planes that had landed there after rain had created furrows in the soil; it wasn't surprising that our Hurricane had fallen foul of a wheel track as it taxied in, finishing up on its nose with a very bent airscrew. This had already been removed, so it wasn't a question of the five of us reversing the procedure carried out at P1."[82]

They were advised that the Hurricane's pilot had gone sick with malaria, so there was no great panic to get the job finished quickly. However, by the following morning, the propeller had been fixed and tested, but since they lacked any coolant for the engine, urine had been substituted. Rex Collis continued:

> "In the afternoon the pilot of the Hurricane turned up to see if his plane was serviceable. He was a young sergeant, [possibly Sgt Bill May of 232 Squadron] not long out of flying training school, still pale from his bout of malaria. He had been lucky to survive so long, and his chances of living much longer seemed pretty remote. He told us that he had been ordered to stand by for take-off to Java at first light the next day. 'There's room for one of you to stow down the fuselage behind the wireless inspection panel; sorry I can't fit you both in.' As Brem and I trudged back to the billet we discussed the prospect and decided we would stick together and take our chance overland. Maybe our luck would hold just a little longer. Anyhow, there was no guarantee that the Hurricane would reach Java safely, especially with our urine in its coolant tank.
>
> At dawn we made our way to the airfield for the last time, pushing the Hurricane clear of the trees that screened it as the young pilot walked over to us, already in his flying gear. 'Who's for a day trip then?' he said, trying to put a brave face on things. I think he felt lonely, just one inexperienced pilot left from a whole squadron that had taken off from the carrier in the Bay of Bengal. I felt rather mean telling him we had decided to stay together. He taxied the plane out clear of the trees, and with the roar of full boost was soon airborne and lifting clear of the surrounding jungle. We watched for as long as it took the lonely Hurricane to diminish to a speck over the southern horizon and then we turned to make our way to the galley."[83]

232 Squadron had also 'abandoned' two of its pilots: Sgts Gordie Dunn and David Kynman had been ordered to stay behind long enough to destroy any Hurricanes that could not be made serviceable:

> "The Station CO was an Aussie [Grp Capt McCauley] and he ordered us out to catch the last train south, and said he would look after any kites before the Nips could get them. He said he had scrounged a Hurricane, had made it serviceable and was going to be the last to leave in this Hurricane. I didn't know his name and never met him again."

Another group of airmen left stranded in Palembang town was the 258 Squadron detachment under Plt Off Macnamara. Having returned from their skirmishes with the Japanese paratroopers on the road to P1, they found that Sgt Scott and his party including Sgt Dusty Miller were missing[84]. Uncertain of what to do next, their problem was solved when an abandoned Dutch motorboat with its engines running came drifting down the river. Flg Off Tudor Jones and a stranded airman AC1 Peter Lamont were able to leap aboard as it came within reach; one engine had seized but Lamont succeeded in getting it working. Meanwhile Tudor Jones rounded up his four companions – Macnamara, Campbell, McCulloch and Cicurel – and with Lamont at the wheel, the craft headed for the railway station, about a mile upstream. Red Campbell provided an account of the adventure:

> "We got back to town and McCulloch showed up at this time. And we had Tudor and this enlisted airman who had found a Dutch river patrol boat. It had two small Ford V8 engines in it and it had a mounting for a machine gun on it. And so we decided to commandeer this thing. The problem with it was, one of the propellers was badly bent. It had apparently run aground somewhere – I guess why it had been left. But we decided to take this and go – we looked at a map and decided we could go up river and intersect the road for P2 and rejoin our people. We arrived there late in the evening and there were people coming down the road heading in the other direction who led us to understand the Japanese were just over the next hill which we found out later was complete cock but at the time we believed them. So we decided then that our only recourse was to stay with the boat and get as far south as we could and get away from the immediate area. So that's what we did. We spent the rest of that day and all night and then the next day on the boat, but anyway we finally were starting to run out of river bottom – we kept running aground. We came to a native village and Ting Macnamara exercised his usual charm and between him and Cicurel, they talked the local natives by sign language and so forth into trading a lorry they had there for this lovely boat which they thought was really great. I don't think they owned the lorry either.
>
> Anyway we took the lorry and all our gear – we had taken all the arms we could carry in the boat. We drove the lorry and we finally came to a bridge that had been blown. This was after I don't know how many miles and by this time it was evening. We got across the river and walked all that night. I carried a rifle, a Tommy gun and two pistols and a knapsack with a lot of my personal gear in it. I don't know how many miles we walked that night."

A gruelling 20-mile walk now began, during which the party split into two groups, Tudor Jones and Campbell forging ahead. They reached Matapoera and were at once offered lifts in a number of cars that were just leaving; realising that there was no room for the others, they decided to press on rather than ask the drivers to wait. Campbell continued:

> "It must have been some place between 15 and 20 miles we walked that night and the next day, and finally came on an intersection in the road where there were people coming down another road and we got a ride down into the south end of Sumatra – probably the last twenty-five miles – where we got passage on a ferry that was going over to Java and that's the way we made our way back to Batavia."

Ting Macnamara and the rest of the party arrived at Matapoera having completed the walk in ten hours, but were totally exhausted. Any hopes of a train were quickly dashed as the last one had gone some time before, and the town had been all but abandoned. Among many wrecked vehicles they discovered a serviceable car but, as they strove to get fuel for it, a truck carrying some Dutch and British sailors arrived, survivors of a minesweeper bombed at Pladjoe. These had arrived purely by chance, having become lost. They were happy to take aboard the British party, who were able to direct them onto the correct road for Oosthaven, along which they drove throughout the night. Following a stop for breakfast in a still-inhabited town, they reached the port on the morning of the 17th, as demolitions were still taking place. A ferry steamer was just about to leave and, getting aboard this moments before it sailed, the RAF men were reunited with the rest of their party, who had arrived some hours earlier.[85]

The losses inflicted on the invading forces by the Hurricanes and the bombers during the day could only delay the inevitable and, as soon as darkness fell, the landing craft were able to proceed to Palembang, the surviving Japanese troops made contact with the paratroop survivors that night – nearly 36 hours behind schedule. A further 96 paratroops were dropped over P1 at about midday. Of the 360 dropped on the first day, almost 25 per cent had become casualties, of whom 37 were killed, a relatively small price to pay for the gains achieved. It was already clear to General Wavell that he could not hope to hold Sumatra.

The Japanese were quick off the mark and their air units began pouring in to the newly acquired airfield at P1, including 16 Ki-27s from the 11th Sentai, 20 Ki-43s from the 64th Sentai, and a part of the 27th Sentai. Soon, all available Ki-43s of both the 59th and 64th Sentais were established at P1, from where they could operate over Western Java with ease. Within two days Japanese forces secured Tandjunkarang, then the 12th Flying Battalion Ki-27s moved to this location. Meanwhile, three C5Ms and 15 A6Ms of the 22nd Air Flotilla Fighter Group moved to Muntok from Borneo. Thus, the arrival of the JAAF in Sumatra allowed the land-based elements of the Navy's 21st and 23rd Air Flotillas to concentrate their attacks on Eastern Java, together with the other islands in the chain towards Australia.

CHAPTER V

LAST STAND AT JAVA

16 February – 8 March

"'Attack everything that comes in, no matter what, and force it to land on Java,' we were told. 'If you do that you will have done your job.'"

Plt Off Red Campbell, 258 Squadron

By now, the second Japanese convoy of troop transports had finally steamed up the Moesi, anchoring at Palembang, where the troops disembarked. The attacks on the landing parties from the first convoy had proved most effective, and had shaken the Japanese somewhat, whilst the resistance to the paratroopers, and the losses inflicted on them, had slowed down their programme substantially. However, the precipitate withdrawal from Oosthaven and elsewhere had resulted in much useful matériel being left behind and, when the last Allied ships left Oosthaven, it was already becoming embarrassingly apparent that the Japanese were not actually on the heels of the fleeing evacuees. An aerial reconnaissance of the Oosthaven-Palembang road showed no immediate occupation of Oosthaven port to be likely and, consequently, it was decided to attempt a salvage operation. Grp Capt G.E. Nicholetts AFC[86] led 50 RAF volunteers drawn from 605 Squadron aboard the Australian minesweeper *Ballarat*, which departed at once for Oosthaven. On arrival, they found the port deserted, and were able to spend 12 hours loading valuable RAF equipment including a Hurricane's Merlin engine and Bofors ammunition, whilst doing as much damage as possible to what remained. Not until they were well away did the first Japanese troops enter the town.

It was, by this time, abundantly clear to the Allies that the panicky withdraw from Palembang had been unnecessarily hasty. Although withdrawal in the face of the stronger forces available to the Japanese would undoubtedly have become inevitable, P2 airfield had not even been discovered at that stage. A resolute fighting defence of the town and harbour, followed by a slow withdrawal towards Oosthaven, would have allowed the still-substantial numbers of aircraft at the jungle airfield to have created more havoc with the landings; possibly even to have rendered the arrival of the second convoy as costly as the first. Instead, panic and confusion had again reigned supreme. The aircrews felt aggrieved, certain that they could have kept up their attacks for much longer; they considered themselves badly let down yet again. Palembang was yet one more in the line of major and minor disasters however, for worse was very soon to come.

The necessity for the Japanese forces to establish themselves on the new airfields in Sumatra ensured that the Allies were able to enjoy a few days of relative quiet in Western Java, where strenuous efforts were expended to form the scattered remnants of the RAF's squadrons into some semblance of an air force. Even as the survivors of the Palembang debacle started arriving on the island, the residue of 488 Squadron had managed to get three Hurricanes fully operational and at readiness at Tjililitan airfield, an L-shaped satellite strip among rubber and coconut plantations a few miles outside Batavia. Plt Off Bunt Pettit provided a description of the airfield:

"Tjililitan was perhaps ten miles outside the centre of Batavia which was pretty close to the coast and had its own port, Tandjong Priok. Like a lot of the airstrips out there, it was simply just grass – a little emergency strip that the Dutch Air Force used although they weren't stationed there when we were there. There was no runway, and no cross-runway, largely because there wasn't a great deal of wind for most of the season. It had a couple of peculiarities. It wasn't a very long strip and was made awkward in that it was perched up slightly above the surrounding countryside. It had been built-up so it was 50 or 60 feet above the rest of the countryside and at one end there was a buffalo wallow. They probably knocked the top off a small hill and flattened it out by spreading the spoil from the middle to the ends. Consequently it had a nasty slope at both ends and, if you were at height, was deceptive in that it looked like flat ground, and that you had a lot more landing area than was there. I never got any closer to the ends of it than I could avoid. We had a dispersal hut and *atap* huts – little shelters basically – where we sat out of the sun, waiting for our scramble."

By the 16th the number of operational Hurricanes at Tjililitan had risen to five. Fifteen had flown in from P2 the previous day, but most were unserviceable on arrival. The decision was now taken to reduce drastically the number of units that were to remain operational, and the first move was the disbandment of 226 (Fighter) Group. With Air Vice-Marshal Pulford and a number of his senior officers missing, overall command of the RAF on Java passed to Air Vice-Marshal Maltby. All squadrons now came under the direction of Westgroup, which Maltby commanded with headquarters at Soekaboemi, whilst Air Commodore Vincent took over the Fighter Control HQ. For the time being ABDAIR remained responsible for the control of the actual operations flown. Maltby was to have the benefit of just two radar units, both salvaged from Singapore and Malaya; these were sited at Batavia. Air Commodore Vincent later wrote:

"Under peacetime conditions the road up to Bandoeng must be one of the most beautiful motor trips in the world. It climbs up out of the heat and damp of Batavia with good surface for about 3,000 feet, with glorious scenery in fertile well-kept countryside, with contented-looking natives. We had a marvellous lunch en route in the most beautiful of hotels, cool and dry, with magnificent views, a golf course, tennis courts and a swimming pool. In Bandoeng we stayed the night in the Savoy Honan Hotel where Sir Richard Peirse [Commander-in-Chief Allied Air Forces] told me he had, the previous night, had the best dinner he had ever eaten in any hotel in the world. I found it was in every respect up to this standard, marvellous food and orchestra, unlimited staff, cool comfortable bedrooms with private bathrooms and every convenience. Charming demoiselles in beautiful evening frocks combined with this to make it hard to believe that we had been running away in acute discomfort for several days and nights ... and that the enemy was advancing towards us as fast as he could manage."[87]

Organisation was much improved at Batavia and, therefore, beneficial to the fighter pilots at Tjililitan, as subsequently reported by Vincent:

"We took over a house and made a small Operations Room which we had functioning in little over a week, with direct radio contact with the aircraft and telephone links with a number of observer posts, on direct lines arranged by the Dutch. HMS *Exeter* also became a very vital link in our chain, usually from about 100 miles north, giving us early warning of formations heading in our direction. The Ops Room was completed with a large-scale 'table' together with telephones to three aerodromes, R/T communication with aircraft, observer corps liaison, communication with gun and searchlight positions and direct lines to Bandoeng and Sourabaya. In addition the filter room was connected up to two RDF sets and two GL sets and three small American sets were being sited but were never actually in use. In this favourable position we were able to bring off several successful interceptions of raids and also obtain something like Battle of Britain figures for enemy shot down in relation to our smaller casualties.

The building was surrounded by an unclimbable spiked bamboo fence and the Dutch works people did a first-class job in a remarkably short time. In addition, a squad of some twenty Dutch girls were trained in a week to become our plotters and filterers. A very attractive collection, they were most keen to wear uniform. They paraded before me in their creations for selection: drill blouses with short skirts, long trousers or mini shorts! I chose the trousers! On one item they all agreed – could they wear the RAF fore and aft cap? I said they certainly could if they made them, as we had none in our stores! However, they never had the chance as the Ops Room very soon had to be broken up and communications wrecked as the enemy once more approached. During the last week or two we managed to reorganise the squadrons into two good units and started evacuating air and groundcrew that could not be employed due to lack of aircraft, so that they could escape to carry on the war elsewhere."[88]

For fighter defence, two squadrons were to be reformed, while 232, 258 and 488 Squadrons were effectively disbanded. Initially the ground party of 242 Squadron, which was still in Java with no air component, was to have the pilots of 232 Squadron transferred to it en masse. Although a dozen of the 51 Hurricanes delivered on 4 February had been handed to the Dutch and 17 more had been sent up to Sumatra, a total of 25 of these fighters were still available (including the survivors of earlier deliveries), and of these 18 were operational. These were now concentrated at Tjililitan in the new 242 Squadron:

242 Squadron – Sqn Ldr R.E.P. Brooker DFC
Flight Commanders – Flt Lt I. Julian RNZAF and Flt Lt B.J. Parker

Plt Off M.C. Fitzherbert
Plt Off R.T. Bainbridge
Plt Off E.C. Gartrell RNZAF
Plt Off W.M. Lockwood RCAF
Plt Off T.W. Watson RCAF
Plt Off R. Mendizabal RCAF
2/Lt N. Anderson SAAF
Sgt R.L. Dovell
Sgt J.A. Sandeman Allen
Sgt I.D. Newlands RNZAF
Sgt A.W. May
Sgt G.J. King
Sgt D. Kynman
Sgt E.M. Porter
Sgt K.H. Holmes
Sgt G.J. Dunn RCAF
Sgt J.P. Fleming RCAF
Sgt I.S. Fairbairn RAAF
Sgt T.W. Young RAAF
Sgt D.J.B. Isdale – one of the replacement pilots

Although Sgt John Fleming was on strength, he was currently very ill with a fever, presumably contracted during his travels down the Malayan coast, and spent four days in a native hotel unable to get out of bed. Fortunately, he made a good recovery and was soon back on operations. At about this time Sgts Ken Holmes, Ron Dovell and Ian Fairbairn[89] learned they had been recommended for field commissions. Flt Lt Julian had arranged for them to be interviewed by Air Vice-Marshal Maltby when a message came through that the AOC had been involved in a car accident the night before and was in hospital. Events moved too fast after that and the interviews never took place. Julian also received a visit from Air Commodore Vincent about the same time, regarding the incident with the Air HQ wing commander at Singapore:

"'Oh Julian,' he said, 'God Almighty! Look at the situation you've put me in – you're supposed to be on a charge!' I said, 'Look we were so tired that we could hardly keep our eyes open and hardly stand on our feet and yet we still had to fly. We didn't mind that because that's our job. But my God, when I find that an officer in ops is actually having his afternoon sleep, then that's the end,' and, I added: 'Yes I did really let him have it, sir.' The Air Commodore got me a drink and said 'Forget it.'"

The second unit to reform was 605 Squadron – again the ground party being available and fresh, although having no aircrew. Sqn Ldr Ricky Wright was posted from 232 Squadron as CO, bringing with him newly promoted Flt Lt Joe Hutton as his deputy, the other pilots being drawn equally from 258 and 488 Squadrons plus a smattering of new arrivals. Sqn Ldr Thomson had called a meeting of 258 Squadron pilots to decide who would remain, Flg Off Dobbyn having been nominated to command the second Flight. Volunteers were called for but only Plt Off Red Campbell and newly arrived Sgt John Vibert stepped forward. Campbell recalled:

> "We had told the people in command that we did not have enough planes. We told them that we had enough experience, we knew the Jap tactics, and we knew we could beat them at their own game if given half a chance. But we had our orders. We were told that Headquarters wanted the Japanese to land on every island on the chain down to Australia, to slow their advance and give the Australians a chance to build up their defences. 'Attack everything that comes in, no matter what, and force it to land on Java,' we were told. 'If you do that you will have done your job.'"[90]

Cards were drawn to decide who would remain with them, Sgts Kelly, Lambert and Healey drawing the low cards, which determined their fate. Sgt Art Sheerin, who had drawn an 'ace', recalled:

> "Cam White and I set off for the railway which was teeming with Navy, Army and Air Force as we discovered this was the only and last train for Tjilatjap. What a trip, the engine ran out of fuel – so what to do? Chop up the seats or anything! Just let us get cracking! We finally reached the port – which was in utter confusion with people shouting, yelling – and panic. I bumped into two Qantas flying boat captains who were about to depart for Darwin – they begged me to come with him but I would not leave Cam. We scrambled on to a small (about 4,000 tons) ship, not knowing where we were going."

605 Squadron – Sqn Ldr E.W. Wright DFM
Flt Lt J.C. Hutton (Deputy)

A (New Zealand) Flight	**B Flight**
Flt Lt F.W.J. Oakden RNZAF	Flg Off H.A. Dobbyn RNZAF
Plt Off N.C. Sharp RNZAF	Plt Off J.A. Campbell (US)
Plt Off H.S. Pettit RNZAF	Plt Off R.L. Cicurel (US)
Plt Off G.P. White RNZAF	Sgt C.T.R. Kelly
Plt Off W.J. Greenhalgh RNZAF	Sgt A. Lambert
Sgt E.E.G. Kuhn RNZAF	Sgt P.M.T. Healey
Sgt W.J.N. MacIntosh RNZAF	Sgt G.D. Binsted
Sgt H.J. Meharry RNZAF	Sgt J.G. Vibert RNZAF
Sgt W.E. Collins	Sgt C.E. Sharp RNZAF
Sgt A.D. Jack	Sgt F.N. Hood RNZAF

Although initially posted to the new unit, Plt Off Wally Greenhalgh and Sgt Jack Meharry were instructed to evacuate, which they did aboard the MV *Deucalion* on 23 February. All of A Flight with the exception of Sgts Bill Collins and Albert Jack were original 488 Squadron pilots. B Flight's Sgts George Binsted, John Vibert, Collis Sharp and Frank Hood were also replacement pilots. It is unlikely that any of the replacement pilots, with the exception of Vibert, were called upon to make any operational flights due to the shortage of Hurricanes. Plt Off Pettit remembered:

> "We weren't privy to the selection process and we were just told that we were to join 605 Squadron. Names weren't picked out of a hat, so I can't explain why I was there, but the

rest of them I would say were the cream of what was left of 488 Squadron. I would say that Noel Sharp, Eddie Kuhn and Jim MacIntosh were chosen because, ability wise, they were top of the list among the pilots. Snow White was also a very good pilot. I believe five were definitely selected on quality. I'd had a few days off with this bit of shrapnel in my arm from an engagement in Singapore, so I suppose they reckoned it was about time I had a bit more fun. We had more pilots than aircraft so we split, the 488 pilots would fly together and the 605 chaps likewise. Depending on how much action there had been by one lot, the other flight might come in early and take over to give the others a bit of relief. We hardly ever saw the other members of 605 Squadron. I knew them after the end of the hostilities really more than I did prior to that. We kept much to ourselves and were flying at different times.

Ricky Wright became CO. Harry Dobbyn was ex-258. Red Campbell was one of those guys who always saw the enemy aircraft before anyone else. He'd been flying as a civilian in the States before the war and went to Britain and joined up because he liked flying and because he couldn't get into the American Air Force, because of his age. He was a very useful chap; a good pilot with fabulous eyesight, possibly because he was busily looking, or used of looking, about the sky."

Of the arrangement between the two flights, Jim MacIntosh wrote:

"We used the same aircraft; we'd come on and relieve them, and they'd go off, and I think the roster system in use was two days on and one day off. The day started at 1 o'clock – you would always relieve the flight at 1 o'clock and stay on till 1 o'clock next day. And they'd come on and relieve you. But it didn't always work."

The young veterans of 488 Squadron had seen much action flying Buffaloes in defence of Singapore – both Noel Sharp and Eddie Kuhn each having been credited with three victories[91]. MacIntosh, who had one shared and three probables to his credit – continued:

"Noel Sharp was as game as Ned Kelly – the bushranger. I felt as though he wanted to be an Albert Ball or a James McCudden of the First World War. That was about the best way I could describe Noel. He was a good bloke, was as game as you would get and he would take anything on, but he was a bit indisciplined in the air. Eddie Kuhn was a good pilot and we flew a lot together. He did very well. Grahame White [Snow] was a good pilot, and a nice reliable chap. I had him fly No.2 with me on several occasions. He was a good sticker alongside you. I don't recall many of the others in the outfit, apart from Red Campbell, the American, and Sgts Kelly, Lambert, Healey and Vibert. They are really the only ones I remember. Of course they [B Flight] were right away on the opposite side of the airfield, down the L-shaped leg. We were over on this side and they were away down at the bottom end there."

Although the two squadrons had sufficient aircraft for only one unit, it was hoped to re-equip 605 Squadron with American P40Es when supplies arrived from Australia[92]. Surplus pilots from 488 Squadron were sent to Kemajoran, where they helped assemble and test newly arrived Hurricanes. The CO, Sqn Ldr Jack Mackenzie, air tested one on 19 February, his first flight in Java. For the hard-working groundcrew, conditions were becoming worse rather than better, as evidenced by entries in LAC Max Boyd's diary:

"A Flight and half of workshops maintenance went to work today [18 February] to an airport about 10 miles out of Batavia. The rest of us filled in time at the barracks. We got a small piece of bread and a slice of bully beef for a meal and to get this we queue up for hours with the queue stretching hundreds of yards. It is easier to go up town and pay for a meal at a cafe, although food seems to be getting harder to obtain now. Last night I believe the English officers had a sign put up outside the premier nightclub reading 'Officers Only'. The Dutch did not take kindly to this and promptly threw out all the English officers. The Dutch are much less class conscious. We went to the open-air pictures this evening and the Dutch colonial officials did try to push in at the head of the queue in front of the troops but the New Zealanders elbowed them aside, unlike the Dutch colonial troops who stood aside. This place is full of contrasts and contradictions.

B Flight went out to the aerodrome today [19 February]. The first thing Leo Arden and I did was to dig ourselves a foxhole near the machine we were looking after. It was very hard work in the sun and we were very weak from no food or sleep for so long. At least the Dutch on the drome have fed us well. The RAF don't care how we eat, we are only colonials. The rotten, dirty, whining, creepy, crawling, little pommies. They ran out of Singapore and we got all their old planes to service. All a pommie can do is strategically retreat. The kind we got in Singapore anyway. The dregs of the country and conscripts at that. The heads all liked to live a rotten, degrading, immoral life, which was the social life in Singapore. Rotten to the core. Too much roughing it in Raffles Hotel, the best hotel in the place. All allegations to the rottenness we read about in the papers are true. Singapore, the cesspool of the East, the perfect place for the second-rate English. 488 Squadron was recognised as the best in Malaya. The services of Singapore were lousy, with dumb stupid pommies making the whole system top-heavy, and with commissioned ranking officers who had the intelligence of a child of two. Why can't we have men of ability running our forces, our mighty armed forces, instead of moneyed socialites who have intermarried for so long, so as to hang on to their money and social position, so that they are now no longer intelligent human beings, but just a pack of doddering imbeciles with one track minds – mainly leading to booze and women. The downfall of Singapore.

A Flight went again today [20 February] to the drome. I went to town and had a feed. Also visited town again at night with Wally [Murray] and we had a meal at a nightclub. The Dutch don't like the English but when they find out we are New Zealanders they cannot do enough for us. B Flight went to the drome today [21 February]. The RAF has taken over the drome and there is no food at all for us. It is all so different to the Dutch who gave us huge meals and tea or coffee. This only confirms my opinion expressed earlier of the incompetence and ruthless attitude of English officers towards their ordinary troops. I spoke to two British soldiers who had been all day out in the boiling hot sun with no shelter at all, manning a light machine-gun post, which was only a hole dug in the ground. They had had but no food or water the whole time. Contemptible treatment. We arrived back so late and had to scrounge for our food."[93]

Next day the unhappy Max Boyd's fortunes changed for the better when he and his companions from 488 Squadron received the news that they were to be evacuated forthwith, and by the evening they were aboard the MV *Deucalion* bound for Australia. Although many others were clearly and understandably unhappy with their lot, newly promoted Flt Lt Jerry Parker revealed:

"We were billeted in the Hotel des Nederlands and, there being rather more pilots than serviceable aircraft, we were on duty day-on and day-off, changing each noon. This allowed us time to go off swimming each day to the sailing club down at Tandjong Priok where the Dutch residents were friendly indeed. We found Java a most pleasant country although hot and humid near Batavia, thick with mosquitoes.

The Dutch had a curious ambivalent attitude towards us. They had been sheltered from the war, except those who had arrived from Holland after the fall of continental Europe to the Nazis, and they wished to pursue their profitable and comfortable life. They had not been particularly alarmed about any threat from Japan prior to December 1941 and viewed our arrival after the fall of Singapore and Sumatra with dislike. They reacted strongly to air raid warnings. That night there was an air raid alarm while we were just about to start our supper, and the hotel staff immediately turned out all the lights. We were starving and lit napkins and menus to serve as torches as we could hear no aircraft, but the management and other patrons were most upset and we were forced to eat in the dark."

Air Commodore Vincent was among the senior officers who shared the opulence of the almost surreal surroundings of the Hotel des Indies:

"Here I stayed for a fortnight in luxury, living a most extraordinary existence, in that during the mornings I was frequently shot-up and bombed out at one of the aerodromes – in fact one day I had one of the closest shaves of my life, to be followed immediately after – having brushed the dust of the slit trenches from my clothes – by a luxurious lunch with an orchestra playing in the company of exquisitely dressed ladies and their escorts. The hotel and its residents completely ignored the air-raid sirens – I wondered whether they had an arrangement with the Japanese not to bomb the town. It never was bombed; all the attacks were confined to the port at Tandjong Priok or the airfields."[94]

Even the NCOs had little to complain about, as testified by Sgt Terry Kelly, he and his companions were beginning to enjoy the break from the constant action and activity they had experienced at Palembang. They were able to enjoy meals in restaurants and to visit nightclubs in Batavia, and, for once, had decent accommodation. He wrote:

"We, the sergeant pilots, now fell properly on our feet having had made available to us a splendid private house, fully staffed and owned by a Naval reservist who had been called up and got his wife and family away to another house he owned near Bandoeng. We saw him just the once when he took us round, showed us where the drinks and cigars were kept, handed us the keys, wished us luck and told us that if we wanted to get away he was hoping at the end to escape in his yacht and there would be places for us. When the time came we forgot all about him – but I don't suppose that signified. If he hadn't already got away by then, he probably didn't anyway. We had issued to us a Bedford van, which we used to park on his front lawn and in which we used to drive to Tjililitan when on readiness.

Apart from drinking and singing squadron songs one was interested in women and if one was fortunate there were very beautiful girls to know in Java. I met such a one. She used to wear glittering sequined evening dresses with glittering sequined skullcaps to match. She was a truly lovely creature with wonderful dark eyes, a husky voice, a superb and memorable body and was sophisticated beyond the wildest dreams of a boy of twenty-one – even my CO used to ask my permission to dance with her. They were golden days those last two weeks in Batavia, to have the contrast of exciting days and luxurious nights."

Sgt Frank Hood added:

"Paid £95. Free and easy for a week. Swimming most days. Boozing at night at the Yen Pin and Black Cat. Posted to 605 at Tjililitan. As usual, no kites. Nothing doing. Raids every day. Previously could have left with 258 Squadron, but destination did not appeal. Wish I had now."

Another pilot bemused by this unreal situation was Sgt Snowy Newlands:

"Walking along the main street of Batavia I was rather irritated at the sight of a cheeky little two-seater Jap recce plane stooging around a few hundred feet up, enjoying the peaceful scene. This was too much for my blood pressure. With a fast draw and careful aim I let him have a few rounds. As there was no noticeable effect I did not claim a possible, but did feel much better! Nobody commented or looked my way. The locals just had no idea the war was heading fast towards Java!

This was shown again a few days later. After a hard afternoon on readiness at nearby Tjililitan, we had returned for evening relaxation as usual in Batavia. After dinner and a picture show, we were having a few drinks at the bar of the Yen Pin, a local cabaret, when two MPs approached me and suggested I handed over my loaded revolver for safe keeping. I was not at all happy with this request as I was due back on dawn patrol in a few hours' time – there were rumours of a pending invasion and it was essential to carry a loaded gun at all times. The boys picked me up from the local jail – complete with revolver – in time for a quick breakfast before I was due at the drome!

This may have been the morning, when hurtling along a narrow causeway between paddy fields, that the road ahead was obstructed by an ox cart that refused to move over in spite of vigorous horn-blasting. We were already running late. Flt Lt Julian put the jeep into four-wheel drive and shouldered the cart, putting the protesting driver and ox into a side ditch. He was lucky to escape my smoking gun!"

* * *

A dozen of the newly erected and tested Hurricanes[95] at Kemajoren had been presented to the Dutch, these being allocated to re-equip 2-VlG-IV at Kalidjati (Java) under the command of 1/Lt R.A.D. Anemaet; this unit still had a few CW-21Bs on strength. The pilots assigned to fly the Hurricanes were:

1/Lt R.A.D. Anemaet	Sgt N. Dejalle
2/Lt A.J. Marinus	Sgt F. Beerling
Ens L.A.M. van der Vossen	Sgt A. Kok
Ens A.W. Hamming	Sgt H.J. Mulder
Sgt Maj P. Boonstoppel	Sgt J.C. Jacobs
Sgt Maj F.J. de Wilde	Sgt R.M.H. Hermans

1/Lt Jan Bruinier[96], who had flown with the RAF in the UK in early 1941 and had, until now, been attached to 3-VlG-V where he had been assisting with the training of the Brewster pilots, was posted in to assist with conversion to the Hurricane. Plt Off John David, 243 Squadron's former Engineer Officer, was attached to the Dutch unit and recalled:

"No spares, ammunition or supplies of any kind were included and no training was offered. At the handing-over ceremony the Dutch colonel receiving the aircraft, not understanding the safety ring on the firing button, enlivened the proceedings by firing a long burst just over the heads of RAF VIPs in the parade! This set the scene for a remarkable do-it-yourself private air force, which survived for several weeks and really gave the Japs quite a bad time, although at great cost."[97]

The Dutch CO, Lt Anemaet, added:

"After a short briefing we flew the planes to Kalidjati, where we got further acquainted with them. They were not equipped with radio and did not have oxygen masks. On heights above 15,000 feet we just took the mouthpiece into our mouths."

Engineer Officer David continued:

"We moved to an improvised grass airfield [Kalidjati] north of Bandoeng in central Java and lived in grass huts in the local village. The squadron CO, Lieutenant Anemaet, was a saturnine individual of daemonic courage. He came from Dutch Guiana, in South

America, and was of very mixed blood. He was also a gentleman of the old school and spoke perfect English. His second-in-command was Lt Bruinier who now acted as training and conversion man. He, too, spoke perfect English and never hid from me his assessment of how hopeless the situation was; at the same time, he did a remarkable job of building the pilots' morale even higher. As their experience had been confined to the Curtiss-Wright CW-21, the Hurricane was an eye-opener for them and they revelled in its speed, rate of climb and, above all, its armament and toughness. The Dutch were brilliant pilots, having had years of training in the peacetime Netherlands East Indies, and the strength of the Hurricane allowed them to take ridiculous liberties with it. Some of our repairs were ridiculous, too, including using the village bicycle repairer (Chinese) to braise damage to the fuselage trusses and the ladies (Javanese) to provide patches for fabric repair.

We worked about 20 hours a day, cutting out dispersal pens in the rubber plantations around the airstrip, getting the locals to dig trenches, checking out the assembly work, stripping the aircraft down, teaching the Dutch pilots to handle liquid-cooled engines and constant-speed props and, above all – vital to morale, it seemed – painting the yellow triangle insignia of the Royal Netherlands Indies Army Air Corps on the aircraft. Knowing the familiar glycol problem, to which was now added a critical shortage of .303 ammunition (the Dutch only had .300 calibre) as well as batteries and equipment for the Hurricanes' TR9D radios, I made many visits to Bandoeng and Batavia to squeeze the official channels – with almost complete failure. I was then reduced to begging from my engineer colleagues dotted about Java and finally to finding out where the most recent crash had occurred. It was then a matter of trying to beat the RAF recovery team to the site. Thanks to our Dutch native airman driver, we usually got there first."[98]

From Tjililitan on 19 February, a patrol of Hurricanes from 242 Squadron had just departed, newly attached Sgt Don Isdale the last to leave, when four A6Ms dived on the airfield, the pilots apparently having not seen each other. The Japanese fighters made one pass before they flew away to seek better targets. Corporals Taff Simmons and Jim Home had just seen their charges safely away:

"The first bullets and shells zipped up off the grass about 20 feet ahead. Some had helmets on, something I never remember having had at any stage. My friend Taff was trying very hard to bury himself into the baked hard ground and imitate a Dutch mole, without too much success. We all held the same terror of strafing and each time did nothing to reduce that fear. That raid did not develop further, though it did show how simple it was for the Japs once our aircraft had left. I noticed Taff's elbow had started to bleed profusely, yet he was unaware that he had been nicked. Then, another fitter yelled out: 'Hey, look what you silly sods have been hiding behind.' We looked at the case contents and found to our horror that each one held six bottles of breathing oxygen, all fully charged!"[99]

Sgt Snowy Newlands was also caught off guard:

"I was walking along the edge of the strip when a Zero zoomed over the jungle, with guns blazing. This was a fairly difficult situation. I ran about 30 yards without touching the ground and dived under a high-octane petrol tanker, drew my gun and fired! I missed and luckily he missed the tanker!"

During this period, Sgt Bertie Lambert recalled:

"Wg Cdr Maguire discussed with other pilots his thoughts for mounting attacks by night by single Hurricanes on P1, in order to strafe enemy aircraft on the ground. The plan was not developed as it was considered that taking into account the distance and lack of any radio 'homing', there would be virtually no chance of any aircraft regaining base."

At dawn the next day (20 February), a number of Hurricanes of 242 Squadron were scrambled from Tjililitan and climbed to 20,000 feet, but one suffered a glycol leak, Sgt Snowy Newlands returning to base early. Despite a ground loop following a crosswind landing, his aircraft (Z5485) was not damaged. Meanwhile the rest of the unit had engaged Japanese aircraft over Bantam Bay; Flt Lt Julian claiming a Ki-27 shot down, while a second was claimed jointly by Plt Off Tom Watson (BE230) and Sgt Jimmy King. On return, Sgt David Kynman overshot on landing and his Hurricane was damaged – earning him seven days as Duty Pilot as a punishment. Later, six more Hurricanes were scrambled over Batavia harbour, where a lone floatplane was sighted at 9,000 feet by Sgts Ron Dovell and Tom Young, the latter firing at extreme range. He recalled:

> "Almost immediately smoke poured from it and he [the Japanese pilot] turned his aircraft towards me and passed so close I could plainly see the pilot. I felt he was anxious to take me with him."

Young was credited with its destruction.

Although there was a Japanese raid directed at Kalidjati airfield on 21 February, which was intercepted by Dutch Brewsters, the RAF Hurricanes at Tjililitan were not engaged, most of the day being spent dispersing the aircraft into 'hideouts' in the surrounding jungle. Around this time Flt Lt Jerry Parker and Plt Off Mike Fitzherbert were sent off to try and catch a reconnaissance aircraft. Parker recalled:

> "We had been warned of no other aircraft in the area but I saw half a dozen specks a very long way off in the distance against some white cloud. It took me about a quarter of an hour of cruising and climbing to get into the right position against the sun and then the pair of us hurtled down against them, only to find they were Dutch Buffaloes. I was very pleased they had not seen us but they joined up with us and we climbed back to 25,000 feet. Soon afterwards I saw the twin-engined recce aircraft a long way below us, almost vertically. I dived steeply down and throttled back in order not to overshoot and we were strung out in a line at the same height as the Jap preparatory to overtaking and firing in turn, when he suddenly increased speed enormously and we were unable to get within 600 yards of him. He just accelerated off to the north and we had no hope of catching him. He had a very fast aeroplane and the pilot had clearly worked out our tactic and flown slowly until we had lost our height and speed."

Their opponent was undoubtedly one of the speedy Ki-46s, probably from the 81st Independent Sentai operating out of P2.

Late in the afternoon, the Hurricane pilots at Tjililitan had a surprise when a squadron of US A-24 dive-bombers from the 91st Bomb Squadron (Light) arrived in their area from Malang airfield, as Plt Off Pettit recalled:

> "We were sent out to intercept these aircraft, dive-bombers, which, when we arrived, anxiously commenced circling. We had a chance to get a good look at them and observe their star markings and as they were obviously friendly and it was getting so near dusk we decided to return to the airfield while we could still see it. So we landed and the Americans followed us in but they had an untold amount of trouble. Being unfamiliar with the strip the first two just ran straight off the edge into the buffalo wallow.
>
> There were probably ten or more of them and I would think about half ended up in the buffalo wallow. They began landing short, doing all sorts of things that they shouldn't have – all because it was a tricky airfield and because, of course, of the poor light. They ended up with something between four and six kites left. I know they took off the next day and were never seen again."[100]

Another witness to the arrival of the dive-bombers was Sgt Perce Killick:

> "They came screaming into the strip, went right down to the far end and [most] tipped over on their noses. They were all piled up at the end of the runway. I don't remember a single aircraft that was flyable. I wouldn't have been surprised if they did it deliberately. They weren't much good to anybody."

The A-24s had been despatched from Malang airfield in Central Java to search for Japanese shipping reported in the Java Sea. Not all were write-offs and at least three were made serviceable within a couple of days or so.

During the morning of 22 February, 605 Squadron's A Flight undertook the unit's first patrol, Flt Lt Oakden (Z5690) leading the New Zealanders. They spotted six bombers and 16 escorting fighters north-west of Java – possibly a force that had just raided Semplak – but lost them in cloud. Sgt Jim MacIntosh, flying BE332, noted:

> "Sharp, Pettit, White, Kuhn and self, led by Oakden, mixed with six Jap bombers escorted by 16 Zero fighters in patchy cloud. Nothing decisive."

A second patrol was flown later by the same six pilots, when they reported seeing AA bursts over Batavia but failed to sight any raiders. This was probably the occasion when half a dozen patrolling 242 Squadron Hurricanes were warned of an enemy aircraft over Batavia. Plt Off Lockwood observed his colleagues dive away, in search of the intruder:

> "I also observed way below, at about 8,000 feet, a lone twin-engined aircraft which I took to be a Jap recce heading north towards the sea. I had difficulty in keeping it in sight as I went into a long dive to intercept it. My canopy fogged up and the Jap, which I had not positively identified, was travelling through thin cloud layers. I gained on the aircraft ahead and below, at which time my engine decided to run and stop intermittently. I tried carb heat with no effect. I followed this aircraft through thin cloud well out of the Java Sea, my engine still not functioning properly. Being aware of my predicament and still not in a firing position, I reversed course for Java and the airfield. As I descended to a still lower altitude around 4,000 to 5,000 feet, my engine decided to run smoothly, I landed back at the airfield."

Following another relatively uneventful day for the RAF Hurricanes at Tjililitan, 24 February was to prove to be far more busy, during which much occurred in the air. In the morning a big JAAF raid was launched over Western Java, 14 Ki-43s of the 59th and 13 of the 64th Sentai sweeping over the area. The Japanese fighters reported meeting seven Hurricanes and two 'P-43s', and claimed five of these shot down. Nine Hurricanes flown by pilots of 242 and 605 Squadrons had scrambled and climbed to 20,000 feet where they spotted two fighter aircraft over Batavia; one of these – assumed to have been Japanese – was shot down by Plt Off Red Campbell of 605 Squadron. In fact, it seems that he had mistaken the identity of the aircraft and attacked and probably shot down a CW-21B of 2-VIG-IV, killing Ensign D. Dekker. His was one of four CW-21Bs that had taken off from Kalidjati to patrol over Batavia; a second aircraft from this unit force-landed and was damaged beyond repair, while a third was reportedly shot down by Dutch AA, the pilot baling out safely. Sgt Jim MacIntosh wrote:

> "We six New Zealanders [A Flight/605 Squadron] were sent out to intercept the usual Jap reconnaissance aircraft that came over about 9 o'clock every morning. Flt Lt Julian was leading the six top Hurricanes [242 Squadron], we were in the middle, and there was another flight further down [B Flight/605 Squadron]. While we were practically over the docks, covering our level, two Dutch Curtiss interceptors appeared. With their radial engines and their orange triangle markings giving the appearance of a red blob, they looked very much like Zeros, and one was shot down by one of 242 Squadron's flight

[sic]. There was a terrible shindig in the Hotel des Indies that night, with the Dutch pilots firing their revolvers into the ceiling, and they were almost shooting one another. They were very distressed about the English [sic] chaps shooting down one of theirs."[101]

Dutch Hurricanes of 2-VIG-IV were also up over Kalidjati. Sgt Jan Jacobs crash-landed after his aircraft was hit while Ensign Hamming crashed into a bomb crater as he attempted to land, his aircraft subsequently being destroyed by strafing fighters. A few days earlier, Japanese fighters had strafed the airfield when the Hurricanes were landing, shooting up three or four but causing no injuries to the pilots concerned. 2-VlG-IV was now reduced to just six serviceable aircraft. Plt Off John, the Engineer Officer, had been caught up in the action:

"The Japanese mounted a major low-level bombing and strafing attack just after our morning patrol had come in. Six aircraft were refuelling, and all were destroyed when the petrol bowsers brewed up. About fifteen of my men were killed or seriously wounded, as were several Dutch pilots. My life was saved by Bruinier, who pushed me into a slit trench and fell on top of me just as another strafing wave came in."[102]

During the afternoon 13 Ki-43s of the 59th and 17 bombers of the 90th Sentai returned to Java, this time to attack Tjililitan. On this occasion ten intercepting Hurricanes were reported by the Japanese pilots and two claimed shot down, while one large and three small aircraft were claimed on the ground. Seven Hurricanes were on readiness at Tjililitan in the afternoon, four 242 Squadron machines and three from 605 Squadron's B Flight; a further six A Flight aircraft were on standby. Sgt Bertie Lambert of B Flight recalled:

"They were well dispersed and there was an agreed signal to be given if we were to scramble. After a most uncomfortable wait in a very high atmospheric temperature of early afternoon, we took off. Due possibly to the wide dispersal prior to take-off and individual take-offs, there was some little confusion in forming up which, I believe, was to be led by Sqn Ldr Wright. A short time after take-off, and whilst still at fairly low altitude, an aircraft came up on my port side, as if looking for a section leader, and then turned underneath my aircraft with the intention of coming into the No.2 position on my starboard side. Unfortunately, the manoeuvre resulted in the other aircraft coming up underneath my starboard mainplane and its propeller cut off the outer half of the wing.

It was immediately obvious that my aircraft would be uncontrollable and I prepared to bale out. Whilst unfastening my oxygen and R/T connections having unfastened the seat straps, the aircraft flipped onto its back and I was shot out – the altitude being low, 1,000-2,000 feet. I pulled the cord immediately and the chute opened at, I would think, 1,000 feet. As I looked down to see where I would land, I saw my aircraft, in an inverted spin, hit the ground. I landed in a paddy field close to a native village, fortunately on a dry path. I wandered into the village and after unsuccessful attempts to communicate, I managed to get a youth to understand that I wanted to get to Batavia. After collecting my chute, which two more youths insisted on carrying, we set off along a path through trees. I recall that on looking round after walking a short way we were leading a procession of what must have been a large percentage of the villagers. We eventually met a native policeman and a Dutch police officer, who had seen the crash and were looking for the pilots. After taking me to their mess, I was given a lift back to base. The other pilot [believed to have been Sgt Pip Healey], I learned on my return, had force-landed with the airscrew reduced to stubs as a result of the collision. He too, was uninjured."

The remaining pilots reported intercepting unescorted bombers as these were attacking Tjililitan, and three were believed to have been shot down, one each by Flt Lt Hutton and Sgt Jimmy King, the other shared by Flt Lt Julian, Plt Off Tom Watson (BE210) and

2/Lt Neil Anderson. Actual losses inflicted on the raiders are not known. It would seem that the escorting fighters of the 59th Sentai had become entangled with the Hurricanes of 605 Squadron's A Flight led by Flt Lt Oakden (Z5690), which had also been scrambled as the raiders, estimated at 40-plus, approached Kalidjati. At 14,000 feet, A Flight became involved with many fighters, and Sgt MacIntosh (flying BE332) reported:

"General mix up. Sharp and Kuhn claimed one each, self fired long burst into Jap fighter but could not follow it due to pressure from many others. With the heavy odds against us, we find it almost impossible to follow up any attack."

Sgt Eddie Kuhn noted:

"I was No.2 to Noel Sharp and we tackled a formation of three head-on. Noel took the middle one and I took the one on the right. I believe Noel got his but it was every man for himself and we were separated."

MacIntosh added, in greater detail:

"Six of us intercepted bombers going in on Kalidjati. We picked them up a long way away; of course a flight of 27 in a tight formation are easy to see. But then these Zeros came behind them, and turned towards us when they saw us coming. Oakden was leading and could see the bombers all right but failed to see the Zeros coming, doing a big sweep round towards us. It seemed a bit ridiculous to me but so often we went out on R/T silence and, in his excitement of trying to point out to Oakden where these Zeros were, Noel Sharp nearly came down on top of me. I was looking right up into the belly of his aeroplane and he almost bumped me as he was waggling his wings and pointing. I was annoyed at Noel and rather alarmed that Oakie couldn't see the Zeros coming round.

We all fired at Japanese aircraft but what the result was I couldn't confirm. I like to think I damaged one. It was a very full deflection shot as they came round and I turned in towards the one I fired on. Whether it went down or not I don't know, as it is very difficult to follow up when you are so hopelessly outnumbered with the others swarming round you like bees on a honey-pot. In practically all the encounters I had, I noticed the Japs appeared to have a set pattern of attacking you, then half rolling and diving down. They had typically gone down and Oakden, Pettit and Kuhn had gone down ostensibly to engage them. So I went down but I finished up in a dive that I couldn't handle. It was the first time I learned that a Hurricane was so uncontrollable in a vertical dive. I'd never experienced it before and I didn't allow it to happen again. Dive them yes, say 45 degrees, but not straight down. Quite often in Buffaloes we did – generally as an escape measure – but the Hurricane was different. I finished up in this speeding vertical dive and was just about ready to undo the straps, detach my oxygen gear and slide back the hood, when I managed to pull out."

MacIntosh continued:

"The Japanese were good pilots, very efficient and, oh! – were they aggressive? Mind you, they could be as they had such tremendous numbers, and we were hopelessly outnumbered. But I would say they were very much copybook pilots – they did everything according to the book and didn't appear to fly so much on their initiative like, I would say, the British. The Japs were very predictable in that they would dive, zoom, stall, turn, and come back down again. My opinion is that if you survived the first five combats, you were quite capable then of combating them. You knew what they were going to do next."

Following his success, Plt Off Sharp had been attacked and his aircraft damaged, forcing him to bale out; he came down in a canal where he was nearly drowned under the weight of his parachute, before two Javanese pulled him out. On recovery, he managed to reach Tjililitan after a trek lasting three days. Plt Off Pettit's aircraft also came under attack:

> "My aircraft was damaged by a Zero, which attacked me from the rear. It was superficially damaged and I was grateful for my armour plating. I was followed down by three fighters but managed to elude them and, having done this, the sky seemed empty with the exception of one aircraft which I chased for some miles, only to find it was another Hurricane."

That the situation in Java was now becoming very serious was clearly emphasised in a letter written by Air Commodore Vincent to Air Vice-Marshal Maltby on 25 February:

> "We are getting very short of fighter defence in this forward sector. This afternoon we are actually down to six serviceable aircraft between the two squadrons. All being well, we shall get back to a total of 10 or 11 tomorrow. We are not likely ever to better that figure owing to daily casualties, and the force is definitely wasting.
>
> The Dutch are, I am told, not using the Hurricanes that we gave them operationally, and they have also removed all their fighters from Tjisaoek so that our meagre force is all there is in the front line. Is it possible for us to get the Hurricanes back, or at least persuade the Dutch to bring them perhaps to Semplak or Tjisaoek to share out some of the very strenuous flying and fighting that our squadrons are doing? If we cannot get any more aircraft I think the time has come to shrink to one squadron, and I would suggest, if this is done, that 605 should go (though the airmen are quite among the very best as workers and 'fighters') and 242 should stay, as they have more pilots. They should take on the few pilots from 605 also.
>
> At the moment Tjisaoek is our reserve aerodrome. I am moving the R & R [Recover and Repair] party from Tjiloungair tomorrow morning, as it is so very much better. I went yesterday to Tjisaoek to ask the Dutch Commandant to carry out any R & R work necessary but found the Dutch had flown. We have no other reserve aerodrome except Tjisomang, which is near Bandoeng and I have not been able to visit that. My Dutch Liaison Officer whom I asked to get particulars, measurements, communications etc., has absconded (with a personal debt of 20 guilders to me) so I am not in the picture I am afraid there. I want to go into the question of an alternative Operations Room further back in case our present one is 'blitzed', perhaps in Buitenzorg or even Bandoeng. I would like to have your views on this, first, however, on the advisability of the labour, wiring, equipment etc. With regard to our few RDF sets do you think we could put one at Tjilatjap where it could at least give warnings – though probably not much more.
>
> I have now spoken to you on the telephone on the first part of this letter but I would like it on paper also."

The JNAF'S 22nd Air Flotilla launched its first major attack on Western Java during the morning, 27 Genzan Ku G3Ms being escorted to Batavia by 13 A6Ms and a C5M from the attached fighter unit. Two-dozen 59th Sentai Ki-43s and 32 light bombers from the JAAF's 3rd Flying Battalion also appeared over the area, in two waves, to attack Semplak. 242 and 605 Squadrons each scrambled Hurricanes from Tjililitan, six aircraft of 605 Squadron's B Flight engaging the Navy fighters.

With the advantage of early warning, Sqn Ldr Wright had briefed his pilots to climb to 33,000 feet. They had devised tactics to combat the manoeuvrability of the opposing Japanese fighters by climbing to maximum height, diving to attack and then continuing in the dive, either to head for home or up to regain altitude. On reaching altitude, the Hurricane pilots saw below them two separate circles of Japanese fighters, each about 15 strong, one above the other, so they peeled off to attack. Sgt Kelly reported:

"We three sergeants [himself, Lambert and Healey] did the planned attack, Campbell did not. What Dobbyn did, we did not see."

The tactics adopted made it impossible to make claims accurately, but Kelly was sure that he had damaged one fighter. Only four of the 605 Squadron Flight returned to Tjililitan, Dobbyn and Campbell both failing to appear. It transpired that each had disregarded the planned tactics and become engaged in dogfighting. Harry Dobbyn's wrecked Hurricane and body were later found in a swamp in the Krawang area, 30 miles north-east of Batavia. Campbell was more fortunate and later reported:

"We were scrambled to intercept a Japanese bombing force with fighter escort. We found them when we arrived over the area of Tandjong Priok. There were fifty-four in each of two groups. I think it was probably the largest raiding force they put in. The first lot of bombers were already there when we arrived and we had no chance to get up to them and do anything about them until they'd released their bombs. So we pulled off slightly from them and continued to climb to gain altitude sufficient to dive on the second lot and try to get them before they bombed – there wasn't much percentage in shooting down bombers that had dropped their load, if you can get the one still loaded.

We were just in position on the second lot and there were, as I recall, nine Zeros circling up from below, trying to intercept us. They were basically between us and the bombers. Having altitude advantage, our intention was to dive right through them on to the bombers, which would have worked quite well except that just as we were getting ready to peel off, I looked up over my shoulder and I saw six Jap fighters coming down from above, catching us cold, coming out of the sun. Ricky Wright, who was leading us, was already peeling in to make the attack, so the only thing to do was to ignore the fighters and dive in. So that's what we did. But we never did get properly into the bombers. The fighters below boxed Ricky in nicely – I saw him go after one and another one fix in right behind him and I thought the thing for me to do was to shoot that one off his tail.

From then on it's a bit hazy. What I do remember is that the Jap fighter I was going after started to take evasive action and I followed him, taking short bursts, and finally he turned upside down. I thought he was going to half roll away from me and dive so I rolled over with him but reflecting on it later I concluded I must have hit him and he was having problems. Anyway he rolled on to his back and stayed there with me on my back behind him. The Hurricane quit running when this happened, so soon I was falling away on my back below him, trying to raise my nose enough to have a shot at him. If he'd have stayed where he was, he'd have gone home happily, but instead he rolled back upright, did a bit of a dive and flew right through my line of fire and he came apart. His port wing came away almost at the wing root, and then there was an explosion and the wing went spinning off and he went spinning off the other way."

This was almost certainly NAP 1/C Suehara Ide, who failed to return and was later reported to have been killed. Campbell was then attacked by another fighter and his aircraft, BE332, received severe damage and went into a dive, half the wing breaking away. He continued:

"Instead of quickly rolling and getting the hell out of there, I rolled over quite gently and watched this thing go down. I was fascinated by it, wondering if the pilot was going to jump out – there was always a doubt in my mind whether they did or did not carry parachutes. Anyway, the next thing I knew there were noises, which sounded like a church bell or a large gong and were caused by cannon fire from another Zero who was firing at me from behind. Fortunately his shells weren't coming through. I kicked rudder and stick over and rolled but only slowly because of my low airspeed. I can remember hearing the church bells all the way through the roll and I thought I'd been hit, personally I mean, because when I was leaning over watching the other fighter I shot down, go down, I had my arm back tightly against the longeron on the left side and when the cannon shell hit the armour plating, the force transmitted through to the seat and it was like being hit on your elbow. The sharp bone suddenly had a tingly feeling and almost paralysis in it. So I thought I'd been hit.

Be that as it may, I suddenly found myself in an extremely fast dive, actually a spiral dive, because of the damage to my Hurricane. I could see huge holes in the wing and that most of it from the aileron sections outwards had come away. It wanted to spin in the dive but as I still had full control on the other aileron, I was able to pull it out and dive fairly straight by using a good deal of force. But when I began to pull out it started to roll on its back again with a sort of skewing action. I realised I was going to have to leave. This created a problem because during the action my canopy had been partially slid back (I had a habit of flying this way because of a tendency to claustrophobia if it was fully closed) and this Jap had apparently done enough damage to the tracks behind the seat to make the canopy inoperative. I couldn't close it and I couldn't open it and when I tried to jettison the escape panel, that wouldn't come away because of being held in place by the track. And of course the canopy itself couldn't be jettisoned unless it was fully closed. So I found myself trapped inside.

At that point the ground was coming up fairly quickly and I can remember looking down at the ground and saying, 'Gee, I'm going to hit that so damn fast that it's not going to hurt. It's all going to be over and that's it.' Anyway I suddenly said, 'No, gee, this is me!' and I jumped up on to the seat, pulled the stick back, getting the aircraft out of the dive and skewing and then I put one foot on the stick, one on the seat, and my back against the canopy and the next thing I knew I was out. As soon as I sprung the canopy with my back to get the wind under it, it literally tore it open because of the damage to the track. I went by the tailplane – fortunately I'd tucked my knees up as I came out – and I went over the horizontal tailplane and right by the rudder, missing it by inches and found myself out of the aircraft."

Campbell delayed opening his parachute too early for fear of being fired on by Japanese fighters:

"So I waited until the ground was closer and then I pulled the ripcord. I was jerked up abruptly and bruised like hell because I wasn't wearing my own parachute, which had got wet jumping into that ditch at Palembang, and the one I'd borrowed didn't fit. Anyway here I was, sitting out with this parachute and two impressions came, one of which was that I felt like I was going back up again. I suddenly had this feeling, 'My gosh, I'm being sucked by some vast up-draught back to the combat area!' And I looked up at the parachute and here was this bloody great dark place on it and I thought, 'Gee this is just impossible.' But all it was, of course, was the pilot parachute now lying on top of the parachute. And the other thing was that looking down I could see my gun falling away from me – when the parachute harness tightened apparently it just snitched the holster right off my belt and sent it hurtling down with a knife I used to carry which I'd picked up in the Middle East."

He then saw a fighter approaching from above:

"I thought here's that Jap going to come down and strafe me. Then I realised it was one of ours – it was a Hurricane – and his path actually brought him very close to me. I was frightened again because I thought he was going to ram me then and he came in above me, probably four or five hundred feet, and passed over the canopy and went out this side into a stall turn, turned and came back and went below me and when he went below me

I could look right down into the cockpit and I could see the pilot hunched over inside. I watched the aircraft go down and crash and later realised it was Harry Dobbyn. I think he must have been killed in the cockpit because the aircraft was basically coming down somewhat out of control. He must have had it trimmed well or else he was fighting with it. I don't know. I have the impression he was probably dead in the cockpit and that's why the aircraft came down in the manner it did.

Next thing was, I thought, well, I'd better get ready for landing. I started doing that and then I thought I was going to go into a river so I tried to work myself back into the swing of the parachute harness to sit in it so as to be able to release the quick-release button so that when I hit the water I could get clear of the 'chute. Then I saw a rice paddy field – just mud, no rice in it, just a big muddy patch, and I grabbed the shrouds and side-slipped to bring myself over there. The ground seemed quite far away at the point I was doing the slipping, but the next thing I realised was that it was coming up very rapidly and I was still side-slipping so I let go of the shroud and the parachute righted itself and the next thing I knew, I'd hit going somewhat backwards and one leg stuck in the mud which put my knee under me and twisted it. The other thing was that I'd strained my back and my neck coming out with the canopy and I still thought I had been wounded and started to try feeling my back, because I was convinced because my arm tingled that I had taken a hit in the spine area, but the only blood I could find was a slight scratch on my right shoulder and I had some shrapnel in my lower area which you could actually pick out with your fingers."

Searching natives found him in the jungle and eventually he was taken to a Dutch officer in a river patrol craft. This same officer had found Dobbyn's remains. Campbell was returned to Tjililitan, arriving at 0300 on the following day.

"I arrived back at the barracks where we were staying at just about dawn. Ting Macnamara was my room mate. He was asleep and when I looked I could see that all my gear was gone. It was quite natural. The fourth pilot, I don't know who it was, had got back and he'd seen my aircraft go down and hadn't actually seen me bale out so he'd presumed that I was dead. So they'd already started to divvy up my gear. I always remember I crawled on the end of the bed, lifted Ting's mosquito net and said: 'I'm the ghost of Red Campbell. You'd better give me my gear back you bastard!'"

The A6M pilots reported meeting eight Spitfires (sic) and claimed four shot down: apart from the loss of NAP 1/C Ide, the reconnaissance C5M also failed to return – probably shot down by Sgt Sandy Allen of 242 Squadron (flying BE202/R), who recalled of his fifth victory:

"I do not remember the detail but I was separated from the section and I was caught by some Zeros. I was claiming damage only to one but Sqn Ldr Wright was in the area, and he confirmed the destruction because the plane nearly hit him as it went down."

The Japanese also claimed two small aircraft destroyed on the ground at Semplak where, in fact, one Hudson under repair was further damaged, but no less than 11 of the Genzan G3Ms were hit by AA fire. The 59th, 1st and 11th Sentai pilots also reported meeting eight interceptors and claimed four shot down, while the JAAF bomber crews claimed the destruction of seven aircraft on the ground; despite the damage inflicted, all the bombers returned safely.

Sgt Jim MacIntosh of 605 Squadron's A Flight flew his new Hurricane (Z5616[103]) over to the Dutch base at Semplak, where it was to have an immediate overhaul. While there, he gained permission to fly one of 2-VlG-V's Brewsters, which had a more powerful engine than the RAF's Buffalo, and undertook two two-hour sorties in B-395. The first was an aerodrome defence patrol, the second as top cover to one of the Dutch unit's missions, leading him to comment in his logbook: "Lone top cover. These Dutch kites are great. Twin-row Cyclones."

With the disbandment of 232, 258 and 488 Squadrons, the personnel no longer required to be shipped out of the fighting zone. Those 488 Squadron pilots[104] not attached to 605 Squadron had departed Tjilatjap (the largest port on the south coast) aboard the MV *Deucalion* for Fremantle (Australia) on the 23rd, leaving in a violent tropical storm. Those 258 Squadron pilots[105] not posted to 605 Squadron, the wounded pilots of 232 Squadron (Plt Off John McKechnie, Sgts Dick Parr and Henry Nicholls[106]) and three or four of the 266 Wing pilots including Sgts Ewen Worts[107] and possibly Sgts Jenson and Lawrence, in addition to surplus groundcrew, were evacuated from Tjilatjap on the night of 26/27 February on the *Kota Gede*. Also aboard this vessel were surplus aircrew and ground personnel from all bomber squadrons, together with those from miscellaneous units. Flt Lt Denny Sharp had arrived in Batavia in time to be evacuated:

> "When we got to Batavia I joined up with the pilots of 258 Squadron. We had no aircraft at all and were billeted out. I would say we were about ten days in Batavia frequenting nightclubs, having big meals at hotels, and sightseeing – generally having a good time. We were getting the odd bomb but it was the waterfront that was being attacked – down where the shipping was. A senior officer, a wing commander, was trying to organise the building of a fighter strip, and singled out two of us for the job. It was so obvious that the damn place was going to cave in that I suggested the main task was to get as many able-bodied people out, beyond the reach of the enemy, so we could operate again. I think he took my advice and a couple of days later arranged for us to board a train at the station at Batavia. And we trained all the way to Tjilatjap, a port on the south-west coast and got aboard a boat called the *Kota Gede*. At dusk on the night that we arrived there, two boats set sail. I remember vividly a tramp steamer went before us, and we followed about a mile astern. As we left the entrance to the harbour, there was a great big monsoonal storm out at sea, and the both of us sailed straight into it. After about three-quarters of an hour we came out of the storm, into the clear air, and the other boat was not in sight. We assumed that it probably went to Australia. We kept on going east and ended up about six days later in Colombo. We were very lucky and got all the way through without incident."

To strengthen the defences in Eastern Java, the Dutch now ordered most of their remaining fighters to move there; therefore the six Hurricanes of 2-VlG-IV led by Lt Anemaet and six Brewsters from Andir flew to the secret Blimbing airfield, Ngoro (south-west of Sourabaya) during the afternoon, from where US P-40s of the 17th Pursuit Squadron were operating. RAF Engineer Officer Plt Off John David, attached to 2-VlG-IV, recalled:

> "Anemaet was ordered to move to Surabaya in east Java, which had been flattened and was expected to be invaded. It was obviously to be a last stand and he absolutely refused to take me with him, saying that they would probably manage only one take-off and that his own groundcrew of about ten men could look after that. We were returned to Bandoeng, already in chaos; some of us were ordered to evacuate and some to stay. I was lucky."[108]

The Japanese air units at Palembang returned to the attack during 27 February, raiding Tandjong Priok during the morning and Buitenzorg in the afternoon, where three Dutch aircraft were destroyed on the ground. Hurricanes from 242 and 605 Squadrons were scrambled to intercept the morning raid, as Plt Off Bill Lockwood recalled:

> "I was flying weaving positions in a V formation, climbing continually into the sun. We climbed to a height of approximately 25,000 feet at which time I lost formation in the sun. I levelled out and was puzzled as to where they had gone without trace. As I looked

around, above and below for my buddies, I noticed a nice, neat formation of Zeros flying about 2,000 to 3,000 feet below to port and in the opposite direction. As I sighted them, they also spotted me and went into a defensive circle to the left. I was also making a left circle above them and was in a quandary as to how to make an attack. The Zeros were standing on their tails momentarily to fire at me, dropping off as they stalled. I maintained height above them and decided to reverse my circle and drop down for a head-on attack as they came around in the opposite direction. This did not prove very effective as I only had time to meet one or two without scoring many hits or being hit. I became surrounded and decided to use the Hurricane's advantage of superior diving speed and returned to base."

The other Hurricanes had made contact with a number of fighters and Flt Lt Hutton possibly claimed one shot down, while Sgt Lambert recalled:

"One which I attacked must surely have been damaged but there was no indication of this. The engagement quickly broke up and we returned to base individually."

One of the replacement pilots, Sgt John Vibert, also encountered the Japanese fighters:

"I had only one encounter with the Japs and that was when I became separated from my companion on a patrol in pairs. I emerged from the side of a cloud to be attacked by two Zeros whose path I was flying across but managed to evade them by hiding in another cloud before they could hit me, although it must have been close as I could see the wisps of tracer above my cockpit cover. I bet the one firing at me thought he was hitting me – it was that close!"

Four of 242 Squadron's aircraft were off again after the Buitenzorg raid, led by Flt Lt Parker. As they commenced the climb, two of the Hurricanes broke away and returned to Tjililitan. With only Sgt Gordie Dunn for company, Parker continued up to about 20,000 feet. Below them at about 17,000 feet they caught sight of a group of distant aircraft against the pale blue of the horizon. Manoeuvring up sun, they counted between 12 and 15 fighters, straggling along and apparently not having seen the two Hurricanes. As they dived onto the group, three of the Japanese aircraft started to dive and turn to port, whilst the others pulled round to starboard and up in a slow climbing turn. Parker kept after the first three and brought his sights to bear on the leader. He later wrote:

"I only needed a little deflection at our angle of approach and I'd have him. To my surprise when I pressed the tit I heard only a couple of rounds from one of my guns and the rest were silent. I didn't know what had stopped them and nearly broke my thumb pressing on the button, but there were no results in the half-dozen seconds it took to overhaul the Zero. I dived within a few feet of him and saw his helmeted head peering coolly around as I passed his tail and then went into a long dive away. That was a very well-disciplined pilot to have remained as a target for so long in order that his friends could come round and take us, particularly when they would anyway have been too late to save him if my guns had fired!"

Sgt Dunn, following his leader in the dive, hesitated before firing, having observed Parker not firing, fearing that he may have misidentified the Japanese fighters for Dutch Brewsters:

"I continued my attack as a practice and I was close enough to see the 'Flaming Arsehole', as we called the Nip roundel; I knocked chucks off one Zero and continued to dive on by."

Parker continued:

"I taxied the Hurricane straight down into the *ulu* in a furious rage, instead of leaving it by the Flight Office to be refuelled and re-armed, and stamped back up to the dispersal hut to sound off about the inefficiency of the armourers. To my surprise, Air Commodore Vincent was there with Sqn Ldr Brooker, and he tore me off a hell of a strip for not having checked my guns and everything about the Hurricane before I'd taken off. Brooker looked very sympathetic and the other pilots were almost mutinous because we all relied on our groundcrews, but we all stood and listened to his tirade. Evidentally he must have heard that we were not too confident of the Hurricanes because he swore they were a match for the Zeros, and to prove it he took one up and threw it about the sky. We were not impressed and had no enthusiasm ourselves for aerobatics, even if the raid was over, and then we had another talk from him."

As if to emphasise the point, Vincent then calmly stated that he was going on readiness and took his place in one of 605 Squadron's aircraft. He declared he would fly No.2 to the section leader Sgt Bertie Lambert. As it happened there was no scramble during the period of the standby, so he did not actually fly, but he obviously had every intention of doing so. Indeed, he had frequently done so during the Battle of Britain – despite his age and seniority – when he had been credited with at least two German aircraft shot down, to add to his Great War victories. Plt Off Red Campbell recalled an earlier incident concerning the Air Commodore:

"I remembered having one chance meeting with Vincent in which I was insolent toward him. He had said something about a Hurricane flying straight and level with a Zero after him and called it a 'damn poor show, to run away,' and that irritated me. I told him: 'You know nothing about fighting Zeros! That Hurricane pilot was me!' And I stormed out."[109]

As the month drew to its end, to the north of Java the Japanese Western Invasion Force was rapidly approaching, a second mighty invasion force heading for Eastern Java in a pincer movement, thus effectively sealing the fate of not only the island but also its British, Dutch and American defenders. Air Vice-Marshal Maltby now ordered Air Commodore Vincent to hand over command of the fighters to Wg Cdr Maguire – who had arrived only the previous day by sea from Palembang with other evacuated RAF personnel – and depart at once with his seven HQ staff for Tjilatjap. Before leaving, Vincent went to see his "gallant fighter boys" to say goodbye to them and write letters to those he was unable to visit. He and Maguire arrived at Tjililitan early in the morning of 28 February, and were introduced to some of the pilots. Vincent recorded:

"I was seemingly deserting them at their very worst hours, and exhorting them to fight to the last moment. Feeling simply dreadful, I left them to it. One has to be practical, of course, and say there was no virtue in remaining to become a prisoner if one could manage to get away and 'live' to fight another day and fortunately I was able to do just this."[110]

Soon after Vincent's arrival at the airfield five Hurricanes were scrambled; they were to provide top cover, in heavy cloud, for the cruisers HMAS *Perth* and the USS *Houston* retiring from the Java Sea Battle[111]. Several aircraft were seen to the north, but they did not approach immediately and were not engaged; however, one C5M of the 22nd Air Flotilla did succeed in evading the fighters and carried out a reconnaissance of Tandjong Priok, the crew observing two flying boats and 14 merchant ships in the harbour. Having seen the Hurricanes off, Vincent and his party stood watching AA bursting over the harbour, when low over the airfield roared a gaggle of Japanese fighters. Everyone headed for the conveniently placed slit trenches. Vincent continued:

"I shouted to those around to take cover and stopped to pick up my helmet at my feet; because of this brief delay I was the last to reach the slit trenches about ten yards away.

The leading Jap saw us running and as I was diving for a trench I saw his guns firing. I landed full length on top of a sergeant as an exploding bullet hit the side of the trench, about a foot above. The pilot, evidently realising that he was attacking across these small trenches, did a circuit and came in again to fire along the length of them. Again three or four strikes came about a foot below the rim at the end of the trench, but we were almost underground by then and were only splattered with earth. We were then able to watch the rest of the attack and were glad that the Hurricanes were away. One Hurricane did return before the Zeros left and he chased them out of the area. When he came back he was fired on, and fortunately missed, by our own AA guns."[112]

A second Hurricane, obviously damaged, returned to the airfield with a Japanese fighter sitting on its tail, steadily firing, while the AA guns tried to force it away. The Hurricane eventually crash-landed without injury to the pilot; this was possibly Sgt Pip Healey. During this attack one Bofors gunner was killed, while Flt Lt Joe Hutton of 605 Squadron was wounded in one leg by bomb splinters and 2/Lt Neil Dummett[113] suffered temporary loss of vision caused by a bomb blast and, as a consequence, his immediate evacuation was arranged. Flt Lt Mike Cooper-Slipper was also quite badly wounded at this time:

"In Batavia I got too near a falling bomb, and I woke up in a Chinese river boat which had been converted to a hospital ship. The Japanese gave us safe conduct and we sailed to Colombo."[114]

Some were enjoying the last few free days of their young lives, including Jerry Parker and his close friend Mike Fitzherbert:

"Mike and I were swimming at Priok when the air raid alarm went and a couple of twin-engined aircraft bombed the shipping in the port nearby. Almost naked in our swimming trunks, we felt amazingly defenceless and dashed to the slit trench next to an anti-aircraft gun installed nearby, only to find it full of the gun crew led by their Javanese NCO. There was no room for more with all those chaps in the slit trench, so we put the best face on it by roaring our heads off with laughter and went to stand behind some palm trees until the raid finished very shortly thereafter – just a few minutes before B Flight led by Julian, appeared on the scene."

By noon *Perth*, *Houston* and the surviving destroyer escort were approaching Tandjong Priok when a single-engined Japanese floatplane was seen attacking a small Dutch patrol boat, whilst above droned two 242 Squadron Hurricanes whose pilots were obviously unaware of what was happening below. The floatplane departed but then another – or perhaps the same one – approached the cruisers from seaward just as *Houston*'s sole surviving scout plane was due from Sourabaya. As soon as the misidentification was realised, shots were exchanged, but the Japanese floatplane apparently escaped unscathed. However, fire from the cruiser's guns almost accounted for the Hurricane patrol, one of which was flown by Sgt Sandy Allen, who recalled:

"We were nearly shot down when on convoy patrol – this was the usual protection job ending as ever with a mistaken identity: she [*Houston*] opened fire on us and the shooting was the most accurate naval gunnery we had met to that date."

605 Squadron's A Flight also provided air cover for the cruisers, Sgt Jim MacIntosh (Z5616) for one flying a number of sorties:

"There was another quite important task we six New Zealanders had – escorting the *Perth* and the *Houston*. The Hurricane didn't have a long endurance and we were limited as to how long we could stay, but we would come back, refuel and then go out again. I can't

> remember how many flights we did that day, but we went out and sat over these two cruisers, which were steaming at full speed for Batavia, for about an hour. They refuelled in Batavia harbour, set out that night and ran into the Japanese battle fleet, right in the entrance of Sunda Straits and were both sunk. We had their crews, those who survived, with us, as PoWs, in Java."[115]

By noon the full extent of the Japanese Western Invasion Force had been realised by the Allies. One body of 11 ships, which were carrying the 230th Regiment, had left the main convoy and were heading for Eretanwetan, just to the north of Kalidjati, while the rest were heading in towards the peninsula between Merak and Bantam Bay, on the far north-western tip of Java. This force would soon divide to land at each of these locations simultaneously. The Eretanwetan force had been sighted while still 50 miles out, escorted by the cruiser *Sendai* and three destroyers, and received the initial weight of the Allied reaction – which was pitifully weak. Only two Hudsons were still serviceable and these joined with the remaining six combat-worthy Blenheims to carry out attacks on the ships. The Dutch could muster 11 serviceable Glenn Martins, seven of which were at Kalidjati, three at Tjisaoek and one at Andir.

The Blenheims took off first, at 1830, some crew then flying three sorties during the course of the evening and night. By the time the attacks ceased, with the arrival of dawn, 26 Blenheim and six Hudson sorties had been flown; by then the crews had almost reached complete exhaustion. The weather had been bad and results difficult to assess, although it was believed that at least two ships had been sunk and others damaged. The Kalidjati-based Glenn Martins had flown a further 17 sorties, their crews claiming hits on a cruiser and a destroyer but they actually achieved only near misses. A Blenheim and one of the two Hudsons were lost, both force-landing. All the Glenn Martins returned safely. In Bantam Bay the landings had gone ahead virtually unopposed on the ground, although much damage had been caused to the invasion force by the naval and air actions. At least two transports and a minesweeper had been sunk, and the invasion force's HQ vessel severely damaged.

CHAPTER VI

THE FINAL DAYS AT JAVA

March 1942

"Now we shut down. Long live our Queen! Goodbye till better times."
The last words from the Netherlands News Agency in Bandoeng

The initial landings on the beaches of north-western Java began soon after midnight on the first day of the month (1 March). Dawn found the Allied air units under orders to counter-attack. The landings at Eretanwetan were the first to be reported and by 0200 the RAF's Hurricanes had been ordered to take off from Tjililitan at first light, while the Dutch Brewsters at Andir were also made ready.

At 0530 therefore, nine Brewsters set out for Eretanwetan. They were joined by three Glenn Martins, also from Andir. At about the same time, Flt Lt Julian led off a section of three Hurricanes of B Flight of 242 Squadron from Tjililitan, to ascertain the exact position of the landings; they were followed by nine more led by Sqn Ldr Brooker. The invasion fleet, when found, was estimated to comprise 11 transports in line astern, 50 yards apart and 200 yards from the shore, flanked by two destroyers with a cruiser standing a mile out to sea. The Hurricanes, which were met by intense AA and rifle fire from the transports and the shore, made their first attack on the *atap* huts along the shoreline in which Japanese soldiers were sheltering: these huts were left in flames. As they turned their attention to the beach itself, which was covered with men and supplies, and the barges just off shore, a voice was heard over the R/T: "Don't strafe those barges."

Plt Off Lockwood remembered:

"... heads turning under canopies and looking at each other in amazement. Undoubtedly someone on the ground on our frequency. We dived into attack through considerable ack-ack. I made one pass each way at water level on a barge midway between the ships and shore, which made it a very unhealthy place to stooge around. The Japs suspended landing ops temporarily. We regained formation and returned to base – no aircraft shot down. On landing I noticed a spent shell hanging beneath my starboard wing."

Sgt Sandy Allen (BE239) recollected that the main landing took place "in a lovely bay 10-15 miles east of Batavia", and added:

"The set-up when we were sent out was a line of ships – nine, I think – with two destroyers. All the ships had guns and the guns were already ashore. We attacked the barges running between the ships and shore and I think more damage was done by the gunfire from the ships and the shore than by us! As we attacked the barges we were followed by much heavier calibre fire from both sides and some barges received direct hits from shells."

One Hurricane failed to return to Tjililitan, Sgt Gordie Dunn having carried out an emergency landing at Batavia:

"My airspeed indicator packed up and I went into a high speed stall over a ring of Jap soldiers on a tarred road, and I did not think I was going to come out of it. When I looked up I could see palm trees but in that instant thought: 'What's the bloody point of killing myself just to kill a few bloody arseholes?', and somehow managed to regain control. Having survived that, I headed for Batavia where there was a long concrete runway.

Unable to judge my airspeed, I just floated over the runway until I was finally able to touch down but overshot and ground-looped into a pile of crushed stone. I switched off before I struck and saved the prop when my starboard wing and wheel crushed onto the stone and supported the kite. Having safely climbed out I phoned the CO at Tjililitan, who was not amused until I told him that I had managed to save the prop. He then changed his tone and said: 'Good boy! I'll send a truck over to pick you up.' Some time later a truck turned up with three groundcrew guys in it, and together we removed the prop, put it in the back of the truck and drove back to Tjililitan."

During this attack the Dutch bomber crews claimed one transport sunk but one Glenn Martin was lost, probably hit by AA fire from the ships. On returning to Andir, a Brewster belly-landed, the pilot unable to lower his undercarriage. The strafe by the Hurricanes was believed to have set fire to six landing craft and three motor vehicles.

242 Squadron carried out two more attacks during the course of the morning, when nearly all Hurricanes suffered damage, mainly from shell splinters, although none were lost. However, Sgt Tom Young's aircraft was hit in the wing when strafing a road convoy and on attempting to land, his engine cut and he belly-landed in a swamp. On wading to dry land he was approached by a Dutch officer who offered him a glass of whisky before driving him back to the airfield. Sandy Allen was also involved in the strafing:

"We went out again and by then the troops were on the move along a long straight road between paddy fields; there was no protection anywhere and I would hate to estimate the casualties involved. I cannot remember who, but one of the lads in this raid left his parachute behind and sat on a tin helmet as the best means of protection when all the trouble was coming up from below."

Sgt Snowy Newlands also made two strafing attacks, flying BE202/R on both occasions:

"They were lined up off the beach. There would have been about 40 – most of them about the same size. There might have been about ten to twelve transports, with troops, and six or eight warships lined up outside them. They were lined up, anchor distance, in parallel lines, about a mile off the beach, and their barges were coming into shore. We zoomed down and first of all saw hundreds of troops riding bicycles, all on this one road, with this swamp either side. They were jumping from their bicycles into the swamp to avoid our bullets. We took turns, the leader going in first, and I was probably the fourth. The causeway was packed for about a mile. It was just murder.

We were pretty close to the warships and the transports. They were just to our left – on the seaward side. I heard some voice over the telephone stating the ack-ack was too heavy and to return to base, and I thought to hell with that. Most of our aircraft turned round and went back to Tjililitan, but I still had some ammo left so I zoomed on a bit further to where I could see barges. They were tethered alongside this little wharf in the corner of a bay, with dense jungle from the back country extending almost to the water's edge. I came in at high speed, zig-zagging, and sure enough the whole jungle was alive with Nips and up came the bullets. I noticed a barge coming in with troops so, as soon as I shot up the jungle and part of the wharf, I made for it across the bay and strafed it. It was all pretty quick. They were firing at me from the ships, and their ack-ack was bursting on the water and some of it went into the barge.

Out of the corner of my eye I observed another Hurricane. He'd got himself in between the warships and the transports and he was right down at sea level, only a few feet above the water. If anyone fired at him they would be firing at each other. I am sure he was from our squadron but I never found out who it was. I also asked a few people about the message about ack-ack fire being too heavy and to return, but they never heard

> it. I was always aggrieved that I never shot any planes down, but that was a most spectacular sortie, and I never got a scratch on the plane. We really got our money's worth that day. If only we had some bombs the war could almost have been turned at this stage, but that was not to be!"

Aircraft from 605 Squadron also carried out attacks during the early morning and, on the first of these, Plt Off Noel Sharp's aircraft was hit by ground fire. Sgt Jim MacIntosh noted:

> "Dawn take-off. Strafing Jap landings at Cheribon, about 90 miles east of Batavia. Sharp shot down and seen to belly-land in paddy field about three miles inland from landing."

He later expanded:

> "We weren't supposed to be on that morning. Sqn Ldr Wright hauled us out of bed about 4 o'clock in the morning to take over this duty. Why he didn't use the other flight I don't know. We were ordered to find and then strafe the landing at Cheribon. The first take-off was at daybreak and the landing wasn't very hard to spot because there were two large troopships, about three miles offshore, disembarking landing barges, carrying about 130 soldiers in each. There were more ships further out – cruisers and destroyers – that put up a terrific ack-ack barrage, although by flying tight down on the beach we managed to keep under most of it. I only went out once – after the first five had taken off I had a bit of trouble with my pneumatics – my pneumatic bottles weren't charging correctly. By the time the groundcrew had taken the panel off and adjusted the charging regulator the others were well cut in front and I took off and went in after them. I was opening fire when an ack-ack shell burst right under me and damaged the bottom of my aircraft. My aircraft [Z5616] also received a hit in the air bottle, which left me without guns and landing brakes. It was taken away and hidden in the rubber trees and we worked on it there to try and get it back serviceable again.
>
> Noel Sharp was shot down during our first operation. Snow White saw Noel turn in from the beach, instead of going in to do a strafe. He was hit, like me, right at the beginning of the approach to the strafing run. Snow saw Noel turn in with smoke coming from his aircraft and he turned off and followed him. They were right down on the beach by this time. He circled and saw Noel do his forced-landing in the paddy field, watched him get out, take the fuel cap off and fire his Very pistol into the fuel tank – and the last he saw of him was treading away across the rice field towards scattered bush and jungle."[116]

Six floatplanes from the floatplane tender *Kamikawa Maru* had flown to Bantam Bay in the morning, two of the F1Ms then flying on to the Eretanwetan area, where they were joined by two more from *Sanyo Maru*. During the early afternoon five Hurricanes of 605 Squadron were again led off by Sqn Ldr Wright. As they approached the area they came across a lone floatplane, which all attacked. It proved very manoeuvrable and, after releasing some bombs, flew in a tight circle and opened fire on Sgt Terry Kelly, who hurriedly broke away. It then attacked a second Hurricane. Again all tried to hit it, attacking from various directions without success and they then held off to give Sqn Ldr Wright a chance to deal with it alone. Although he used all his remaining ammunition, he was unable to shoot down the gallant Japanese pilot, and eventually broke away, returning to Tjililitan with three of his flight. Their opponent had been a *Kamikawa Maru* F1M flown by Wt Off Yatomaru, who landed to report that he had shot down three of his five opponents! Meanwhile, Kelly still had sufficient ammunition left to attack the invasion forces and set off alone to do so. He observed many boats ferrying troops ashore and then saw two floatplanes in the bay, which he attacked although under fire from AA positions, setting one on fire before returning to Tjililitan.

Having re-armed and refuelled, the Hurricanes set out again including one flown by Sgt Kelly, who reflected on his second sortie:

> "I was having my own private little war as a lone pilot attacking the Japanese force and, as I was the sole object on which they could carry out target practice, I was getting the full attention of the escorting warships and to improve my chances doing my strafing from little more than treetop height. It was on one of my sorties that I saw my first Japanese close to. He was wearing a green shirt and yellow shorts and crouching in the surf – and as it has to be far easier for a man with twelve machine guns firing simultaneously to kill another lying on an unprotected beach than for a few warships, however enthusiastically they blaze away, to hit a small aircraft flying low at about three hundred miles an hour it was reasonable for this fellow to be even more frightened than I was and frightened he certainly was."

A little later another section from 605 Squadron set out, led by Flt Lt Jack Oakden (Z5602). They completed a quick sweep around the beach area and came under fire from vessels lying offshore. The beach appeared to be clear of troops, so they headed inland and came across a troop convoy. Plt Off Bunt Pettit recalled:

> "We were flying very low during this operation and in fact probably would have done better if we had used a bit more height and attacked more steeply. The Japanese were remarkably steady under fire and continued to use their rifles against the low-flying aircraft, on many occasions not even attempting to take cover. The accuracy of their fire was evidenced by a few holes in my Hurricane. I could not help admiring these troops, as I suspect I should have been looking for cover had I been shot at by eight Browning machine guns in a low-flying aircraft. It was during this time that a seaplane, which was probably a reconnaissance aircraft with an observer acting as a rear gunner, and fitted with machine guns firing forward, attacked. Fortunately Eddie Kuhn removed it before I even saw its approach."

Kuhn attacked the floatplane and shot it down for his fifth victory:

> "I saw a floatplane down below barely a mile or two from the bay we had just finished strafing, so I did a u-turn and got onto his tail. It had come off a boat and was a slow observation type. I fired one burst at it from very close range and the aircraft ploughed into bush and trees. There was another in the distance but it was too far away so I rejoined the others."

Meanwhile, disaster struck the RAF's bomber base at Kalidjati. Although Eretanwetan was only some 30 miles from Kalidjati, orders for the surviving Blenheims and Hudsons to be evacuated had not been given until 1000, when it was confirmed that fighting was underway in nearby Soebang, even though the Glenn Martins had already departed. By then it was too late. The airfield was soon overrun, with many RAF casualties, while only a few aircraft managed to get away. Of the 350 British troops defending the airfield, about one third were killed or captured, as were all 30 of the RAF defence personnel and the Station CO, Grp Capt George Whistondale.[117]

At midday, A Flight pilots of 242 Squadron arrived at Tjililitan to take over from B Flight. By now the larger landings at Bantam and Merak had been discovered, and during the afternoon some of the efforts of the remaining Hurricanes were to be directed here as well. Strafing continued to inflict casualties on the invaders and, of one such sortie carried out by Flt Lt Parker with Plt Offs Mike Fitzherbert and Dizzy Mendizabal, Parker later recorded:

> "I led off with Mike and Dizzy in the only three aircraft available and kept the palm trees as much as possible between us and the seashore. Our first intimation that we'd reached

the landing point was groups of shells exploding in the trees below and around us. We were obviously not surprising the Japs and, rather than fly straight and level at low altitude for the benefit of their gunners, I corkscrewed along a few hundred feet higher. Then we saw the transports and a couple of warships just offshore with three further smaller boats moving between. We each attacked a barge and then Dizzy and I turned away to the shore to aim at the troops working on the beach and in the village.

Mike turned out to sea and aimed at the destroyer, which was banging away at us, but I doubt whether he damaged it at all. I spotted some troops dashing into a bamboo hut roofed with palm leaves and fired at it, seeing my shots breaking on the walls. When I pulled out of my dive and round to attack again, the hut was on fire and a squad of men were lined up nearby with rifles aimed, whilst others ran out of the smoke. The riflemen had little chance to get off more than one shot at me and none hit the aircraft – before my fire was bursting on and around them, and then I'd run through my ammunition and pulled up and inland, out of effective range of the AA guns.

Almost immediately, I was joined by Mike and Dizzy and we flew back to Tjililitan. My aircraft and Dizzy's were still unscathed but Mike had collected the nose-cap of a heavy shell in the mainspar of his wing. On the way back, at fairly low level, we found we were receiving machine-gun fire from the ground, so I moved up to about 5,000 feet. My starboard oil tank had been hit and there was a black stream of oil over the wing, which worried me considerably. I kept a close eye on both the temperature and the oil gauge and flow but suffered no other difficulty. Of course, we taxied the aircraft straight down into the *ulu* for repairs and checking as soon as we landed. I think that very probably the Dutch (for they could have been no others) machine-gunners fired on us in error."

Having all three landed safely, Plt Off Fitzherbert related that he had spotted two 'flying boats' that had just alighted on the sea and had destroyed both in a strafing attack. The Japanese recorded that one F1M floatplane from the *Kamikawa Maru* had been burnt during the day's attacks and others badly damaged, presumably one of these being Sgt Kelly's victim.

After joining the British aircraft in the initial attack on the Eretanwetan landings, all Dutch effort was switched towards the larger force off the Kragan/Rembang area to the east. From their secret base at Ngoro/Blimbing, six Hurricanes of 2-VIG-IV joined six Brewsters and nine US P-40s to attack shipping, during which three of the Hurricanes were hit by AA fire and damaged: Sgt Maj Boonstoppel force-landed at Maospati airfield, while Sgt de Wilde, flying Z5664, came down in similar circumstances near Bodjonegoro, but 2/Lt Marinus was able to get his damaged aircraft back to Ngoro, where 1/Lt Bruinier and Sgts Dejalle and Beerling had landed; Bruinier had flown so low that the propeller of his Hurricane had clipped one of the boats he was strafing, although he managed to return and land safely. The P-40s had fared badly, three being shot down and the other six all returning with varying degrees of damage, all being rendered operationally unserviceable. None of the Brewsters were lost. While refuelling for another strike, a Dutch courier aircraft landed at Ngoro, followed closely by a flight of A6Ms of the Tainan Ku from Bali. The Japanese pilots had spotted the aircraft about to land and then observed the secret airfield. Diving down to carry out a strafe, the courier aircraft was promptly destroyed, as were all ten P-40s on the airfield, plus two Hurricanes, five Glenn Martins and two LB-30s.

By late afternoon, owing to the shortage of Hurricanes, 605 Squadron was ordered to stand down and its remaining four serviceable Hurricanes were handed to 242 Squadron. The pilots of the New Zealand Flight were initially ordered to remain. Jim MacIntosh recalled:

"Jack Oakden and Eddie Kuhn were the only two go out on the last strafing raid – in the afternoon. While they were away, Sqn Ldr Wright turned up and gathered up all 605 personnel, and he told us to take our remaining aircraft and go and join 242 Squadron under Sqn Ldr Brooker. When Kuhn and Oakden came back they enquired as to where everyone was and we replied we didn't know but that they had evacuated the aerodrome. It was getting towards late evening when Brooker came across to address the five of us. He had more pilots than aircraft so he took over our Hurricanes and said as far as we were concerned it was finished – we couldn't do any more. We had a little Chevrolet utility and he told us to take it and get ourselves across Java to the south coast. There was a ship convoy leaving which we should be able to get out on."

Meanwhile, Sqn Ldr Wright had been ordered to take the rest of his men including those of the 258 Squadron detachment to Tjilatjap, where – he also was informed – ships would be waiting to take them to Australia. The party reached the port during the evening in two Ford cars after a nightmarish dash across Java, in the belief that their vessel would sail at dawn. They were closely followed by the pilots of the New Zealand Flight, released from their attachment to 242 Squadron, who had piled into a truck and set off, as Sgt Jim MacIntosh later wrote:

"So we went back into Batavia, to the Tandjong Priok flats hotel where we were billeted, and we waited there till midnight, hoping Noel Sharp would turn up. Some Army personnel appeared and advised us to get out urgently because the Japs had not only landed at Cheribon, but opposite the Sunda Straits and they were forming a pincer movement around Batavia. A senior Dutch officer said that Batavia had been declared an open city, which meant that all military personnel must leave. So we had no option but to go and we travelled all that night armed with Dutch rifles and a Tommy gun. The route as far as Bandoeng was very congested with troop movements coming and going and roadblocks. However we arrived there about 9am on 2 March."

Sgt John Vibert was with this party, and he recalled:

"When we got to Bandoeng we saw some P-40s there in railway sidings in their crates, which belonged to the Dutch. We waited, for there was talk of the groundcrew assembling them, but we were then ordered to try and get down to Tjilatjap."[118]

MacIntosh continued:

"There [at Bandoeng] we were informed to carry on to the south coast of Java, to a small port called Tjilatjap, where the RAF were organising the evacuation of all non-effective aircrews. So after refuelling our truck we carried on. We had to keep a sharp lookout for aircraft all day and frequently had to take cover as Jap fighters and dive-bombers were very active. Our route took us through Garoet and Tjamis. Late that night we arrived at a small place called Poerwerkerta, a few miles out from Tjilatjap, where quite a number of RAF personnel had gathered in a sugar factory. We stayed somewhere there in a cottage near a stream that particular night. Wg Cdr Noble was there and so was Sqn Ldr de la Perrelle with some of his crowd. Noble was trying to assemble everybody he could to take them all down to the south coast to Tjilatjap."

The tension and discomfort of the journey had been heightened by lack of knowledge of how far the Japanese invaders had infiltrated; however, arrival brought the appalled realization that the port was empty. Many other units swarmed around the deserted quays, all anxiously awaiting the arrival of ships to get them away from the rapidly deteriorating situation. MacIntosh continued:

"Next day, 3 March, Plt Offs Pettit and White and Sgt Kuhn and I made a trip down to

Tjilatjap in our truck to have a look at the port. The town and port were small with only a few small ships it. Everything there was very quiet and up until then the Japs had not bombed the place. On the night of 4 March, a full trainload of RAF personnel left Poerwerkerta for the port. Our trip was very slow due to a very small engine on a large train and we didn't arrive there till daylight. We assembled in numerous groups along a roadside between the railway station and the docks in some bush. Two fairly big ships (about 8,000 tons) had arrived and it was on one of these that we were to go out. At about 10am while we were just sitting around beside the road, we heard large numbers of Jap planes approaching. These appeared out of the clouds from all directions – fighters, dive-bombers and heavy bombers. They proceeded to bomb the town and port and it was one of the worst bombings we had experienced from the Japs. The town and docks were practically flattened and the two ships sunk. Any chance of evacuation was gone and everyone left to his own resources. The four of us left the port and camped with a large number of RAF personnel in some bush on the outskirts of the town for the night. That night mosquitoes were bad and fires from the oil tanks by the docks were terrific.

Another of the small party, Sgt Eddie Kuhn, added:

"All this occurred over a very small area and the death toll was enormous. Having survived the intense bombing we assisted rescue squads to find survivors. Many air raid shelters received hits and all that remained were pieces of people, so consequently these areas had to be simply filled with earth. Once again this was a sickening experience which can never be forgotten."

* * *

Meanwhile, at Tjililitan at dawn on the morning of 2 March, three of 242 Squadron's Hurricanes led by Flt Lt Parker again set out for the Eretanwetan area. Whilst two attacked targets of opportunity, including a large group of Japanese cycle troops, Parker decided to try and silence one of the light AA guns firing at them.

"We set off before dawn in aircraft hastily repaired overnight. Upon arrival we were met with a concerted fire from several light anti-aircraft guns firing tracer. Whilst the other two immediately started to attack any other targets they could see – which were not as plentiful as on the previous day – I decided to take on the guns. I believed that they would fire an eight-round magazine and then would re-load, so I flew just out of range of one of them, watched the tracers falling below me and turned to attack just after I had counted seven. The eighth shell came up as I skidded into my attack and it missed by a long way and by then I'd centred the controls, aimed at the sandbagged gun emplacement and poured on the de Wilde. However, I'd no idea as to how long it would take the protected gunners to change the magazine and the gun went off again as I wheeled over it. I don't know by how much they missed but the flash from the gun barrel seemed to reach my wingtips.

I had a great contempt for AA fire against a jinking fighter aircraft, provided the plane was not aimed at the gun in order to exchange shots, because at say 5,000 feet the gunners had to aim so far ahead that a pilot had only to change direction slightly to be safe. Of course, the same did not apply to box barrages, aimed at bombers on their bomb runs. I did not care to risk another low-level attack on this gun but I wanted very much to knock it off, so I climbed away from it to over 6,000 feet, weaved back until I was overhead and slowly peeled off into a vertical dive. I had only a short time to fire but was happy that no shells followed me as I pulled out of the dive. I then joined Mike [Fitzherbert] and the other pilot, who had apparently found a large group of Japanese troops who dismounted from bicycles and stood in the road to fire rifles at the aircraft. They had of course been badly mauled already but I also put in a couple of attacks on these troops, many of whom had taken to the ditches before I emptied my magazines."

On returning from this raid, completely undamaged, Parker was advised that he was to immediately take his section to Andir, the airfield just outside Bandoeng, from where they were to attack Japanese-occupied Kalidjati.

"We had a couple more aircraft serviceable by then and, delayed by contradictory orders for some time, we flew up to Bandoeng after lunch. Brooker, the only one with an aerial map of Java, led us and the rest of us had to make do with some rather featureless road maps. He led a section of three and Sergeant Dunn and I brought up the rear. We found cloud overhead at about 3,000 feet when we got to Bandoeng and, as usual, I dropped back about half a mile as we approached the airfield. We were only at about 1,000 feet but, to my alarm, heavy AA shells started to burst around Brooker's formation. Soon we too were receiving intermittent shellfire but I had already commenced mild evasive action and nothing worse happened than that an oil leak appeared in my airscrew and a fine mist covered the windscreen. Brooker led us around the airfield until the shelling stopped and then he landed, apparently quite confident that the gunners had mistaken our identity. He was right."

Heading for the nearby town of Bandoeng at the same time as the Hurricanes arrived at Andir was Plt Off James McEwan, an IO attached to one of the Vildebeest squadrons. He witnessed the greeting received by the Hurricanes:

"Just as we were climbing into our trucks again a flight of Hurricanes came in to land. The unexpected sight of the familiar and well-loved shapes in the sky kindled a great warmth of patriotic fervour in all our hearts. For a while the machines circled low over the airfield, waiting instructions to land. Then, as we watched, we saw, under the wing of one of the aircraft the white puff of an exploding shell. Immediately every anti-aircraft gun in Bandoeng seemed to open up on the hapless machines. The Hurricanes took instant action to announce their identity. They fired their recognition cartridges, they dipped their wings, they came down to an even lower altitude where their RAF roundels seemed to protest blankly at the demented gunners. Apart from anything else, the Hurricane was one of the most distinctive aircraft of the war. Had the gunners lost their recognition signals or had Japanese attacks made them jittery? Clearly it was going to be only a matter of seconds till one of the machines was shot down.

Spellbound with horror, we sat and watched helplessly. Then one of the Hurricanes – presumably the squadron commander – peeled out of the circuit and streaked away northwards from the town, immediately followed by the others. We had seen no machines actually shot down, but some must have been peppered by shrapnel, and their escape from Bandoeng did not end their troubles, for where were they now to go? The northern Javanese airfields were probably in Japanese hands and their fuel supply running low. Perhaps the best they could hope for was a speedy return to sanity on the part of the Bandoeng gunners, which would allow them to return and land."[119]

Obviously McEwan did not witness the eventual safe landing of the Hurricanes.

The first Ki-48s of the 75th Sentai had already arrived at Kalidjati in the early morning, three Hurricanes being ordered off to strafe this airfield. As they approached out of the sun, Flt Lt Julian warned that Japanese fighters were in the air, and then proceeded to fly straight up the centre of the airfield. Sgt Geoff Hardie, flying his first sortie since being shot down over Singapore, turned to starboard and flew around the airfield, followed by Sgt John Fleming:

"I came in last – saw the Japs but disregarded them and proceeded to strafe three bombers

> sitting in the corner of the airfield with their engines running. Set them on fire – a lot of smoke and fire and Hardie thought it was I who had crashed. As I broke away I saw three Japs blazing away at me. Radiator punctured and engine temperature rose sharply. I managed to fly about 20 or 30 miles back towards Batavia, then baled out in front-lines and landed in a rice paddy. I was immediately strafed by a Jap who had followed my glycol trail. Five passes he made, and I sustained a wound in my left arm. Local natives were very kind and took me to a first aid station in Dutch territory, from where I was driven by ambulance to Batavia, arriving about six or seven in the evening."

Unfortunately, he became one of the first RAF fighter pilots on Java to be captured when the hospital was overrun by Japanese troops the following day. His fate was not known for some considerable time, as his two companions reported, on their return to Tjililitan, that they thought he had crashed on the airfield, having seen much fire and smoke. It is believed that the Hurricanes' opponents were Ki-27s of one of the 12th Flying Battalion's sentais.

Once the Hurricanes had been re-armed and refuelled they were off again, although in the hands of fresh pilots. Plt Off Tom Watson led the trio to the Serang area, Sgt Newlands returning early when his aircraft ('J') developed a bad oil leak. Nearing the target area, Watson's aircraft also developed engine trouble but he decided to carry on, he and Sgt Sandy Allen (BE239) attacking many troops. As with others on previous occasions, these troops fearlessly stood their ground and fired incessantly at the Hurricanes. Inevitably, Watson's troublesome aircraft (BE130) received several hits in the engine, which seized, obliging him to crash-land in a paddy field. Shortly after Sandy Allen's lone return to Tjililitan, a scramble of standby Hurricanes was ordered to intercept a retaliatory raid by Japanese fighters. The Squadron received a reasonable amount of notice to become airborne but, once in the air, they failed to receive any further direction over the R/T. A fight occurred over the airfield at 12,000 feet, Sgt King claiming one shot down. The RAF noted that the airfield was under frequent attack during the day, as 242 Squadron's LAC Pat Cowle had cause to remember:

> "Our airfield was soon discovered by the Japs and became untenable. The first visit by 15 bombers found me in the centre of the airfield robbing a crashed Hurricane of parts, and shook me up a bit when they unloaded all at once. The airfield was strafed by Jap fighters and many planes destroyed, although only one round passed through a hangar full of Hurricanes being assembled. This round passed through an engine, so we removed the airscrew from this machine to fit on another that had its prop badly damaged being towed from the docks."

During the course of the morning Plt Off Bill Lockwood was detailed to fly to Buitenzorg, there to sketch a map showing the location of a Japanese convoy that had been reported approaching the city:

> "I found the Japs just west of Buitenzorg, or rather they found me stooging along at 1,000 feet over the jungle-enclosed road. I was fired at but received no hits. Not being detailed to strafe, I completed the sketch on my knee. I sketched this map on the inside of the hard cover of a book and dropped it to the Dutch on a golf course at the north-eastern outskirts of Buitenzorg, and then returned to base."

At Tjililitan, by early afternoon, more Hurricanes had been made serviceable and Sqn Ldr Brooker informed his men that the unit was to carry out a full-scale raid on Kalidjati. The operation was again to be flown from Andir, as the advancing Japanese were now only 30 miles away from Tjililitan. Even as the Hurricanes were on their way, a Japanese bomber formation estimated to be 50 strong was also heading for Bandoeng and comprised aircraft from the 27th Sentai escorted by 59th and 64th Sentai Ki-43s.

Most of the bombers turned back due to bad weather, but the fighters of the 59th continued. They arrived soon after the Hurricanes had landed at Andir, and when an air raid warning was sounded four Dutch CW-21Bs were scrambled, closely followed by the last three Brewsters. The RAF pilots soon witnessed a short, sharp engagement and one Dutch pilot was observed floating down under his parachute.

After a conference with his flight commanders, Sqn Ldr Brooker decided that he would lead a strike on Kalidjati that evening, enabling the Hurricanes to return under cover of darkness. At dusk therefore, six Hurricanes set off (the seventh having become unserviceable), but as they approached the target Sgt Gordie Dunn saw a single fighter diving on them:

> "I shouted a warning and the CO also shouted and we went into a defensive circle. One Hurricane was out of the circle and was attacked. The Zero had the advantage that he could fire at anything because he was alone, but in the dark we were at a disadvantage. As my part of the circle came round I found that I could not aim at the Zero but I fired anyway and he broke off. The Zero had attacked Sgt Ron Dovell. He managed to limp back and I formated on him but neither of us had noted our return course. Ernie Gartrell picked us up and led the way home. The CO gave us a real blast when we got back, though he let me off the hook for firing and chasing the Zero, but then tore me off a strip for not checking on the return course – which had been an oversight on my part due to inexperience."

Once the Hurricanes were safely back, the job of refuelling was undertaken by Flt Lt Parker – who was not on this mission:

> "There being no squadron groundcrews around to re-fuel the aircraft, I went round with a bowser to fill all the wing tanks. This took some time and I remember being very fed-up on filling a port wing tank to find the starboard tank mostly shot away so that the aircraft had to stay unserviceable anyway. In fact, they were able to take the airscrew off it during the night and fit it to my plane for the morning.
>
> All the pilots slept the night in two rooms of the Savoy Honan Hotel, quite a good modern one but crowded with refugees at the time. The water supplies were off and we were filthy in sweat-soaked clothes but, as it was dark by the time we reached town, we had no opportunity to buy others. We slept naked and climbed back into our dirty clothes and flying boots in what seemed the middle of the night. Somehow we still had four [sic] serviceable aircraft and Brooker, Mike and I and Dizzy were to attack the Kalidjati airfield before dawn."

There was no let-up in the fighting, most of which was occurring in Western Java. Early in the morning of 3 March, all seven RAF Hurricanes set off from Andir to attack Kalidjati again, Sqn Ldr Brooker ordering Flt Lt Parker and Plt Off Mendizabal to remain above as top cover while he led the rest of the squadron down to strafe. Parker:

> "We got off all right in clear skies with the dawn just a paleness in the east, crossed the hills and came over to Kalidjati. Dizzy and I were to remain as top cover until the others had completed their field strafing and then, if there were no Zeros up, we also were to attack them on the ground. The light AA guns opened up as soon as we approached and I watched the flickering exhausts of the others pull down into the attack, the flashing of the multiple guns, and the lines of bullets streaking onto targets and ricocheting away in all directions like Christmas sparklers. One or two fires started, there seemed to be no Zeros in the air and the AA guns continued to pump shells up into the air behind us as we weaved around the field. I soon decided that the time had come for us to have a go and we went down in a steep dive in line astern.
>
> I found a line of twin-engined aircraft and brought my guns up over them and a

> bowser standing by the last one – at least one of the aircraft and the bowser caught fire. I had no time to look about for, as I pulled up out of my dive a Hurricane, closely followed by a Zero, crossed my line of flight. I turned in behind the Zero and fired – to no apparent effect other than to draw attention to myself. He whipped round in a tight turn to come at me from behind but I still had quite a lot of speed from my initial dive and climbed away from him. I circled overhead once more but saw no more Hurricanes about and as several Zeros were climbing up towards me, I returned to Bandoeng, which the other Hurricanes reached first. We had apparently inflicted some damage on the enemy but had certainly not put them out of action."

Plt Off Mendizabal – the victim of the attack – was not so lucky, and his aircraft was badly shot-up; he managed to get some miles from the airfield before he was obliged to bale out. A running fight then developed as the Hurricanes sought to get away, during which three victories were claimed by Plt Offs Gartrell and Fitzherbert, and Sgt Jimmy King. No further Hurricanes were lost, but nearly all were damaged and Gartrell was slightly wounded. He remembered:

> "We came down at first light, through the clouds right over the top of Kalidjati, where we viewed the Japanese aircraft lined up in a long stretch on the tarmac, with Dutch and British aircraft left intact where they had been caught. We ignored those and went straight for the Zeros. We attacked in line astern and went up and down the runway. The Japs were using small arms and machine guns to fire at us. There was no ack-ack used at all. We used up our ammunition and were on our way back, individually, when two Zeros, that had evidently got off the ground, came chasing us. I got shot-up. My aircraft didn't fly again."

The presence of the Hurricanes at Andir had left Batavia unprotected and, in their absence, the airfields at Tjililitan and Kemajoran had been bombed. As the Japanese formation headed for home, A6M pilot NAP 2/C Kazuo Yokokawa of the Tainan Ku formation, spotted a fighter which he identified as a P-40 and claimed it probably shot down. This may have been a Dutch Hurricane, one of the surviving pair belonging to the ill-fated 2-VIG-IV, that had been flown from Ngoro to Bandoeng during the day, piloted by 2/Lt Marinus and Ensign N. Vink. Marinus force-landed near Soerakarta en route, the aircraft being wrecked.

The movement of Japanese units to Kalidjati was now accelerating fast, the rest of the 59th and 75th Sentais arriving during the day, followed by the 64th and 90th next day, together with six A6Ms of the 22nd Air Flotilla and five A5M fighters attached to the Mihoro Ku, which had recently reached Sumatra. Alarmed by the rapid deterioration of the situation, and aware of their inability to defend the port of Batavia adequately, the Dutch authorities declared it an open city to prevent unnecessary damage and suffering.

On the ground, following the capture of Kalidjati, the elements of the Japanese 30th Infantry Regiment responsible had moved westwards to take Tjikampek airfield, which they reached by 3 March. Meanwhile the rest of the regiment had headed south from Eretenwetan and concentrated at Soebang, south-east of Kalidjati, where they were to regroup after the securing of Tjikampek. The force from the Merak/Bantam Bay area meantime, had split into two columns, one heading for Batavia, the other towards Buitenzorg and Bandoeng. The route of the latter, more southerly thrust, was barred by defending forces which included the British/Australian elements: these forces hoped to deny access to river crossings in front of Buitenzorg, while Dutch forces which had been engaged in the Merak area had now fallen back to Serang, where the invaders captured an important road junction. In an effort to prevent a two-pronged advance on the capital, a Dutch mobile force from Bandoeng struck north, engaging the 230th Regiment at Soebang. A small force of tanks actually penetrated right into the centre of the town, but the infantry was unable to follow up and give the necessary support, and a withdrawal followed. A reserve regiment at Buitenzorg was ordered to move to Soebang in support, but when 20 miles short of its objective, it was spotted by Japanese reconnaissance aircraft and at once came under sustained attack by the JAAF units at Kalidjati. Throughout the afternoon and evening waves of light bombers and army co-operation aircraft attacked, the column becoming completely scattered. Next day all available forces were withdrawn by the Dutch command, to concentrate on the defence of Bandoeng.

The only sustained Allied activity in the air on 4 March involved the RAF Hurricanes at Andir. One of the servicing party, Corporal Jim Home, remembered:

> "We set to work servicing our four [A Flight] aircraft to get them airborne. We were armed and had pilots who still seemed to be spoiling for a fight in spite of the ridiculous odds. The drome was large and spacious and one could see across a wide expanse toward the mountain ranges."[120]

The four Hurricanes were off at first light, heading for the Sunda Straits area where Japanese troops were to be attacked. Jerry Parker takes up the story:

> "A Flight reported to the airfield with B Flight and were told that Japanese columns had landed just east of the Sunda Straits and we were to go to strafe them. I wasn't at all happy about these ground attacks on troops as, according to the terms of the Geneva Convention, it was definitely illegal to use explosive ammunition but we had no ball ammo for our guns. We agreed that upon finding the target, I was to stay overhead as top cover with Mike [Fitzherbert], until Taffy Julian and Ernie Gartrell had cleared their ammunition. We flew west for about 20 minutes and then saw a long column of horse-drawn transport on a straight tree-lined road. Taffy and Ernie peeled off to investigate, found they were fired on by khaki-clad troops – the Dutch had green uniforms – and opened up.
>
> They attacked several times whilst Mike and I divided our time between watching them and anxiously searching around the skies above and then it was our turn. I felt it was unfair on the horses to shoot them with the explosive de Wilde but there was nothing else for it, and I went down to add my share to the shambles. I made only one dive and saw there was little further needed besides which I wanted to keep some ammo in case we were attacked by Zeros. The road was blocked by fallen horses and overturned cars, some of which were on fire, although I suppose the mess would not have taken long to clear up and the Japs would have lost only a portion of their fighting strength. As I pulled the nose of the plane over the trees, I saw a single horseman racing away from me towards a thicket some distance away. He never made it because I put my nose down again and got both him and the horse in a short burst whilst he still had far to go. I climbed up to the others who were waiting above and found them as anxious to get back to Tjililitan as I was.
>
> We had time to re-fuel, go off again and attack more horse transport and cyclists before we had lunch but we were constantly aware of our vulnerability at low level should the Zeros appear, particularly when returning with almost no ammunition, so we were most relieved at meeting none at all. We had some sandwiches at the field and were preparing to go off again for more ground attacks when word came through that we were to return to Andir. B Flight carried out another ground level attack to the west with whatever aircraft were serviceable."

As soon as everyone was ready, B Flight led by Sqn Ldr Brooker took off for Kalidjati, six of the Hurricanes going down to strafe, while Plt Off Lockwood, 2/Lt Anderson and Sgt Sandy Allen remained above as cover. Sgt Snowy Newlands (Z5691) reported:

> "We took off in the morning and I think there were at least six of us – there might have been more. Whoever was leading our formation must have been a bit late in picking up

the drome and just dived straight down. We were diving far too steeply, came in too fast, and were in line abreast instead of line astern. I had a hell of a job pulling up anyhow. I could see a bomber, lined him up and gave him a few bursts. I think I hit it, and may have even destroyed it, but nothing spectacular occurred like blowing up. As I flew at a right angle across the runway I saw a Jap fighter taking off and I only just missed him. I was going too fast to get a bead on him. I had barely gone another couple of seconds and I looked in my rear vision mirror and the bloke taking off had actually turned his plane in, and had his four bloody guns going straight behind me. I couldn't believe how he could have taken off that fast and got his guns into action. So I didn't hang around. I just kept down at ground level until I found myself going up this mountain pass, getting steeper and steeper. I barely got over the saddle. Just after I left the plain I saw two other aircraft heading off, so I thought they were our blokes. I tried to join up with them, but they probably thought that I was Japanese, and they didn't wait for me."

Unable to observe much from the height at which they were flying, the top cover followed the others down. Lockwood recalled:

"As Lt Anderson followed me down, I met at around 6,000-8,000 feet, two Navy 0s climbing. As I went past them and was about to pull around, I noticed a transport of the DC-3 type below and in a landing circuit. I dove in behind this aircraft and was about to open fire when I remembered a remark made by someone before we took off about there still being a few Dutch aircraft around and not to shoot down a Dutchman. I climbed slightly and to the right of the aircraft to check. I saw the 'fried eggs' on the wings. He also saw me and turned away to port with wheels and flaps down. I looked in my rear view mirror and saw two Zeros on my tail. I made a hurried diving attack on the transport and went to treetop level, heading I knew not where, but hoping Bandoeng. The Japs were close behind and firing. I weaved and put the throttle through the gate. I had a slight speed edge. Flying straight and very low, I flew south for some minutes and presently came over a range of mountains and there was Andir airfield. I landed. Lt Anderson did not come in. I never saw him again."

Sgt Sandy Allen remembered:

"The Zeros came in underneath and we had a simple target for the first few vital moments, after which we were so heavily outnumbered that we got into serious trouble. I managed to shoot down one Zero which swerved into another and I was credited with two Zeros destroyed, one probable and one damaged, but crawled back to the aerodrome with 28 cannon-shell and 43 bullet holes in the machine (BE239) and with slight wounds to my head and legs. I remember being given a cup of tea and I was shaking so badly it stirred itself! However, I took off in a fresh plane 10 minutes later so that I was able to recover my nerve."

Most of the other Hurricanes returned with varying degrees of damage. Although saddened by the loss of the South African Neil Anderson (who was taken prisoner but died in captivity two days later), the pilots were jubilant for they believed that they had shot down six of the intercepting fighters – two by Sgt Jimmy King, his fourth in three days, and one each by Brooker and Julian to add to the pair credited to Sandy Allen. What the Japanese losses were in the air is not known, but their fighter pilots – apparently from the 22nd Air Flotilla – also believed that they had shot down five of the Hurricanes. On the ground one light bomber was destroyed by fire, with two more and one reconnaissance aircraft badly damaged, while one of each plus one Ki-48 were damaged to a lesser extent.

While the Hurricanes were away, A Flight pilots drove to Bandoeng in the Buick, which Plt Off Cicurel had found, as Parker recalled:

"The neat villages and clear roads of Java were a pleasure to drive along in the sunlight and there were smiling children everywhere along the way. The only tiresome thing was that the alarm gongs (of bamboo) sounded any time any aircraft were heard and we were forced by the police to get off the road. We arrived at Bandoeng in the late afternoon and went straight to the airfield. As Andir airfield was located in the fertile valley close to Bandoeng and had been used previously only for smaller civil aircraft, it was not very large and there was no jungle or rubber plantation nearby in which to park the aircraft. We had still only four aircraft serviceable despite the work of the groundcrews at Batavia who were coming by road to Bandoeng that evening."

Soon after arrival a message was received requiring a Hurricane to reconnoitre the road leading southwards from Kalidjati to Bandoeng, since Japanese forces had been reported advancing down this in strength. Flt Lt Parker was detailed to undertake this sortie, Plt Off Fitzherbert volunteering to act as escort. Whilst discussing the job in hand a raid by Kanoya Ku bombers occurred:

"We were talking this over and keeping an eye out for the Zeros we could see patrolling the hills a few miles away when we saw the familiar sight of twenty-plus bombers, closely escorted by fighters, coming in towards the field as high as they could get under the cloud layer. I was very relieved that there was no thought in anybody's mind that we should take off and try to intercept this formation – there was no time, anyway, and the Zeros would have hacked us down. We dived into slit trenches and held our heads whilst the anti-personnel bombs exploded all over the field and buildings. Luckily, the Japs had aimed at the main buildings and hangars some way from us where most of the larger aircraft were parked and no bombs landed very close to us.

Immediately afterwards, Mike and I ran out to our planes, started up and taxied between the bomb craters to the end of the runway. At the same time I was strapping on my parachute, Sutton harness and helmet and clipping in my oxygen and radio connections (although I had little hope the latter would work). I turned at the end of the runway in a cloud of dust and opened up the throttle without waiting for the engine to warm up to test the plugs. As the plane came off the ground and I pulled up the wheels, I switched on the gun sight and twisted the gun button to 'Fire' from the 'Safe' position. We were heading to the west end of the valley under lower clouds there and then I would turn north and later east to bring me to the Kalidjati road. I looked over to Mike who had come up very quickly on my right and found him signalling frantically to me to turn round and go back to Andir. I checked my instruments with a quick glance but all seemed in order, yet when I looked at Mike again he gritted his teeth (he had no oxygen mask on), stabbed his finger furiously downwards and pulled over and down back to base. I had only just pulled around to follow in my turn when I saw my engine temperature gauge had gone right off the clock and glycol vapour started coming through the cockpit of which the cover was still locked open.

I didn't know the cause of the engine overheating and the glycol vaporizing but I was scared stiff of the cloud of vapour, which I knew I had to expect. I was still very low but Andir was close and I left closing the throttle as long as I dared and pulled around in a final steep diving slipping turn just short of the runway and to one side of it, streaming vapour from the cockpit but mercifully able to see where I was going. The undercart was still up and I'd had no time to do anything about the flaps, which I'd set for 30 degrees down for a quick take-off. I saw I would hit the ground close to a Dutch bomber, which was being re-armed. The groundcrew looked up and started to run, but they had no time to get very far before I kicked over the stick and rudder and levelled just before I hit, a few feet in front of the bomber. The Hurricane thumped into the tarmac and slid past the bomber and the running men with a tremendous clatter and clouds of vapour. However, I was strapped in just as tightly as usual and the plane did not overturn as it came to a stop minus flaps, airscrew, radiator and much of its under-surface. I had the engine switched off in no time and, although there seemed to be no fuel leaking from its tanks, I left it very smartly in case of fire. A tender dashed up and the Dutch groundcrew shook my hand many times, thanking me evidently for finally pulling away from them, although, of course, I was rather more anxious not to crash on to their bomb trolleys than they were. In the middle of all this I remembered my maps and went back to the Hurricane, which was still steaming and making hissing noises, and found the gun sight and button still switched to 'On'. By the time I'd turned them off and collected my helmet and parachute, the vapour had stopped and Brooker had come down with a car to take me back to the office."

The pilots adjourned to the Savoy Honan Hotel in Bandoeng for the night, and during dinner Sqn Ldr Brooker announced that two Dutch transport aircraft were due in that night to begin evacuating pilots. In the first instance wounded pilots would accompany Wg Cdr Maguire and himself, while four more pilots would have seats – to be settled by drawing lots. On his departure, Flt Lt Julian was to take command of the remaining pilots and aircraft. In the event, as somewhat of an anti-climax, the evacuating aircraft did not put in an appearance that night.

Two of 242 Squadron's pilots, Sgts Gordie Dunn and Tom Young – who had volunteered to drive a petrol bowser from Tjililitan – had not yet arrived at Bandoeng, but they were on their way. The bowser had been loaded with pilots' personal possessions, including a number of gramophone records. Their journey was anything but uneventful. They had set off with Dunn driving, and were shortly overtaken by an Army convoy, as he recalled:

"An Army sergeant enquired of our destination and on establishing this, said he would drive back from time to time to make sure we were not in trouble. We continued on our way, quite uneventfully until we reached the mountainous area, when the engine started to overheat. Pulling into the side of the road near a paddy field, we found an old tin and with this gathered water from the field and refilled the radiator. Within a short while of recommencing the journey we came to a steep decline, at the bottom of which was a stream with a narrow bridge. As there was a matching steep incline the other side, I decided to accelerate, aiming the vehicle at the centre of the bridge. I noted that the speed had reached 50mph when Tom shouted a warning. An old man with a donkey and cart suddenly appeared on the bridge. There was nothing I could do, so half expecting a collision, we careered across the bridge, missing the man and his donkey but hitting the back of the cart, before shooting up the other side!"

Apart from the radiator overheating again, the rest of the trip was relatively uneventful until evening time. As they parked for the night a Dutch officer approached them with a request for some fuel for his car. After facilitating him, they experienced difficulty in turning off the tap and lost about 100 gallons of fuel. In return for the petrol, the officer found them accommodation and placed an armed guard on the bowser. Next morning however, they found that they could not communicate with the guard, who spoke only Javanese and would not let them enter the vehicle; they had to wait for the return of the officer before they could get underway. Andir was eventually reached without further mishap, but not before they had noticed a stencilled warning sign on the side of the bowser: 'This vehicle not to exceed 15mph.' They were hardly surprised therefore, when they later learned that the bowser would no longer travel faster than 2mph! Their main regret however, was that the gramophone records had practically melted away in the intense heat of the glove compartment, where they had been placed.

Wg Cdr Maguire and Sqn Ldr Brooker spent much of the morning of 5 March in

Bandoeng, where they experienced great difficulties with the Dutch officials. Since many of the senior officers considered that further resistance was useless, and were divided in their wish to surrender, or to assist the RAF in continuing the fight, pleas for assistance failed; however, when verbal threats were employed, supplies of fuel – but not oxygen – were forthcoming. The RAF was not aware of the on-goings in Batavia, which was about to surrender. The story of its fall was later told by the war correspondent of a Tokyo newspaper:

> "On the afternoon of Thursday March 5, the Japanese arrived at a narrow river, some four miles to the north of the city, where they were met by a group of Dutch and Indonesians carrying white flags, who stated that they represented the Government in Batavia and were waiting to convey a message of surrender. Learning that Batavia had been declared an open city and that the Allied troops had been withdrawn, the Japanese commander gave the order to enter, and at 2030 his troops marched in. Following a meeting with the Mayor and the provincial Governor, the Japanese commander issued a proclamation, in which he declared that he had taken over the duties of the Governor-General; that local laws would remain valid where they did not interfere with the military administration, and that the Japanese authorities would respect the lives, religion and rightful property of the people, who in turn must respect the orders of the Japanese Army and officials. Wilful violation of Japanese orders, communication with the 'enemy', destruction of property, etc., would be severely dealt with. [He said that] the military administration aims at the rapid restoration of peace and order and normal conditions in the Netherlands East Indies, on the principles of co-existence and co-prosperity for all."

In the meantime at Tjililitan, Flt Lt Parker set off to carry out the reconnaissance he had failed to complete the previous day – on this occasion with Plt Off Lockwood as escort. They took off as soon as sufficient cloud had formed to offer some refuge should Japanese fighters appear. Parker wrote:

> "Bill Lockwood was to escort me on the recce trip. He was terribly keen but very inexperienced and I was not at all happy. We could see no Zeros but we waited until the clear skies gave way to cloud over the hills to the north before we taxied out and took off. A few miles to the west the cloud layer actually covered the tops of the hills so I signalled Bill to stay behind and map-read my way around the valleys just under the cloud until I saw Kalidjati in the distance and came across the road I was to reconnoitre. I dropped low over it so as not to be seen from Kalidjati and then followed it back towards Bandoeng. Half the time, of course, I was studying the sky above and around me but I saw nothing but a bright yellow and white bus and no troops or fighting whatsoever.
>
> It took me only a few minutes to reach the foothills and, as I approached, I saw a couple of aircraft in the distance, mere specks, apparently circling a few hundred feet above ground level. I prepared to pull away and into the cloud in case they turned out to be Zeros, although I naturally did not want to do this with so many hills in the clouds, but in moments I was able to identify them as twin-engined bombers, almost certainly Japanese. They evidently had not seen me coming from the north and below them and by the time I had closed to 400 yards to the one travelling ahead and turning to port in front of me, I could see the Japanese insignia. I opened fire and easily followed him round without too much deflection. After a few moments his starboard engine streamed smoke, his nose came up, then he dropped over on his back and dived straight downward. I turned away to starboard as I was then facing Kalidjati towards which the other bomber was streaking and I lost sight of the damaged bomber under my wing for a moment. When I looked again, I saw the parabola of his smoke trail in the sky and at the end of it on the ground a fierce fire where the plane was burning.
>
> I pulled farther round to the south for home and up towards the cloud base, safely

crossed the hills and started down to Andir. Unfortunately the cloud base did not extend to the southern slopes of the hills and, as I hustled along and searched the skies above, I saw four Zeros coming from the left and above me. They only had to turn a little, as they immediately did, to stay between me and the cloud and there was not the slightest chance of my getting back in there without their knocking me off. I had no option but to keep going down towards Andir and hoping they wouldn't follow. They easily overhauled me until I could see in the rear view mirror the closest one opening fire and, when I looked back in fright, I saw two were shooting and the others lying back and above. I knew I daren't turn to try to fight; I had to keep going flat out for any help the AA guns at Andir might offer. The trouble was compounded by the slowness of the Hurricane which, no matter how I tried to shove the throttle past its stop, would rake up no more than 270mph. I'll never forget the glimpse, which I thought would be my last, I had of the dazzling white clouds behind me, the blue skies, red roofs below, green paddies and trees and, above all, the black shining shapes of the Zeros above and the flashes of their guns.

I then banged the throttle shut, slammed the pitch into 'fine', wrenched at the stick and strained at the rudder. The wing went down, the nose came up, the straps held me tight and the aircraft seemed to stop. But no Jap had passed me. They were still there shooting, only now very much closer. I pushed the stick forward and over to the other side, reversed the rudder and opened the throttle again. The engine stuttered and pulled – the Japs were still behind me and still shooting but they hadn't hit me. Andir came up ahead and I centred the stick and concentrated on skidding at hangar height across the airfield, frantically willing the Bofors guns to open up. Nothing happened.

I pulled around the hangars to the centre of Bandoeng to port and found the tower of the Savoy Honan ahead. Although I was still in fine pitch and full throttle, I set the flaps to 'down' and hauled the Hurricane around the tower, knowing the great risk of hitting the tower that any following fighter must take in trying a deflection shot. Still I'd not heard the clang of any hits on my aircraft and, having completed 180 degrees around the tower I shot off back to the airfield again. This time the gunners were ready and, as I whistled across the field at ground level, I found myself overtaken by their bright orange shells. Mike told me later that the Zeros had broken off on my first pass over the field, although he was the only one who had shot at them – with a rifle snatched from an Indonesian infantryman. Unaware of this, I had nothing left but panic."

Watching the exhibition of low-level flying from the safety of the airfield was 242 Squadron's Corporal Jim Home:

"In one particular cleft in the range, a pass or a valley, aircraft buzzed round like tiny dots. Maybe a dogfight was taking place over an area of some importance – perhaps the Hurricanes were being harassed by Zeros as they endeavoured to strafe enemy forces. Our quiet session was broken by a single shout of: 'Look out! They are coming this way.' 'They' could have been either our Hurricanes or their Zeros; no one could tell at that distance, but we no longer took any chances. Off we dashed to a nearby bungalow, which stood empty at the airfield entrance; a few preferred the shelter of nearby pomelo trees. The planes were both ours and theirs – and the first Hurricane came roaring over with a Zero on its tail. Then came another Hurricane with yet another Zero on its tail [this was obviously Parker's Hurricane on its second circuit]. It was a grand sight to see them zoom, climb and dive as each tried to rid himself of his encumbrance. Not a shot was fired. Then, almost without warning, the planes broke away as though by pre-planned arrangement – there was no accounting for what had looked more like a terrific air display than an act of aggression."[121]

Meanwhile, Parker was fleeing for his life:

"Attacked at my own base by enemy aircraft and 'friendly' gunners, I'd had enough and fled. I hared over paddy fields and trees and reached the other side of the valley before I realised I was alone. Not only alone – but gradually ashamed and indignant at my own behaviour. I'd been airborne for only 20 minutes, had enough petrol in my tanks for another hour's flying and I knew the location of a satellite airfield at Pameungpeuk on the south coast. I decided I could safely have a go at the Zeros and laboriously climbed to 20,000 feet, the maximum I dared without oxygen. I planned to come down at them at 400 or 500mph, pick off one or two and land either at Andir or Pameungpeuk. Unfortunately I lost sight of the valley and mistook it when I dived down between the clouds, finding neither Zeros nor Andir. For more than half an hour I searched, staying just under the clouds and following all the valleys, anxiously watching the petrol gauges and worrying about the Zeros, but I was hopelessly lost. Finally, I pulled away to starboard on sighting another fighter approaching dead ahead. He did the same and to my great relief turned out to be another Hurricane, Bill Lockwood still keen to escort me. Luckily, having no map, he'd patrolled only a few valleys close to Andir and he was able to lead me safely back to Bandoeng."

With a great sense of relief and self preservation, Parker landed safely at Andir, physically and mentally drained by his experience:

"When I landed I discovered that Brooker had been quite upset over my apparent end and had devoted himself to his papers with the grim comment that 'Sprog's dead and I'm to blame!' He seemed quite relieved and happy to see me back for a few minutes and then returned to his normal businesslike self. Maguire congratulated me on the phone on the demise of the bomber but found it hard to believe there were no troops on the road."

The bombers Parker had encountered were undoubtedly part of a force from the 75th and 90th Sentais that had raided Andir soon after he had left to undertake the reconnaissance. Some Hurricanes had scrambled to intercept without success, but one of these (Z5691) flown by Sgt Snowy Newlands was swiftly in trouble. No sooner was he airborne than he noticed glycol fumes entering the cockpit and, after a quick circuit, he landed again within five minutes of take-off. Of the incident, he later wrote:

"Some erk twit had not secured my glycol cap and my windscreen fogged up and the cockpit was full of fumes. I did a circuit almost within the aerodrome and was on the deck in less than five minutes. I taxied at about 40mph to the bomb bay as another wave of low-level bombers approached. I parked the kite and dived into a slit trench as a stick of bombs straddled me. One hit a Dutch bomber facing my direction about 40 yards away and set it alight. Each time I poked my head out of the trench, machine guns on the bomber – due to the heat – fired over my head!"

By the time the bomber had burnt out Newland's temper had also cooled down. He had been intent on finding the person who had not secured the glycol cap on his aircraft and exacting some sort of revenge.

One of the missing Hurricane pilots returned to the fold during the morning when Plt Off Tom Watson unexpectedly arrived in Bandoeng, looking the worse for wear and with quite a story to tell following his crash four days earlier:

"I managed to crash-land, wheels up, in a rice paddy not too far away from the Japanese. Apart from a small bump on the head, I was OK. I got as far away from the scene of the crash as I could, and as fast as I could, and then started my trek back. The Japanese were between me and Batavia and I suppose I rather advanced with them, trying to keep out of sight. I threw away my flying helmet, put dirt on my face and tried to look as much like a native as possible. However, I had two problems. One that I have been bald since my late teens and the sun gave me hell, and the other was we had no proper flying equipment and all I had on my feet were low shoes. However, I found an old native straw hat after the first day, which kept the sun off my head but at night it rained and the mud in my shoes started to wear on my flesh so that my feet became somewhat raw.

Most of the Indonesians were afraid of me but one young boy really helped me. He could speak some English. There was no food to be had, water I drank out of any place I could find it, and I didn't dare go to sleep. Japanese patrols were about quite a bit and once I hid while they passed. I was lucky that there was something like a haystack to hide in. The second day the boy walked with me most of the time and was able, by talking to other Indonesians, to ascertain where the Japanese were. It soon became obvious that I could not get back to Batavia and I headed for the hills. I eventually reached the Tjililitan river and crossed it downstream from where the Japanese were repairing the main bridge that had been destroyed."

Watson then met an elderly native who helped him put together some bamboo poles to form a raft and, although it would not hold his weight, it acted as a support for him in pushing his way across the river. He decided to make for Tjililitan and shortly after crossing the river saw a horse cart and driver, which he commandeered to take him to his destination. However, he soon met a Dutch cavalry patrol that had suffered some casualties, including their officer, and therefore they had spare horses. He joined up with them, and he realised they were also heading for Tjililitan:

"My experience as a horseman was not great at any time, and galloping with them through the jungle was rather harrowing. I was dead tired and my feet were in poor shape. We finally reached this town in the hills at about the same time as the Japanese. An Australian Army captain saw me and told me to get into his truck with him, which I did. He was heading for the mountains where what was left of the Dutch and Australian troops planned to put up sonic sort of a last stand. I also vaguely recall that my Australian friend had the responsibility of blowing up bridges after we crossed them to impede the advance of the Japanese. We arrived at this mountain base at night. From walking and riding horseback I was very stiff and riding in the truck had not helped. My feet were so sore that when I got out of the truck I could not stand up for a while. Here I learned that Batavia had fallen and what was left of the air force had established at Andir aerodrome in Bandoeng. A Dutch captain got me a car and driver and gave me a letter for his wife in Bandoeng. I must have arrived at his home about midnight. His wife took off my shoes, bathed my feet, gave me sleeping clothes and I slept the night there. In the morning she found me socks and two canvas shoes which weren't exactly a pair but were more comfortable as they were soft. I then set off to find 242 Squadron."

On locating the squadron's HQ in Bandoeng, it was arranged that he should be driven to the airfield. Watson's traumatic adventure was not yet over however, and was about to take a turn for the better, but first:

"Sandy Allen was driving me to the drome at a good clip when a truck was pushed across the road and we crashed into it. I went through the windshield and received rather bad cuts on the forehead. I came to with three rather beautiful young Dutch women caring for me. I tried to have them take me to a civilian doctor, as I did not wish to be taken PoW at this stage, which would most likely happen if I went to a military hospital. However, I did end up in one. I was given an anaesthetic and an Australian doctor operated on me. I was rather lucky not to lose an eye."

Undaunted by its diminishing resources, the small RAF fighter contingent continued to operate, although from Andir the pilots could hear gunfire in the hills and watched Japanese aircraft patrolling over the fighting area. A rumour rapidly spread that the remaining Dutch Brewster fighters, fitted with extra fuel tanks, were preparing to evacuate Java, their destination being Australia! The disturbing factor was that the few remaining Hurricanes were to act as a decoy to allow them to get away unmolested. The rumour appeared to become reality when Wg Cdr Maguire – although totally opposed to such a plan, but having been over-ruled by the AOC – detailed newly promoted Sqn Ldr Julian – who had just been advised by Air Vice-Marshal Maltby that he was to take command of the unit following the decision to evacuate Sqn Ldr Brooker – to carry out the operation. With only six Hurricanes now available it fell to the senior pilots to undertake the task. Flt Lt Parker, one of those detailed to fly, wrote:

> "We were to take off immediately. The plan, said Taffy, was that he and Ernie Gartrell would be the first section. We would divert the Zeros and the Buffaloes would take off. I said they could stuff the Buffaloes and himself too. He knew as well as I did the Zeros could have us before we reached the end of the field and who'd benefit? 'We'll have no more of that', said Taffy, looking sideways at the others who were looking very relieved at not being detailed for this. 'Those are the orders and we've just got to go.' Ernie looked anxious and Bill [Lockwood] quite untroubled by this, but neither said anything. Taffy's conviction fell off a bit when I pointed out that I'd give it a go in half an hour or so when the clouds that were forming would provide some cover if we could sneak off. I suggested a smoke screen on the north side of the airfield and he went off to pass this on to Maguire. The answer was negative when it returned, but the query took so long to pass up to the top and back again that at least we had plenty of cloud cover. Taffy and Ernie went off first and we were only fifty or a hundred yards behind them."

As soon as sufficient cloud had formed to provide some sort of cover, the Hurricanes took off in pairs. However, Sgt Jimmy King's engine cut just as he had become airborne and he was obliged to force-land in a swamp. His No.2 circled overhead and was relieved to see him emerge unhurt, but by this time contact with the other four fighters had been lost and his companion was forced to return to base. Sqn Ldr Julian led the remaining four Hurricanes into cloud, the formation having evidently escaped the notice of patrolling Japanese fighters. The section separated, Julian and Gartrell heading for the Lembang area while Parker and Lockwood flew towards Kalidjati, as Parker later related:

> "I was greatly relieved that the Zeros above the hills didn't come down at us. Taffy followed the route I'd taken the previous day but I led Bill to the south and up to 10,000 feet, keeping the valley in sight and whipping down half an hour later – under the cloud, round the hills and north towards Kalidjati. I had seen no movement by the Buffalos but was not at all worried by that. Then I saw a Jap bomber making its way north, presumably returning to land, and hared off to overtake it. Bill had left me as he'd sighted another pair of bombers wheeling off to our right. I was closing on my target rapidly but I suppose I must have opened fire at over 400 yards, so scared was I at flying north deeper into enemy territory. I fired one long burst of probably about 12 seconds and saw some, but not much, de Wilde bursting on the wings. Some smoke appeared from the starboard engine of the bomber but as soon as my guns stopped firing. I turned back the way I'd come. I was very fed up at passing another Jap bomber only yards away when I had empty guns. This must have been the partner of the one, which, unknown to me, Bill had just shot down. I went back round the end of the hills to the west, hedge-hopped back to Andir and landed, to find everyone in fine humour. Taffy and Ernie had each claimed a bomber half-an-hour earlier and none of us had seen any Zeros once we were in the air."

Plt Off Lockwood had at last secured his first confirmed victory. He reported:

> "We climbed west and also north in the direction of Kalidjati, high over the range of

mountains over which we had seen Navy 0s patrolling from the ground. We crossed the range and descended into a murky sky at lower altitude. Presently I noticed two twin-engined bombers slightly below, to starboard and flying in the direction of Andir. I called Parker on the R/T but received no reply. I pulled to starboard and the two bombers turned around and headed back to Kalidjati. I made a diving attack from the starboard side of the rear bomber. Nothing happened, so I decided that was enough of that nonsense and I pulled around and came up directly behind it. I opened fire very close in, about 100 yards, with a hosing action. Presently the port engine caught fire so I moved over and concentrated on the starboard engine. It also caught fire. By this time my windscreen was covered with oil from its ruptured tanks and I had to open the hatch and look out the side. Being unable to see forward clearly to pursue the other aircraft, I returned to Andir. Presently Parker returned. He confirmed having seen a blazing aircraft in the jungle."

Plt Off Gartrell had not, however, returned to Andir but news soon came in that he had landed his damaged aircraft at Tasikmalaja, a few miles to the east. He claimed a bomber shot down plus a second as a probable. On his return to Andir, Sqn Ldr Julian was informed that there had been no evacuation of Dutch Brewsters after all (only two such aircraft remained serviceable in any case) and it transpired that their proposed departure was nothing more than a rumour! That afternoon the three serviceable Hurricanes were ordered to patrol the mountain area to the north of Bandoeng, Julian leading off Parker and Lockwood. The strain was beginning to tell by now, Jerry Parker recording:

"I was getting a bit fed up with this. On the ground I was scared stiff of having to take off and I was suffering from 'pink-eye', not at all happy to look up into the sun. However, I was more ashamed to appear scared in front of the others whilst we had a fair chance of survival."

They flew through scattered cloud and, on emerging from it, were amazed to see a large formation of Japanese fighters just a matter of feet above them and travelling in the opposite direction, but the Hurricanes were not spotted. Bill Lockwood recalled:

"... we proceeded on our respective ways. As we came round on a southerly course – I was flying the last aircraft of a V formation – I noticed far off to starboard, at our level, two aircraft. I called on the R/T and receiving no reply, decided to investigate on my own. As I came closer to the two aircraft, I took them to be two-seater dive-bombers. Coming in at the rear and setting up the reflector sight in what I judged to be the correct wingspan, I had everything in order and was about to open fire when the two aircraft made a sharp pull around to the left. I turned inside of one and at right angles and in a stalled position, hanging on to the prop, fired a short burst at the aircraft as it went past, see-sawing in a vertical bank. After regaining airspeed and coming round slightly above for another attack, I noticed that the gunner in the rear was busy with his tracers. About this time something shook my aircraft and I didn't know if I was being fired on by the other dive-bomber as well, or by some of the 0s I had seen shortly before. I decided to dive away and returned to base."

Meanwhile, the other two Hurricanes had continued with the patrol, flying above the clouds. After about an hour, unaware of Lockwood's combat with the dive-bombers, Julian suddenly peeled off and dived away from the direction of Andir. Assuming that his leader had spotted a target, Parker checked the sky above and then followed him down:

"There was a tremendous thump in the middle of my back and the dreadful clatter in my earphones as heavy calibre bullets burst on the Hurricane from behind. The stick was already well forward and, with the breath knocked out of me, I was unable for several seconds to pull it back. In that time, whilst I was kicking on the rudder and twisting in the dive, I passed between the clouds and only narrowly managed to pull out of the dive about the trees. I was quite panic-stricken, expecting at any moment to collect some more trouble and I pulled around in a skidding turn to the south. Then I went into my routine of sliding and slipping and crazy flying. I searched the air behind me, twisting my head frantically to see the enemy aircraft, but there were none in sight so I tried to maintain the speed of well over 400mph, which had built up in the dive.

I was some miles to the east of Bandoeng and Andir and I passed them on my southerly flight in moments. I could see that one cannon or heavy machine gun shell had exploded in my starboard petrol tank, making an awful mess of the wing root but there was no fire and the engine was running quite regularly. There was no pain in my back but there was a trickle of blood down the lower part of my spine. I kept checking the sky and the instruments and decided that, in the circumstances, I should go to Pameungpeuk rather than try to sneak into Andir. I had no idea what had become of Taffy and didn't at all care. Pameungpeuk on the south coast was best located by flying roughly south-west from Bandoeng until one reached the coast and then turned east. I flew as near to south as I dared without risking hitting the coast too far to the east for I had not visited Pameungpeuk before and I was worried about how much fuel I had left. My back started to ache and stiffen up and, having felt with my gloved fingers the torn metal of the back of the seat, I feared I was bleeding to death. Looking in the mirror as I flew over the hills, I could see the tail unit was scored and tattered but the rudder and elevators seemed to be working in good order. When I arrived at the south coast, the clouds were much lower and within a few minutes I saw a small landing field, which I correctly identified as Pameungpeuk."

After landing and being greeted by some Dutch officers, he requested that this aircraft be refuelled, as he planned to return to Andir just before dusk. Fortunately Parker had been wearing a Dutch parachute, which had thick webbing crossing in the middle of the back, which had undoubtedly saved him from serious injury. A heavy calibre shell had pierced the armour plating of his seat and most of the fragments of this and the seat were embedded in the webbing of the parachute. However, several pieces had penetrated his back, just to the right of his spine.

"I had a glass of milk and the Dutch officers sent for their doctor to look at my back. He was a very pleasant, mild and bespectacled young man, a lieutenant in the air force, but unfortunately he was quite black and, in my naiveté, I suspected he was some sort of witch doctor. I said hurriedly that I thought my back would hold out and I fear I may have offended him as nobody pressed his services upon me. I realised later of course that he was probably quite as well qualified as any other service doctor, but I'd never met a black doctor and I was a bit shaken up. I sat there for a while watching the mechanics working on the aileron. I was biting my nails with anxiety to get back to Andir but eventually the mechanics confessed they could not fix the plane that night.

The Dutch were very kind and took me off to stay with a Danish tea planter and his wife who ran an estate in the foothills a few miles away. I bathed very carefully for my back was most tender and then I sat about in a dressing gown whilst we had supper. The Danes were very depressed about the conflict in Java, as, although their country had been over-run by the Germans and had not declared war on Japan, they had no idea as to how the Japanese would treat them if they were victorious. In addition, they had their industrial worries in that the labour on the plantation was pro-Japanese and quite disinclined to work during these exciting days. I was exhausted from my day and, having to rise early the following morning, soon went off to bed to sleep very soundly on my stomach."

With the onset of nightfall, three Dutch Lodestars and a KNILM DC-3 landed on a road near Bandoeng, to make one of the last evacuation flights out of Java. Again the RAF was allocated just eight seats in one Lodestar, which were earmarked for Wg Cdr Maguire, Sqn Ldr Brooker (both of whom had been ordered to leave), the injured Plt Off Tom Watson, who had been collected from hospital, Sgt Sandy Allen (who had shrapnel wounds to the back of his legs and had suffered further injury in the motor accident) and Sgt Geoff Hardie[122], who was still suffering from ear trouble. Lot-drawing amongst the other pilots for the remaining seats brought allocations for Sgts Jimmy King and Ian Fairbairn, while Plt Offs Mike Fitzherbert and Reg Bainbridge, and Sgt Mark Porter were to stand by in case there should be sufficient room for them. The aircraft were crammed with 15 very senior Dutch officials and their families including Dr van Mook, Lt Governor-General of the East Indies, and the pilots were very anxious to get away. When Wg Cdr Maguire discovered that the cargo holds were being loaded with luggage he got out of his aircraft to try and persuade the groundcrew to offload this to let more of his pilots aboard. The engines were running and a crowd of people, anxious to board the aircraft, were being held back by guards with fixed bayonets. While Maguire was arguing with the groundcrew, someone closed the door and the Lodestar taxied out and took off. Sandy Allen recalled:

> "On realising the Wing Commander was being left behind, I drew my revolver and ordered the pilot to stop. But it was too late and the aircraft was already gathering speed and couldn't or wouldn't stop."

Sgt Fairbairn was also left behind. Having gained an allocation in the draw, he and fellow Australian Tom Young had retired to have a farewell drink and meal, but, on returning to Andir, found that the aircraft had already departed. Red Campbell, among those left behind, was understandably bitter and spoke for his companions:

> "The Dutch in Java, upon whom we depended for ground support, never fought a major battle there, and they refused to fight now. They surrendered the island and declared Batavia an open city. Some of them even stole the Lockheed Lodestars that were supposed to be our transportation and used them to fly their wives and children out to Australia. Those of us who were left had to take to the hills and exist like guerrillas for the next three weeks. Churchill had said that the RAF would fight to the last aircraft and then take to the hills and fight to the last man. That was us!"[123]

Sqn Ldr Julian commented:

> "We managed to get away some of our pilots and then we had to have volunteers to stay behind and put up the last desperate effort. I'd hardly say we were volunteers since all our names were read out – as volunteers! So we just carried on the best we could."

The remaining members of 242 Squadron had been ordered to Tasikmalaja from Andir, but bad weather and darkness prevented them completing the flight and they landed again at Andir to await morning. Following the heavy bombing of shipping at Tjilatjap there was now little hope of anyone getting away by sea, so a considerable body of mostly unarmed RAF and RAAF men (about 2,500), who had amassed at Poerwerkerta, about 30 miles inland from the port, were now to be moved westwards by rail. Their destination was Tasikmalaja airfield, 50 miles south-east of Bandoeng. By the evening of 6 March, two trains had arrived at Poerwerkerta, each made up of a few carriages and a number of freight vans, the first of which was carrying a load of high-octane fuel and aircraft spares. This train, packed with airmen, departed at about 1900, heading south to the junction with the main east-west line at Maos, a short distance from the Serajoe river. The second train followed about two hours later but soon caught up with the heavily-laden, slow-moving first train. At least 600 airmen were packed on the two trains. At 2215 when seven miles north of the junction, near the trackside *kampong* at Sampang, the first train was ambushed by advanced units of the Japanese 56th Regiment, part of the force that had landed at Kragan and had infiltrated the area. Attacking with mortars, machine guns and hand grenades, they blew several of the metal freight vans off the track. The second train was forced to stop and also came under attack. Surprisingly, there were not many casualties at this stage and groups of survivors made their way southwards along the track towards Maos, eventually to be taken prisoner, although a number were killed in skirmishes en route.

At dawn on 7 March, the last five serviceable Hurricanes flew over to Tasikmalaja, finding the airfield practically deserted. The fighters were dispersed and covered with branches, the pilots then heading for the headquarters in town. Shortly after the arrival of the Hurricanes, two light bombers of the 75th Sentai and six 59th Sentai Ki-43s attacked, concentrating on aircraft in pens. They claimed two large aircraft burnt and eight others damaged. Certainly they managed to destroy one Hurricane and damage a second. One of the Ki-43s, that flown by Sgt Yasuhiko Sakakibara, was shot down by AA fire and the pilot was killed – the final JAAF aerial loss of the campaign, from which the 59th Sentai's top scorer – Sgt Maj Hiroshi Onozaki – emerged with ten victories including eight Hurricanes.

Meanwhile at Tasikmalaja, no orders were forthcoming for the RAF contingent. During the day Sgt Snowy Newlands was enjoying himself by providing a meal:

> "By resting the barrel of my .38 Smith & Wesson on the window sill, I managed to shoot a couple of tame ducks, which we grilled on a bit of wire netting over an open fire. The owner of the ducks wasn't very happy, but war is war. This gave me a total score of two ducks and numerous near misses for the .38. My Hurricane score wasn't much better!"

Shortly thereafter, Newlands was approached by Sqn Ldr Julian:

> "I was offered a job escorting a Dutch Buffalo pilot on a strafing trip in the mountains, where the Japs were hand-fighting the Dutch, but there were strong rumours that Java was about to capitulate and I declined."

The Hurricane pilots were close to exhaustion and, when darkness came, 242 Squadron had not flown any sorties during the day; only two aircraft remained serviceable. The day also saw the last operation by Dutch fighters, one Brewster being shot down with the loss of the CO, a second being written off in a crash-landing; the Dutch also had only two fighters remaining. Meanwhile, Flt Lt Parker and his damaged Hurricane remained at Pameungpeuk:

> "I awoke early in the spare room of the Danish plantation manager near the airstrip. Apart from soreness, my back wound was not troubling me as it seemed to have been cauterised by the hot metal so I preferred to have it looked at by our own doctors in Bandoeng rather than have first aid at Pameungpeuk. I crawled into my shirt and shorts, socks, overalls and flying boots in the darkness before washing and sitting down on the verandah until a car came for me at five o'clock. I left a thank you note for my host and a few minutes later was discussing the state of the aircraft with the Dutch fitter. He had been quite unable to repair the cable and they had nothing there with which he could replace it. He'd fixed a wooden wedge on the aileron, which he said it should hold in place. I thought to myself that I had carried out some violent manoeuvres with the damaged aircraft, flown a hundred odd miles and landed with it in no worse condition, so I'd prefer to get back to Bandoeng with it.
>
> Full daylight was coming as I strapped myself in as tightly as I could, lowered the seat as far as possible and locked back the cockpit canopy. There was no breeze, the engine

fired easily and the mags were fine. Before he jumped down from beside the cockpit, the Dutch captain shouted to me to keep well away from Tjilatjap where there were so many Japanese aircraft about. I lowered the flaps by a third, revved up the engine and roared down the field with the gun button and gun sight switched on. In taking off, one automatically and without conscious effort compensates for any tendency in the aircraft to dip or swing out of line. Thus it was not until I was just airborne that I realised that, although I was climbing slightly, the port wing was dropping badly and I had the stick right over to its starboard stop. This was the result of the torque created by the airscrew, which is normally controlled easily enough by the ailerons but one aileron was not enough to counter it. I opened the throttle fully to increase the speed of the air over the one aileron but the effect was to disastrously increase the torque, so that I had not lifted more than 50 feet above the ground before the wings had tilted over beyond the vertical and the engine cut out. I had only a moment to see the horizon turning and revolving swiftly ahead and, looking out under the top of the upside-down windscreen, the barbed wire and machine-gun posts of the airfield perimeter flashing past below me. As always in moments of crisis, time seemed to stand still and I took my hand off the throttle and switched off the ignition.

The violence of the crash was appalling. The port wing and the nose seemed to hit the ground almost simultaneously and the whole aircraft cartwheeled for a couple of hundred yards whilst I was helplessly strapped inside. Guns, wheels, ammunition and parts of the wings were scattered as far as 350 yards from the fuselage but the cockpit retained its integrity and I was quite uninjured for a few seconds, except for a scratch on my shin. The fuselage had come to rest facing the direction opposite that of my take-off and I found myself with the gravity tank almost in my lap and petrol splashing out through the bottom. I was hardly aware of this before I was struck on the head by the rudder pin and stunned. The back of the aircraft had been broken and the tail unit had fallen on to the cockpit. I pulled myself together again, pushed the stick and petrol tank aside, clambered out of the cockpit and picked up my parachute. Several Dutch officers, who hurtled down the airstrip in a car, were surprised to see me emerge from the dust and they congratulated me on a remarkable escape. They organised an old Chevrolet car with a Dutch sergeant as driver to take me to Bandoeng, which we reached about noon.

The town was in chaos, the Japanese ground troops being fairly close, and I found the Squadron had been moved to a small airstrip near Tasikmalaja, rather further to the east. There was a lot of traffic on the roads but we got there in the late afternoon and the sergeant, instead of taking me to the airfield, left me where the pilots were billeted. They had been unable to contact Pameungpeuk and it had generally been assumed on the previous afternoon that I was dead. Taffy had landed all right at Andir and at the time of my arrival at Tasikmalaja was round at Air HQ in the town. An RAF doctor came round to see me at the billet after dark and I lay on a bamboo frame whilst he dug out the bits of metal in my back under local anaesthetic. There was no electricity so Mike held a torch as various angles under the doctor's direction until he was unable to avoid being sick and somebody else took over. The bits had gone quite a long way in and I was very lucky that they had not hit my spine.

Taffy came back with the news that the British troops near Tasik, mostly 5,000 RAF men with a couple of battalions of Australians and some anti-aircraft gunners, would form a guerrilla force in the hills of southern Java and try to hold out long enough to hope for escape by sea and to maintain some resistance. The Dutch intended to surrender on the following day, and at daybreak, our last two Hurricanes were to survey the road to the south-west up which I'd travelled a few hours earlier to ensure that the would-be guerrilla force could get through and that the Japs were not near it.

We visited the remains of my Hurricane, which impressed the other pilots, and the

Danish plantation manager, whose anxiety had increased considerably, and who talked of a menacing future. His workforce had become very unsettled since the news of the Dutch capitulation had come through and he had to reconsider his whole work schedules. I needed a rest badly and at first I was very relieved that the fighting was over. During the previous seven weeks I'd flown more than anybody in the remnants of the two 232 Squadrons – as much as eight hours in a day sometimes – and the strain right from our disastrous first day had been most severe. Of the original ten officer pilots I was the only one left after the first two weeks and was astonished I had survived so long. In addition to the aerial combat there had been the several days of strafing troops and convoys on the roads and in barges and I'd been involved in four crashes."

Dawn on 8 March saw the last two Hurricanes, flown by Plt Offs Bill Lockwood and Reg Bainbridge, undertake the road reconnaissance to Garoet, just to the north of Tasikmalaja. When they landed, at 0800, their mission completed, the aircraft were destroyed on the orders of Air HQ. Corporal Bill Yeardye, a Canadian with 242 Squadron, was given the honour of setting fire to them. Jerry Parker continued:

"We took the radios from the Hurricanes and pulled up the undercarts whilst taxiing them along the field but we were under very strict orders not to burn anything as this might antagonise the Dutch. My back had been well dressed and strapped up and did not bother me but the others, who had seen the extent of the damage, wouldn't let me lift a finger. Despite the delay whilst we smashed whatever we could, we managed to get on the road in a commandeered Buick and some trucks before most of the other troops and in two days we were in the hills to the north of Pameungpeuk on a tea plantation called Pameungatan."

At midday, the Netherlands News Agency in Bandoeng sent a last message to the outside world:

"The situation in Java, at least in the west part of the island, had become critical as the result of a Japanese break-through of the defences of the north side of the volcano of Tangkuban Prahu crater – a success achieved the previous day in the face of desperate resistance by the Netherlands East Indies troops. The Dutch were not only far inferior in numbers, but they were continuously harassed by the Japanese Air Force, against which the Allies could no longer put up effective resistance. The tragedy now unfolding itself in the previously peaceful valleys north of the Tangkuban Prahu crater – known to thousands of tourists for its beauty is the more heartrending for Dutch people when they recall that a great part of the Dutch Air Force was lost in the unavailing defence of Malaya. In the Netherlands East Indies there had been some criticism of the way in which the Allies had conducted the campaign in Malaya and Singapore, but now that Dutchmen had to fight in the same circumstances, judgement might be less severe. However, the conditions in Java were even more unfavourable than in Malaya, since the Japanese were probably in the proportion of at least five to one to say nothing of their superiority in the air, where they had absolute mastery. After they had overcome Dutch resistance at sea and in the air, the Japanese had practically free play. Nothing could prevent them from landing just as many men and as much matériel as they wanted. Without sufficient protection in the air the troops were practically powerless. So Batavia had to be abandoned, and the Dutch forces were concentrated on the plains around Bandoeng, since this was easier to defend than the flat country of the north coast."

On Java all fighting was now virtually over. In the east, Sourabaya had been entered from the west and south during the day, most of the remaining Dutch defenders withdrawing to the island of Madoera for their last stand. Tjilatjap had fallen and Bandoeng had little chance of holding on much longer.

A Japanese war correspondent later reported that shortly before midnight on Saturday 7 March, a Dutch general, carrying a white flag, had approached the Japanese lines and offered to open negotiations for surrender. The next afternoon, at 1500, the commander of the Japanese forces met the Dutch Governor-General, Jonkheer A.W.L. Tjarda van Starkenborgh Stachouwer, at Kalidjati. It appears that the Governor-General consented initially to the surrender only of the troops in the Bandoeng sector, but on the Japanese commander insisting on the unconditional surrender of all the Dutch forces on the island, Stachouwer promised to order the cessation of hostilities at 1000 on the following morning. A contemporary account of the unconditional surrender of the Dutch forces was published by the Japanese News Agency:

> "Cars displaying the white flag draw up before the buildings on Kalidjati aerodrome. The men who descend from them are General ter Poorten (the Dutch Commander-in-Chief), his Chief-of-Staff, Lt General Buckels, a staff officer and two interpreters. They stride into the building behind the guides, and take the seats to which they are motioned. The conference begins. The Japanese commander permits ter Poorten and other officers, to be named by ter Poorten, to keep their swords. Ter Poorten smiles faintly in thanks. Then he brings out a list of armaments and weapons in Java, and places it on the blue and white striped tablecloth. He explains the items in a tired voice. Our commander bends over the list, and glances up in amazement. 'The number of guns you have is very small,' he says, 'it does not amount to the artillery brought here by us. Whatever made you fight in the circumstances?' Ter Poorten smiles in his embarrassment, 'That's true. It is certainly true,' he says."

CHAPTER VII

INTO THE BAG

March 1942 – September 1945

"They have broken the commandments of God, and their defeat is their punishment. To show them mercy is to prolong the war."

Japan Times & Advertiser, 24 April 1942

At first it was intended that the Hurricane pilots should join the armed element of the British force – known as 'Blackforce' after its Australian leader Colonel Black – and take to the hills, to continue resistance as a guerrilla force until rescue could be achieved. Among this group was Sgt Eddie Horton, a Canadian pilot from 266 (Fighter) Wing:

"When Java fell I was in hospital at Bandoeng RAF HQ. A large battle took place outside town and the Japs moved in and the hospital was taken. The hospital patients who could be moved were placed in trucks and taken out of Bandoeng in front of the advancing Japs. This convoy picked up stragglers as it went along, mostly members of the British army; quite a few guns and some supplies were possessed by this party, which numbered about 1,000. They finally found a spot where they intended to make use of the supplies and make a stand against the Japs, but they received orders by a runner from the GHQ to give up, as the Dutch had capitulated."

Apart from the many thousands of British Commonwealth prisoners, the Japanese also captured some 42,000 Dutch troops; 2,522 Dutch officers and men had been killed during the fighting. Although some 7,000 British and Commonwealth air force personnel had been evacuated since 18 February, more than 5,000 remained at the time of the surrender. Air Vice-Marshal Paul Maltby, AOC Java, was the most senior RAF officer to be taken prisoner, together with a bevy of air commodores, group captains including E.B. Rice[124], former AOC 224(F) Group, Singapore, many wing commanders and so forth. Once the few evacuation flights to Australia had ceased, there was no escape from Java except for a handful of opportunists, although many others tried.

A fair number of undamaged or only slightly damaged aircraft also fell into Japanese hands, in Malaya and Singapore, but particularly in the Indies. At Kalidjati a substantial number of Blenheims had been captured during the surprise attack on this airfield, as had five Glenn Martins. About 16 more of these bombers remained undestroyed on Java on 8 March, to add to others found on Singapore. Indeed, so many Glenn Martins did the Japanese find in their possession that nine were subsequently passed to the Royal Thai Air Force to supplement their aircraft of this type. Other types included at least one CW-21B Interceptor, a number of Dutch Brewsters, one or two RAF Buffaloes and several Hurricanes, one of which was a Dutch machine. At least two Hurricanes were repaired and air tested by the 64th Sentai, 2/Lt Aito Kikuchi losing his life when one of these crashed at Palembang on 10 March – the final, if Pyrrhic victory – for the Hurricanes.

One small group of fighter pilots managed to avoid capture and escaped in a somewhat bizarre and daring fashion. Plt Off Dizzy Mendizabal, one of 242 Squadron's Canadians who had been shot down on 3 March, had reached the Dutch airfield at Pameungpeuk, where he was befriended by Australian Sgts Stuart Munroe and Alan

Martin, New Zealander Sgt Doug Jones (all three ex-266 Fighter Wing) but, more importantly, by Dutch Brewster pilot Ensign Frits Pelder. All had one aim in common – to escape. Pelder was able to use his influence with the commander of a Dutch Lockheed 212 squadron, in obtaining permission to repair one of the unit's aircraft with a view to flying it to Ceylon. Following a search amongst the abandoned Lockheeds, aircraft L-201 was found to he the only one that had not had its undercarriage deliberately retracted, having had its tail section rammed by a tractor instead to immobilise it! The five men got to work, as Sgt Martin recalled:

> "We found three Lockheeds, which had been damaged by the Dutch. One had its tail missing, and another its nose. We took the tail off the second plane and fixed it on the first, patching it with ropes and pieces of bamboo. We completed the job with bits and pieces from the third plane, and filled the tanks with petrol drawn from the other two."

Two 40-gallon wing fuel tanks were removed from an unserviceable fighter aircraft, and were installed within the cabin. Extra cans of fuel were loaded into the aircraft and a rubber tube run from the main tanks in the wings through a hole cut in the side of the fuselage. This makeshift arrangement allowed fuel to be fed into the tanks in flight, via a hand pump. With machine guns fitted in the dorsal turret and nose position, the escapers felt confident of their chances. However, there was a further problem to surmount, as Mendizabal later related:

> "The field had been thoroughly bombed, and there was blown-up wreckage strewn everywhere. We managed to clear a semblance of a path, marking it with sticks between the craters."

At 0900 on 9 March therefore, L-201 took off with Pelder at the controls and headed for Medan, 1,200 miles distant in northern Sumatra, which they had been advised was still in Dutch hands. During the seven-hour flight all five pilots took turns in flying the aircraft, reporting that it handled well, and eventually a safe landing was made. Following a day when the aircraft was thoroughly checked over and prepared for the next stage of the journey, L-201 departed Medan early on the morning of 11 March for Lho'nga, on the northern tip of Sumatra, the final refuelling stop. On arrival, willing hands hastily pushed the aircraft under cover as a Japanese reconnaissance aircraft circled above. The Lockheed's tanks were speedily topped up and Pelder took off just as nine bombers were reported heading for the airfield. As he pulled the aircraft out to sea, two Japanese bombers were seen diving down but the Lockheed was not attacked. By late afternoon, following an uneventful eight-hour flight during which each pilot again took a turn at the controls, Ceylon was sighted. Unable to find an airfield, a Hurricane was fortuitously seen cruising by and this was followed to Colombo, where a safe landing was made at Ratmalana airfield.

They were the lucky ones[125].

* * *

Plt Off Red Campbell was in a group that included 242/605 Squadron survivors who, with others, decided to remain in the hills, living off the land and sleeping in abandoned tea plantations. Campbell recalled:

> "In effect, this was the end. At one Javanese town that the Japanese had not yet taken over, the grounded pilots and their remaining crew members appealed to the Dutch officer in command for help. Instead, the fliers were told that the Dutch had surrendered in order to prevent suffering for their families, and the airmen must turn in their weapons also. The fliers refused to comply and escaped in the truck they had acquired. In the resulting

exchange of gunfire, one of their members was killed.

However, food was scarce, as were medical supplies, and the Javanese natives would not help for fear of reprisals. Many men were in poor shape, so the party finally surrendered. The British Army men with us started raiding for food. We were on the south coast of Java, and soon a Japanese patrol picked us up. One of our men started to run and was shot dead. The rest of us surrendered. The date was 20 March."[126]

Another on the run was the adventurous Sgt Newlands:

"Dave Kynman and I decided to try and escape to the south coast but Dave sprained his ankle. So I packed an empty parachute bag with a few tins of food, a canvas bed roll, a single bed sheet, plus revolver, and set off up the jungle slopes, steering by the sun – and that was the last I saw of the squadron boys for three and a half years. The jungle was not lonely. Multi-coloured snakes had to be avoided on the ground and, up above, various monkeys and large black cat-like creatures followed me along, necessitating more firing practice. After varied adventures and a bit worse for wear, I was persuaded to stay on a rubber plantation until orders came out for all white Dutch to report for interrogation. It was thus deemed expedient to give my beloved .38 a sad burial and join a passing Army convoy back to Garoet School, an interim holding camp for Air Force personnel."

The small party of 605 Squadron New Zealanders – Plt Offs Pettit and White, Sgts Kuhn and MacIntosh – were free for a few days, as the latter recalled:

"On 6 March, word was sent to us to return inland again and we were to be taken by rail to Bandoeng where rumour had it that a last stand was to be made by the combined services against the Japs. So we just took to shank's pony [walking], arriving at a small station on the main Bandoeng line after dark. We slept on the platform until about 1am on 7 March, when a train arrived travelling in the direction of Bandoeng. This we all boarded, crowded in with just standing room. Next morning we arrived at Garoet and detrained and spent the rest of the day in a large clump of bush. No one seemed to know what we were to do. That night 605 Squadron slept in a native schoolhouse. During the last few days since we had left Batavia, the native population appeared completely indifferent as to what we did or what was about to happen and seemed little concerned about a Japanese victory over the country. What train travel we did we seemed to pass quite a large amount of war material in railway wagons at the various sidings, such as unassembled P-40 fighter aircraft, wagon loads of bombs, field guns and other war material.

8 March was a very black day for us, for during the morning we were to learn that the British and Dutch forces had capitulated to the Japanese. We had left Garoet about 9am in a motor convoy of trucks and cars for Bandoeng. A few miles out at about 10.30am, while held up in a convoy jam, word was passed along to us about the capitulation. When we realised what had happened the whole convoy just split up, everybody going his own way. Some went back to the aerodrome at Tjamis and waited, others to Bandoeng, but in most cases they went to the south coast with the chance of sailing a sampan or a boat that would make it to Australia. Sgt Kuhn and I left the truck we were in as the rest of those on board decided to return to Tjamis aerodrome. Our plan was to head for the coast. In a small town I saw some natives playing with a motorcycle so I took it and after refuelling Eddie got on the back with me, and we headed off down to the coast.

We had been informed not to go out to the airfield at Garoet, because it was due to be bombed by the Japanese anytime. Had we known better and gone there, so we were told afterwards, when prisoners of war, there were two American B-17s at that airfield wanting to take out any aircrews that they could cram in. During our run down to the coast that afternoon, we passed a lot of our equipment destroyed or being destroyed, such as armoured trucks mounted with machine guns, burning or run into the river, Bren-gun carriers and some guns that were blown up. Late in the afternoon we arrived at quite a large tea factory about 25 miles from the coast. Quite a large party of RAF had gathered there, including most of 605 Squadron. We stayed there, sleeping in the factory that night. There was Air Commodore Staton, as far as I can remember, who was organising everyone into a general party. The following day those of our Squadron learned that the rest of our chaps were further down near the coast, so we left the factory in two trucks that night and arrived at a small place called Poemompoke. Here we stayed until we were taken in by the Japs about a fortnight later.

It was not a port, but there was a small aerodrome, with some Dutch Lockheeds on it, and a couple of Buffaloes, but they had run a bulldozer into them all. The Dutch had done all they could to stop us from escaping, and rumour had it that they wanted to set up a puppet government under the Japs. We had a radio van with us and were in contact with the Allied Command in Australia. Word was that they might send in Catalina flying boats to get the aircrews out. They had quite considerable numbers of P-40s arriving in Australia, with no operational pilots to fly them, so they desperately wanted us. But the Catalinas never turned up and we heard afterwards they had been bombed in Broome harbour – the Japanese had carried out a bombing raid on Broome and destroyed them. There were also reports that they were going to try and get us out by submarine. Well that never came to anything either, because, by that time, the Jap fleet had come through the Sunda Flores Straits and they had completely encircled Java. We were becoming fatalistic then, and realised that we weren't going to get out. There was talk about taking to the jungle, going guerrilla, like a lot of the Dutch did but Wing Commander Noble said it would be a pretty desperate move to do so without medical supplies, equipment or even armaments. He said word had been sent in by the Javanese that we either came in and surrendered or there would be complete extermination. He didn't want a bloodbath on his hands and ordered us to go into Garoet. So we all climbed aboard lorries and went into this school at Garoet where we were received by the Japanese."

Many of the pilots and others still free were suffering from various illnesses and ailments, including Sgt Kuhn:

"Although we searched the coastline for a boat, with thoughts of somehow sailing to Australia, we were eventually taken prisoner, and were herded into the local jail and locked in a cell which was packed tight with other prisoners, many of whom were ill and suffering from diarrhoea etc and this coupled with the intense heat made conditions incredibly bad. After about a week we were allowed out of the cell into the courtyard, which was a great relief. The only food we received was rice, and eventually I found I was suffering from beri-beri [resulting from a lack of Vitamin B], and in my case it affected my eyes. Eventually I was put on a diet of kataniqu which fortunately corrected my deficiency and my eyesight returned, leaving my right eye slightly affected."

A small party of reinforcement pilots from 266 Wing remained at large for almost nine weeks, as Sgt Frank Hood sporadically recorded in his improvised diary:

9 March: Panic rumour. Away west in a big hurry in afternoon. Lots of rain. End of road at dusk. Nightmare track. Still hoping to get away. Lost kit. Night on beach. 10 March: Started hiking in morning. 11 March: Arrived Tjanda evening. Rented chief's home. Guide supposed to have taken us to fishing village. Scouting parties learn no boats but Nips about. Taken over in boat. Signalling each night. 21 March: Most of blokes left to surrender. Still hurry on, but perhaps wiser to have gone in. Ron, Tommy and Phil arrived. Radio gen not much. Not many left on beach. Nothing doing our place. 28 March: Bill James poisoned feet. Collis [Sharp] malaria. Hiking east. Camp below Tandjong. Plans

for raft. Trouble getting workmen. Attempt for boat. No go. Food very scarce. Plenty on odd days. Half bowl rice two days, 17 bananas one sitting later. Raft finished in a hurry on account of panic. Celebration, cigars and champagne. 17 April: Disappointment. Surf much too heavy. Think OK in calmer water but no hope here. 18 April: Hiking east. Bill James in bad way. Stretcher for him with carriers. Bill into Pam (native doctor). Us there next day. Hope to go on without Bill. Trapped into staying night at Pam. 20 April: In morning native police. Well armed. Ultimative. Go to Garoet with them or outlaws to be shot on sight. None of us very fit. Money low. No future. Estimate two years as PoW. By truck to Garoet."

Sadly, Sgt Bill James did not recover from his infection and died in captivity three months later, on 21 July. In addition to Sgts Hood , James and Collis Sharp, the group included four Australian Hurricane pilots, Sgts Bill Belford, Norm Hobbs (who also contracted malaria), Kevin Wiley and Bill Williams, and may have also included Sgts Albert Jack (who was fated to die as a prisoner on 19 July 1944 at Pangkalan Bali, Sumatra), Tony Payne, George Binsted, Keith Collins, and James Hamilton, who were all taken prisoner at this time. The two Canadian Pilot Officers, Angus Morris and Gordon Palin were also taken prisoner.

Flt Lt Jerry Parker of 242 Squadron, who was also taken prisoner, provides a detailed account of his last few days of freedom:

"It was quite evident that 'Blackforce' would be no fighting unit whatsoever. The RAF men, many of whom had very recently joined up, were unfit to fight, even with full supplies and ammunition laid on. As guerrillas, they couldn't even think of how to live off the land and they seemed to have no notion of the most elementary rural hygiene. The most senior officers accepted that the force could do little but wait for the Japanese to intern us. Meanwhile, the Javanese people, prompted no doubt by wireless broadcasts, welcomed the invaders as liberating them from the colonial Dutch and some amongst them would undoubtedly have betrayed to the Japanese any Europeans they might have found in the jungle and plantations.

The Javanese people in the villages through which we passed seemed to be as happy as ever and there was little sign of the war. We stopped to buy bread and canned provisions but were disappointed to find there were no chicken eggs, only ducks' eggs. Each night we drove down to the beach, hoping a submarine would appear to take us away but, as we could raise no reply on our radios – which wasn't surprising – we had to rely on rumours about a possible escape from the HQ people whom Taffy [Julian] contacted daily. The 300 men for whom we now found ourselves responsible, luckily with the support of some older officers from the Stores, Accounts, Engineering and Administration divisions, were billeted in the main shed of the tea factory whilst the six of us -Taffy, Ernie [Gartrell], Mike [Fitzherbert], Reg [Bainbridge] and Bill [Lockwood] and myself lived in the manager's office. We were able to get showers every day. I had very few clothes, but did have a cotton blanket, a mosquito net, a light mattress and parts of my parachute, much the same as the others. We had to consider the material needs of our men and none of us were very good at it. We learned fast, only time being on our side."

Sqn Ldr Julian added:

"My main objective was to get to the south coast and find a boat, but the Dutch hadn't been good to the natives in Java and anyone who was white was looked on with great hostility by them. Instead of friendliness, which we thought would be the case, they were most anti-European and all boats had been hidden, or destroyed, so there was no chance of making it to Australia, as was my aim. So eventually we were picked up in a tea plantation up north, up in the mountains. I believe the Japanese lined up some women and children and shot them, and word was that for every Japanese that was killed they'd do ten women and children. They meant it unless we surrendered. Reluctantly we just had to go into the bag."

The 242 Squadron pilots going 'into the bag' to join those of 605 Squadron included Sqn Ldr Taffy Julian, Flt Lt Jerry Parker, Plt Offs Mike Fitzherbert, Ernie Gartrell, Reg Bainbridge and Bill Lockwood, Sgts Ron Dovell, Tom Young, Bill May, Gordie Dunn, John Fleming, Ken Holmes, Snowy Newlands, Ian Fairbairn, Mark Porter, Dave Kynman and replacement pilot Sgt Don Isdale (who died as a PoW at Hintok on 18 June 1943). Sgt Gordie Dunn was amongst those who had been on the run but eventually decided to surrender:

"We reached a train station and the train was sitting there, waiting. It was early in the morning, about 7 o'clock, and the CO lined us all up. The Jap CO ordered a count. One man short – our CO said there were 300 present, but the Japs counted only 299. Big trouble time. We were still there at noon and our CO was walking around with other officers, apparently concocting a plan. Eventually, our CO approached the Jap CO and asked if he himself had been counted. 'Ah! No!' replied the Jap CO – and we were allowed to get on the train."

The train took the prisoners to a tea factory outside Batavia:

"When we reported to the factory, we just hung around before they marched us to a prison camp in Batavia. The prison camp was just a compound of *atap* huts. We named it the Atap Hilton. When we arrived, a Jap guard gave a guy with a big, red beard a hard time, so he smacked the Jap and knocked him about a bit. There was a big parade to find out who this guy was, but they didn't twig him because he'd shaved his beard off.

At the camp every time our Nip guard walked by, with a rifle bigger than he was, we were supposed to get up and bow. One day some poor little slob of a guard accidentally discharged his rife through the roof. The Jap Commandant was furious – he came out of his office, took his sword out and cut off a big piece of bamboo and whacked hell out of the guard with it – cut his shirt right off his back. Now, he may have done that to show us guys not to step out of line, but it was a poor example of discipline and just increased our hatred."

Some of the prisoners including Sgts Dunn, Horton, May, Holmes, Porter, Dovell, Young, Kynman, and Fairbairn were taken to Kalidjati, where they were forced to work on the aerodrome. Some men were treated better than others. Dunn later testified:

"Shortly after our arrival questionnaires were distributed and asked questions such as 'How many flying hours each person had?' 'Where had they trained?' 'What the Allies used as aircrew diet?' The wing commander in charge explained that the papers should not be filled out."

The officer who gave that instruction, Wg Cdr Edward Steedman[127], a 37-year-old Londoner, protested to the Japanese Commandant that under the Geneva Convention a prisoner of war was obliged to give no more information than his name, rank and number. The Commandant replied that although the Japanese representative had indeed signed the Convention, the Japanese Government had never ratified it and, that, if he did not obey the orders of the Japanese Army, he would be shot. The Wing Commander persisted that he would not transmit such an order to the officers and men in his charge. He was shot the next morning (17 May 1942). Gordie Dunn and most of the others were not aware of this:

"Next morning about 20 of us were taken for private interrogation by a Jap lieutenant who spoke English very well. We were taken, one at a time, and were beaten by third-degree methods. [Sgt] David Kynman was placed on the floor during his interrogation and his wrists and ankles tied together behind him. A rope was thrown over a rafter, tied to his wrists and ankles and he was raised off the floor. A lighted candle was placed on the floor under him and he was then raised and lowered so that the flame would burn his bare chest.

When it was my turn, the interrogator asked, 'Did you fly an aeroplane?' I said yes and he said he wanted to know about it. Was it very fast? I replied that I couldn't tell him stuff like that, it's classified material, so he took his sandal off and hit me on the back of the neck – which kinda hurt. I was infuriated but couldn't do anything. At one stage the Jap officer said, 'I am in trouble over this and if you don't answer me I will be a failure and I will have to cut open my stomach' – or words to that effect. A wicked thought went through my mind: 'I wish you'd do it now if you're so keen to have a 'coming-out' party – be my guest.' Personally I didn't think he had the guts!

This guy then came up with a stick in his hand and poked me with it, so I pushed it away. Another guy took a whack at me. I made out I was unconscious and sort of fell on him, so he pushed me down on the chair and started yakking. He took another slap at me and put me in another room. They put other guys in the outer room, too – to work us over gradually. I did think they were going to kill us. I guess we thought this was going to be a sticky wicket."

When it was his turn, Horton recalled:

"I was threatened and beaten and taken out and stood up against a wall as a threat of execution. We were then put into a small room. We'd had no food or water since the previous day and were still under threat of execution. Some of the guys had cigarettes hidden on their persons and, being extremely nervous, decided to smoke. Jap guards came in, slapped the entire party about considerably, took all cigarettes and said we were to be executed at 4 o'clock. Guards began picking up bits of personal clothing for their own use after the execution. The squadron leader in charge of the party devised a code we could use and advised filling in the questionnaire, which seemed to be the only alternative, using the code he had devised. This gave no definite information and seemed to pacify the Japs. We were then all put in to a large room and given some food and water."

Dunn added:

"So I filled in the questionnaire. Where it asked how many flying hours did I have when training, I put 260 although it was only 26! The next question was: 'What information were you given on completion of training?' I wrote, 'Stay away from girls and don't drink alcohol!' Another asked if there was more than one rudder bar on a Hurricane? So I called the Jap over and said there is only one. He said the question meant how many bars like a ladder, so we wrote, 'One for tall guys, and one for short guys!'"

Another pilot wrote that he had been trained on hot air balloons and was most experienced on all types of aircraft with more than six engines. One pilot was asked if he carried his sword in his aircraft, and when he replied that fighter pilots did not carry swords he was told emphatically that was the reason why Japanese fighter pilots were superior. These replies were accepted without comment, probably because the Japanese were not qualified to assess the value of the information supplied. However, on learning of the execution of Wg Cdr Steedman, many of the pilots were later worried about some of the frivolous answers they had given. The gloom was lifted about two weeks later they were advised by the CO that a Japanese clerk in the office had 'mislaid' the forms – undoubtedly with a little outside help from a light-fingered prisoner – and that the forms would have to be filled out again. Gordie commented: "No problem. That officer really saved our bacon over those forms!"

Following his capture, Sgt Jim MacIntosh was taken to a different camp:

"After we'd surrendered the Japanese used us to repair Kemajoran, the civil airport near the wharf at Priok. The Dutch had blown it up and the Japanese used British prisoners of war to fill in these craters. They were taken out there for weeks at a time, filling in bomb craters with an old steam engine road roller. Some of us were used at an old school they wanted cleaned out for use as a Japanese barracks. It was on this detail, when we were cleaning out these barracks, that I saw this Japanese soldier reading a magazine, issued to their troops as a newspaper. Like any soldier he chucked it aside, when he finished, and I picked it up and casually looked through it. I noticed a full page print featuring this Hurricane coming in, which intrigued me immensely, and I asked the guard what this represented. He explained that was a Japanese artist's impression of aircraft strafing the Japanese landing at Cheribon. Well I immediately knew that was our attack. So quite innocently I threw the magazine down in front of him and, as he moved away with some of the other guards, without him noticing, I retrieved it and ripped the page out and shoved it in my pocket. I took it back and hid it with my logbook."[128]

Sgt Terence Kelly provides a graphic picture of the early days of his captivity:

"Boei Glodok was Batavia's gaol and as their Dutch masters regarded the native Javanese as of small account, the facilities now made available for the soldiers, sailors and airmen hastily dispatched in a vain effort to stem the Japanese advance, were sorely limited. The entrance was unprepossessing: a crude, unpainted concrete portico shaded a set of iron doors with barred openings above. On our arrival the centre pair of doors was open and inside two Japanese soldiers awaited us: the one to count off batches of six, the other to act as tallyman; every sixth man got a booting in and at each booting the tallyman made a mark. Once within we were roughly dispatched through a forward area towards a 'U' of large cells into which we were counted by more or less the same process and when each cell was considered sufficiently filled, its iron door was clanged shut. In my cell [K.8] were about one hundred and fifty. It had a concrete floor and concrete walls and high above a timber roof. It was slightly more oblong than square with the two opposite walls unrelieved by openings while of the other two, one was pierced at high level by a more or less continuous shallow barred opening through which could be seen a line of western sky, while the fourth, which overlooked the courtyard around which the 'U' of cells was built, had the door in the northern corner and barred openings whose sills were about chest high. In the centre of the cell was the lavatory that consisted of a hole in the floor and two lines of glazed tiles on which one was supposed to squat.

A week or two after we had arrived, the Japanese decided it was time we did something to earn our keep and sent us out to Kemajoran Airport to help repair the damage to the runways which the Dutch had mined. To the imprisoned Hurricane pilots there was a curious irony in this. We had arrived in Java by flying our Hurricanes off the aircraft carrier *Indomitable* from some point in the Indian Ocean close to Christmas Island, forty-eight young men cock-a-hoop with confidence they would soon sweep the Japanese with their wooden biplanes out of the skies of Malaya and Singapore. I happened to be in the first batch of sixteen to land and we arrived to welcoming drinks and lunch in the glittering airport terminal building which overlooked the runways from which we would fly up to Singapore on the following day. There were five survivors in Glodok, Lambert and Healey being with me in K.8 and we worked beside each other filling in the craters in mined runways.

To get to the airport we had to march for three miles through contrasting sections of what had been to us a very beautiful and fascinating town. And so to the airfield which, a bare three months ago, we had beat up in formation before breaking into pairs and taxiing to that glittering terminal for our welcome feast. That glittering terminal! What was it now? A nondescript mess of broken glass and twisted metal. The Dutch had certainly done a splendidly efficient job of mining and the runways had been rendered unusable by huge, neatly round and very deep craters with the resulting debris surrounding them. Our job was the simple one of pitching the debris back in again. Meanwhile the airfield was in operation for there was plenty of room for aircraft to take off and land on its grassed areas and it was with savage chagrin and desperate jealousy that Lambert, Healey and I watched this activity. But soon it occurred to us that herein lay the only possible method of escape from Java. If, we reasoned, we could steal an aircraft of sufficient range with a bit of luck we could make Australia.

Scattered around the field were the burnt out remnants of allied aircraft but amongst them the almost intact fuselage of a Lockheed Hudson. One of us could, we decided, slip into it when the guards were occupied and stay behind, spend a night casing the [security] precautions taken and satisfy ourselves which aircraft were fully fuelled. We saw little difficulty in this initial exercise or in organising things so that one should not be missed through the rough and ready roll call of many hundred men returning to camp – and indeed as future experience was to demonstrate, covering up one missing man would have presented little problem. It was a risky idea but it might very well have worked. We had no chance of finding out, for another group of pilots, again three in number, upstaged us, attempted almost exactly what we had in mind, were caught and summarily beheaded. Moreover the Japanese made it clear and had it put around that in future if escapes, or attempted escapes took place, they would presume that those who slept on either side of the offenders were of necessity in the know and would suffer a similar penalty."

The unfortunate trio included two of the 266 (Fighter) Wing pilots, the Canadian pair of Sgts Howard Low and Russell Smith, the former having been wounded at Palembang. During early April the two friends together with Plt Off Red Campbell of 605 Squadron, and two Hudson aircrew, hatched a plot to escape from the prison camp and attempt to steal a Ki-56 transport aircraft, which they had seen parked at nearby Batavia airport. At the eleventh hour however, one of the Hudson aircrew went down with a bout of malaria and was forced to drop out, then, the day before the planned breakout, Campbell informed the others that he had seen Japanese personnel testing the engines of the transport aircraft and that one engine had developed an obvious fault. His doubts, however, failed to deter the other three – Low, Smith and Flg Off Harry Siddell, the Hudson pilot – from making an attempt to escape that night. Armed with revolvers and knives, they apparently killed a guard and managed to get one engine started before being captured. They were beaten unconscious with rifle butts and dragged to the guardhouse. It was rumoured that they were tortured by Kempetei in an attempt to extract information about any others who might be involved in the escape plot, and were then taken to a corner of the airfield and shot. A Javanese civilian[129] later testified to the Allies as to what he had witnessed:

"With my friend, I was standing near the gates at the railway crossing. I saw five Japanese soldiers approaching the plantation with three airmen. The men were blindfolded and wearing flying boots. They wore light brown shirts and their trousers were tucked into their flying boots. The airmen and their escort appeared to come from the direction of Glodok jail. Before the shooting took place other Japanese called at the *kampong* about 8am and obtained from nearby the services of three Indonesians to dig three graves in the plantation. The airmen and their escort arrived about 10 o'clock. Blindfolded, they were placed facing their respective graves in a standing position. They were not allowed to pray before they were shot. The airmen were shot from a distance of about one yard. Two Japanese did the shooting. Two airmen were shot first and death appeared to be instantaneous. They were shot with revolvers. The Japanese soldier who shot the second airman then turned his revolver on the airman who I now learn was R79670 R.C. Smith (RCAF) and whose identification disc I saw when his remains were exhumed. When the soldier turned his revolver on the airman R.C. Smith he, too, was shot outright. The three airmen had their hands tied behind their backs. Just before the shooting, the three Indonesians were sent away but were recalled after the execution to close the graves. I do not know why the airmen were executed and I could not recognise the Japanese soldiers again."

Russell Smith died just eight days before his 20th birthday; Howard Low was four years older[130]. It did not end with their deaths. Their friends and acquaintances and some who shared the same quarters were interrogated and tortured. Some were hung up by their ankles from the ceiling and beaten with truncheons. Shortly after, all prisoners were ordered to sign a piece of paper to undertake formally not to attempt to escape. 'Beery' Noble[131], the Senior British Officer and former OC RAF Kota Bharu and Lahat, issued an order that no one was to sign, and was severely beaten for his pains, and ten men were thrown into solitary confinement, without food or water, until everyone had signed. Noble relented and agreed for all to sign, pointing out that as signatures were obtained under duress they were without effect.

There occurred a further four executions of RAF personnel at Malang on 4 May following an unsuccessful attempt to escape; one of these was another 266 (Fighter) Wing pilot, Sgt Dennis Poland, a 22-year-old from Lancashire. Corporal Jim Home of 242 Squadron witnessed their deaths:

"One day, when arriving back from our working party, we were told of an attempted escape made by four RAF men. Two were ex-planters, one a sergeant pilot and the fourth was a Malayan warrant officer of the Singapore Training Corps. They had gone the previous night without being missed until they were picked up. Their chances had been relatively good as only the sergeant pilot had not lived in the East, one man was coloured and between them they had ample funds. They had reigned two nights. Apparently the original plan had been a mass escape. Later it was decided a smaller party would be more suitable for the initial attempt, as the four would be 'testing the water'. If they could have quickly found a friendly *kampong* or contacts, it was just possible they may have succeeded. But now what?

We were kept on parade at *Tenko* and the four men were paraded before us; it seemed that the natives had preferred their rewards to risking their skins by helping escapees. The four were given an unholy beating, then tied up and taken to the guardroom. They were already in a sorry state having obviously been 'helped' along the way from the moment they were caught: every available boot would have been put in with great relish. On such occasions the guards quickly lined up to work themselves into frenzy, until they lost whatever reason they might have possessed. Later, the four were placed in a bamboo cage like wild animals, with no regard to even the most fundamental rules of warfare. Each night we were assembled on *Tenko* to witness them receive yet another beating before being returned to their cage. About a week later, in the middle of this disgusting display of cruel sadism, a lorryload of soldiers with machine guns entered the arena. They dispersed their machine guns with an expert efficiency to surround us all – those butterflies were back and flapping around in my stomach. Our first thought was that there was going to be a mass annihilation for which we were not in any way prepared. I know of at least two that prayed – I'm sure there were many more – and I was maturing very quickly.

The Camp Commandant and his interpreter made their appearance on the scene in grand style as though playing some rôle in *Shogun* – they were dressed as though to attend their noble Emperor. The Commandant told us that for every man who attempted to escape, at least ten others would die. Was he now to pick the 'chosen' forty to die along with the four he now held as an example? Was that why they needed to surround us with a battery of machine guns in case there was a reaction from ourselves? The answer was not long in coming and it was devastating. The four escapees were already lined up as though for execution and the guard in charge was attempting to blindfold the first. He was the sergeant pilot and he was refusing to be blindfolded. Two others accepted rather quietly and the fourth broke down to plead. I have many times hoped that in those last dreadful moments that the sergeant suffered, he realised how proud we all were of him – we no doubt wondered if we could show the same raw courage.

Whilst this was taking place the ranks began to sway to and fro as though to break. I doubt if anyone had considered ever being in such a hopeless situation. An order rumbled through and along the ranks, 'Hold it and don't be stupid.' It was very good advice. No doubt our captors would have welcomed some trigger practice on hot-headed prisoners. Standing there together the four escapees were shot and a Jap officer followed through with his revolver to put a bullet into each. The whole affair had been carried out with great aplomb; the four now had the respect of their enemy as they were dead. We now understood a little more about our captors. It was said that the prisoners had earlier been forced to dig their own graves. The firing squad had turned out in beautiful white uniforms and were drilled with a trained respect for those they intended to kill. The four were buried and a small cross was placed at the head of each. In the eyes of the Japs the four were now dead but also honourable!"[132]

Elsewhere on Java small groups of airmen were frustrated in their attempts to render various abandoned aircraft airworthy in bids to escape. At Andir, a Dutch Glenn Martin had been discovered with only slight damage. Repairs were secretly carried out and an overload fuel tank fitted, but the senior RAF officer refused permission for the volunteer crew to leave, as it was feared that reprisals would be taken against those remaining. A similar decision was made at another airfield camp when a Tiger Moth was located unassembled in a crate. Over a period of ten days, the aircraft was assembled and fitted with extra fuel tanks to give it an estimated 800-mile range. The night before the planned departure, the Japanese Commandant informed the senior RAF officer that severe reprisals would be taken if any of the men under his command attempted to escape. The Tiger Moth was duly destroyed. Many others attempted to escape by sea in various craft, but only one party of 20 airmen made it all the way to Australia. At Tasikmalaja, where 2,000 mainly RAF and RAAF personnel had gathered, the arrival of the Japanese was awaited with trepidation. LAC Don Peacock later wrote an account[133] of his time at Tasikmalaja:

"We could have lived happily ever after but for one slight problem: the Nips. They first disturbed our peace on our second day on the airfield. We were lined up on one of those wretched parades without which, unfortunately, service life seems quite unable to function, when a formation of bombers, with fighters weaving behind them, came screaming in at us little more than palm high. Every nerve in our bodies urged us to dive for cover as we had learned to do over the past three months. The ranks wavered, but the officer in charge, moustache bristling, his face puce with anger, bawled at us to stand fast. And when it came to the choice of facing the bombers or the wrath of the Wing Commander [Wg Cdr Gregson[134]] it had to be the bombers. We stood there petrified as the planes kept diving at us. Quite likely, we reasoned, their pilots had been bombing and strafing as long as we had been ducking and running. Could they now kick that unfortunate habit? They could and they did. A few more low passes over the parade, and off they flew.

A few days later we met our hosts eyeball to eyeball. We stared at the Nips. The Nips stared at us. They crouched along the sides of the truck, scruffy and undersized, holding their rifles grimly between their knees. In their washed-out uniforms, with cloth streamers dangling from their peaked hats like tatty pigtails, they could scarcely have looked less like conquering heroes. Gradually a curious crowd gathered around them. The silent battle of stares intensified. Then, neither side meeting quite the hostility it feared, eased off again. The swarthy faces began to relax. Here and there came the suspicion of a smile. Despite our inner feelings, some of us grinned back. This was apparently what the Nips wanted. Simply beaming now, they quickly moved into the rôle of indulgent victors. Soon they were all jabbering away at once. So many of them spoke intelligible English that it seemed obvious that they had been specially picked for this reconnaissance. For the moment they all seemed anxious to please: over-anxious perhaps. Some even went so far as to throw us cigarettes, which weren't refused. For a few more minutes they simply oozed goodwill. Then they drove off as suddenly as they had arrived. Presumably they went back to report that we were a pretty docile bunch unlikely to cause much trouble. They had performed their role efficiently. No doubt they would have done their duty just as adequately had they been sent in to mow us down."

So far, so good – for the time being:

"We became a trifle uneasy . . . when we found that an enterprising group of aircrew types were busy trying to repair a damaged American bomber that had been left in a corner of the airfield. The affair put our senior officers on the spot. Should they help the aircrew to carry out their undoubted duty to try to escape; or act to protect those who would be left to face the music, if not the firing squad? There were mutterings that this wildcat scheme should not be allowed to put our necks at risk. Wasn't the future grim enough without deliberately inviting trouble? The issue was finally settled when the officers sent a party of only too-willing volunteers to slash the bomber's tyres and sabotage any hope of getting it off the ground. The frustrated flyers were not too happy about this. They swore to see that those responsible were court-martialled as soon as we were freed. But freedom proved much farther away than any of us dreamed, even in our most despairing moments.

Gardens to keep us in veg seemed a good idea. We started digging in the fond hope that Tasikmalaja was to be our permanent home. Then we felt no good prison camp would be complete without its home-produced entertainments, so we got up a concert. A secret radio was a must. Our officers produced one. I went along each day to take down as much of the BBC Overseas Service news as my inadequate shorthand would allow. The result was the *Tasikmalaja Times*, which an officer read out to anyone interested. The news was always terrible, though everyone was interested to hear that London had us still up in the hills harassing the enemy in the true Churchillian spirit. Of course there had to be some sporting activities. Some officers took up hunting: hunting the flies, which bred in fantastic numbers in the open trench latrines we had dug. Enthusiasts set themselves a target of 500 a day. The champ, I think, a fighter pilot, set up a record kill of 94 at one swipe, using slightly-off bully beef as bait.

Then there were shopping expeditions to the fence. So far the Nips had shown no interest in our private market. I made one important purchase. I bought one of those large plate-shaped basketwork hats worn by natives in the paddy fields. It brought a few ribald comments, and hints that the sun had got me already, but had I been able to foretell the future I could not have made a better buy. Most of our companions had come into prison camp more or less straight off the boat from Liverpool, pausing only for a quick pint in a Batavia bar. So we old hands wiled away pleasant hours hunting out newcomers from our hometowns who could tell us if the Odeon was still standing and if they still had the same barmaid in the Red Lion."

After some time at Tasikmalaja, Don Peacock was among a party of 200 PoWs sent to Semarang to construct an airfield:

> "A Japanese bomber pilot, who dropped in unexpectedly, delighted us with a skidding broadside that would have done credit to a dirt-track ace when he noticed, rather belatedly, that our light railway lay right across his path. It was several days before his plane was fit to take off again. There was a slapstick serial provided by a gang trying to get a plane into the air pulling a drogue target. Time after time the target caught on some obstruction or other, the rope snapped, the whiplash scattered the Nips, and the plane took off towing nothing but a piece of string.
>
> Dive-bombing practice was often great fun too, with the bombs tending to fall anywhere but on the target. One pilot made a very creditable attempt to close the main railway line. But we were not always in the best position to appreciate the joke. We had one or two narrow escapes. The dive-bombers had left three unexploded bombs somewhere in the swamp. The order was, 'Find them.' I had never felt that bomb disposal work was really me, so I spent the day paddling around knee-deep in ooze, making sure that I neither found nor disposed of anything. Fortunately, suicidally inclined comrades quickly unearthed two bombs, and long muddy hours later the third turned up. I kept my distance while the three were dragged together. They were then blown up... together with one over-enthusiastic Nip.
>
> This interlude of comparative peace was marred by a tragedy in what we called the cookhouse, an *atap* roof supported by four bamboo poles. Our food was prepared in *wejangs*, huge conical cast-iron cooking pots, balanced on dwarf stonewalls over log-fires. We were waiting for the evening meal to be ladled out when the whisper went round that the mangy body of a kampong cat had been found floating in the stew *wejang*. We hoped that death was due to drowning after slipping off the roof, and not to rabies or some dread tropical disease. Nobody actually refused his meal, but the idea of even a healthy cat swimming in the stew did not improve our appetites. We had yet to rid ourselves of our absurd fussiness over our food."

Later still, when at Haruku camp, Peacock recalled:

> "Whatever the reason, it was the sick who benefited from a new dog-trapping campaign launched by the Gunzo. His victims still found themselves slung into the air in Heath Robinson bamboo traps, but he was now beating them to death with his bamboo pole instead of beheading them. And, surprisingly, they were now handed over to the cookhouse specifically for the hospital stew."

Another prisoner commented:

> "Dogs did not last long if they strayed into our camp. What a grand meal, if only we had salt to put on it. Cats were easy to catch – so sweet, white fleshed. We boiled the animals in oil drums and hid the meat in the soup mixture given to us."

By late 1942, the Japanese attitude towards the prisoners began to harden and beatings became commonplace. A proclamation by Colonel Masanobu Tsuji, Chief of Operations and Planning staff of the victorious Japanese 25th Army, that prisoners should be shown no mercy had obviously gone a long way towards changing attitudes. His words were echoed in an article, printed on 24 April 1942, in the influential and widely read *Japan Times & Advertiser*:

> "They [the Allies] surrender after sacrificing all the lives they can, except their own, for a cause which they know well is futile; they surrender merely to save their own skins. They have broken the commandments of God, and their defeat is their punishment. To show them mercy is to prolong the war. They have shown themselves to be utterly selfish

throughout all the campaigns, and they cannot be treated as ordinary prisoners of war. Their motto has been, 'Absolute unscrupulousness.' They have not cared what means they employed in their operations. An eye for an eye, a tooth for a tooth. The Japanese Forces are crusaders in a holy war. Hesitation is uncalled for, and the wrongdoers must be wiped out."

The prisoners would be kept in camps in Java for some months, and then most were transferred to Japan. Some 28,000 prisoners were despatched to Japan from Singapore, Java and Hong Kong to work in mines and heavy industry, since most of the young Japanese men were in the forces. To transport these men, cargo vessels were fitted with staging so that floor space was doubled or even trebled, although some ships had no staging and prisoners had to lie on top of cargo. Toilet facilities were negligible, comprising wooden crates hung over the sides of the ships. Washing and exercise were impossible aboard many of the vessels and food and water always in short supply. While life was desperately hard, the mortality rate was not nearly as high as amongst those who had been captured in Malaya and Singapore and who ended up working on the infamous Burma-Thai railway[135]; most of the Java captives survived to return home at the conclusion of hostilities. Only one RAF man managed to successfully escape, Sgt Charles McCormac of 205 Squadron[136]. Another, Aircraftman Gordon Coates of 100 Squadron, a 25-year-old from Co. Durham, managed to evade capture for nine months. Sadly, when he was eventually taken he was accused of being involved in espionage and was executed on 1 February 1943.

Meanwhile, Sgts Kelly, Lambert and Healey were incarcerated in the goal with other pilots, including Sgt Snowy Newlands, and were at Boei Glodok for seven months. Kelly later wrote:

"I was fortunate in being able to share a cell with Lambert and Healey. We had come halfway round the world together, we had fought the Japanese in Singapore and Sumatra and having all three of us drawn low cards that vital morning on the stoep of the Hotel der Nederlanden in Batavia, we had gone on to fight them in Java. We had seen close friends killed and wounded and said goodbye to others who escaped to Australia and Ceylon. And in the end after more death and injury we had been the last three of the original squadron to fly against the enemy. And then with no aircraft left we had tried to escape together, failed do so, shared the same native hut and entered Glodok side by side.

In a normal civilian life we would not necessarily have chosen each other for company but circumstances had so arranged things that it did not occur to us to look elsewhere and naturally we stayed close in Glodok. The effect of this was blinkering. We were not unaware of the suffering around us and did not entirely escape it, but we did not apply the possibility of dying to ourselves. When we felt depressed we escaped by strolling the courtyard together, looking at the cumulus longingly, reminiscing and deluding ourselves that we would one day fly again. Fortunately we were equally poor and thus there was no risk of envy creeping in and, importantly, each of us, because of the other two, was obliged to maintain his self-respect. As fighter pilots we had counted ourselves rather special and if this speciality was to be retained then we could not have anything to do with being unshaven, unwashed, unkempt nor with begging cigarettes from our captors or toadying to those who were by prison standards rich men. We felt moreover a sort of responsibility to those around us, which sprang from the automatic but very positive respect that ground staff always gave to aircrew. After all pilots are what air forces are all about."

With so many hundreds of undernourished men packed into very small confined areas, illness and sickness was rife, although loss of life at this stage was not excessive. Kelly continued:

"Another malady was known as 'Strawberry Balls'. Presumably there is a medical term for this as well but if there is I have never heard it. It was obviously another complaint springing from vitamin deficiency and there were few who did not suffer from it in smaller or greater degree. It attacked the testicles from which one daily lost a skin and the area soon itched, grew sore and became a surprising colour. Occasionally septicaemia set in and I believe in other camps, though not, I think, in Glodok, some deaths resulted. There were of course doctors who'd been taken prisoner but neither they, nor their Japanese counterparts, had the slightest notion how to deal with it. Many exposed the affected parts to the presumed beneficent rays of a tropical sun. On an appointed day all sufferers were instructed to attend a course of treatment on 'The Green'. The length of exposure was to be timed and limited and at a given word of command all were to be instructed to expose their testicles. At the preliminary briefing it was pointed out that the penis was likely to cast a shadow and all patients must make appropriate arrangements to see this didn't happen. Much ingenuity was displayed: there were slings with tapes, which tied around the neck; there were tripods; there were posts and strings.

The hunger of men given, over a lengthy period, insufficient food to satisfy their wants yet just sufficient to keep life going has curious consequences, which vary according to attitude, character and sense of purpose. But, in one way, all are affected equally: the sex urge entirely vanishes. And not only does it become impossible to think of women sexually but extremely difficult to think of them at all. To pass the time one might try to conjure up sexual images but the result was dismal failure. You just could not hold in your mind the idea of a girl lying naked on a bed; the best you might do was imagine one in a pretty dress on a summer lawn, with the chink of teacups rather more important than her voice; and quite soon you'd forgotten the girl and the teacups and your mind had shifted to steak and chips.

So we [Kelly, Lambert and Healey] were a little apart from the hundreds of men about us and to a degree sufficient in ourselves. This was to end abruptly. The 'we', so far as I was concerned was to become 'I', and Bertie and Pip, as I knew them, were to go out of my life and I was not to see them again until after the war was over. On 21 October 1942, almost exactly seven months after entering Glodok, I left as one of a batch being transferred to Japan. Thus one day life was pretty much a routine business shared with two friends, who had become very close, and the next I was parading at the gate and they were saying goodbye. I was sad to leave them but young enough to be glad that the pointless stagnation of life in Boei Glodok was at an end. Without the least idea of our destination, blessedly unaware of what the next few months would hold, I felt once more the tingling of adventure. And I was fortunate. Both Lambert and Healey (who were subsequently sent to help build airfield on the island of Ambon) had a grimmer tale to tell."

Kelly's party – about 500 strong under the command of Sqn Ldr Ricky Wright – was taken to Tandjong Priok, where they embarked on a very small vessel, the 3,000-ton *Yoseda Maru*. Conditions aboard were almost indescribable. The space between decks was subdivided horizontally so as to provide layers of men with just about enough head height to be able to sit up, but who were so close side by side that when one turned, his neighbour was more or less obliged to do the same. The 500 British prisoners were packed into one hold; the other three holds contained about 2,500 mainly Dutch and Javanese prisoners. Crammed in like this, they were transported to Singapore:

"We docked in Keppel Harbour. Here was evidence of a shaming defeat, which would change forever the opinion of the Oriental towards the British: scuttled ships, deserted godowns, piles of scrap. For two days we lay by, before we were filed ashore for inspection and disinfectation. The inspection was by means of a glass rod thrust up our anuses; the disinfectation was as unforgettable. It was a ship, which had been especially converted and had a curious wooden structure like an endless sheep dip along which we progressed naked into a warm bath, which smelt of lime and was of the colour of mashed potato. In it we were required totally to immerse ourselves until, presumably, we were rid of germs and then we returned to re-dress ourselves in the same germ-ridden clothes."

They were then transferred to the ancient, rusting, decrepit but much larger *Dai Nichi Maru* (15,000-tons). Kelly continued:

"I knew only a few of the 285 men in the hold, although one I did know was Sgt Bill May of 242 Squadron. The hold measured 80 feet by 60 feet and was illuminated by a single light bulb. It was infested with rats, flies and cockroaches. Other holds contained up to 1,000 more prisoners, while on the deck were about 1,000 Japanese soldiers going home, for the destination was Japan. On arrival at Takao, Formosa's southernmost port, we took on board some American prisoners. After several days in turbulent seas, severe diarrhoea broke out among the tightly packed prisoners, and soon the troughs were blocked. They had to be cleared by those not affected by diarrhoea and dysentery. Permission was forthcoming for those able to, to go up on deck to obtain water.

We slid and slipped our way across the pitching deck, pausing when the slope was too much against us, grasping at anything to hand to hold us back when too steep. To sluice out the troughs we used buckets on ropes, which we hurled over the side and hauled up, swaying wildly, crashing against the rusty sides and losing half their contents. We threw the water into the troughs to sluice them out. The troughs were hideous. Everything was choked together: blood and slime and excreta bound by bloodied paper and bloodied rags. It resisted shifting and was evil beyond words being not just the remnants of what men had eaten but part of men themselves. It was abominable and obdurate and it stank of death. We threw the water at it and the water was contaminated and picked up by the wind and whipped into contaminated spray, which drenched us. It was a long, cold, unpleasant job sluicing out those troughs three times a day."

Men began to die in large numbers. Another aboard the *Dai Nichi Maru* was Sgt Ed Horton:

"During the journey food was entirely inadequate. The Japs furnished one half pint of tea twice a day. Suffering from extreme hunger and partial suffocation, two members of the British Army broke into Jap stores and for punishment the entire hold was locked and of the 500 PoWs only ten men at a time were allowed on deck."

Incarcerated with about 3,000 other unfortunate prisoners aboard the *Singapore Maru*, also destined for Singapore, was Sgt Gordie Dunn. Another prisoner on board the same vessel wrote:

"We were transported to the *Singapore Maru* to Singapore, taking eight days. Three thousand of us (mostly Dutch) were packed in the hold of the ship like sardines. This was a real hellhole as conditions were bad and many suffered from dysentery. We were fed three cups of rice a day covered with two spoonfuls of soup. On arrival at Singapore we were marched about 14 miles to Changi [prison camp]. Some of the PoWs [including Dunn] were left in the boat and more crowded in."

Eighty-five prisoners died during the journey to Singapore. Sgt Snowy Newlands was among those sent briefly to Changi:

"While in Changi I visited Sgts Fleming[137] and Margarson[138] and swapped news. They weren't in the stone prison, but in an adjacent area living in some little huts they had made themselves. Margie seemed to have made a fair sort of recovery from his wounds. I had last seen him in a very bad shape at the main Singapore hospital just before the surrender of Singapore."

The two vessels plus a third, the *Tofuku Maru*, in which Newlands now found himself, set out for Japan. Horton continued:

"Two weeks from Japan, a severe epidemic of dysentery broke out and conditions following cannot be described. At least fourteen Air Force PoWs died. When the ship reached harbour, she lay at anchor for three days and no one was taken off. Finally, all of the fit were taken off and the ill left in the hold. The very ill were put on board the *Singapore Maru*. Thirty were left on the *Dai Nichi Maru*, too sick to move, some dead. PoWs were finally taken off transports and taken to Moji. About 48 hours later the Japs brought food but the majority of the PoWs were too ill to eat. Shortly after, about 20 American PoWs, including Navy corpsmen and six medical officers, and two Australian medical officers arrived. Eighteen died during the first night."

Eighty deaths had been recorded aboard the *Dai Nichi Maru* by the time she eventually arrived at Moji. Sgt Gordie Dunn, aboard the *Singapore Maru*, painfully remembered:

"The boat stopped at Saigon for two or three days. We thought we would get off there. The weather and seas were so bad. Dysentery broke out and the guys died like flies. Dysentery travels fast and they did let us up on top every now and again. We saw sea snakes all around us. We had a little dachshund dog called Fritzy, which used to bark at the Jap guard – the cruel bugger threw him overboard. The last we saw of poor Fritzy he was swimming in the wake. One or two of the boys figured the easy way out would be to step overboard, but they never did. My mother used to say I was so stubborn that if my arse itched I'd scratch my ear – you have to be stubborn sometimes. Some guys broke into the storehouse but I was too sick to worry about that, but they clued me as to what had happened. They found some watermelons and made them into a stew. When we landed at Moji I was really sick and I was taken to the YMCA camp."

He added:

"During the dysentery epidemic – December 1942 to January 1943 – the bodies of victims were placed in the sick bay beside patients. At one time they collected five days' victims that had been allowed to accumulate."

Snowy Newlands' journey aboard the *Tofuku Maru* had been similarly tortuous:

"The boats were old small freighters converted to troopships – Japanese style – with decks built around the cargo holds, giving room to sit up only, and so crammed with prisoners that there was scarcely room to lie down. Fever and dysentery were soon rife. At first the bodies were buried at sea over the side, but later nobody was able to care much and sanitation buckets and bodies fell to the bottom of the hold as we struck typhoon conditions. I would say between one-fifth and one-quarter died before reaching Japan. Those not able to walk on arrival at Moji – with snow falling and us dressed in open shirts – were taken by truck to a makeshift hospital with concrete floors, with eight patients to a room about 12 feet by 10 feet. We slept on a layer of straw on the concrete but had some blankets. It was possibly -15° centigrade, with approximately 18 inches of snow. Most of us had extreme diarrhoea. One chap was moved from our room, very ill. He also had extreme beri-beri. Another chap took his place from next door. He was getting lonely as the other seven had already been cremated."[139]

The surviving prisoners were divided into two groups. One group including Sgt Bill May was sent to Mukaishima, while Sgt Kelly's group was put on a tug and taken to Innoshima, thence to Habu Camp, where Sqn Ldr Wright became the SBO. Without sufficient time to recover from the arduous sea journey, the survivors were put to work. At Moji, Sgts Dunn and Horton found themselves working together, as the latter recalled:

> "On about 2 February [1943], both myself and Dunn began working, loading cement on ships. I worked three 24-hour shifts in one week, and for three weeks I was so ill I could not go out of camp. Food decreased in quantity all the time.
>
> The first man in charge of the Moji camp was an American-educated Japanese lieutenant, who was fairly strict and yet quite honest. He only stayed a few months. The next, who remained until the PoWs were released by Allied forces, was Captain Saito, who was a tyrant from the beginning. At first he made slight improvements. Then he began taking Red Cross parcels belonging to the PoWs and issuing them to the guards, except the bits he rationed to the PoWs. When a spokesman for the PoWs protested, he took one complete shipment of parcels, had them all opened up and the contents placed in wooden buckets in the square, and ordered that it must all be eaten by lights out that night. Much of the perishable stuff was wasted because most of the PoWs were too ill to take advantage of the quantity.
>
> In the early spring a reign of terror began in the camp. Mass punishments started. The Jap guards would line up and take turns beating the PoWs with shovels and belts. One Javanese boy was beaten until he almost died and then forced to go out on a working party. Once a party was being celebrated by the Japs and all the guards got drunk and walked around camp with big sticks and rifles hitting PoWs over the head. A captain doctor was knocked unconscious for two days and was in a stunned condition for weeks. Every Jap holiday was cause for mass punishment. Every Allied victory caused PoWs intense mistreatment. This condition got worse as time went on and raids by Allied aircraft increased. Every alert in the Moji area was cause for worse treatment.
>
> For infractions of one of Saito's vague rules, I was hit over the head by him with a sword. I was also paraded before the guardhouse one day for not having my shoes shined. I was hit over the mouth. When I reported to the sick bay to have my mouth dressed a Jap NCO asked how I had hurt my mouth. I pointed to the guard who had struck me and his name was taken down. When the NCO left, all the guards jumped on me and beat me up for approximately two hours with sticks. I was then tied up in such a way that my arms went numb."

Gordie Dunn had more benevolent memories:

> "Guys there gave us bread – four inches wide and six inches long. They said when we were stronger they would give us some work – we were going stir crazy! When stronger we were taken to the boatyard to move sacks of salt, heavy old things. The Jap stevedores knew we were trying so they were not bad to us. They had bread allowances and said we could make our own.
>
> We also unloaded coal from barges but one time we were on a tramp steamer, just as it was getting dark, loading coal. They told us to hurry, hurry, hurry – we were hurrying, but we didn't care. All of a sudden the ship started going – the ship had started its engine – and it swung around a buoy in the harbour. I guess they wanted to get their anchor chains off the buoy. This little head suddenly pops over the rail and called down on us on the barge. We looked up and saw it was the captain of the steamer. He yelled 'hurry, hurry, hurry' and we, all sweaty and exhausted, called back for him to 'get lost' and to 'fuck off!' He disappeared and after that the ship started off down the harbour and we were still loading the coal, with us guys in the barge still anchored against the side. We were beginning to get into the swells of the outer harbour before some crew workmen came down into the barge and cast off – and there we were, sitting in the barge and bobbing about in the harbour. When the steamer was about a couple of miles up the harbour, he

turned about and finally took us under tow back to Moji. We just sat there, talking, laughing and enjoying the scenery."

Both Dunn and Horton[140] later testified that they had seen white-painted Japanese ships carrying Red Cross markings being loaded with field guns and ammunition, and confirmed that PoWs were employed handling bombs from 25lbs to 1,000lbs, and also ammunition and high-octane fuel.

Red Campbell, in a different camp, although burning with a hatred for his captors, later reflected on the punishment meted out by the Japanese amongst themselves:

"Japanese Army discipline on its own troops was rough. I saw an officer beat a Japanese enlisted man with his metal sword carrier almost to death, in the name of discipline. Another did beat a Jap soldier to death with a heavy bamboo club.

The Japanese could never understand why we complained. They said we were treated no worse than any others. They fed us enough food to keep us active, because they wanted us for working parties. Some of the parties sent to the outer islands never got back."

One of the prisoners at Habu Camp, Plt Off John Fletcher-Cooke, wrote of this period[141]:

"There was little enough we could do in the camp to control our own destinies. Ricky Wright had shown great persistence in his protests to Nomoto [Captain Akira Nomoto, the camp Commandant]. He had protested about the food, about the treatment of the sick, about the lack of baths, about the overcoats, about the futility of officers standing about in the dockyard without any control over their men; in short, he had protested about almost everything. Eventually, Nomoto had refused to see him. Undaunted, Ricky Wright was now engaged in preparing a written memorandum of all his protests.

A rumour went round that officers were to be permitted to wear their own uniforms in camp. I received this news with mixed feelings. I was already wearing mine under my Japanese uniform; it was still very cold. In due course Nomoto issued the order and the rumour became a fact. Ricky Wright, who was the only officer who had his RAF blues with him, looked resplendent in his squadron leader's uniform. All the Japanese camp staff, including Nomoto, regarded him with admiration, touching every part of his uniform with curious fingers, like children.

Before he was taken prisoner in Java, Ricky Wright had bought a magnificent pair of brown boots, which he had intended to wear while flying. As all our boots and shoes were rapidly disintegrating he had decided to have these cut down so that he could wear them. He had entrusted these boots to one of the PoWs, who was doing his best at boot repairing, to have the tops cut off. Nomoto had spotted them and paid us an unofficial visit, in the hope of persuading Ricky to sell them to him. Unfortunately, Ricky had to tell him that the boots had already been decapitated. Nomoto was as heart-broken as a child who had lost its favourite teddy bear. Nomoto was a lonely man."

Some 2,200 RAF PoWs were sent to the Molucca Islands to build airfields and included Flt Lt de la Perrelle, Plt Offs Ernie Gartrell, Bill Lockwood, Bunt Pettit, Snow White and Sgts Pip Healey, Bertie Lambert, and Harley Monsell, the latter being one of the replacement pilots, who reported:

"The voyage to the [Molucca] Islands took approximately 60 days in very cramped quarters. Food and water were scarce. We had two meals, one at 10am and one at 4pm, consisting of a pint of rice each meal with occasionally a little fish or greens. Dysentery and malaria were prevalent and though no lives were actually lost on the voyage many died shortly after disembarking. The Nips on this voyage were very cruel and many beatings took place. One Nipponese warrant officer nicknamed Yellow Boots was exceptionally cruel, making dysentery patients stand at attention around open hatches in the hope that they would become dizzy and fall in.

Our first port of call was Amahai [on Ceram Island] where we were forced to unload bombs and machinery. The next port of call was Amboina. On arriving here we were bombed by American planes but not hit. We were put on smaller lighters and transferred to the island of Haroku about 45 kilometres from Amboina. Plt Off Lockwood was also on the island with me and kept an accurate diary of people that he buried. This was a small coral island and contained no camp whatever or any housing. There was nothing but jungle. On arrival we received no food or water for 48 hours and the sick, of which I was one, were made to lie down in the jungle. The treatment on this island was very bad and Sgt Mori, although not Commandant of the camp, had complete charge. There were 4,000 of us on that island, English, Dutch and a few Canadians.

For the first day's work party, 1,500 were demanded but there were about 600 sick. When the number required by the Nips was not supplied, the sick were forced to go on parade and asked if they would work. When they said they couldn't they were beaten with bamboo poles and left to get back to their quarters as best they could. Food was very scarce and a market was run by the Japs but exorbitant prices were charged, making it almost impossible for the prisoners to buy anything. Dysentery, tropical ulcers, beri-beri and malaria were very prevalent and medical supplies were nil. Eighty-four per cent of the prisoners in this camp died or were killed in the bombings. The island was such a hell place that even the Nip guards made attempts to escape from it.

I was one of the first crowd to leave the Islands around 20 November 1943. We were put on a coaling ship [the *Maros Maru*], which had one great front hold. There was a small opening about 3 feet by 6 feet, which was the only means of air or light in the hold. The bottom of the hold was covered with about two feet of coal dust and water. The draft consisted of about 600 men, 100 of which were stretcher cases. These were put on top of the hatch uncovered from weather. The remainder were forced down into the hold. We were allowed to go on deck for air but the majority of the prisoners were too weak to climb the ladder. I was unconscious after about two days. We remained on this ship for a week and then were transferred at Amboina to a bigger and much cleaner boat. Some of the draft was transferred to another, supposedly hospital ship, which bore a Red Cross, and carried Jap soldiers, our own prisoners and guards, aeroplanes and guns. This ship [the *Suez Maru*] was torpedoed, I believe. We never saw any of the boys who went on that boat.

The trip from Amboina to Sourabaya was made in 60 days. Conditions were fairly reasonable except for the shortage of food and water. We received a pint of rice at 10am and a pint of rice at 4pm and about a half-inch of tea in the bottom of a mug at 8 at night. Eighteen men died on the return trip. On arrival at Sourabaya we were forced to lie on deck all night in the rain. Many men were beaten up for getting up to go to the toilet and trying to assist others who had dysentery. The next day we were put on a train and taken to Batavia. On arrival in Batavia the Jap officers were so shocked at our condition that [we] were confined to a separate camp within the prison at Cycle Camp and were not permitted to converse or see any of the other prisoners. Medical supplies such as vitamin B and sulphur drugs were given and some extra food, most of which was donated by the other prisoners, causing them to deprive themselves of much needed food."

Wg Cdr Maguire, Senior British Officer at Cycle Camp, recalled:

"I personally witnessed the initial return of some of the survivors to Cycle Camp, and the sight inside those lorries beggars description. It was the result of a deliberately evil policy by a military clique, which professed to despise those who allowed themselves to be taken prisoner, but when the tables were turned almost to a man failed to take the 'honourable way.'"[142]

He added:

> "En route to the Far East [as OC 266 (Fighter) Wing] lectures on the area were given to the less experienced by those who had served there before[143]. One such lecture was given on our ship by a widely travelled army doctor. In it he said, with considerable emphasis, that if we were going to operate in the jungle we would find that casualties from tropical diseases would outnumber those caused by enemy action. Most of us with overseas experience thought he was being unduly pessimistic. Were not malaria and dysentery under control, and was not cholera a memory? But it was sad and true."[144]

Of the voyage back to Java, Bill Lockwood, who assisted with the funerals, recorded the names of the 295 men who died, including 185 RAF, reflected:

> "The most utterly depressing, body and soul destroying experience of my PoW life, was aboard the *Maros Maru*, on which I was one of just over 600 prisoners. We spent two months on that ship in transit from an island called Haroku, south of Ceram, to Java. Approximately 300 of us managed to survive the trip."

Another survivor of the nightmarish journey, Corporal Jim Home of 242 Squadron, provides a graphic and disturbing record:

> "Scenes of indescribable horror continued until they became commonplace: men picked their way through the tangled mass of humanity which lay around the narrow ship; and orderlies carried the naked and wasted bodies of the dead to the side of the ship where men like Bill Lockwood (242 Squadron) helped to cast the weighted bodies into the sea.
>
> Tongues began to blacken, and raw shoulders peeled and bled whilst the last drops of sanity left many men as each night was filled with the tortured yells and moans of the dying. They were joined by the curses of the more able who tried so hard to gain a little rest, hoping to sleep away their worries if only for an hour. Some of the more chronically ill developed an awful sounding symptom that seemed to affect a man about to die of beri-beri – a loud lasting period of violent hiccupping. Another youngster, delirious and distraught with sunstroke, shouted out the thoughts of a demented and distorted mind for thirty long hours before he became too weak to utter a single word. By this time men were dying like flies in the winter, their bodies being thrown overboard at regular intervals at the rate of about eight men each day."[145]

There were many such dreadful voyages that had to be endured by the prisoners of war. There were ten shiploads in 1942, twelve in 1943, seventeen in 1944 and six in 1945. Altogether some 34,000 prisoners were transhipped. These figures exclude the many voyages made between conquered territories such as from Singapore to Sumatra and Java to Ambon, which were equally unpleasant. Tragically, a number of Japanese vessels transporting prisoners were sunk by Allied submarines and aircraft, the crews of which were totally ignorant of their victims' cargoes. The first of these tragic incidents occurred on 29 November 1943, when the US submarine *Bonefish* sank the *Suez Maru* near the island of Kangean, north of Bali, while en route from the Molucca Islands to Java. Although marked with a Red Cross, she carried damaged aircraft on her deck. There were no survivors. Among the 214 RAF men lost out of the total of 548 fatalities was 488/605 Squadron's Flt Lt Grahame (Snow) White, a survivor of both Singapore and Java. Between June and November 1944, no fewer than eight Japanese vessels carrying PoWs were sunk by the Allies (three by US submarines, two by RN submarines and three by US aircraft), when 3,713 prisoners lost their lives including 163 airmen, although no further Hurricane pilots were involved.

Life for prisoners who remained on Java was, on the whole, more bearable. One of these, Wg Cdr Gerald Bell[146], who had been OC Kallang, wrote:

"From time to time, depending upon space available in each camp, theatrical shows were extremely popular. In one camp a particularly enterprising party put on variety shows once a month. The Japanese came to some of these and appeared to enjoy them, although their reaction might have been different had they understood some of the jokes at their expense. Some activities ended in disaster. One group was intent upon distilling a hideously potent spirit made from fermented maize. Unfortunately, their still proved unequal to the task and blew up during the night. The Japanese took a lot of convincing that the still was not, in fact, a bomb factory!

A companion of mine and I embarked upon a duck hatchery. We converted an old-fashioned icebox into an incubator, heat was supplied by an electric light bulb and the temperature controlled by opening and shutting sliding glass doors. This entailed adjustments every 20 minutes or so and the apparatus, therefore, required 24-hour attention. Unfortunately, during the dark of one night a Korean guard saw the glowing windows and was convinced that this must be a wireless set. Twenty-four hours later, after much shouting and some personal violence, the guards were convinced of the authenticity of the apparatus but, by that time, it was wrecked and the eggs addled. The sequel was that the Korean guards were so impressed by the incubator idea that they ordered the manufacture of a jumbo model in the camp workshop. The 500-egg monster was finally constructed, fired by a number of paraffin lamps. At the end of ten days an impatient Korean guard enquired where the little ducks were. It was explained to him that nature dictated a timetable on these affairs but this he would not accept. He thereupon turned up the heat with the result of 500 hard-boiled eggs.

A less amusing episode concerned two pregnant sows, which were introduced into the camp by the guards with the commendable idea of improving the prisoners' diet. The pigs were to be fed from leftovers from the cookhouse. Unfortunately for the plan, almost nothing was ever left over by the permanently hungry prisoners, so when the time came for the sows to farrow, a mere two or three runts were produced, who promptly died. Again this was considered a case of non co-operation and the unfortunate sows were given such a beating with bamboo poles that they failed to recover."

Plt Off Fletcher-Cooke provides another pig story – this one relatively lighthearted – that originated in his camp at Habu, shortly following the end of the war:

"As I returned to my hut, I passed by the cookhouse and had a word with one of the cooks. He told me an amusing tale. When the camp Commandant had told the Dutch interpreter that the war was over and that the two pigs would have to be slaughtered, the PoW butcher promptly went off and killed one of the pigs. The carcass was hung up in the cookhouse.

During the afternoon and evening of the same day the camp Commandant, and the camp staff, had become convinced that some 'fire-eating' general was making a last-ditch stand on Kyushu and that hostilities had broken out again. Thereupon the Japanese cooks and butchers left their own cookhouse and descended en masse on the PoW cookhouse. They demanded the carcass of the pig, which, they claimed, had been prematurely killed by the over-eager PoW butcher. Hostilities broke out between the staffs of the rival cookhouses and in the struggle the pig's head came off. The Japanese, however, obtained the greater part of the carcass. When [next day] it appeared that the rumours of a last-ditch stand in Kyushu were not based on fact, the PoW cooks and butchers mounted a raid on the Japanese cookhouse. After a bitter struggle, during which the pig's legs were pulled off, the PoWs succeeded in recovering the greater part of this meat.

A number of Japanese civilians who worked in the PoW cookhouse as clerks and storekeepers now entered the lists. Believing that the war was over and thinking of their famished families and the probability of unemployment ahead, they took the opportunity of the PoW cooks' rest period to reduce the remnants of the pig into even smaller pieces, which they concealed about their persons. When the PoW cooks returned, after the Japanese civilians had left, there was nothing of the pig left except the severed head. The Japanese civilians did not, however, get very far with their loot. When they were searched by the Japanese guards at the camp gate, the remnants of the pig were found and removed from them. The Japanese guards on duty wasted no time. They grilled the remains there and then and consumed them on the spot. On learning of this, the PoW butcher went out and slaughtered the second pig. It was reported that he slept with the carcass until it was ready for the stew."[147]

Sgt Gordie Dunn found himself inadvertently, and literally, involved in yet another pig incident while at Moji, also at the end of the war:

"The Japs had decided they would raise a couple of pigs in a little cage at the back of our shower stalls. So they got these pigs going and they used to come in and get slop from the Jap kitchen – they didn't get much slop from our kitchen – that's what they gave us to eat. I guess the pigs were about 60-70lbs when the Nips went 'boom' [the end of the war]. We were all just hanging around, nobody was working and the camp Commandant had given us a speech on how we should look after ourselves. I forget whom it was who came up to me, but he said that the officers had decided to kill one of the pigs and that we would have to do it, so that the men could have some pork chops. He told me that they wanted me to look after it and that there were two or three farm boys in our group who knew how to slaughter a pig. I asked where we should kill it and he said the bathhouse would be the best place. We were going to need some way of holding the pig, so we built a gate from two rectangular scrap pieces of wood and we tied a piece of cord around them, then took the pig down to the bathhouse. The pig didn't really want to go to the bathhouse – I guess he figured something was going to happen to him – but we four got him there. One guy grabbed him by the tail, and one by his ears and we pushed him in.

They gave me an old axe – I don't why me, perhaps they thought being a Canadian somehow made me a farm boy – and said I was going to have to hit him on the head between the eyes and stun him, then one of the others was going to knife him. So it sounded quite good, except the pig wasn't going to co-operate. The guys got him standing there while the pig did his best to get away. Someone said, 'OK, count one, two, three, then wham him.' So I counted 'one, two, three' and, as I swung the axe down, the pig moved his head and instead of hitting between the eyes, I hit him bang on the forehead side of one eye – and his eye popped out on to his cheek. The pig let out a dreadful scream and with blood spurting out decided to move somewhere else. I don't know how exactly he managed to push a couple of guys onto their behinds, but he took off and went screaming through the door – I mean through the door – the door was closed! Oh man! Everybody kinda looked back on it as a funny experience, except the pig, of course! Anyway, the pig went darting out and around the camp, spurting blood all over the place until the guys finally shooed him back into his pen. And that was it. No pork chops. An officer asked what had happened – I kinda told him I wasn't a butcher. That solved the pig's problem. One of the doctors went to have a look at him; I think he put some sulphur powder into the pig's eye, but after that I would imagine he was sight-impaired! I don't know whatever happened to the pigs after that – and that was the sad story of one of the two little pigs."

Several of the pilots helped to build, or conceal, wireless sets ingeniously manufactured out of scrap. One of those involved in this highly dangerous activity was the American Red Campbell:

"The Japanese even used to conduct body searches for the radios they suspected we had concealed. Once an Aussie named McNally [Plt Off John McNally RAAF of 84 Squadron] got by with an exceptionally gutsy trick. Usually we had the radio buried in the ground in a tin box, where it couldn't be seen. This time we had been caught by surprise, and the radio was lying in the open, under a bedroll. After he had been body-searched, McNally whispered to me to try and keep him hidden a bit. Then he stepped back, picked up the radio, and put it in some clothing he had tucked under his arm. Since he was now among the prisoners who had already been searched, the Japanese did not notice the radio in spite of its bulk, and he was not searched again. During a period when our radio was not working, I came to suspect that a group of Dutch pilots had one. There was a technique to finding out where the camp radio was. It got so that you could sense it from the comments of the men in the vicinity – slips of the tongue, occasional mention of what sounded like fresh news. I made a point of checking in with one of the Dutch pilots I knew and suspected of having a radio, at an hour when it was customary to pick up broadcasts. Finally he said to me: 'Well, you might as well know,' and they let me listen in on the reports.

We quickly learned that the news we gathered had to be restricted, for the safety of the PoWs in general. If too many people learned about up-to-date news happenings too quickly, inevitably they would talk, and the Japanese would overhear conversations indicating that these prisoners were extremely well informed. Then they would track news sources down and seize our equipment, and execute the operators. It got so bad that we had to hold up news reports, sometimes for weeks, until comments by the Japanese guards made it obvious that they were familiar with the more recent developments. Then, when we passed this sometimes outdated but corrected information to the PoWs and they started to talk, the Japanese did not pay much attention since this was old news – stuff that would come out gradually anyway just with the passage of time. The worst blabbermouths were the Dutch. We learned to keep everything from the Dutch PoWs for the longest periods so that there would be the least amount of suspicion."[148]

Others involved with secret wireless sets included the Canadian Sgt John Fleming who, when in Kutching PoW Camp in Borneo, worked with Corporal Len Beckett who had built a set, which they operated for the whole term of imprisonment. Fleming subsequently received a mention in despatches, having by then been commissioned, the citation stating:

'Flight Lieutenant Fleming was captured by the Japanese in the war and was transferred to the prisoner of war camp at Kutching, Borneo, in 1942. At an obvious risk, a plan was laid to build a small wireless set. Those responsible were faced with severe punishment and perhaps death if discovered. A Royal Air Force warrant officer [Beckett, at the time a Corporal] elected to build the set with the aid of a few selected volunteers who obtained scraps and bits and pieces of makeshift materials and finally the valves. Flight Lieutenant Fleming undertook the task of officer in charge of security and organised an ingenious scheme of warning fuses, lookouts and hiding places for the set, which, despite vigorous searches, successfully avoided discovery. During a period of over two years, Flight Lieutenant Fleming guarded the tiny set. As the responsible officer, his punishment if caught was certain. By his disregard for his own safety he won the admiration of his fellows and contributed materially to their high standard of morale.'

Beckett also received a mention in despatches, as did another of the Hurricane pilots, the American Plt Off Leon Cicurel, awarded for his services to the dying and sick during his internment in various camps in Java. He, like so many others, had been threatened with execution after failing to answer questions under interrogation. Others so recognised included Sqn Ldr Vic de la Perrelle and Plt Off Reg Bainbridge.

Frequently, men would be beaten for no apparent reason – and senior officers were not precluded from receiving such punishment. Corporal Jim Home witnessed Wg Cdr Maguire take one such beating shortly before the end of the war, when he was SBO at Bandoeng:

> "The only other incident I had recorded from this camp happened, I'm certain, in the month of July [1945] just before we left. It was the beating up of our senior officers. One evening at *Tenko* the Japs had demanded a list of skilled men. Names from the British section were not forthcoming so Kasiyama ordered all officers to the Jap guardroom to be given the third degree. Then, up came Mori, whom I hadn't seen since leaving the *Maros Maru*. The sea journey had not mellowed him in any visible way; and demanding to know what was going on he took over.
>
> It looked to be yet another set-up job. Mori started screaming and bawling in his own inimitable way, then, surprisingly, he dismissed them all only to call back the most senior officers within minutes of having been dismissed. Mori then proceeded to beat up about fifteen officers individually, and at one time there were three officers lying on the ground, unconscious. Mori then made a special attack on Wg Cdr Maguire. He was hit by a chair which, fortunately, broke, for it was very heavy and may otherwise have badly injured him – as it was, he was only knocked out. Whilst Mori was having his grand slam, Kasiyama was following around 'mopping up' with his fists and feet any officer on the ground. We had christened those two well; the titles of 'Blood' and 'Slime' could not have suited them better."[149]

Fortunately, for the surviving prisoners, the end of the war was nigh.

* * *

Flt Lt Jerry Parker

The experience of every PoW held by the Japanese was, of course, unique, but the story of what happened to many is necessarily similar. However, some were treated more harshly than others and many hundreds died of malnutrition, illness and sheer brutality. Those who remained in Java generally fared better than those who were sent to Japan or the Indonesian islands. One of those incarcerated in Java was Flt Lt Jerry Parker. This is his story:

> "Our way of life was determined of course almost entirely by the Japanese and the camp routines followed the arrangements laid down throughout their 'Greater East Asia Co-Prosperity Sphere'. In whatever camp we were in Java, at 6am every morning we and millions of other people under their direct control had five minutes of broadcast PT to a standard rhythm, counting up to ten continuously in Japanese. We had roll call, then whatever breakfast was available – perhaps a slice of bread and tea from the cookhouse – then work.
>
> Throughout the following three-and-a-half years we, i.e. Mike [Fitzherbert] and I and those who were with us for most of this time – Spike and Jeff and the Doc – owned apiece a mug, plate, knife, fork and spoon, working shorts and shirt and a pair of wooden clogs, parade shirt and shorts, stockings and marching boots, (these last to be treasured for journeys between prison camps), a sheet and a thin blanket, pillow and case and mosquito net, towel, toilet gear and a watch. I also had an autostrop razor and three blades with which I was able to keep myself shaved every other day until we were released. Mike had his RAF side-cap and I, having lost mine in Palembang, wore the khaki peaked cap of 2/Lt Anderson, a SAAF lad who was killed in the last days of the war in Java.
>
> The Japanese allocated few guards to maintain order in the camps, in each of which there would be several hundred or thousands of Allied prisoners. Nobody escaped from Java after capture because the nearest possible destinations were some hundreds of miles

away. In the circumstances our captors maintained control over us through our own internal discipline, from the senior officer in the camp down through the officers and NCOs. As a result, accommodation was generally allocated separately amongst the ranks and, where room was short, equitably. In some camps everybody would just about have room to roll over on the hard boards or mattresses and in others men could sleep comparatively spaciously.

In all the camps there were sentries on the gates and sometimes in watch-towers, as well as odd sentries on roving patrols, so that at any time during the day or night, when a sort of brown-out was in force, a Japanese or more often a Korean private armed with rifle and bayonet would be ambling around. Whenever any sentry passed or was passed by a PoW or civilian, the nearest person of whatever rank was required to shout *'Kyotski – Kin – Nown – Yasmi'* – 'Attention – salute – finish salute – as you were.' The salute – or bow, if one were hatless – had to be held until it had been acknowledged and one generally wore a cap in order to avoid the need to bow. Many of the patrolling guards seized these opportunities to be gratuitously sadistic towards the captives and they needed no excuses to beat up anybody whose expression they might not like. Nevertheless, if they wanted to pretend righteousness, the camp rules were such that pretexts were not difficult for them to find.

For instance, anybody smoking a cigarette had to have beside him a clean ashtray of some sort, half-full of water. On the call of *'Kyotski'* the cigarette had, of course, to be extinguished, thereby dirtying the ashtray – a misdemeanour. Japanese and Korean NCOs and senior privates were permitted to beat and kick their subordinates, as well as PoWs as they wished, so that we were not treated any worse than their own men in general, except by those who had developed either hatred or contempt for us. It would happen that, after bad news of the progress of the war, some guards would react against the PoWs. Dependent upon the characters of the British CO and the Japanese camp Commandant, protests might be submitted in cases of injustice but none were remedied. The camp commandants were normally Japanese junior officers with perhaps Japanese NCOs and, always, Korean guards. These were often bitter, having been promised farms to work in Java and then instead found themselves inducted into the Japanese Army on arrival. We never knew how loyal they were to the Japanese. They never had any thought of disobeying authority unless they were sure of benefit to themselves and safe from punishment, but nearly always there would be some among the guards who would be willing to buy watches from the prisoners and smuggle in food and soap.

We air crew had very little money when we were captured and, since we were 232 Squadron pilots newly supported by 242 Squadron's ground staff, we were not acquainted with the Accounts Officer and the Adjutant. A large number of the RAF officers were either recent enlistments into the Air Force from civilian life as engineers or planters in Malaya or were new recruits from England. One pilot officer under training as an air controller had been a bank official until three weeks before he'd been put aboard a ship for Singapore. Some of these people, having no duties or responsibilities since arriving in the Far East, had looked after themselves by drawing cash from the banks or by holding impress funds from the Air Force. At least one had some thousands of guilders on 8 March.

We saw little of this and started our PoW life unpromisingly by selling surplus gear such as fountain pens. Soon however, we were reduced to writing cheques and cashing them with those who preferred funds after their eventual anticipated release to money in their pockets in prison camp. After we'd been inside a year or two, I paid a cheque for £20 for twenty sulphur pills, which were smuggled in by the guards, probably having been looted from the Red Cross parcels which never reached us. However, I was able to clear all my debts on my return to England in 1945. Our first camp at Semplak near Buitenzorg (nostalgically renamed 'Bognor') was in an enormous old single-storied farmhouse near the airfield and there were fifty RAF officers and 300 airmen. There were about thirty Japanese guards headed by a very smart NCO who had considerable authority but who appeared to understand and partly sympathise with us. He did not press the saluting and humiliating procedures at first and we had several days in which to settle down. We had to fill in forms giving rather more information than name, rank and number but, since there was very little information we could provide the Japanese which could help their war effort, they didn't ask for much. We pilots gave the branch of the RAF in which we served as General Duties, hoping that this would not lead them to believe that we were aircrew. This was perhaps a useful precaution for in the first evenings of our stay there, the Japanese guards, who were assault troops, visited all the quarters to chat to us.

Julian, Gartrell, Bainbridge, Jeff Skinner (an RAF Signals Officer), Mike and I had a stone-floored room to ourselves and we knocked up beds for ourselves from lumber we found about the farmhouse with nails we extracted from it and straightened out. We had carried our thin mattresses, blankets and mosquito nets from Pamegatan, had varying amounts in our pockets and were temporarily well set-up. On our first evening there we were paraded and counted before a meal was issued, the members of each room forming a mess and sending two representatives to collect the mess's share. Reg Bainbridge and Jeff Skinner volunteered to go and left the other four of us awaiting their return. Taffy Julian and Ernie Gartrell were both from New Zealand and I don't suppose that in other circumstances they would have been particularly friendly, Taffy being a somewhat large and coarse fellow and Ernie a reserved and thoughtful junior chartered accountant. Mike and I had grown quite close, having been flying together as a section during the closing days of the campaign, and I was particularly grateful to him for his friendship whilst I was recovering from the wound in my back.

Before Jeff and Reg returned, the open door into our room was darkened by the figure of a short Japanese in uniform, except for wearing slippers instead of puttees and boots. He wore a big smile and a long forked beard, which he constantly stroked with either or both hands. 'I, Ito,' he announced. 'Corporal. You?' He sat down comfortably on Taffy's bed and looked enquiringly at him. 'Julian,' he replied, 'Squadron Leader.' 'Parker,' 'Gartrell,' and 'Fitzherbert,' we added in response to his smiling gaze. I lay on my stomach when he came in and, because of the wound in the middle of my back, turned my head away to avoid conversing with him and explaining how I had come by it. Mike had to tell him that I was down with malaria. We didn't quite know what our attitude to this unwelcome visit should be, but at that time we had not spoken to any other Japanese. In his very limited English he asked us questions about our homes and families and nothing about our service life. We responded politely to these enquiries and offered nothing more than admiration for the photographs of his wife and children, having none of our own to show him. Reg and Jeff returned before this visit was over but he left as soon as he had had a little conversation with them, so we were able to get on with our meal.

The next room to ours, a much larger one, was occupied by about eight senior officers, including Wing Commander Alexander[150], and later that evening an orderly was sent from there with a notice to all ranks, advising them of the arrangements for the following morning's parade, which was to take place at 6am. There would be two ranks in front of the farmhouse, officers, NCOs and airmen being grouped independently. Everybody should wear hats and clothes in which to work on the airfield. One of our officers, a Pilot Officer MacDonald, had studied the Japanese language sufficiently to be able to help in the interpretation of the Commandant's wishes when he held discussions with the wing commander. He was something of a portly academic, although portliness was not an attribute he was able to maintain much longer, and apt to attract to himself rather more authority than he actually possessed. I walked to the other rooms occupied by officers until I found MacDonald and asked him whether I was to parade the following morning: 'If you are fit, you are to parade.'

'I've been shot in the back and I think I'm going down with malaria.' He replied: 'You are to parade tomorrow morning with everybody else, but you will probably be excused work at the airfield.' We were relieved by this information because we knew that some of the PoWs were not above petty theft and, slight though our personal possessions were, we would prefer not to have them stolen. If I were to spend the day in our room, then my friends could leave their watches, pens and cash in confidence.

On parade in the morning, the men were regrouped in sections with NCOs and officers allocated to each and marched off to the airfield, leaving only the sick and a few cooks and nursing orderlies behind. Doc Morgan, who had been the Station Medical Officer at Kallang remained behind whilst Doc Dawson accompanied the men to the airfield. I was given quite a good meal by the remaining cooks, and having found some books and magazines to read, since many Dutch homes contained English books and American magazines, I enjoyed quite a pleasant day. I did not notice the prisoners who were under guard and fencing in with barbed wire the extensive grounds of the farmhouse.

When the others returned in the evening, they told me of their day. After about forty men had been detailed to fence the camp, the rest were told to stack on to captured British lorries some hundreds of flimsy four-gallon tin cans of petrol with the officers and NCOs supervising. This had not been too successful as too many of the cans leaked when banged on the ground or the trucks and the Commandant easily demonstrated how to carry such unwieldy loads by shouldering a bamboo pole with a can at each end. He was able to jog along with such a load in the easy rhythm with which we had seen Javanese men and women carry burdens of water or produce.

However, the leakage continued until an airman pissed against the wheel of a captured British truck. The Commandant called to a Japanese NCO who detailed two guards to take the man to one side and beat him unconscious with their rifle buffs. Since the truck had become the property of the Imperial Japanese Army, his behaviour had been extremely insulting. Thereafter, the prisoners appreciated that any punishment would not be lenient. When the petrol had been trucked away, the men were set to filling in the bomb craters on the airfield. There were very many of these and the work would take some days. On their return to the camp and parade for counting the adjutant asked for volunteers to go to Batavia to collect a steamroller to assist in the work. A Sergeant Green and a mate had offered to go and would leave on the morrow. I said I thought this was aiding the enemy. The others disagreed but before we could resolve our views Ernie and Mike returned with the evening meal, accompanied by Ito. My heart sank for, no matter how pleasant a fellow Ito might be, he was an enemy with whom we had nothing in common and we now had much to discuss quite urgently. He had brought in a canvas bag three large bottles of Heineken beer, which had to be shared out right away, as he had to take the bottles back. It was warm beer and not particularly welcome, but not to be refused. He sat there, chaffing away and volunteered that he had taken part in the landing north of Kalidjati. It was difficult to believe that he did not realise that we were pilots for we were the youngest officers in the camp – indeed he knew that I had only just turned 20 and that I held the rank of captain – and we were members of the RAF.

'American Air Force,' he said with much gesticulation, 'are very cowardly. American airplanes fly very high where our guns cannot reach them. British airplanes fly low. We shoot them, they shoot us, but they very bad. My friend next to me in small boat. One airplane shoot and bullet in here.' He pointed to the side of his head, just in front of his right ear. 'Here, small hole. Here,' pointing to the left side of his head, 'nothing! Very bad!' 'Oh, Ito,' I said, 'That is war. Terrible, terrible. But you were all right?' 'Yes, I was very lucky. Now I must go.' 'Well, goodnight, Ito. Thank you very much for the beer.' 'Don't mention it. Goodnight.'

Some of us had a quite unreasonable belief in a rumoured Javanese legend that a white race would rule there for 300 years, a yellow one for three months and a brown one ever after. Despite the fact that the Japanese were attacking Australia 1,500 miles away and had won almost all the islands in the Pacific we hoped they would be pushed back just as fast, as had been happening in the North African desert. We were not at all keen to aid in the work to which we had been put and, even though there were frequent beatings for slacking, the repairs to the airfield did not go ahead very quickly. Added to which the officers felt they should not do any manual work and refused to do so in the absence of the Japanese CO. There were one or two nasty incidents of officers being beaten up but faced with their absolutely vehement arguments in sign language that the Geneva Convention required that officers were not to be forced to work, the Japanese guards were unsure of their ground and feared the rage of the commander. When he returned to the camp that night, he summoned Wing Commander Alexander and told him that Japan had not signed the convention and that, if the officers did not assist in the labour, they would be shot. Alexander returned and called a meeting, at which it was resolved that the officers would hold out. I felt quite strongly about this, believing it would be a terrible humiliation for a holder of the King's Commission. I was young enough not to be greatly concerned about being shot although a threat of being beaten or bayoneted to death would probably have brought about a considerable change of heart.

Again the following day we didn't work and again there were tense incidents, with the guards still refraining from inflicting serious injury. In the evening Alexander was called to the office and didn't return. An hour or so later Matthews was taken across and returned very quickly to summon another meeting. He said that Alexander had been shot [not so] and he himself was to return and confirm that we would work the next day or the same would happen to him. Violent arguments then broke out but naturally the wing commanders and squadron leaders, having family responsibilities and being evidently more likely to be shot than we junior and younger ones, were rather more vulnerable than we. Eventually we were ordered to carry out the physical work and Matthews went back to the Japanese to advise them of our surrender. Those who would have preferred to refuse the instruction were told that there could be no exceptions without damaging the relationship of the survivors with the Japanese and with the British airmen and NCOs who would lose even the slight protection of the officers if they were all shot. In my rather weak state I wept about this abject defeat but later in our camp life we would look back on these days and wonder at the forbearance of the Japanese NCO and our own stupidity. Several of the Japanese officers we saw afterwards would not have scrupled to have the whole lot bayoneted.

On the following morning's work parade the Japanese Commandant was present and the officers were grouped together after the roll call and asked individually by him, 'Will you work?' I had hoped to shirk and avoid the work, if I could, to maintain my self-respect but I'd lost the battle the night before and hadn't the moral courage alone to deny it. Shamefacedly we all agreed. The officers never did work very hard at Buitenzorg, unless they felt like it, but we were not allowed to spend all day merely supervising the men. The guards always threatened to take us to the Commandant if we didn't go through the motions of working for a few minutes so that eventually we accepted the situation entirely and did as much as the men.

A little later at one evening roll call we were told that, in common with all Japanese troops, we were to have our hair cropped. Clippers were delivered to our own barbers for that purpose. Again, there was suggested resistance from the officers but this time the

Commandant came to the following evening roll call with extra guards, beat up Matthews, who was rather a dapper little man, and threatened severe trouble for those who did not have their hair clipped by the following evening. We all had our hair cropped.

Among the officers was Squadron Leader Dave Grant, who had been a reporter for the *Daily Mirror* and early in the war had been commissioned as some sort of press officer. He'd been in France attached to Cobber Kain's squadron and had seen a lot of the political and the social side of the war. He had a great and harmless sense of humour and for some days after we had our hair cut he had his scalp semi-cropped in a sort of Victory V shape to demonstrate his indomitable spirit. There were many lizards in the old farmhouse and many insects, large and small, used to venture in and rest on the cool walls. We used to watch the lizards creep up on them and then, quick as a flash, they would cover the last six inches or so and grab the insects in their jaws. One evening Dave was left to himself in the senior officers room for half an hour or so and amused himself by drawing a butterfly and a lizard on the wall and sat staring at them when he heard approaching footsteps. The next officer coming along saw Dave staring and waiting for the lizard to pounce and joined him. After a couple of minutes Dave burst into laughter and looked around to see whom he'd caught with his joke and found the Japanese Commandant. He didn't get beaten up but he did have his hair properly cropped.

In the early days at Semplak, Mike and I considered whether we could escape – walking out of the camp would be easy enough at night – and cycle down to the south coast to look for a boat, assuming that all other stragglers would have been mopped up and intensive searches would have been over within a couple of weeks of the surrender. However, Sergeant Green, driving the steamroller back from Batavia, came in one day with a story of a couple of sergeants who had light-heartedly walked out of another camp and were picked up within three hours. They were badly beaten with pick handles when returned to camp and the following day roped to posts and used for bayonet practice. We stopped considering escape for a while.

Once the bomb damage around the airstrip had been cleared up, Jap aircraft used to pass through, on their way down towards Australia along the archipelago we assumed, as the types and numbers varied. I kept a record for a year in the belief that we would soon have a means of communication with the outside world (perhaps through escaping), and there was no work for our men, apart from camp cleaning. I used to give lectures on English grammar, carefully swotting a textbook each evening, and I myself learnt to type under the tuition of the orderly room corporal, Morgan, who had run a secretarial school in South Wales before the war. He was of course an expert and eventually was spirited away by the Japanese for some secret work and never seen again.

In the evening we had football matches, the greatest delight of the airmen being when one of their teams played the officers. They felt at liberty to call us the most obscene names in great good humour, probably because we did not take their deliberate fouls too seriously and we were not realistic contenders for the camp championship. Occasionally we had a concert which the little Commandant used to attend, there being a good deal of amateur talent. Somebody re-wrote the words of a popular song, 'Goodnight, Sweetheart' to start 'Goodnight Semplak, see you in the morning' and it went down very well.

So our first few months in prison camp were not too onerous and we were quite well fed, but soon we were marched to the train and taken to Batavia with what gear we could carry. Our normal wear around the camps consisted of caps, shorts and wooden *klompen* or clompers. These started as the equivalent of modern plastic flip-flops but were made with webbing or leather straps across the insteps nailed on to foot-shaped pieces of wood, which were replaced as they wore through. After a few months' skilful woodworkers and their mates were able to carve hardwood to fit individual feet and even toes; they further refined them with the addition of pieces of motor tyre nailed or screwed on as soles and heels. They were useful for wearing around the camp but no good at all for marching or working parties. Thus we normally had little need for extensive wardrobes but we liked to have reserve clothes – and indeed each hastened to acquire a stout pair of army boots and woollen socks – in case we were moved from Java. When we left Semplak we wore our better shirts and shorts, stockings and shoes and carried our water bottles, eating irons, bedrolls and mosquito nets and any spare clothing. We also had one or two tins of bully beef we'd been hoarding and our packs weighed around 60-80 pounds.

We marched through Buitenzorg to the railway station and were miserable at seeing some Dutch women and children, who started singing 'There'll always be an England' alongside us, being slapped and beaten by the guards. We had some acorn valves and others parts taken from our aircraft radio sets with us hidden in socks but had had no opportunity to convert them into small radio receivers. Any sort of thorough search, such as we were later accustomed to, would easily have uncovered these but none took place. We waited for hours in the sun at the station near Buitenzorg for a train to take us to Batavia and arrived about midday, drinking water and eating a little rice prepared by a cooking crew.

During our stay at Semplak my friendship with Mike Fitzherbert had greatly strengthened. He was a year or two older than I and we had both been to British public schools before we became aircrew whereas Ernie and Taffy were from New Zealand. His family was from Eire and his father had fought in the Royal Flying Corps. During the last weeks of the campaign over Java Mike had flown as my wingman and we had roomed together, brought a second-hand Packard roadster and swum and sunbathed at Tandjong Priok. He had brought my clothing from Bandoeng to Tasikmalaja to await my return after my crash at Pameungpeuk. Mike hated to be caged and we continually discussed ever more daring and complicated schemes to get to Australia. The one he pressed most and which sent me into shivers of dismay relied upon Javanese villagers accepting paper promises from us on behalf of the British Government to purchase bicycles and a boat. On the cycles we were to proceed to the south coast and we would sail to Australia in the boat. Only the news of the punishment of other failed escapers finally killed this scheme.

From the station at Batavia we were marched off to Makasser camp adjacent to our former airfield at Tjililitan, about seven miles or so outside the town on the main road. It was in a large plantation of coconut palms surrounded by a tall barbed wire fence with about a dozen long newly erected huts constructed of plaited bamboo walls with palm-leaf roofs. Each hut had an earthen floor and was about seventeen feet wide and at the peak of the sloping roof about ten feet high. There was an opening in each hut-end, which served as a door and on each side down the length of the hut was a shelf of plaited bamboo on supports about seven feet wide and eighteen inches off the ground. Ventilation came between the top of the sidewalls and the eaves and each of us had about three feet of bed space on the shelf, sufficient for a mattress and a mosquito net. There were some thousands of men in the camp and the officers slept and messed together in a section of each hut, separated from the men by curtains of sacking. There were also openings in the walls every quarter of a length of each hut serving as side doors so that there was no congestion anywhere in any of the huts and the guards could stroll down and through them, generally with adequate warning amongst ourselves.

At night there were low-wattage lamps throughout the huts, providing sufficient light for the guards to see the prisoners as they patrolled through the quarters and incidentally for games of cards, although not sufficiently bright for reading. We quickly strung wire (unravelled barbed wire) along the bamboo posts supporting the roof at the foot of the shelf/beds and against the walls so that we were able to tie up our mosquito nets. During the day these would be folded up or hung outside to air but when the prisoners retired to bed at night the effect on any guard moving through the huts would be of walking down a long corridor between walls of cotton sheeting. There would be little of interest to see so that the guards preferred at that time to stroll in the cooler air, disturbed only by the chirping of crickets and the occasional prisoner visiting the latrines.

This was a new camp and we found we were the first occupants so that, as at Semplak, we had no trouble with bedbugs, later to become such pests. These spade-shaped flat (unless bloated with blood) insects grew up to a quarter-inch long and infested the masonry in the older prisons and barracks to which we were later moved. They came out at night to bite a sleeper, burrowing between sheets and mosquito nets and hiding in the seams of clothing and nets when disturbed and in the daytime. Thus, they were transferred from camp to camp by those who did not inspect their gear regularly or when they found themselves bitten.

We soon discovered that Makasser was a transit camp for PoWs and internees being taken off either to Malaya or down to the islands near New Guinea and there was comparatively little work to be carried out at or near the camp. The entrance was on the side away from the road a few yards from a large house, which had evidently been occupied by a Dutch planter or farm manager. This large two-storied stone building was taken over by the Japs as their guardhouse and we were transferred from the charge of the front-line forces to whom we'd surrendered to an organization with particular responsibility for PoWs. We rarely saw a Japanese officer and the camp was run by two or three sergeants commanding a couple of dozen Korean soldiers.

Within a week of our arrival at Makasser our familiarisation with the discipline required by Dai Nippon Gun was advanced. After an early evening roll call we were shown how to bow and salute in the Japanese style and to offer these courtesies to the lowliest private. Although the Japanese claimed that they had not ratified the Geneva Convention covering the treatment of PoWs, they treated us no worse in Java than their own soldiery and soon introduced a system of paying us pocket money. This amounted to 25 sen a day[151] for officers, 15 sen for NCOs and 10 sen for other ranks. We found the Japanese had instituted their own currency for Java, with paper money and aluminium coins. Careful records were kept of these payments, which were to have been recovered from us after the war. A Chinese contractor was authorised to visit the camp for a few minutes each day and we were allowed to buy soap, fruit, a crude variety of sugar, hardboiled ducks' eggs and other provisions. A few PoWs were employed as servants in the guardroom and barracks and there were one or two outside working parties but most of the time was passed in cleaning and improving the camp.

The small daily ration of rice, offal, flour and vegetables provided only a plate of rice, watery soup, a slice of bread and unsweetened black tea so the additional foods bought from the contractor, both by individuals and any messes, were really life saving. The introduction of money and a market in which to spend it immediately resulted in the initiative of individuals setting up their own enterprises. The men on working parties brought back odd tools, timber, metal from crashed aircraft on the airstrip, old tyres and textiles and indeed anything which might serve as raw material for saleable manufactured goods. Newly interned Dutch civilians would sell their valuables in order to buy food before they were transported elsewhere. These in turn, together with exquisitely manufactured model aircraft, etc., might be sold to the guards or to the catering contractor and we all benefited greatly from a little extra fruit. All British and Commonwealth officers subscribed to a fund to purchase extra rations for the sick and the Commandant agreed to the purchase of some basic medicines.

Somehow about 200 of us from Semplak had become the permanent staff of this transit camp and we were surprised and pleased when draft after draft was taken away and we remained. We had discovered when we left Semplak that our Wing Commander, Alexander, had not after all been shot by the Japanese for disobeying orders but had been placed in secret and solitary confinement. He was restored as our CO and, together with Pilot Officer MacDonald, liaised most effectively with the guard commanders at Makasser. The senior amongst these seemed to be a very smart, slight man who rarely came inside the camp but was a strict disciplinarian to his own men. He came to be known amongst us as 'Slapsie Maxie', a reference to his favoured response to misdemeanour.

Between the camp and the guardhouse there was an empty space on which the guards were paraded and exercised and where they used to throw baseballs to one another for amusement when off duty. We eventually had sufficient funds to buy footballs but there was insufficient clear area amongst the palm trees, so we rigged up basketball nets and established a league. Some people acquired expensive tennis shoes, others played in bare feet, but I made shoes out of old footballs by cutting out the panels and sewing them together in the right shape. So our physical conditions were really not uncomfortable and we had sufficient able-bodied men to be able to maintain and improve the camp sanitation, the hospital, the kitchens and the general tidiness of the camp.

Thus, during the day we were fairly busy and in the warm evenings most PoWs sat out on benches, chatting, blowing smoke at the mosquitoes and watching the flying foxes by the camp floodlights. It was in this period that Jeff Skinner, our signals officer, with Mike's help, was at last able to construct a radio receiver. Jeff had only just come down from Cambridge on the outbreak of war and he was a genius.

Amongst the private enterprises set up in the camp were those fitters who worked on aircraft models cut out of duralumin from the crashed aircraft and Mike had little difficulty in obtaining a soldering iron. Jeff used this to wire up some small dry batteries in series and to manufacture a small radio from the acorn valves we had taken from our own aircraft when we sabotaged them at Tasikmalaja and other components we now obtained from new Dutch arrivals in the camp. Jeff successfully operated the radio inside his own mosquito net with a thin wire aerial pinned up inside it and nobody but we pilots, Jeff and Doc Morgan knew what was going on. However, the batteries soon expired and we found we could not rely on constantly buying more, for this would be a complete give-away, so very shortly Jeff made up a transformer system and plugged it into the mains after the nets were up every night.

Of course, PoW camps were hotbeds of rumour at every level. There were rumours regarding our treatment in individual camps, of atrocities and beatings-up, of new privileges, of lost privileges, of PoW movements, of the progress of the war, of life in Java outside the camps, of attempted escapes from other camps – in fact, of every possible development which could reflect upon our way of life and its duration. Even though the news from the BBC in 1942 was generally discouraging, it was at least real and, if not as hopeful as some of the rumours in the camp, it was better than some of the others. The news from the radio was therefore a real boon and soon, whenever there were only British troops and officers in the camp, we were producing daily bulletins to the officers to be passed around by word of mouth. We were aware that this definite world news would reach the NCOs and men but we were really anxious that the reality of the radio was not generally known.

The reason for this was that amongst the Dutch troops there were a very small number of Nazi sympathisers and they were known to enjoy extra rations and other privileges in return for providing the Japanese with information. If any one of these were to suspect a secret radio, the camp would have been most thoroughly searched. The total unreality of the Japanese version of the progress of the war, as published in newssheets occasionally issued to us, rendered utterly incredible the facts reaching us over the radio if one was ignorant of the source.

Many of the Dutch troops who entered and left Makasser en route to the steamers to take them down the archipelago to build airfields were reservists who had only taken up arms just prior to the invasion. As soon as peace was restored they resumed their civilian occupations under surveillance until it was convenient for the Japanese to replace them. Occasionally the quotas were short and some of the British troops in the camp would be drafted in to make up the numbers. We therefore prepared for the contingency that we might ourselves be drafted out.

Jeff's final radio at Makasser was fitted into a water bottle, which had a compartment actually containing water. The earphones and power pack were in similar bottles and these were their hiding places in camp. The routine at night was that Jeff would have one earphone and tune the radio with a small screwdriver and I would have another and make notes as fast as I could. We would immediately whisper the news to Mike and the Doc of course and I would type out my notes the following day – not a suspicious activity in itself as I was constantly practicing my typing.

Our particular concerns and worries of course were only that our radio would be discovered, that we would be shipped out on a draft and, underlying everything, what would the Japanese do with the PoWs when, as was inevitable, they lost the war. Few had any doubt but that they would fight to the last and would massacre the prisoners. Apart from these concerns, it might be considered that we had a pretty good time. We had sufficient food to keep us alive, were able to study and exercise without much interference and we could follow the progress of the war.

1943 arrived and with it the Japanese New Year. The Korean guards celebrated and drank more than was good for them; the following day we were covertly amused to see them sweating off their symptoms at drill in full kit and being pretty well thrashed by Slapsie Maxie.

Flies were a problem. Batavia has a hot and humid climate and lies just six degrees below the equator. A visiting Japanese officer decided that a campaign to kill them should be instituted and every prisoner must kill ten flies every day. These were to be produced for inspection and destruction at every evening roll call. It was easy on the first day. On evening parade we each held out our hands with ten flies upon them to be tipped into a bag. On the following day we managed quite well although those farthest from the cookhouse and the septic tanks found difficulty in filling their quotas. On the third day I was approached by an airman after the morning roll call. 'Are you having a problem with your flies, sir? I nodded for I had spent several hours on the previous day keeping an eye out, with other officers, for a fly to swat. 'I can offer you good, big flies for 2 sen each, or ten for 10 sen.' I managed to bargain the price down to 7 sen for ten and was presented with a twist of paper containing ten flies. I don't know how he managed to produce them in quantity so soon after the inauguration of the daily check – for other officers bought them too – but it wasn't long before they were being commercially reared. The Japanese enthusiasm for this exercise died after a while but it was re-ignited for a few days at a time whenever the problem arose again.

A few weeks later lists were produced of another work party of mainly Commonwealth troops and Mike and I were horrified to find that he and I were included in this draft and Jeff and Doc Morgan were not. Naturally Jeff would keep the radio and, as usual, nobody knew whither the draft was bound; it could be Japan, Burma, Malaya or down the islands. The British doctors were responsible for ensuring that all nominated men were fit and would not, on ethical grounds and to avoid Japanese distrust of their integrity, issue a false sickness certificate. Despite the Doc being a member of our very close group, he would not help us to hoodwink the senior medical officer and I was reconciled to having to leave with Mike.

However, a couple of nights before we were rumoured to be marching out, Mike went out to the latrine in the small hours of the night and some time later I heard him calling me. I found him crouched over a small bamboo bridge over an earthen drainage ditch, wearing just his night sarong and with one of his clogs some feet away in the ditch. 'What's the trouble?' I asked. 'I think I've broken my ankle.' 'How did that happen?' Although it was obvious that one of the bamboo stems had broken and others gone with it. He must have dropped a couple of feet to the bottom of the ditch and wrenched it somehow. He just grunted and it was obvious that he was in some pain. I said I'd get the Doc and went into the hut to get him out of his mosquito net next to me. The Doc was a heavy sleeper and didn't like to be awakened in the middle of the night, although this happened quite frequently.

Doc muttered to himself and followed me to the door and out to the spot, only a few feet away, where Mike was sitting on the ground with his feet through the bamboo structure. We managed to lift him so that he could help lever himself up with his other leg and we got him back on to his section of the communal bed. The light wasn't good enough for Doc to attend to it right away but he confirmed in the morning that it was indeed broken.

I spent the night worrying about my own prospects, as well as thinking of how lucky Mike had been to suffer this accident at such a convenient time, for there would be no question of his leaving on a work party within a week. It looked like an accident and neither the doctors nor I put it to him that it wasn't. I think he would have said something to me if it was deliberate but he was also one of the most determined men I have ever known and, if he decided that he wasn't going, this is how he would have engineered it.

Nevertheless, this left me as the only one of the four to be leaving and I didn't like it at all. I wasn't brave enough to break a limb and in any case such an accident would have been too much of a coincidence. I spent much of the following day putting on a brave face and preparing my gear for the miserable journey. There were now only two days before the PoWs had been advised that the draft would leave and I was afraid that I would never again see those who had been my closest friends.

That night I was overtaken by severe cramps in my stomach. I developed high temperatures, vomiting, fearful sweating and a rash. Doc was again woken in the night; indeed he could hardly have slept through my writhing around next to him. Worse, he couldn't get to sleep again for there was nothing he could do to relieve my extreme discomfort, which was real enough. In the morning he asked the other doctors, who were naturally suspicious of this fortuitous ailment, for advice and they were confident that they would be able to get me fit in time for the draft. However, I spent the day vomiting and quite unable to keep down any food. The Doc was very worried indeed for my life, since nobody was able to diagnose my condition. News came that the draft was to be delayed by four days. My name stayed on the list.

There were few medicines in the camp and I was prescribed dosages of the one or two which might be thought effective at least to relieve the symptoms, but there was no improvement in my condition. Day after day two or three doctors would visit me and I would grow weaker even after the draft was delayed a further three days. In all eleven days passed, four days after the ship had left, before my condition started to improve and I was able to keep down my food. Like everybody else, I was pitifully underweight before my illness and it took me several weeks to recover even to that level afterwards. There were many puzzled people around the camp and many half-joking queries about my convenient illness but the doctors were in no doubt of my condition and brooked no criticism. I never admitted to any deception. I had remembered that during my schooldays it was believed that one could become quite ill if one ate tobacco and thus avoided unwelcome tests or examinations: I had got hold of some very old and dried native tobacco and kept myself topped up for more than a week.

When the camp at Makasser was closed down, we were marched into the centre of Batavia where there was a walled civil prison known as Boei Glodok. Once again, there were about three hundred British and Commonwealth troops under Wing Commander Alexander and when we arrived the place was empty and had been prepared by the Japanese so that we could manufacture string and heavy sacks of sisal on primitive machinery.

On the night before our march from Makasser we filled the water compartments in the radio-carrying water bottles and discovered that one leaked and we should not be able to put water in it with the radio or power pack. Many of the troops carried food with them and water bottles were convenient containers for sugar, so we filled the leaking water compartment with sugar and had only three with radios and water. This proved to be no problem.

The following morning we were paraded outside the camp and had to empty our backpacks and stand behind our kits dressed to march whilst every item that could conceal anything that might be of interest to our captors was inspected. We marched off with our enormous packs and the guards accompanying us carried only rifles, bayonets and bandoliers. Nevertheless, by the time we reached the outskirts of Batavia they were demanding water from the bottles of the prisoners who still had some. As soon as this began, Jeff, Mike, Doc and I moved into the two central files of the four ranks in which we were marching but even so Jeff was asked to give a guard a drink from his bottle. He indicated graphically that he was suffering from dysentery and the guard was very pleased, if somewhat surprised, to accept an offer of water from one of his neighbours. The others of us emptied our false water bottles so that we should not be similarly embarrassed later in the march. Upon arrival outside Boei Glodok our kit was again similarly searched but nothing objectionable was found on either occasion.

When we entered the prison we found that the big double gates and 20-foot high walls surrounded a number of individual compounds of varying sizes. There were several, big enough for about thirty men each, which consisted of a large stone room with one door and one window abutting on to a veranda, an open drain, a wash house, a couple of lavatories and a large earthen yard. The room and veranda comprised one side of the yard and the other three sides had walls about 14 feet high with a single door in the wall opposite the large cell. All the buildings were separated from the high outer wall by an open passage about ten feet wide and from the administrative buildings by a couple of gates and a large recreation yard, upon which we did our PT and roll-calls. There were watchtowers on the walls in which sentries were placed, although in our circumstances they were unnecessary, and the guards patrolled the passage outside the compounds.

Apart from the larger cells and compounds there were two units next to the recreation ground, which had in them two small cells each and relatively smaller yards. Alexander and his adjutant, Pat Young, knew of course that we had brought our radio with us and, since there were no officers senior to a flight lieutenant except himself and his alternate, a lieutenant-colonel, in the camp, they took one of these small compounds and we had the other. This could be passed off since, although Jeff was a Flying Officer and Mike a Pilot Officer, Doc Morgan and I were Flight Lieutenants, so we thought we were senior enough to have the allocation explained if the Japs should query these comparatively young officers enjoying the most commodious quarters.

Mike, who was an exceptionally capable handyman, became officer in charge of workshops or Clerk of Works, Doc had his medical duties and Jeff and I were put in charge of string rooms. We already had a camp bed apiece and Mike fixed us up with a couple of deck chairs made from reinforcing bars and canvas, three hard wooden chairs and a table with a false top. We kept the hinges on the door of the compound unoiled and squeaky and contrived to keep it closed, when it was not held open, by a piece of rope, a pulley and a brick. Also of course, we were able to put nails into the walls and small shelves on them. We were allocated a servant who looked after our washing and our cooking and life was even more comfortable than it was at Makasser. Officers and men now received enhanced pay in Japanese occupation money, which meant that we could buy more fruit and eggs as well as additional liver and milk for those who fell ill. Everyone was able to cultivate a few plants in the gardens of the compounds although most only grew tomatoes and lettuce.

Mike and Jeff set about organising the radio in our new quarters and we soon had a very good drill. The two cells were each about eight feet by eight feet and Mike and Jeff occupied one and Doc and I the other. There was a surface light switch just inside the doorway to each cell and Jeff drilled two small holes in it so that the bare copper ends of the power cable from the radio, when fully pushed in, would give current but could be easily snatched out in an emergency. The wire to hang the mosquito nets ran across the middle of the cell from just above the switch and its ends were insulated from the nails holding it. The table with the false top was placed underneath the switch and the three chairs around it, one almost in the doorway. Every night we got the radio out of its very secure hiding place and put it in the table, which was partly covered by a green cloth on which there were three hands of gin rummy already dealt and with score paper and pencil. The top of the table consisted of three narrow boards, the outer two of which were screwed down as usual, but the centre one hinged up against the wall at one end. When closed, it was secured by nail through a drilled hole in a flange and the table frame.

When, as happened occasionally, a guard opened the squeaky door at the end of the compound about 15 yards away, whoever was on guard in the deckchair on the veranda with a book would shout *'Kyotski!'* He and the player seen by the door would leap to attention, ensuring the guard could not immediately see into the cell. Jeff and his assistant would disconnect the power cable, unclip the aerial from the mosquito netting wire, place them both with the earphones in the false tabletop where the radio was already lying, quietly lower the centre board of the table and put the nail in the hole. If the guard were to venture as far as the door of the cell he would find all three at attention with the green cloth over the table, the three hands of cards and perhaps some mugs of cooling tea. Much of the space in the tabletop was occupied by tins of bully beef and Blue Cross margarine. If there should be a very thorough search of the camp during the daytime, which never actually took place, and the hiding place in the table were discovered, there would be no radio set there and the need for the secret table would be explicable as a safe place to hide the food from pilferers.

Our most vulnerable time was a few seconds each evening as we took the radio from its permanent hiding place to the top of the table and returned it later. The larger compounds were equipped with latrines although we eight in the four death cells (as we believed they were before the war), had to use a small lavatory about twenty yards down the main passage. The purpose of the gully, which ran through all the compounds just below the verandas, was to carry away rainwater and the water used in the bathhouses. In private houses, hotels and barracks alike in Java then the system of showers was very simple: a big stone tank of water was located in a shower room with a corrugated tile floor sloping towards a drain. One filled a dipper – generally of about a gallon capacity – with water and poured it over oneself, repeating this as often as one needed. In the prison compounds these tanks, whose water level was regulated by ballcocks, were located over the open gullies and nothing could be simpler. But it was underneath our bathroom and up the galley that we located our perfect hiding place.

The galley was about eighteen inches wide at the top and narrower at the bottom of its cross-section, about a foot deep and fashioned from concrete slabs. About two feet up the galley under the bathroom the top of one of the sides had not been properly concreted and we could reach into a small cavity there between the earth and the concrete slab. In our first few nights there we were able to excavate this somewhat so that, although we did not have to scramble up the galley, we were able to reach our left shoulders right up alongside the cavity and then thrust our arms back down and parallel to the galley. An Englishman would have had to be told how to reach the radio by lying in the galley; most Japanese would have been too short to do so, even if they were told where it was. We were able to carry out the excavation unobserved because for about an hour after the evening roll-call until dark everybody was allowed to wander round the barrack block and the recreation ground so that at that time of the evening we could place a lookout of our own outside our door to warn of a sentry's approach. After dark nobody, except privileged officers such as the doctors, the camp adjutant and the CO, was allowed out of his compound. Out of a heavy Sidcot flying suit which we had persuaded somebody to cut down to jacket size I had sewn a tough waterproof bag with a zipper and the radio was put into this before being stuffed behind the galley.

We took turns about this task, which was unenviable as men in the upper compounds, despite instructions being given that they were not to do so, were occasionally not bothered to use the latrines and urinated instead into the galley. So our routine every evening at about ten to eight was to arrange the chairs, table and cards, check the passage and one of us would then strip off and retrieve the radio and then shower. We'd listen to the radio news and take notes for 15 minutes, repack the radio, check the passage and restore the radio. Soon after that we'd be joined by the adjutant and discuss the news for half an hour or so before turning in. As we were all British or Australian in the camp, everybody was told the news the following day and nowhere else did we enjoy such a snug and secure arrangement.

Very shortly after we moved in, the guards were still curious about what we did in the evenings and often looked in. On one particular occasion we were actually receiving the news and I was sitting in the deckchair on the veranda whilst the other three were at the card table listening to the radio. The outer door set up its squeak and a rifle and bayonet appeared around it, closely followed by a small Korean guard. I immediately set up a shout of *'Kyotski'* and heard the stealthy noises of the table being closed as my friends loudly scraped their chairs on the floor and they stood up. He looked suspiciously around at our batman's hut and at the earth, which we had been digging up in order to plant vegetables and then shuffled up the paved central path towards me. After four or five yards he stopped because there was a cat standing on the path and looking at him over its shoulder. This was most unusual because most cats and dogs fled at the sight of a Japanese uniform for the soldiers appeared to dislike them and often threw stones at them. He moved two steps closer and the cat didn't move a muscle, so he brought down his rifle and bayonet and prodded towards the animal. Conscious of my standing there in front of him, awaiting his salute, he grasped his rifle by the stock and lunged and lunged even more closely at the cat. As it still didn't move, he swung backwards and then struck the cat under its ribs with the bayonet. He was surprised to see it loop swiftly into the shadows under the wall three yards away where it lay with straight legs, silent and unmoving. We'd found the cat in the cell when we arrived and I'd had the notion of using it to play for a few perhaps precious seconds.

All this time he had not acknowledged me so I was standing on the verandah at the salute with my cap on, not knowing whether to laugh or be scared at the beating I could foresee, and the others without caps, were bowing in the cell behind me. The sentry looked at the cat and then he looked at me about five paces away, bawled *'Currah'*, which seemed to be a general word of challenge and interrogation, and came on a bit. I shouted the word for 'Stand at ease' and explained wholly in English, but with what I hoped were suitable gestures and expressions, that we had been expecting the adjutant and hoped to play this innocent little joke on him. I would never dream of offering it disrespectfully to a representative of the Emperor. He looked at me blankly, bellowed that I was *'hai-kura'* and told us not to mention the incident but to get rid of the cat. I was greatly relieved, although we'd missed the news, and I discovered later that *hai-kura* was apparently derived from 'high-collar' meaning a toffee-nosed person. I think he must have been impressed by my white silk pyjamas, made from a piece of parachute, and my SAAF peaked cap.

A few weeks later I was again on watch on the verandah during the news. The routine was quite humdrum now and I was genuinely immersed in the book I was reading. The door squeaked but I paid it no attention. Suddenly there was a vast bellow of *'Kyotski'* from Mike right behind and above me and I leapt to my feet with Rudolph, the Korean interpreter almost on top of me. He was a bit taken aback by this enormous shout and was anyway quite a diffident fellow who tried hard to steer clear of trouble. He asked timidly if he could see the Doc who was peering out of the door, having cleared the table. The Doc was always very efficient when conducting any medical business but also rather brusque. Absolutely no bedside manner. Quite evidently he saw some duty or other coming up for he put on his business expression and barked at Rudolph, 'What d'you want?' and Rudolph unbuttoned his trousers and exhibited his penis. Doc was accustomed to dealing with the guards when they caught the clap and came to see him when they were on duty. They were thus able to avoid punishment through discovery by their own medical orderlies or doctors. Now he told Rudolph he wasn't infected. 'Yes,' replied Rudolph, 'but is it big enough?' We almost hooted with laughter and relief, but I was considerably embarrassed by having been so careless.

The work at Glodok was not very demanding and the whole camp quickly fell into a routine. The Commandant was a stocky stolid lieutenant called Yamamoto, reputed to have been a schoolteacher. He appeared to allow his men freedom to treat the prisoners as they would their own subordinates and to be more concerned about output than anything else. There were occasional incidents but these were rare in comparison with other camps and there were few searches.

In most compounds the men started brews from sweet potatoes, bananas, peas, etc., and yeast from the bakery, and some of the stuff was quite good, generally rather sweet (through not having been allowed to brew long enough) and strong. Unfortunately, some were found drinking it just before Christmas 1943 and were beaten up. The matter was reported to Yamamoto, the camp searched and all brews poured away. It was just too difficult to hide a four-gallon can of fermenting liquor in a cramped cell.

Just past the administration buildings and guardhouse by the main gate on the other side of the recreation ground was the string factory. The end product, which was produced elsewhere, was a heavy sisal sack of which we were shown an example. We were given the sisal to spin the string of which the sack was woven. The factory consisted of a number of large rooms, which housed long tables, down each side of which six or eight men could work. Each man had in front of him a wooden reel about a foot in diameter revolving on a horizontal axis at right angles to the table. These reels were powered by a system of belts and one man at the end of the table pedalled to keep them all going. A few strands of sisal were attached to the hub of the reel, held by the spinner and twisted into string. As the strand knit, so the spinner added more sisal, stepped back and so 'grew' the string. The rooms were large enough to allow the men on both sides to move back half a dozen paces before catching the string near the reel, snagging it forward and thus having it wound on the reel before they unsnagged it and recommenced spinning string. After a little practice it was easy enough, with care, to spin sisal string of regular diameter thin enough for the coarse sacks. It was deadly boring and dusty and, when the men added too much sisal at any one time to the string they were spinning, it developed lumps so that the theme for good string was 'little and often'.

I was put in charge of a string room with about twenty men and my assistant was Pilot

Officer Ben Dougal, a quantity surveyor in Malaya who had been given a commission in the Air Ministry Works Department on the outbreak of war there. Yamamoto was quite patient in the first few days and I remember his coming into my room, complaining that the string looked like a snake which had swallowed ostrich eggs and carefully demonstrating how it should be done. A little corporal named Uwazami (known as 'Rosemarie' to the men) was in charge of about half a dozen rooms and he used to come around and check that Ben and I were supervising the quality of string. The men had become quite clever at making clumsy careless thick string at the start of a reel and then covering it with well-spun string in the last layers. However, there was really not enough work for both Ben and me to walk around and supervise and so, after mid-morning break, by which time the previous day's completed reels had been checked in and supplies of sisal drawn, Rosemarie allowed Ben and me to alternate our duty, taking time out in our compounds. I don't know what Ben or any of the others did with this spare time but I would be practising typing, gardening or learning Russian or Spanish – anything but Dutch, Malay or Japanese – or sewing basketball shoes.

A few months after we'd started in the string factory I had some trouble, which I suppose was fairly typical of the sort of incident, which used to take place every week or two. Rosemarie complained that the men's string was bad – a regular criticism in order to maintain quality control – and he pushed one of the men aside and spun a few feet of string as an example although of course everybody knew by then how to spin well. However, on this occasion Rosemarie made a mistake and I pointed out that there was a lump in his string, so therefore even the best spinners sometimes suffered faults. He didn't take the comment kindly, started up at me for some seconds and left. That afternoon Ben was on duty in the factory and I was in my compound practising my typing on a small portable borrowed from the orderly room when Rosemarie came storming in with an armed sentry. He took me off to the guardroom and complained to Yamamoto that Ben and I were derelict in our duty – apparently Ben had gone to the toilet so that for a minute or two there was no supervisory officer in our room. Yamamoto, who deliberately picked occasions on which he lost his temper, stayed calm and put us in solitary confinement in the cells opposite the guardroom. Our personal particulars were recorded in some sort of punishment book and I remember the guards' surprise that I was a Flight Lieutenant at 21 and Ben a Pilot Officer at 42. We occupied two of the four solitary cells in a row about half a dozen yards from the sentry standing by the gate leading from the factory to the recreation ground. The cells themselves were about six feet by four, each with a concrete bunk to serve as a bed, an oriental type water closet and a low water tap. A tiny yard about the same size, concrete-floored between the walls, connected the cell with the open-barred gate. Both areas were open to the sky and steel bars ran across the top. No food was to be provided for the duration of our sentences.

All the prisoners working in the factory had to pass between the solitary cells and the sentry four times a day and that evening Mike muttered that he'd bring food the following morning. Sure enough, I grabbed a packet from him as he passed in the crowd and retired to the cell to dispose of it. It consisted of bread, a peeled banana and a shelled hard-boiled egg and the wrapping paper contained a short summary of last night's news in a simple code. I shredded the string in which it was bound and ate the food and paper by the time all the men had passed. Unfortunately, Ben had found some old tobacco in his cell, contrived to roll a cigarette and lit it. The guard had either heard him striking a flint or seen the smoke after the workers had all passed and raised the alarm over this irregularity. They searched the cells and found that Ben had also a fresh banana that he was keeping for later, as I discovered afterwards.

Yamamoto was called and blew his top. He had the gate to my cell opened and yelled '*Comeer*' several times until I understood he meant, 'Come here'. I took a couple of paces to the threshold and he kicked me in the stomach. I doubled up and clutched the sides of the gate and he yelled again *'Comeer'*. When I straightened up again he kicked me again and we repeated the exercise several times. Then he lashed my cap off with his cane and beat my head with it until it had broken and the jagged splinters had dealt me superficial but badly bleeding cuts about my temples. I was then taken to his office and asked who had given me the tobacco and banana. I denied I had any and then was clubbed several times until I lost consciousness.

I recovered my wits as I felt the skin being torn from my bare feet in the dirt and dust while two guards dragged me by my arms across to the punishment cell. It was a slight relief to be left lying on the concrete floor and the gate was banged shut and locked. The guard on duty threw my wooden clogs at me through the bars. I writhed feebly to ease the cuts and bruises against the hot concrete but the dust clung to my sweat and blood. My shirt had gone, my ragged shorts my only garment and no protection against the heat of the day and the night to come. The flies were already stinging. Time passed without my knowing. The guard were changed two or three times without their shouts and stamps disturbing me and the sun had gone when I opened my least damaged eye and saw the floodlight blazing above. I was conscious only of pain and thirst.

The tap at the back of the cell was only a few yards away but I couldn't move towards it and I lay back on the floor. But my thirst tormented me until I was forced to make the attempt to drag myself by my hands across to the back wall. My hips and ankles scraped on the dirty concrete but at last I reached the tap. I put my head under it and, when I twisted the faucet, there was a warm dribble for a few moments only which brought me no relief. I lay there, exhausted, and squirmed across to the filthy bowl of the toilet. A weak dry stench told me there was nothing there, but a knotted string above was attached to the cistern. I managed to reach up to it, pulled it, heard a dry clank and I fell back on to the concrete. The pain, the thirst and the mosquitoes were more than I could bear without some sort of relief and I tried to call for help from the guard. I could only raise a rattle in my throat. I'd have to get back to the gate and so started the interminable journey again. I blacked out time and again and didn't reach the gate. Warm water trickled over my cropped and bloody scalp and the sergeant of the guard was standing over me with a small tin can, soon empty. Gasping, I lay on my back whilst he told the sentry to refill the can. It was placed just inside the gate and they stood back to watch me drinking. I muttered my thanks to them but no more water was forthcoming. I was helpless and my situation hopeless. There was nothing to be done about my physical problems of the cuts and broken teeth and bruises, the almost certain septicaemia and ulcers, but surely Yamamoto wanted me alive? My trifling offence didn't warrant an official execution and he would have killed me on the spot if his consuming rage had been so great. When dawn came, I'd know what more would befall me. With this, I passed out again, waking only when I could hear the whole camp astir.

It was nearly seven o'clock when the prisoners plodded by on their way to the factory building and no one stopped to look at me. I was able to drag myself to my feet against the bars and caught the eye of the Adjutant, Pat Young, as he passed. I hoped he would be able to do something but nothing happened and I slumped against the wall by the gate and wondered what I could do. There was no water in the can and I knew the present guard as a monster of sadism, so there'd be no help from him. I hoped that Uwazami sought only to punish me and that my roomful of prisoners would not suffer from my folly. Perhaps Yamamoto's rage had been exhausted and, if he ran true to form, he would consider a formal punishment that morning. The worst could be solitary confinement for about a month in that hellhole and wouldn't be easy to survive. The cuts would turn to sores and ulcers and every day there would be the torment of at least two hours with the sun directly overhead and no possible protection. The mosquitoes of the night were now replaced by the buzz and stinging bites of the blowflies and, no matter how I shifted my body about, there was no respite from the pain and ache of my cuts and bruises.

Well, whatever they did, I thought, they'd never know how much I'd done to their comrades at Palembang and Cheribon and the memory of those slaughters provided some bitter and encouraging consolation. Those I'd killed were the lucky ones amongst them and the wounded survivors of my explosive and incendiary ammunition would carry the scars and deformities for the rest of their lives. If they'd known, they might even envy me. Strengthened by hatred and these triumphant memories, I found my stamina returning, with a little of my normal optimism. But there was still nothing I could do, no option but to wait. Following the example of Job, prayer was the Catholic remedy in such circumstances and I accepted it as the means to pass the painful hours. The formal prayers, 'Our Fathers' and 'Hail Marys' were my first recourse and I muttered them to myself as fervently as when I had seen Zeros above me in the days of combat. Time still dragged and I set myself to recall the less familiar rhythms, eventually composing my own which I entitled 'Prayers for Those in Hopeless Plights' and tried to commit to my memory. I thought then with regret of the little compound I'd shared for the last few months with Mike and Jeff and Doc and the quiet evenings when we'd passed the dark hours in discussing the latest news. How luxurious it all seemed in comparison with the day I'd spent in the cell.

The shadow of the wall crept down and across the floor so that there was no respite from the solid beating of the sun. The guard had changed and, hoping for the best, I leant against the bars and rattled the empty can. The guard was only slightly less antagonistic than the other, slouched across, delivered the usual angry tirade at the top of his lungs and thus brought the sergeant from the guardroom across to the cell. He looked down at me, so I shifted the tiny can towards him, at which he gave an approving shout to the sentry and moved off again. Some time later, footsteps and an exchange of shouts heralded the welcome sight of the adjutant at the gate, accompanied by the guard commander and Rudolph, the interpreter. I hauled myself to my feet again and tried, but failed, to bow. When the gate was unlocked, I fell completely to the ground. The guard was sent for some water, which I swallowed frantically. Pat Young said, 'Take it easy. Things'll get better soon,' and was roundly cursed by the sergeant.

The sergeant shouted, Rudolph whispered his almost unintelligible English and Pat said, 'You're going to be in here for four days without food. Don't answer and I'll tell them you need water to drink and medical attention.' I didn't think the situation could get any worse and burst out, 'That crapper's dry and filthy. I've got to wash it out.' Rudolph explained this to the sergeant who stared into my eyes for a long time and padded by me to inspect the toilet, returning with an expression of disgust. 'Something will be done,' said Pat, and added 'and Doc Morgan will come and see you this evening.' With that the gate was locked again and I was left in solitary torment. I went back to my prayers and memories and after a while the sentry brought in a prisoner with a bucket of water and a mop. Accompanied by much shouting the toilet was cleaned out but the guard ignored my signs of another bucketful with which to clean myself. A lot more time passed and then I heard water running into the cistern at the back of the cell and, dragging myself there, I found I could fill the little can from the tap. Before the men came out of the factory, Rudolph and Doc came with stinging disinfectant and paper bandages. The wounds were cleaned up and whenever Doc got an opportunity he gave me a cheery grin and even a fleeting wink. These were so much out of character in the circumstances that I thought there must be some tremendous news from the BBC.

After the evening roll call I heard a lot of shouting in Japanese from the parade ground just round the corner from the cells. I could make out that Yamamoto was delivering a speech, interspersed with Rudolph's English versions. Of course I learned afterwards that, whilst I was being beaten silly in his office, Yamamoto was told by Rudolph that the banana and tobacco were not in my cell, but in Ben's. Hence I was dragged back to my cell and Ben produced in the office. He swore that the tobacco was in his cell before he got there and that he had not seen anybody drop the banana through the gate. I can only assume that Yamamoto's rage had been exhausted on me and that the sight of respectable-looking Ben, who was about the same age as he, appealed to his schoolmasterly sympathy, for Ben wasn't touched at all. The matter was left until the evening roll call and then the watchtowers around the parade ground were manned and a machine gun produced and trained on the mass of prisoners. There was some nervous comic relief when a private was sent for a bamboo mat on which the machine-gunner should lie behind his weapon but, when it arrived, the unfortunate man put the gun on it and lay down in the dust again.

Nobody immediately responded to Yamamoto's call for the culprit to own up and Rudolph shouted that everybody would remain where they were for 'one day, two days – rain or shine.' Eventually, Jeff confessed to passing the banana, Yamamoto put him into solitary, simmered down and the affair blew over. When darkness fell and the guard had been changed, I took off my wretched shorts and washed them under the tap. This brought no response from the watching sentry and I used the wet garment to clean myself as much as I could. Exhausted again, I collapsed until I was woken by the shuffling past of the prisoners going to the factory on the following morning.

Despite my lack of food and the hard concrete bunk, I was able to lie in a state of semi-consciousness for the next couple of days. I didn't discover what it was that so cheered up the Doc when first he visited me in the cell, so perhaps he was just glad to see that I was not as ill as I looked. No more food or news was dropped in to me and of course with Jeff and me both out of action it would have been unwise of Mike and Doc to try to operate the radio. Mosquitoes and flies still troubled me but the bandages covering my injuries reduced their nuisance considerably. When eventually Jeff and I were released, Doc was able to ease the sores and of course, I ate and drank as much as was available. We slipped back into the camp routine, tried to enjoy reasonable amounts of food, spent leisurely evenings discussing the progress of the war and there were no further dangerous incidents. In the string room Uwazami behaved as before and I took good care not to cross him.

For some reason, perhaps we were producing more string than the sack makers could use, insufficient sisal was brought in to occupy all the men full time, so Yamamoto made arrangements for about half the prisoners to work in the prison gardens between the walled jail and a canal. The land, except odd groves of banana trees, had gone dry as soon as the civil prisoners had been removed, so we had to recultivate it. A Dutch civilian agricultural expert was co-opted to advise and Mike's workshop devised a pump worked by four men to bring water up from the canal. Just across the water we could see the Javanese women living in this suburb of Batavia washing their clothes, brushing their teeth and completing their toilets in the muddy water but they looked quite healthy. Yamamoto was most interested in this farming and rushed up and down the paths between the waterbeds on a bicycle issuing instructions. We grew crops of spinach, tomatoes, lettuces, eggplants, cucumbers, radishes and sweet potatoes and it seemed that there was nothing that would not grow in that soil in that climate. It was very much more enjoyable than working in the factory although Yamamoto's presence was always menacing and somebody was beaten up almost daily.

Then, in the early months of 1944, we were all moved to a camp at Tandjong Priok, the main port near Batavia.Tandjong Priok camp was a former military camp covering a very large area and divided into sub-camps of single storey buildings. There would be anything from a hundred prisoners to one or two thousand in each sub-camp, each of which was surrounded by barbed wire and barbed wire surrounded the whole area.

We were marched there from Boei Glodok of course and experienced two searches, one on leaving and one on arriving, en route. Nothing objectionable was found, other than tools considered to be ever-useful to prisoners. Our water bottles with radios were unchallenged, but we were very nervous on every march and particularly when standing behind our unrolled bedding during searches. Our contingent from Glodok was moved into a large sub-camp already occupied by several hundred Dutch troops and we were allocated some bug-infested buildings. There was great confusion amongst the Japanese during the first roll call until they managed to get us into some sort of order. The different nationalities, ranks, numbers in sick bays and in cooking squads were difficult to allocate and we spent some time initially just standing around being repeatedly counted.

Gradually the prisoners' administration won the approval of the Japanese to sorting ourselves out by nationalities and we were moved from sub-camp to sub-camp until the routine was greatly eased. The smallest sub-camp was reserved to the Americans of whom there were only a few sailors from the *Houston* and a couple of bomber crews. But it happened that this small isolated building held the most suitable small rooms for us to operate the radio. With the collusion of the Senior British Officer, who of course was advised by Wing Commander Alexander, Mike and Jeff and Doc and I became nominal American citizens and moved in.

Priok held several thousand prisoners, mostly Dutch, and there was no question of a general distribution of the news. There were, however, one or two Dutch officers whom we contacted who had had receivers, which they'd been forced to ditch, and to these and to the British officers and to the personnel of the American sub-camp we passed the news as received. The Japanese did not closely supervise such a large camp as Priok, except that nobody was allowed to leave his sub-camp at night and there were guards patrolling between them. Many of the men went out on working parties in the docks during the daytime but most of our days were empty. It was here that we were able to refine our arrangements for concealing the radio whilst we were on the move, for we were very concerned about the Japanese discovering by chance the secret of the water bottles.

By this time the clogs, which nearly everybody wore, had become very sophisticated. The majority were made of a single piece of hardwood, thick and deep, with straps screwed to the sides and raised insteps and hollows for the balls of our feet and heels. On to the flat bottom of each were tacked two pieces of motorcar tyre, which became the sole and heel of the clog. Thus Mike was able to carve a pair of clogs deep enough to accommodate two earphones in the heels and the power pack and the radio itself in the soles. They could still support the weight of a man for a short time, such as during a snap search, but were not safe for marching. Whilst we were in the American camp, there was no question of a guard entering without good warning and none ever came near. We were able to put up a good, big aerial and the Americans were much entertained when San Francisco came through loud enough for them to listen to comedy shows.

At Priok, Mike had the idea that two of us could sail to Australia in a homemade catamaran. I thought it was quite hopeless but he took it very seriously and for some weeks he and Jeff worked on their preparations. They believed that, during one night, they would be able to escape from the beach and reach an island about 30 miles to the north, which somebody had told them was uninhabited. They proposed to lie up there the following day and clear the Sunda Straits on the following night. They beat out and re-soldered petrol cans together into the hulls of their boat and I sewed sails for them out of the remains of our parachutes. They bought up tins of bully beef and constructed water containers but had finally to concede that they could not escape with a boat big enough to take themselves, food and particularly water for the 1500-mile trip to Australia. Knowing so little of Japanese and Javanese activities outside the camps, I thought they would have to be very, very lucky even to reach the beach only a mile or two away, never mind cross to the island.

There were constant drafts of Dutch internees and soldiers arriving and leaving the camp and the influx of cash with these enabled very many of the private industries to flourish. As well as the production of clogs and simple clothing, cooked and processed foods were sold both as take-away and at tables and benches. The Americans were very successful with roasted peanuts and Southern foods, the operators paying a tax to their CO, which he put towards the provision of medicine. In each sub-camp there would be a brew going, officially outside the knowledge of the senior officers, and there would even be occasions when one would visit a bar, although we preferred to brew our own. Our beers became quite sophisticated, except that they rarely cleared and were always more alcoholic than bitter, and generally a light milky orange colour, being brewed from sweet potatoes. We got ambitious and Jeff and the Doc between them found the answer. With Mike's help they made a still out of a couple of 4-gallon petrol cans and some copper pipe. They took the top off one can and soldered on a pyramid-shaped top through the apex of which a copper pipe protruded, pouring the brew in through a screw cap in the side. The vapour came through the copper pipe spiralling through another can of cold water to assist condensation and we drew off the 'gin' at the bottom. We had some very good parties and one doctor, an enormous Scotsman, could not be persuaded to remain in our camp overnight and intended to march over to the guardroom and beat up all the Japanese there. Luckily the din he kicked up was not checked by the guards and he fell asleep trying to negotiate the barbed wire out of our compound.

One brew that we put in to the still had not been properly filtered however. I was tending to the fire underneath it and Jeff was checking the temperature of the distillate with Doc's thermometer. The mash bubbled up in the can and a pea lodged in the entrance to the copper pipe, effectively blocking it. Suddenly Jeff said, 'The tin's bulging at the corners! It's going round!' I looked up from the fire and saw steam spurting through the soldered seams near Jeff squatting over his beaker of clear distillate. I shouted, 'Look out!' and moved back. There was a very loud bang, steam and boiling water went all over the place and I jumped well clear of the explosion. Everybody commented that, whilst Jeff was quite badly burned, he made no sound, and was taken to sick quarters, I was unscathed and my shout (of alarm of course) was heard all over the camp.

Once again, over the Japanese New Year we were amused to watch the Korean guards repenting their sins. This time there was no trouble over drinking too much but about a fortnight later a dozen of them spent the morning running round the football pitch, dressed in full winter clothing with backpacks and rifles. Every lap or two, Slapsie Maxie, in running gear, still with us, accompanied the last man around the pitch thumping him with a baseball bat in one hand. They had patronised some bad ladies.

The Japanese administration at Priok was very liberal and the PoWs, having developed a real economy from which we were provided with more adequate rations, were allowed to make good use of the sports grounds in the camp. Soccer of course was the most popular sport, although some were even foolhardy enough to play rugger on that very hard ground and in the heat. The Americans had acquired baseball bats, softballs and gloves and amused themselves with these. No cricket equipment was available.

There were one or two professional actors and these set up a dramatic society and put on some good shows. I heard comments that these were as good as anything seen in the West End but I don't think they were quite of that standard. The Japanese Commandant was invited along to see some of these and responded by allowing relaxation of the evening curfew between sub-camps, so everybody had an opportunity for a change of routine. We also enjoyed talks from a great variety of people who had followed all sorts of orthodox and other professions before the war. The lives of which they spoke now seemed so remote that burglars and bookmakers were remarkably frank about their techniques.

However, this idyllic life came to an end as numbers dwindled and we were marched to Cycle Camp in central Batavia. Once again, our secrets survived the double search at the beginning and end of the short journey. The Cycle Camp, as it was known to us, had been the central barracks in Batavia of the Dutch bicycle-equipped troops and was well constructed with airy modern buildings. The long barrack blocks were raised above ground so that the torrential rains ran off into wide open gullies surrounding them, the floors were covered in well-glazed tiles and the accommodation was in cubicles facing on to a central passageway. There were wide verandas on each side. The camp held about 5,000 men and had a big hospital, library, kitchens and communal bathhouses. The toilet blocks were separate and consisted of cubicles over long, frequently flushed deep trenches very easy to keep clean.

The barrack blocks were about fifty yards long, the only entrances being on both sides midway down each block. Mike and I, Jeff and Doc were allocated two cells in the far corner and with the help of a Dutch officer who was officially in charge of the camp electrics we had a concealed plug installed in Jeff s cell. There were about forty British officers and their belongings between us and the entrance, so there was never any chance of a guard catching us unawares. Spot searches in the camps were now comparatively rare and we were able to maintain our news service to the officers in our block and to the senior British officers, who included several wing commanders and Lt Colonel Laurens van der Post.

By this time the number of captured allied troops remaining in Java had been greatly reduced by the contingents sent off on the Japanese working parties but in all the camps the senior officers helped as far as they could to keep anybody holding a radio set out of the drafts. As camps were closed down, so more and more of the remnants were brought together in the remaining ones. Thus, at Cycle Camp we met Dutch, both civilian and service personnel, Australians, Americans and other British officers who had radio sets or parts of them and who were able to liaise and swap rare components. Two of these were Lieutenant Hector Arnold and Lieutenant Collins, who was nicknamed 'Bones', being tall and particularly thin, both of the Royal Corps of Signals.

Food was much more scarce in Cycle Camp and presumably throughout Java since no contractor was allowed to sell to the prisoners. The Commandant was a Lieutenant Soni who appeared to be affected by the phases of the moon as about once a month he would carry out a blitz on some facility, such as the sick quarters, the cookhouse, the library or the officers quarters. He would cycle through the camp swiftly on his bicycle to his target, carrying a pick handle or a baseball bat and then break or beat anything or anybody until his rage was exhausted. Whereas shouts of *'Kyotski'* would precede any guard patrolling in the camp minutes before he actually arrived, Soni's raids were a real danger but luckily he never targeted our hut.

Cycle Camp was very crowded at this time and there was no room for football pitches or basketball courts, but we had managed to clear sufficient space for a badminton court. There were few working parties but some weeks before we were transferred to another camp at Bandoeng the Japanese instituted an island-wide campaign to grow castor-oil trees and we were instructed to dig up the badminton court and plant some. However, we were not closely supervised as the court was tucked away behind some buildings and we actually dug about four feet down all around the court so we didn't have to stop playing before we left.

One morning, whilst we were engaged on digging around the badminton court we heard a great deal of shouting not far away. We suspected that this heralded another outburst from Soni but it transpired that a small contingent of survivors from one of the work-parties had arrived and the guards were ordered to segregate them from the rest of us. These were six men lying on the parade ground and they were hardly alive. Quickly, a part of the hospital was cordoned off into an isolation unit, the men were carried in by medical orderlies and doctors summoned to attend them. They were closely guarded in hospital for a month or so and were not allowed to communicate with the medical attendants. Nobody else could go near them. Their condition improved until at last they were put into separate cells inside the camp. There they remained isolated for another couple of months and were eventually released to join the rest of us.

Among them was Reg Simpson, who became a good friend of mine in the few years that remained to him after the war. One day I found him sitting by himself on a verandah in Cycle Camp and asked him about the draft he'd been on. 'It was real hell,' he said. 'They put 800 of us on that bloody steamer and we hadn't the foggiest notion of where we were going. There were shelves built into the holds so that each man and officer had about 24 cubic feet of space. It was as hot as hell, the latrines were almost impossible to find and fetid holes when you got there. During the daytime the ship lay up near the coast to avoid air raids and the prisoners were all battened down under the hatches. During the nights we were allowed up on deck in small batches so that we had very little time in the open air at all. As the men died off and were thrown overboard, our diminishing numbers meant that we were able to spend more time on deck. We found out that we went up to the Celebes and then down past Timor to some remote island near New Guinea. It took eight bloody weeks and there were only just over three hundred of us left by the time we got there. There was an air raid on but the Japs made us each take a four-gallon drum of petrol overboard and swim to the shore with it, whether we were suffering from dysentery, avitaminosis, malaria, dengue, ulcers or the lot. The beach was just coral and you know what that means.'

Nobody who was unused to clogs could have avoided knocking them against his ankle at some time and, lacking food and effective medicine, such sores swiftly became ulcers very difficult to heal and were endemic. In dirty conditions they would spread up inside the leg, eating away the bone and eventually killing. Coral sores were even more malignant. There were no bandages or medicine and the flies were horrific. We were supposed to construct an air base on this island with picks and shovels, because the natives had just moved out into the jungle to avoid the Japs and the air raids. We hadn't a hope of following their example. Despite the extra rations provided to these survivors by 'taxing' all the fit PoWs in the camp, they only just managed to make headway against their illnesses and poor Simpson died of their effects very shortly after the war's end.

In October 1944 we were transferred to a former Dutch barracks by Andir airfield near Bandoeng. There were the usual close searches but by this time our kits were reduced to the simplest necessities of life and the radio, being stored in one pair of clogs, was carried only by one of us, generally Mike. The barrack blocks were open huts without cubicles but some of them had open verandahs at the ends and were raised three feet above the ground. Despite the torrential rain every few days, there was a water shortage at the camp and only a trickle came through to the bath-houses in the early hours, so that I would have to rise at 3am to enjoy a shower. It was considerably cooler at that hour up in the mountains than at Batavia so that the shower was not, in fact, tremendously enjoyable. We were not long in this camp, which also accommodated many Dutch troops, and had no opportunity to establish our radio. Our 'secure' hiding place, for it was a hollowed-out bed support under Mike and me, with which we were not very happy, but it proved adequate in the only serious search of the camp itself. However, Hector and Bones had been allocated a small end verandah and they enclosed it with groundsheets to keep out the rain and thereby preserved their privacy. They used to get the news under their mosquito nets at night and we'd have it from them the following morning.

Bones had joined the army as an apprentice at the age of 14 and had risen through the ranks out of sheer ambition. Despite his slender physique, he was a strong character and also something of a scrounger and believer in free enterprise. In prison camp he applied himself to watch-making and developed a good business in buying watches, particularly Rolex and Omega automatic ones, from those who had to sell them for food and he re-sold them to Korean guards who had a market outside the camp. As well as currency, he bought items of food, such as good bread, ghee, sugar and fruit from the guards who smuggled them in since there was no official contractor allowed in at Bandoeng at that time. These visits used to take place at night of course and, though Bones tried to make arrangements, which would not involve risk to the radio, on one or two occasions Hector had to stop reception when a guard arrived unexpectedly with food to sell and money for watches. Those who didn't know of Bones' other illegal activity referred to him as a 'white' Nip on account of his apparent friendship with the guards but this indeed served us in good stead on one particular occasion.

Early one evening a Korean guard arrived at Bones' place to buy a watch or two and to sell some white bread, butter and sugar. Bones completed the transactions, stored the provisions under his bed and was taken by surprise when the guard returned an hour or so later in a state of extreme panic. He insisted that all trace of illicit substances must disappear for there was to be an extremely thorough search early the following morning by the Kempetai, the dreaded Japanese military police. Accordingly we ate all the provisions and made sure that the radio equipment could not be found. Sure enough, early the following morning everybody in the camp was paraded, and this time it was my turn to have the radio-holding clogs amongst my kit, standing under the hot sun for several hours whilst the military police checked all kit and searched minutely through the camp.

I was greatly relieved when the two Kempetai privates inspecting my kit passed on. It was later disclosed that some young Dutch officers, who must have temporarily lost their reason, broke out of the camp two nights previously and into the guards' area, which was not difficult. They removed the tyres of a car in the compound and cut away the upholstery out of which on the following day they made sandals and pairs of shorts. Of course all this stuff was found and the culprits heavily punished but, thanks to Bones' Korean accomplice, no radio components were discovered.

We spent only a few weeks at this camp before the numbers of its inmates had so dwindled that we were transferred to another much more comfortable one for a short period. In this we four – Mike, Jeff, Doc and myself – shared a small villa with some officers of a Welsh anti-aircraft regiment who had arrived in Java just in time to be captured. They were very pleased indeed to receive the latest news of the war, the progress of which was eagerly debated every evening. One of them was an energetic scrounger named Alan Reardon-Smith, constantly organizing one-up ploys against the Japanese, the Dutch or the senior British officers. He managed to survive by employing great charm against his indignant victims.

However, we were allowed to remain in that camp only for a short time before we were again transferred, together with the soldiers, to yet another camp in the Bandoeng area. This had been a large day school from which all the furniture had been removed. There were only officers interned there and we were provided with lots of whitewood, nails and tools with which to knock up sufficient bunks for 1,500 men, probably all the officer prisoners left on Java. The effective Commandant was a sergeant-major Mori, known as 'Bamboo Mon.' He held the prisoners in the greatest contempt and was rumoured to have won the highest Japanese decoration for bravery, a very broad, strong man over whom his senior officers had very little control. He always carried a club of some sort and enjoyed using it.

By this time it was early 1945 and a ship carrying Red Cross supplies reached Java through the American air and submarine blockade. It offloaded at Batavia and some of the parcels and medicines, our first, reached our camp where they were stacked in the middle of the central parade ground. No distribution took place then but on the following day everybody was paraded and harangued by Mon through an interpreter. Some wicked Chinese people on Java had telephoned the Americans that the Japanese had loaded the Red Cross ship with war supplies and it had been sunk soon after it left Batavia. Towards the end of Mon's tirade he issued threats, which I interpreted as rhetorical but the senior officers, who were lined up in a separate group, misinterpreted them. Mon made a beckoning gesture and the first in line stepped up to him and was felled by his club, followed by the second and all the rest. The first one had returned to his place in the ranks, but quite inexplicably led the whole lot up to Mon for a second thump. Eventually the parcels were distributed, about one to every four officers. We were intrigued by the products and the packaging – floating soap, powdered eggs and Spam indeed, as well as such items as chocolate bars and chewing gum.

Not long after this we were returned to Cycle Camp in Batavia. Now we found ourselves to be among the last few PoWs left on Java. There had been many detachments leaving over the past few months, but we had no idea of their destination or success in avoiding the blockade. We were only thankful to be spared. Nevertheless, rations were shorter, camp security tighter and we were very worried about what the Japanese would do to us as the war neared its conclusion. The British through Burma and the Americans across the Pacific had cut us off from mainland China and Japan but it could be a long time before they were able to reach Singapore.

Occasionally, American and British bombers flew at low level over the camp dropping leaflets, which was greatly encouraging, but on the radio we heard of the burning in caves perpetrated upon the surviving PoWs in the Philippines by the Japanese to avoid their being released by MacArthur's troops. However, we had more immediate problems. Ernie Gartrell, whom we had not seen for many months, had been appointed Quartermaster for the British troops in Cycle Camp and had through necessity to arrange the cooking schedules to provide breakfast in the early mornings and to receive and check rations into his stores late at night. There was now no hope of operating our radio in the cubicles in the barrack blocks for there were many Dutch troops in the same block and there were still informers in the camp. We were therefore lucky that we were able to arrange with Ernie that every night he took two of us to his stores for half-an-hour or so, supposedly to check rations. Nobody other than such workers were allowed to move out of the barrack blocks after dark, so Ernie's assistance was vital. We walked across the few paces on our clogs with the radios inside, spent some minutes locked in the store and plugged into the power supply, listened to the news and then returned with Ernie to the barracks. This was a regular nightly trip, but our former secure routine was also complicated in other ways.

When we reached Cycle Camp we found that we were to repair car and truck engines in what had been a Ford assembly plant at Tandjong Priok. B-29s had been over and bombed the port area so that the Javanese no longer turned up to work there. Every morning about an hour before sunrise we marched down to the station, took the train to Priok not far from our old camp and marched to the plant. There we were supervised by *Hai-hos*, Javanese levies working for the Japanese, and these were sometimes more vicious than either the Koreans or Japanese. There appeared to be nobody of great technical skill in the plant except an old Japanese who could not possibly supervise all the work. Very little was done. I spent a week grinding the valves of an eight-cylinder engine, doing nothing if no *Hai-ho* was in sight and merely twiddling one valve in each hand in its seat if anybody was looking. Unfortunately, one *Hai-ho* turned out to be quite knowledgeable; he shouted and bawled at me and finally showed me how the grinding should be done.

Alan Reardon-Smith, who had spent some years at sea for his sins, had opted to work the overhead gantry in the great shed. It was his habit to climb the ladder to the gantry cage, hop in and move the gantry away from the ladder, there to snooze until awakened by rare bellows from below or by a natural break. The same guard that caught me out also gave him a dressing-down and Alan nearly provoked a bashing for himself by clowning his misunderstanding of the guard's criticisms of him in the racket of the workshops. When we broke for our midday meal, he swore that he would even up matters with the *Hai-ho*, at which we scoffed. After the break he busied himself with running his gantry above the central walkway with a bundle of heavy rope hanging from the hook about four feet from the one end of the shed and awaited the arrival of the *Hai-ho* who, with his rifle and bayonet dragging along the ground, strolled down the middle away from the gantry. He was oblivious to the noise of the gantry accelerating above and behind him with the heavy rope bundle until it clouted him full-length. Reardon-Smith was hidden away inside his cage as he hauled up the rope and stopped the gantry and the guard was unable to get at him before his shift was changed. Alan roared his head off in triumph when he eventually rejoined us.

Rations had diminished to such an extent that even those who, like ourselves, had remained on Java through the years were now lacking nourishment. Nearly all of the poor fellows who survived the work-parties to the south-east and returned to Java found themselves without the additional nourishment they so badly needed to recover, despite the supplementary food and liver they drew, and succumbed to their ulcers and malnutrition. Mike and I therefore put our names down for voluntary work in the camp cookhouse and in the outside bakery. Mike, who was very strong, was accepted for the cookhouse and I was finally able to arrange to work in the bakery, which operated in alternate shifts of 24 hours each. There were about fifty men, including one or two officers, on each shift, but all were working under the supervision of a master baker. We were producing some 12,000 loaves daily for the inmates of the prison and internment camps, mainly women and children of Dutch nationality. Under the Dutch regime anybody of part-Dutch descent was granted full Dutch national status and tens of thousands of men of mixed blood insisted on their Dutch nationality despite brutal pressure from the Japanese. Whilst their men folk were sent away on work-parties, their families remained on Java.

It was really horrible bread, made mostly from tapioca, really just a solid wedge with a crust over it, although it looked impressive to the unskilled eye just before entering or immediately after coming out of the oven. However, not only did we in the bakery have access to unlimited bread of a sort, but also our rations were a bit better than those we had in the camp. The work was heavy, hot and hard and there seemed to be a continuous stream of four-loaf baking tins being rammed into the big ovens by Australian bakers or coming out, very hot indeed and very fast, off their long sweeps. We, the unskilled catchers, had pieces of sacking on our hands with which we caught the hot tins like slip catches. It was very painful indeed to miss a catch or to let the sacking hang off one's hands.

As we ticked off the months of 1945 and heard the news of the American successes against the Japanese, the only campaign of significance to us, we watched the routine of our guards, even in that backwater of the eastern theatre of war, gradually become less mechanical and efficient and more subject to hesitancy. Daily there would be civil disturbances and demonstrations interrupting our short journeys between the camp and the bakery as the Javanese became more restive.

In about July, Jeff was taken off on a draft to Singapore but he left the radio with us since he'd not be able to use it aboard ship and didn't know whether the steamer would be able to run the blockade. We had heard that at least one of the transports carrying PoWs had been sunk. So Mike used most often to go off with Ernie to operate the set in the storehouse at about 10pm. The following morning I would be told the latest news on my return from the bakery but on odd occasions when I was not on shift I would operate the set with Ernie.

Of course, we became more excited and anxious as the Americans moved closer to Japan and the great fire raids on the cities developed. The end was certain but we were deathly afraid of what would happen to us and all other prisoners in the hands of the Japanese forces. We knew well enough that a command to execute the PoWs from anybody more senior than a sergeant would be put into effect and that the vast majority of Japanese troops would see defeat as a disgrace with which they could allow neither themselves nor us to live. It was therefore essential for our survival that we prepared to escape before we were rounded up for massacre. Outside the camps Java was in ferment as those Indonesians who had fretted for decades under the Dutch administration took up arms to fight for their independence from the Dutch who had already been defeated and from the Japanese whose defeat was imminent. The weakened Japanese troops were hated for following their promise of liberation of South-East Asia by a more intense colonization and the Indonesians wanted to overthrow them before the Dutch were able to return under the protection of the Allies. If we went too early, we might therefore flee the almost certain death at the hands of the Japanese into a less certain but possibly more frightful fate from the Indonesians if they believed we were either Dutch or their friends.

One night in August, Ernie and I started out for the store and met a sentry. Ernie shouted *'Kyotski!'* and then *'Kin!'* and we held our salutes as the patrolling guard grunted *'Kurra?'* a couple of yards away. I was wearing the important clogs and Ernie was accustomed to these night encounters so he was able to satisfy the guard that our visit to the stores was essential. Ernie shouted *'Naoni!'* and *'Yasmi!'* We dropped our salutes and went on our way. Having locked ourselves in and tuned to London, we found that reception was poor and, having been delayed by the sentry, we were a few minutes late. We gathered that it was probable that the Japanese would soon surrender since the Russians had declared war on them and were invading Manchuria, in addition to some far more important disaster, which we could not identify. An invasion of Japan so soon by the Americans had not been anticipated and we were therefore unable to understand what major catastrophe for the Japanese could have occurred. On the way back to the barrack we passed the sentry without any untoward incident and stayed up late debating the likely event. I left before dawn as usual for the bakery and, apart from more rumours of disturbances in the streets from our guard on the open truck, I noticed no changes in the demeanour of any of them and had to wait until my return to Cycle Camp on the following morning for the news of the atom bomb which had been dropped.

Then began a very anxious time for us. News of a possible defeat for Japan evidently reached the garrison command in Java for sandbagged machine-gun posts were sited outside the camp wire with weapons aimed at the entrances of all buildings. We were still vulnerable to Japanese discipline and dared not be caught with the radio. Nevertheless, news of the bomb and of the Japanese surrender was common knowledge by the end of August, whilst we watched carefully to time our escape from the camp. The rioting and demonstrations became so violent that on several occasions we were unable to reach the bakery or return from it on schedule after our shift. We and the senior British officers were aware that the Emperor had sent a senior member of his family in a white transport aircraft to explain to his troops outside Japan the reasons for his 'conferring the boon of peace upon the world', as it was explained, but it was also reported on the radio that the garrisons on certain islands did not accept the fact of defeat and refused to surrender.

However, one day we saw the white aircraft with the red crosses on it fly over the town into Kemajoran airfield and a day or two later the senior Allied officers in the camp were officially told of the reversal of the situation. It was agreed that in view of the unrest in the town the Japanese would continue to guard the camp, but to ensure the safety of the PoWs rather than their continued detention. Regulations concerning saluting and other aspects of our relationship with the guards were of course cancelled and they were no longer seen inside the camp. Nobody bothered to try to beat up the guards in response to their brutality over the years as we all realised that they had suffered under the same code, if not to the same extent, as had we.

With the acceptance of defeat by the Japanese garrison on Java we were preoccupied by events in the town of Batavia. The Australian Government had pronounced in favour of the Indonesians in their efforts to free themselves from a return of the Dutch administration and it was believed that this would result in Javanese friendliness to the Australian ex-prisoners. Some of the Australians in camp sought to test this by going through the wire into the town, only a few yards away, in their own Australian bush hats. They reported a friendly reception and returned with some warm beer. Then it was announced that there were many Dutch civilians in camps across the town and volunteers were requested to help in their camp maintenance. I took a party of about 30 men in a truck every day for a couple of weeks to a camp, which held about 11,000 women and children. We were escorted by an armed Japanese sentry but, since the population knew that we were harmless and not hostile to them, the guard was unnecessary and often rather frightened. The Indonesians had aroused their audiences to such an extent that they had assaulted the Japanese barracks on one day and on another had forced two light tanks to retreat.

The reason for our delayed departure was that a seaborne relief of Java must await that of Singapore and then navigable lanes had to be cleared in the mine-strewn shallow seas north of Java. A few British troops, mainly medical orderlies with supplies of the latest drugs, were first parachuted and then flown into Kemajoran. Better food and medication by the most modern drugs for some of the sick cases in the camp hospital produced apparently miraculous remedies, particularly for those suffering from beri-beri and other forms of malnutrition, but many men were past relief. Letters from home were also arriving and not all of these contained good news for husbands and fathers. Some had to be consoled by an infantryman who had been blinded and lost both his hands by a mine just before the surrender three and a half years earlier and who, from pleading to be killed at that time, had developed a singularly relaxed and happy attitude to his misfortunes.

Our first few days visiting the women's camp were most interesting. It was a large permanent single-storied military camp with lawns and gardens between the barrack blocks. The buildings actually formed the perimeter so that, apart from the main gate, there was not an exit. The Japanese had guards at the entrance for the protection of the internees but they were not attacked by the Indonesians. Our men were not to visit the women's living quarters but were to assist with the heavier cooking jobs and with the sanitation. In fact, the women had been carrying out this work themselves for years so our presence was not at all necessary. I spent most of the first day trying to find out what needed to be done but it appeared that the women were just happy to have a few men around. They cheered us up somewhat but they were undernourished of course and had been through very hard times, short of food and other supplies. The men told me that on their first day in the cookhouse they found some of the women there, mostly hefty ones capable of lifting the heavy urns and pots, were naked to the waist in order to ease the discomfort of the heat. On the second day, they were all dressed in blouses and inside a week they had surrendered the heavy work to the men and somehow, as with all the others, they had found some supplies of cosmetics.

After breakfast every morning we were driven in an open truck to the women's camp and returned just before dusk. By mid-afternoon the men were doing little work, other than helping individual women when asked to do so, so that about an hour before our departure each man would be seated amongst a group of women, sipping tea and trying to maintain polite conversation. One or two progressed very quickly with the more forward girls and contrived to find quiet corners in which to compensate for the lost years. By the second and third nights it became very difficult indeed to trace them all, particularly as some of them had made arrangements to hide and remain overnight.

Unfortunately, the civil demonstrations were getting more and more out of hand and it became imperative that we returned to Cycle Camp in full daylight so that we would be recognised as Allied PoWs by the mobs, armed as they were with parangs and spears. With as many as possible wearing Australian bush hats and hiding the Japanese guard in the middle of the truck, we had several times to detour through the town to avoid crowds on their way to demonstrate in the central square. On the last day we found ourselves sandwiched between two mobs going in the same direction. We turned down a side-street, made the sentry lie on the floor of the truck and found ourselves facing yet another crowd of banner-waving, shouting youths, moving to join the others. We hastily turned into the drive of a large deserted house, where we waited until all had passed before cautiously navigating around the outskirts back to camp. These daily journeys across the town whereby we achieved little but a purely social function in no way justified the risk of our becoming involved in clashes, so the arrangement ceased and we found ourselves unemployed and waiting impatiently to be released.

The Australian and New Zealand governments had proportionately far better resources in the area than the British and a stronger will to get their men home. They laid on ships to take them away from Malaya and flying boats to pick up the few hundred left in Java. As aircrew, Mike and I volunteered to act as Movement Control Officers at the jetty at Tandjong Priok, marshalling the jubilant Aussies aboard the Sunderlands and we saw Taffy Julian and Ernie Gartrell off for good. As the numbers remaining lessened, Mike and I calculated how long it would be before there was accommodation on a flying boat for us and we took our small packs with toiletries in them down to the jetty daily. We did not want to wait for the last flying boat, though, for we feared that any empty seats might be filled by high-priority passengers, such as journalists. Whilst there were still a few Aussies remaining, although not down at the jetty, we found some unoccupied seats one evening and so we quietly moved ourselves off Java, saving at least three weeks, for the seaborne relieving forces were still about a week away.

On arrival at Singapore we were given accommodation in a transit camp and kitted out in jungle-green baffle dress and shoes and were able to draw some cash. Although we enjoyed a few cool beers, we had no inclination to visit whatever nightclubs there may have been and we spent our days pestering the Movements Control people to get us away. There was a transport leaving in a few days for the UK and we were allocated berths. Most of the ex-prisoners from Malaya had already left. When we boarded the troopship we found there was no alcohol aboard and it would take about six weeks to reach England. We disembarked and returned to the RAF Movements Control people, pointed out that we were members of the trade union of aircrew and demanded priority. The wing commander in charge asked us if we were so ill that we should be repatriated by air immediately and, on our confirming this, gave us the same priority as the press gang. We had to wait about a week longer and then, just as the prisoners from Java arrived by sea, we boarded a Sunderland flying boat to go to Ceylon. The Wingco was unable to arrange our priorities thereafter; we would be on our own.

When we got to Ratmalana in Ceylon the crew of the aircraft, who were of course familiar with the station routine there, vanished in their own transport and we, the only two passengers, found ourselves facing an ambulance and a sergeant who enquired for the two very ill ex-PoWs he had been told to collect. He was not at all unhappy to discover that we were they and was full of advice as to how we should set about making ourselves comfortable and arranging our onward passages. It took three days of very comfortable living, three mornings of chasing around offices and three afternoons on the beaches of Mount Lavinia and the Galle Face Hotel before we found ourselves aboard a York transport aircraft which landed four days later at Lyneham, after night-stopping at Karachi, Cairo West and Malta."[152]

* * *

Other survivors, having suffered even greater trauma, believed they were saved by the use of atomic bombs on the Japaneses cities of Hiroshima and Nagasaki. One of these was Sgt Ian Fairbairn, who had found himself transported to the Burma-Thai border:

"At the finish, a couple of hundred of us were sent up on the Thai-Burma border near the Three Pagoda Pass, digging great holes ten metres long and three metres deep. After a while a machine gun was placed at each end and we were told that on the 24th 'all men sleepo!', which was in a few days time. I guess that the enormity of it didn't sink in at the time. Then something happened and we were confined to our huts. Things were very tense and jumpy. We didn't know it, but we were saved by the bomb. It was another five days before we knew that the war was over, and why. The anti-climax was immensely traumatic."

Sgt Jim MacIntosh was another:

"Shortly after the firebombing raids, we were informed by the Japanese that the Americans had dropped a 'death-ray' bomb on Hiroshima. They called it a death-ray bomb, and they explained to us that the only protection against this bomb was to be accommodated in concrete shelters. Concrete was the only thing that would deflect its harm, but they didn't sound very hopeful if we ever got one. Well strangely enough just after – about two days after – we witnessed the dropping of the atom bomb on Nagasaki. I had been on night shift – we had to work eight-hour shifts in the factory. I think about eight in the morning, we'd been relieved – and I'd come back with the others from the night shift and we were having a bath. The air raid sirens went and we were herded out. We were allowed to sit on top of the air raid shelter, with those that were sick in the camp, and the Japanese guards, and we saw this B-29 coming extremely high, from the south-east through patches of cloud. We saw the bomber pass over Nagasaki – there was ack-ack and guns going off all round us. They couldn't have got within thousands of feet of this B-29, it was so high – it was just like a silver moth. But we saw this object coming down with a big cluster of parachutes on it. We didn't know what it was, and it came right down over Nagasaki, and was about 1,500 feet up when this blinding flash went off. It was just like looking at an electric arc welder. The intensity was like thousands of arc welders going off – we were completely blinded. By the time I could see again, though a milky sort of haze, there was a great big bone with a halo ring round it.

There was no work because the factory was out of action and shortly after that the Japanese Commandant appeared before us and declared: 'The war is over, we are now all friends.' A South African was our CO and was immediately asked to take over control of the camp. The Japs just stood aside and we formed our own guard."

For Sqn Ldr Julian – and so many others – the end of the war could not have come any sooner. Having been imprisoned in Java, Singapore, Formosa and Japan, he was then sent to Manchuria, being held at a camp at Mukden, 30 miles from Harbin. Here, germ warfare experiments were underway and Julian was due to be part of the next batch for experiment when the war ended. His comment: "None of the previous batches had emerged alive."

Sgt Gordie Dunn, still at Moji, reflected:

> "I weighed 108 pounds at the end. I had a friend at Moji named Jones, who was so thin that I called him 'Bones Jones' – the name stuck. He used to call me 'One-Gun Dunn.' We couldn't have made it through another winter. If they hadn't dropped the atom bombs – the Japs would have fought on."

He added, however:

> "The ship that evacuated us had to call in at the Philippines, where we remained for about two weeks. There, the Americans were so appalled by our physical condition that they made available mountains of food – I reckon I put on a pound per day while I was there!"

Others wanted to extract revenge on their tormentors, including Plt Off Red Campbell:

> "What kept me alive was a burning desire to live long enough to kill a Jap and skin him alive. I mean that literally. Hate will do that. But looking back, I must say they never treated us worse than they treated their own people. A Korean guard treated us worse than the Japanese ever did. Finally my hatred died, and I accepted the fact that the Japanese had to do what they did."

Plt Off Mike Fitzherbert just may have fulfilled his similar desire. On his release, he apparently requested the loan of a revolver from his RN brother-in-law (one of the evacuation party) and presumably settled a few old scores. Elsewhere, Sgt Kelly, having survived the rigours of imprisonment, managed to enjoy his early days of freedom:

> "Another visitor was Bill May, the Hurricane pilot with whom I had played bridge on the out on *Indomitable* and who had had shared the same hold with me on the *Dai Nichi Maru*. He came over by boat from Mukaishima camp to see me, bringing with him Walter B. Ross, lieutenant bombardier, one of the crew of a B-29 shot down a few days before the end of the war. Being on the mainland and their self-assurance bolstered by a group of Americans super confident of their country's might, the prisoners in Mukaishima were very much more in control and knew so much more than we did.The party stayed only for an hour on Innoshima and they took me back with them to see things from the other side.
>
> This proved to be a memorable experience. Bill suggested I might like to take some *sake* [Japanese rice whiskey] back with me. 'We can buy as much as you want at 200 yen a crate,' he told me. I pointed out I didn't have 5 yen let alone 200. 'No trouble,' he said. 'All we need are some red armbands and I'll lend you the money and you can pay it back later on.' Mystified, I accompanied him to a godown. We each put a bit of red ribbon round our arms and entered the official sake store, plonked the 200 yen Bill had lent me on the counter and ordered a crate of *sake*. It was supplied without demur. Somewhat bemused I reached out to lift the crate but Bill shook his head and signalled to a nearby Jap to carry it outside, which he did. We were immediately besieged by other Japanese begging to buy bottles from us. Bill said: 'Black market price is 200 yen a bottle,' and, taking one out of the crate, he sold it and pocketed the money. 'If you want you can sell the lot and go in and buy more and be a yen millionaire in no time!'"

On 30 August 1945, it was revealed that General Itagaki, Japanese Commander at Singapore, had notified Field-Marshal Terauchi of his intention to fight on, that "the Japanese armies remained undefeated in battle." Terauchi's reply to Itagaki was to the effect that further resistance would disgrace the honour of the Japanese Army, a continued defence of Singapore would erase all hope of retaining any Japanese Army – whereas acceptance of unconditional surrender might permit the retention of a nucleus force. Itagaki thought again, and acted wisely. It was actually he who made the final surrender to Admiral Mountbatten at Singapore, Count Terauchi being too ill to attend.

CHAPTER FOOTNOTES

PREAMBLE

1 See *The Grand Alliance*, Volume III of Sir Winston Churchill's *The Second World War*.
2 Germany and the Soviet Union had signed a Non-Aggression Pact in 1940.
3 See *The Grand Alliance*.
4 Flt Lt Ricky Wright won his DFM during the Battle of Britain, when he was credited with at least nine victories including three shared and three probables.
5 See *Caged Eagles* by Vern Haugland.
6 According to his brother John, Graham gained his unusual nickname when, as a baby, an elderly aunt used to tweak his cheeks whilst twittering 'ting, ting, ting!' The names stuck and he was known as 'Ting' throughout his life.
7 Plt Off Don Geffene later escaped from Spanish internment and rejoined 258 Squadron at Ceylon, where he was killed in action in April 1942.
8 258 Squadron's four American pilots were Flg Off Art Donahue, Plt Off John Campbell (known as 'Red' due to the colour of his hair), Plt Off Don Geffene and Plt Off Cardell Kleckner; a fifth, Plt Off Leon Cicurel, had been left behind when the Squadron departed but would travel out to the Far East with 266 (Fighter) Wing. When the Japanese attacked Pearl Harbor, many American pilots then serving with the two Eagle Squadrons in the UK wanted to immediately join the US Air Corps. When this was turned down, 71 (Eagle) Squadron pilots volunteered en masse to go to Singapore to fight the Japanese, an offer also declined by RAF Fighter Command.
9 Shortly before 232 Squadron left England, its European pilots were posted away since they were not allowed, at that stage, to operate outside of the UK. Volunteers to fill their ranks were called for from the neighbouring unit at Ouston, 43 Squadron; those who joined 232 Squadron were Canadian Plt Offs Tom Watson and John McKecknie, New Zealanders Plt Off Ernie Gartrell, Sgts Bill Moodie and Ian Newlands, and Sgt David Kynman from Hull.
10 Spare pilots included Sgts W.F. Burke, P. Tanner, W. Brown and W.H. Swann, all of 232 Squadron, together with, it is believed, Sgts D.N. Caldwell RAAF and D. Gallagher of 258 Squadron.
11 See *Sea Flight* by Hugh Popham.
12 See *A Gremlin on my Shoulder* by Ron Cundy.
13 See forthcoming title in this series, *Fighters over Burma*, for an account of 267 (Fighter) Wing in Burma.
14 Leslie Landels had flown briefly with 3 Squadron before joining 615 Squadron towards the end of the Battle of Britain. He had claimed a Bf109 shot down but had been shot down and wounded by another.
15 Flt Lt Mike Cooper-Slipper was by far the most combat-experienced of the group, having been credited with six victories during the Battle of Britain.
16 When the *Aoranji*, which was also carrying the 6th Anti-Aircraft Regiment, arrived at Durban, one of the gunner officers skipped ship and disappeared with operating and service manuals relating to the new Mark II radar sets with which the Regiment had been issued.

CHAPTER I

17 Although the RAF pilots frequently referred to all Japanese non-fixed undercarriage fighters as the Navy 0 or Zero when invariably their opponents were Ki-43s, their nomenclature is retained; where known the correct reference is made in the narrative.
18 Air Vice-Marshal Pulford, who had taken up his position as Commander of the RAF in the Far East and AOC Singapore in April 1941, had, in 1926, led the first formation flight from Cairo to Cape Town, and from there back to England, the first great transcontinental flight by the RAF. During WWI, he operated from HMS *Ark Royal* during the tragic Gallipoli campaign before taking command of 1 Squadron. At the outbreak of WWII he commanded 20 Group in the UK until his posting to Singapore.
19 Report by Air Vice-Marshal Sir Paul Maltby on RAF Operations in Malaya and NEI 1941-42, published as a Supplement to the *London Gazette*, 26 February 1948.
20 See *Suez to Singapore* by Cecil Brown.

21 Not all 51 Hurricanes were assembled: two were found to be damaged when their crates were opened and were presumably used for spares although the airframes may have been two of six that were later loaded, still in their crates, aboard the freighter SS *Derrymore* shortly before the fall of Singapore and were lost when the ship was torpedoed and sunk on 13 February 1942 (see Appendix III).
22 See *Suez to Singapore*.

CHAPTER II

23 See *Suez to Singapore*.
24 *Ibid.*
25 See *Life and Death in Changi* by Brian Kitching.
26 Ron Dovell, born in Kensal Rise in 1920, had attended Kilburn Grammar School, where he was swimming captain, and was also a member of 8th Willesden Scouts and Willesden Swimming and Cycling Clubs; and the Kensal Rise Aero Club. Before joining the RAF in August 1940, he worked as a clerk for American Express in London. He gained his wings in July 1941, following which he was posted to 17 Squadron.
27 Plt Off Norman Williams was later evacuated to India via Batavia.
28 It is interesting to note that surviving Japanese records report missing personnel only, not missing aircraft from which the crew survived. Therefore, it must be assumed that Japanese losses of aircraft were invariably greater than those admitted.
29 Sqn Ldr Brooker, known to his friends as 'Boy', had flown with 56 Squadron during the Battle of Britain before taking command of 1 Squadron. He was credited with at least six victories including two probables, to which he would add three more in action against the Japanese.
30 Air Vice-Marshal Sir Paul Maltby later reflected on the day's operations and losses: "The first sortie was a disastrous one, despite the very great gallantry of all those who took part. It was a ghastly mistake to have sent that squadron into action before it had been given some sort of training as a unit – but I suppose that poor Pulford [the AOC] and Rice [OC 224 Fighter Wing] felt that the time could not be spared for the purpose. Yet I can't help feeling – hindsight is very easy – that very much more would have been achieved, despite the urgency of getting these machines into action, if some small amount of available time had been given to training them as a unit. It is a point which I shall never be able to put out of my mind." Letter to 232 Squadron's Adjutant, Flt Lt Norman Welch.
31 See *Epics of the Fighting RAF* by Leonard Gribble.
32 See *Suez to Singapore*.
33 See *Singapore Slip* by Herb Plenty.
34 See *Angry Skies* by Mike Hayes.
35 See *Life and Death in Changi*.
36 These were BE584, BE585, BE632, BE640, BG723, BG800, BG809, BG845, and BM900; at least three replacements including BG718, BG722 and BM899 were received following the 27 January raid in which four of 488 Squadron's Hurricanes were destroyed.
37 Sqn Ldr Mackenzie, grandson of a former Prime Minister of New Zealand, had flown Spitfires during the Battle of Britain and had been credited with six victories.
38 See *Life and Death in Changi*.
39 *Ibid.*
40 See *Epics of the Fighting RAF*.
41 *Ibid.*
42 Sgt Keith Minton RNZAF.
43 See *Epics of the Fighting RAF*.
44 *Ibid.*
45 See *Life and Death in Changi*.

CHAPTER III

46 See *Sea Flight*.
47 *Ibid.*
48 Plt Off Terry Marra RNZAF of 243 Squadron.
49 See *Hawker Hurricane* by Robert Jackson.

50 One of the damaged Hurricanes was BD892, which, after being repaired, was flown to Palembang on 14 February, where it crash-landed following combat.
51 See *Caged Eagles*.
52 Plt Off Bruce McAlister had been credited with a Bf109 destroyed in June 1941.
53 This list of credits was copied by the author from a note compiled by Sqn Ldr Brooker and inserted in his logbook. On his eventual return to the UK these details were supplied to the Air Ministry and were used in the reconstruction of events. The handwritten scrap of paper has been preserved by the family.
54 See *Bloody Shambles Volume One* for more detail.
55 Sgt Peter Balland RNZAF of 4AACU.
56 BE208/O was apparently repaired by the Japanese and flown and evaluated for a short time by Japanese pilots, before being turned over to the Tachikawa Giken branch at Singapore. It is not known if this was the Hurricane crashed by a Japanese pilot on 10 March at Palembang.
57 See *Malayan Postscript* by Ian Morrison.
58 Sgt Bill Moodie's older brother John (aged 24) had died two months earlier (7 December 1941) while serving in the UK as a Pilot Officer with 3 Delivery Flight; his aircraft crashed near Birkenhead. The brothers hailed from Howick near Auckland, New Zealand.
59 Despite the praise heaped upon Sgt Ivan Yanovich, his services went unrecognised.
60 The Tiger Moths, each armed with two 20lb bombs and flown by Flt Lt Henry Dane and Sgt R.V.E. Nathan, returned safely. Dane died as a PoW on 1 December 1942, having been recommended for a DSO, which was granted posthumously in 1946.
61 During one particular attack on the *Empire Star*, evacuated Staff Nurses Anderson and Torney were caught on deck tending the wounded. Despite the obvious danger, they continued nursing and protected their patients with their own bodies when Japanese aircraft dived to strafe the vessel. Margaret Anderson received the George Medal and Veronica Torney the MBE in recognition of their bravery.
62 See *Angry Skies*. John Gorton later flew with 77 RAAF Squadron in Australia, where he suffered a second bad crash. Following a distinguished postwar career in politics he became Australia's nineteenth Prime Minister in 1968.
63 In his subsequent report on the campaign, Air Vice-Marshal Sir Paul Maltby wrote: "Air Vice-Marshal Pulford, despite ill health, worked unceasingly and uncomplainingly to overcome the many difficulties with which he was faced when preparing his Command for war and after hostilities had broken out. He never flinched from meeting an overwhelming situation with very inadequate means. No man could have striven more wholeheartedly to carry a burden, which was far beyond one man's capacity. All his decisions were reached with complete disregard for self and entirely in the interests of what he felt to be his duty according to the situation and to his instructions. He refused to leave Singapore until all [sic] his men had been evacuated. His selfless devotion to duty and his loyalty to all those around him, both senior and junior, were an inspiration to all."
64 See *Escape from the Rising Sun* by Ian Skidmore.

CHAPTER IV

65 Wg Cdr Horace Darley, known as George to his friends, had commanded 609 Squadron during the Battle of Britain and had been credited with five victories when awarded the DSO for his leadership.
66 See *History of 226 (Fighter) Group*, a potted history compiled by Air Vice-Marshal Vincent.
67 Since no official list of the pilots assigned to 266 (Fighter) Wing has come to light, this listing has been compiled from various sources and may contain inaccuracies.
68 Sgt Ken Glynn hailed from a village near Fakenham in Norfolk, the son of Lt Cdr A.E. Glynn RN; his younger brother Glyn was killed on Active Service in 1946; he was also 20 when he died and was a Sub Lt in the RNVR.
69 Flt Sgts Andy Chandler and John Rees were each awarded a BEM for their performances.
70 Flg Off John McKechnie, who had narrowly avoided losing his life at Singapore, was killed when the Blenheim – V6465 flown by Sgt B.W. Turner – in which he was flying as a passenger, crashed in India on 4 July 1942.
71 Wg Cdr John Jeudwine DSO DFC.

72 Sgt Ken Lister, 84 Squadron.
73 It is believed that Sgt Fred Bidewell, who hailed from Cleethorpes, was transported to Batavia from where he was evacuated. By 1944, then a Warrant Officer, he was serving with 1685 Bomber (Defence) Training Flight flying Tomahawks on fighter affiliation duties.
74 In the course of the crash-landing Ting Macnamara injured his back, resulting in the protrusion of an intervertebral disc. He was evacuated with the surplus pilots from Tjilatjap on the night of 26/27 February, and reached Ceylon, from where he was transferred to India on 21 April before being invalided to South Africa on 11 July 1942. He wrote in his logbook, "Doctors have told me my flying days are over. It is hard to take. This will be my final entry in my logbook and with a heavy heart and a prayer for those who died and the ones taken prisoner, I write the last word – *Finis*." Eventually spondylitis was diagnosed; Ting would later undergo surgery but was left severely disabled, and his premature death in his native Rhodesia followed more than three years of hospitalization.
75 McCulloch continued: "The next morning more paratroops were dropped and we evacuated at 1100 hrs; the wounded spent three days on the roads before arriving in Batavia. Our medical officers were marvellous, sleeping very little during those three days and doing everything possible for us. I spent four days in the Princess Juliana Hospital at Batavia and from there shipped home to Australia via Colombo."
76 Sqn Ldr Mackenzie was due to lead a further six Hurricanes from Tjililitan to P1 the following day: "To me the most amazing aspect was that they all made it back. When I got the horrible news I just had to sit down and wait for a couple of days. Hutch, Noel Sharp and Jack Meharry all arrived back on the 17th, after making their way by road and rail. It was a marvellous job. It was bloody near VC stuff."
77 See *Flying Fever* by Air Vice-Marshal Stanley Vincent.
78 One source suggests that New Zealander Sgt Harry Jenson, known to his friends as 'Horry', claimed a Japanese aircraft shot down while at Palembang or in Java. This has not been substantiated.
79 The names of Jenson and Lawrence do not appear in the list of Japanese PoWs (see *Unsung Heroes of the RAF*, which also includes RAAF and RNZAF personnel) although Lawrence's name does appear in a list of missing Air Force PoWs dated March 1945, but not in the CWGC records as deceased.
80 Flg Off Matthys Taute, a South African in the RAF, was later awarded the Military Cross for his efforts at Palembang.
81 A few days after Flt Lt Sharp's force-landing at Singkep, a party of escapees departed from the island in a motor sampan and a small launch and set out for Djambi in Sumtara, some 70 miles distant, the navigating officer using the compass removed from Sharp's aircraft, BG830.
82 See *The Tattered Eagle* by Geoffrey Rex Collis.
83 *Ibid.*
84 Unbeknown to their colleagues, Sgts Nelson Scott and Lorne Miller plus survivors of their group had been cut off in the fighting, so they had headed for the railway station, eventually reaching Oosthaven by train. Although the ship they boarded called in at a Javanese port, the captain refused to allow Scott and Miller ashore to rejoin their squadron, and they were taken to Ceylon.
85 Ting Macnamara was apparently recommended for the award of the Military Cross for his performance over these two days, though the award was either not approved at higher level, or the recommendation was lost in the chaos of the campaign.

CHAPTER V

86 Grp Capt Gilbert Nicholetts was a pioneer of flying boats and in 1933 had set a world air record, in company with Sqn Ldr O.R. Gayford, when he flew a Fairey monoplane non-stop from Cranwell to Walvis Bay, South West Africa in 57 hours 25 minutes. Following the outbreak of WWII, he commanded a flying boat squadron in the Middle East before being posted to Singapore. He was taken prisoner and received a mention in despatches on his release.
87 See *Flying Fever*.
88 *Ibid.*
89 Surprisingly, Sgt Sandeman Allen was overlooked for a commission at this time, somewhat

strange since he had originally been accepted for a Short Service Commission in August 1939; however, somewhere along the line his papers had been mislaid and he was actually called up for service when the war broke out, joining the RAF as an Aircraftman and being employed as a driver before he was selected for pilot training. His commission was eventually approved in 1943, following his return to the UK (also see note 122).

90 See *Caged Eagles*.

91 See *Buffaloes over Singapore*.

92 The old US aircraft carrier USS *Langley*, carrying 32 fully assembled P-40s lashed to her deck, was originally destined for Burma, but was now diverted to Java, to accompany the British freighter *Sea Witch* with a further 27 P-40s in crates; three other cargo vessels between them carrying ten crated P-40s were also headed for Tjilatjap. Some of these aircraft were to re-equip the US 17th Pursuit Squadron, and others were earmarked for use by the RAF but, on 27 February, the carrier was attacked and sunk by JNAF G4Ms. Meanwhile, *Sea Witch* and the other freighters safely reached Tjilatjap, where the 37 crated P-40s and six crated DB-7Bs for the Dutch Naval Air Arm were unloaded, although it was now deemed too late to assemble and use the fighters. The P-40s were allegedly unloaded onto lighters and sunk in the harbour to deny them to the Japanese. However, the Japanese recovered so many P-40s that it would seem that not all the aircraft were thus destroyed. In fact, at least ten P-40s were flown operationally by the 12th and 50th Sentais in Burma during 1943.

93 Max Boyd later commented (in 1990): "This is absolutely verbatim from my diary and shows the depth of feeling felt towards the Far Eastern Command. How I ever came to write in such terms amazes me now, and I find it hard after almost 50 years to realise that I expressed my feelings so strongly."

94 See *Flying Fever*.

95 It is believed the Hurricanes were in the serial range Z56?? and included Z5644.

96 1/Lt Jan Bruinier had flown Spitfires with the RAF's 92 Squadron in the UK in early 1941 and had been awarded the Dutch Flying Cross for his performance.

97 See Robert Jackson's *Hawker Hurricane*.

98 *Ibid*.

99 See *Their Last Tenko* by James Home.

100 On the afternoon of 27 February, the three serviceable A-24s took off to attack Japanese transports reported in the Java Sea, rendezvousing with ten P-40s of the 17th Pursuit Squadron from Malang. The pilots witnessed the opening shots of the disastrous Battle of the Java Sea before returning to Malang.

101 Jim MacIntosh had this incident recorded under 21 February, but it is believed it occurred on 24 February.

102 See *Hawker Hurricane*.

103 On the cowling panel and beneath the cockpit of Z5616 Sgt MacIntosh had painted the names *Miss Carronvale* and *Sgt Mac, Carronvale* being the name of his father's farm back in New Zealand.

104 Two of the 488 Squadron pilots initially posted to 605 Squadron, Plt Off Wally Greenhalgh and Sgt Jack Meharry were, however, instructed to evacuate, which they did; Meharry was later posted to the UK where he was killed in action on 5 August 1944. Flt Lt John Hutcheson also left at this time, soon to be awarded a DFC for his performance. At the same time, the award of a DFM for Sgt Eddie Kuhn was announced, though he was destined to become a prisoner.

105 These included Sqn Ldr Thomson (who was promoted to Wg Cdr and given charge of Racecourse Airfield), Flt Lt Denny Sharp, Flg Off Art Donahue (wounded), Plt Offs Ting Macnamara (injured), Micky Nash (wounded), Plt Off Art Brown, Doug Nicholls, Cam Campbell-White, Ambrose Milnes, Ted Tremlett, Jock McCulloch, Sgts Nelson Scott and Dusty Miller – most of whom found themselves in action against the first Japanese air attack against Ceylon on 9 April 1942; during this action 258 Squadron lost seven Hurricanes with five pilots killed including Plt Off Teddy Tremlett. Amongst the claimants were Sharp (one destroyed and one damaged), Campbell-White (one destroyed), Brown (one damaged) and Nicholls (one damaged).

Of the survivors from Java, then Acting Sqn Ldr Art Donahue (awarded a DFC and recovered from his wounds) was apparently shot down by return fire from a Ju88 he claimed destroyed over the English Channel in September 1942; Flt Lt Art Brown failed to return from an operational sortie on 5 December 1943, while two weeks later, on 19 December, Flt Lt Micky Nash was sadly killed in a bizarre accident during a mock dogfight when his colleague erroneously fired his machine guns instead of his ciné gun-camera. A fourth veteran of the dwindling band, Flt Lt Nelson Scott, failed to return from an operational sortie on 11 January 1944; both Sqn Ldrs Denny Sharp and Doug Nicholls successfully flew further tours and were each awarded a DFC.

106 Sgt Henry Nicholls was posted to India, where he joined 155 Squadron flying Mohawks, before returning to the UK. He was commissioned and joined 137 Squadron flying Typhoons but in September 1944 was shot down by flak, badly burned and ended up in Stalag Luft III.

107 Other 266 (Fighter) Wing pilots who were evacuated may have included Sgts Jenson, Lawrence, Dickson, Ambrose, Gratton and Boyd.

108 See *Hawker Hurricane*.

109 See *Caged Eagles*.

110 See *Flying Fever*.

111 See *Battle of the Java Sea* by David Thomas; and *The Ghost That Died at Sunda Straits* by W.G. Winslow.

112 Following the raid, Vincent and his staff made their way to Tjilatjap where they went aboard a Dutch merchantman, which initially set sail for Colombo, but in the event diverted to Fremantle instead.

113 2/Lt Neil Dummett was back in South Africa by 23 March 1942. He did not return to operations. His RAF secondment ceased in April 1943 and he became a flying instructor at 23 Air School (South Africa) in September of that year, but was sadly killed in a flying accident on 26 February 1944.

114 From Colombo Flt Lt Cooper-Slipper was sent to Bombay, and then to the British General Hospital at Poona, spending about six months there before he was fully recovered. He died in 2004, following a postwar career as a test pilot with Avro Canada in the 1950s.

115 By late evening *Perth* and *Houston* had sailed, heading for the Sunda Straits and Ceylon. For superstitious sailors aboard Perth the fact that the ship's cat named Red Lead had repeatedly tried to leave the ship before it sailed from Tandjong Priok was a bad omen. Both cruisers were sunk that night in battle with a Japanese naval force, *Perth* going down with the loss of 353 lives (Red Lead also perished), the *Houston* with the loss of 655. Of the 782 survivors from the two vessels lucky enough to reach shore, more than a quarter would die as prisoners of war.

CHAPTER VI

116 Plt Off Noel Sharp was not seen again and was presumed to have been killed by Japanese troops. He had been recommended for a DFC before his death and this award was promulgated shortly thereafter.

117 34-year-old Grp Capt George Whistondale was clearly suffering from severe stress and was last seen returning to his quarters to collect his prized stamp collection.

118 Sgt John Vibert added: "After we were taken prisoner, on the way back through Bandoeng, we saw the P-40s again. They were still in the railway sidings in their crates – not even destroyed."

119 See *The Remorseless Road* by James McEwan.

120 See *Their Last Tenko*.

121 *Ibid*.

122 Sqn Ldr Brooker, together with Plt Off Watson and Sgts Sandy Allen, Jimmy King and Geoff Hardie, following a suitable rest, were seconded to the RAAF. Following a brief spell with the newly formed 77 RAAF Squadron, Brooker helped form 76 RAAF Squadron before flying to New Zealand where he assisted with the formation on 14 RNZAF Squadron, all three squadrons equipped with the US-supplied P-40 Kittyhawk. Meanwhile, Plt Off Watson and Sgts Allen, King and Hardie were also seconded to 77 RAAF Squadron, with which they remained for several months (see forthcoming *Fighters over Darwin* by Brian Cull and Dennis Newton, to be published by Grub Street). In March 1942, Brooker was advised of the award of a Bar to his DFC, while both Sgt Ron Dovell (by then a PoW) and Sgt Sandy Allen were awarded the DFM. On 16 April 1945, Wg Cdr Brooker DSO DFC was killed in action as leader of 122 Tempest Wing; Sgt (Wt Off) Sandy Allen DFM also returned to operations and was severely wounded while flying

a Typhoon, on 30 June 1943, and was eventually medically discharged following plastic surgery. Sgt (Sqn Ldr) Jimmy King was commissioned, flew a tour on Typhoons and was awarded a belated DFC. He was killed in a flying accident postwar. Plt Off (Sqn Ldr) Tom Watson was also awarded a DFC later in the war, having retrained on multi-engined aircraft. He flew a tour on Liberators in the Far East. The remaining member of the fivesome, Sgt (Flg Off) Geoff Hardie was also commissioned and became an instructor in the UK, where he was killed in a flying accident on 10 April 1944.

In his subsequent report on the campaign, Air Vice-Marshal Sir Paul Maltby wrote: "232 (F) Squadron, under the leadership of Squadron Leader Brooker, who volunteered to take command at a critical moment, was in constant action from the time it arrived in Singapore in mid-January until fighting ceased in Java. It inflicted severe casualties on the enemy in the air, on landing craft and on the ground. It volunteered [sic] to remain in Java as the last fighter squadron. Great credit is due to all ranks of a magnificent squadron, drawn as they were from the ranks of several different fighter units."

123 See *Caged Eagles*.

CHAPTER VII

124 Grp Capt Edward Rice, AOC 224 (Fighter) Group Singapore, died while a PoW at Shirakawa, Taiwan on 5 September 1943. He was awarded a posthumous mention in despatches. In his official report on the ill-fated campaign, Air Vice-Marshal Sir Paul Maltby wrote: "Group Captain Rice, Fighter Defence Commander of Singapore, and Wing Commander Chignell [also awarded a posthumous mention], his CASO, were outstanding in their selfless devotion to duty. They were primarily responsible for the good morale which the small fighter force at Kallang maintained throughout the campaign in the face of a numerous and better armed enemy."

125 While they may have been considered the lucky ones to escape from Java, sadly, none of the Commonwealth quartet survived the war: Plt Off Dizzy Mendizabal later joined 5 Squadron in India and was killed in a flying accident on 10 August 1943. The New Zealander Sgt Doug Jones returned to New Zealand, was commissioned and flew a tour on RNZAF P-40s; he was killed in action on 9 January 1944. Of the two Australians, Sgt Alan Martin lost his life in a flying accident in Australia on 21 May 1942, while newly commissioned Plt Off Stuart Munro was killed flying a Kittyhawk at Port Moresby on 27 August 1942.

126 See *Caged Eagles*.

127 Wg Cdr Steedman, a former pilot, twice received a mention in despatches.

128 Jim MacIntosh managed to keep his logbook and other documents including photographs hidden for the whole of his time as a prisoner.

129 One Ismail Il Bin Rabiin, in a testimony to an Australian investigation team at the end of the war (see *Hell on Earth* by Dave McIntosh). The main suspects in the execution were Lt Takeo Kambiyashi, Sgt Kunio Nogami (in charge of the killing detail) and Einichi Sonia, Kantaro Tanaka and Hisao Yamamoto. They were all later identified, charged and bought to trial but their fate is unknown. There occurred a tragic sequel to this incident when, in 1946, an Australian War Crimes investigation team, having located the burial site and removed the remains to the British military cemetery at Menteng, Batavia, was ambushed and killed by Indonesian insurgents.

130 All three were awarded a posthumous mention in despatches.

131 Wg Cdr Noble received the OBE for his services as a PoW.

132 See *Their Last Tenko*. The other three executed with Sgt Poland were Flt Lt R. Gordon, 152 MU, Flg Off A.G.F. Cheesewright, AHQ, and Wt Off C.A. Kennison, a civilian with the AMWD.

133 See *The Emperor's Guest* by Don Peacock.

134 Wg Cdr O.G. Gregson, former OC Transit Camp, Singapore, was awarded an OBE for his services as a PoW.

135 In addition to the 16,000 Allied prisoners who died working on the Burma-Siam railway, an estimated 100,000 Chinese, Tamil, Malay, Burmese, Javanese and Dutch-Indonesian impressed labourers also died there.

136 See *You'll Die in Singapore* by Charles McCormac.

137 Of life at Kutching, Sgt Fleming wrote later: "I was informed, by other prisoners in the camp, of one execution and many cruelties but I was not an eyewitness to any of them. I was an

eyewitness of many beatings, which were regular and collective punishments of a group for offences of others, but I do not know the names of those responsible. The food was very poor for the first six months and became progressively worse as time went on. I received one Red Cross parcel which had to be divided among six other prisoners of war and this was the only occasion during the two years that I received any such parcels and other PoWs received the same. Red Cross officials from neutral countries or Japan did not visit the camp at any time during my imprisonment. The majority of the prisoners of war were forced to work on the aerodrome building new landing strips and dock facilities at Kutching and also laying keels for new ships. They were forced to work from 7 o'clock in the morning until 7 or 8 o'clock in the evening. Three British officers were strong characters and as the Japs left the running of the camp pretty much in their hands, it was well run, conditions being comparatively good, although medical supplies were inadequate."

138 Sgt Fred Margarson was later sent to work on the Burma-Thailand Railway. He was one of the survivors.

139 As told to the author.

140 Sgts Horton and Dunn provided testimonies that helped convict Yoshyuki Ikeda, Tadoshi Takano and Yosika Yagi of crimes and each was sentenced to 15 years imprisonment, while Camp Commandant Lt Yuhichi Sakamoto received a life sentence, later commuted to 10 years.

141 See *The Emperor's Guest* by John Fletcher-Cooke.

142 See *Their Last Tenko.*

143 Irish-born Wg Cdr Maguire, who had joined the RAF in 1933, had served on flying boats in Egypt and the Far East prewar before returning to the UK to retrain as a fighter pilot and instructor. He commanded 229 Squadron at the time of the Dunkirk evacuation in 1940 and during the Battle of Britain. He was OC Training Wing at 56 OTU before taking command of 266 (Fighter) Wing. He retired from the RAF in 1968 as Air Marshal, having been knighted in 1966, and sadly died in 2003 (see also note 152).

144 See *Their Last Tenko.*

145 *Ibid.*

146 Wg Cdr G.B.M. Bell, first CO of 243 Buffalo Squadron, was awarded an OBE for his services as a PoW.

147 See *The Emperor's Guest* (Fletcher-Cooke).

148 See *Caged Eagles.*

149 See *Their Last Tenko.*

150 Wg Cdr G.F. Alexander was awarded the OBE for his services as a PoW.

151 25 sen equals about 12p in today's currency.

152 A few months after his return to the UK, Flt Lt Jerry Parker was advised that he had been awarded a DFC. At the same time, Wg Cdr Harold Maguire was awarded the DSO, and DFCs were announced for Sqn Ldr Taffy Julian, Sqn Ldr Ricky Wright DFM, Flt Lt Joe Hutton, and Plt Offs Mike Fitzherbert, Red Campbell, and Ernie Gartrell. Having survived the rigours of imprisonment, Fitzherbert tragically fell to his death in 1951 while helping a friend repair a roof. Ricky Wright remained in the RAF postwar and retired as an Air Commodore in 1973; Ernie Gartrell remained in the RNZAF and retired as an Air Vice-Marshal, while Joe Hutton retired as a Wing Commander.

APPENDIX I

ROLL OF HONOUR

Hurricane pilots who lost their lives
Singapore, Sumatra and Java, or as prisoners of war

Singapore

20/1/42	Sqn Ldr Leslie N. LANDELS	232 (P) Sqn	KiA	BM906
	Plt Off Alphonso C. MARCHBANKS (US)	232 (P) Sqn	KiA	BG848
21/1/42	Sgt Peter D. LOWE	232 (P) Sqn	KiA	BE577
22/1/42	Flt Lt Hugh A. FARTHING	232 (P) Sqn	KiA	BG796
	Plt Off Brian P. DANIEL	232 (P) Sqn	KiA	BG804
	Sgt Joseph H. LEETHAM RCAF	232 (P) Sqn	KiA	BE579
25/1/42	Sgt Carl F. MARSH RCAF	232 (P) Sqn	KoAS	BE641
	Sgt Alan V. COUTIE RAAF	232 (P) Sqn	KoAS	BE589
27/1/42	Sgt Charles D.G. CHRISTIAN	232 (P) Sqn	KiA	BE590
31/1/42	Plt Off Bruce A. McALISTER RNZAF	258 Sqn	KiA	
7/2/42	Sqn Ldr Arthur J.A. LLEWELLIN	232 Sqn	KiFA	Z5482
9/2/42	Sgt William A. MOODIE RNZAF	232 Sqn	KiA	BG797

Palembang

6/2/42	Plt Off Cardell KLECKNER RCAF (US)	258 Sqn	KiA	
	Plt Off Keith DAWSON-SCOTT	258 Sqn	KoAS (ground)	
7/2/42	Sgt Roy B. KEEDWELL RCAF	258 Sqn	DoW	
	Sgt Kenneth A. GLYNN	258 Sqn	KiA	
8/2/42	Flt Lt Edwin MURRAY TAYLOR	232 Sqn	KiA	BE115
	Sgt Samuel N. HACKFORTH	232 Sqn	KiA	BE219
13/2/42	Plt Off Leslie A. EMMERTON (Rhod)	232 Sqn	KiA	BG693

Java

25/2/42	Flt Lt Henry A. DOBBYN RNZAF	605 Sqn	KiA
1/3/42	Plt Off Noel C. SHARP RNZAF	605 Sqn	KiA

(believed killed by Japanese troops following crash-landing)

4/3/42	2/Lt Neil ANDERSON SAAF	242 Sqn	KiA

Prisoners of war

15/4/42	Sgt Howard P. LOW RCAF	266 Wing	KoAS (executed)
	Sgt Russell C. SMITH RCAF	266 Wing	KoAS (executed)
4/5/42	Sgt Dennis A. POLAND	266 Wing	KoAS (executed)
21/7/42	Sgt William H. JAMES RCAF	266 Wing	DoAS (infection)
18/6/43	Sgt Donald J.P. ISDALE	242 Sqn	DoAS
29/11/43	Flt Lt Grahame P. WHITE RNZAF	605 Sqn	KoAS

(sinking of *Suez Maru*)

19/7/44	Sgt Albert D. JACK	266 Wing	DoAS

APPENDIX II

KNOWN CLAIMS & CREDITS

20 January – 6 March 1942

Singapore – 232 (Provisional) Squadron

20/1/42		Plt Off B.J. Parker	Ki-43
		Sgt H.T. Nicholls	Ki-43
		Sgt R.L. Dovell	Ki-43
		Flt Lt E. Murray Taylor	2 Ki-21
	BG720	Sgt S.N. Hackforth	2 K-21, Ki-21 probable
	BG810	Sgt G. Hardie	2 Ki-21, Ki-21 probable
	BE579	Sgt J.H. Leetham RCAF	2 Ki-21, K-21 probable
21/1/42	BG796	Flt Lt H.A. Farthing	2 G3M, G3M probable
	BG804	Plt Off B.P. Daniel	G3M
22/1/42		Flt Lt T.P.M. Cooper-Slipper	2 G3M
		Flt Lt E. Murray Taylor	G3M
	BG720	Sgt S.N. Hackforth	2 G3M
	BG810	Sgt G. Hardie	G3M, G3M probable
	BM903	Plt Off R. Mendizabal RCAF	G3M probable
		Plt Off B.J. Parker	G3M probable
	BG796	Flt Lt H.A. Farthing	A6M
		Sgt H.T. Nicholls	A6M
23/1/42	BG846	Sgt G.W. Schaffer RAAF	Ki-43
		Sgt C.F. Marsh RCAF	Ki-21
	BM898	Plt Off W.N. McCulloch RAAF	Ki-43
	BE639	Sgt I.S. Fairbairn RAAF	Ki-43 probable
26/1/42		Sqn Ldr R.E.P. Brooker	Ki-27
		Plt Off B.J. Parker	Ki-43, Ki-27
		Flt Lt E. Murray Taylor	Ki-27
		Sgt H.T. Nicholls	2 Ki-27 (two sorties)
		Sgt R.L. Dovell	4 Ki-27 (two sorties)
		Plt Off R. Mendizabal RCAF	Ki-27 probable
	BG828	Sgt J.P. Fleming RCAF	Ki-27 probable
29/1/42	BG808	Plt Off R. Mendizabal RCAF	G3M, G3M probable
30/1/42		Flt Lt E. Murray Taylor	Ki-27, Ki-21 probable
		Plt Off W.N. McCulloch RAAF	Ki-21 probable
		Sgt H.T. Nicholls	Ki-27 probable
31/1/42		Sgt R.L. Dovell	Ki-43
		Plt Off J.A. Campbell (US)	Ki-43 258 Sqn Singapore
		Flt Lt D.J.T. Sharp (NZ)	Ki-21 258 Sqn Singapore
5/2/42		Plt Off E.C. Gartrell RNZAF	Ki-21 232 Sqn Singapore
		Sgt G.J. King	Ki-21 232 Sqn Singapore
		Flt Lt I. Julian RNZAF	Ki-43 probable 232 Sqn Singapore
6/2/42		Plt Off M.C. Fitzherbert	Ki-27 232 Sqn Singapore
		Plt Off R.T. Bainbridge	Ki-43 232 Sqn Palembang
7/2/42		Plt Off J.C. Hutton	Ki-27 232 Sqn Singapore
		Plt Off J.A. Campbell (US)	Ki-43 258 Sqn Palembang
		Plt Off A.H. Milnes	Ki-43 258 Sqn Palembang
8/2/42	BE195	2/Lt J. Stewart SAAF	Ki-21 232 Sqn Singapore
	Z5667	Sgt J.A. Sandeman Allen	Ki-21 probable 232 Sqn Singapore

	BE115	Flt Lt E. Murray Taylor	Ki-43 probable 232 Sqn Palembang
	BE219	Sgt S.N. Hackforth	Ki-43 probable 232 Sqn Palembang
9/2/42		Plt Off E.C. Gartrell RNZAF	G3M, G3M probable 232 Sqn Singapore
		Flt Lt I. Julian RNZAF	G3M, G3M probable, Ki-30 probable (2 sorties)
	Z5667	Sgt J.A. Sandeman Allen	2 Ki-30, 2 A6M probable (2 sorties)
		Sgt T.W. Young RAAF	Ki-21 probable 232 Sqn Singapore
		Sgt P.M.T. Healey	G3M 258 Sqn Singapore

Palembang

13/2/42		Wg Cdr H.J. Maguire }	Ki-43 266 Wing
		Sgt H.T. Nicholls }	232 Sqn
		Sgt H.T. Nicholls	Ki-43 probable 232 Sqn
		Sqn Ldr R.E.P. Brooker	Ki-21 232 Sqn
	Z5667	Sgt J.A. Sandeman Allen	2 Ki-43, Ki-21 probable 232 Sqn
		Plt Off E.C. Gartrell RNZAF	Ki-43 probable 232 Sqn
		Flt Lt T.P.M. Cooper-Slipper	2 Ki-21 probable 232 Sqn
14/2/42		Plt Off W.McG. Lockwood RCAF	Ki-21 probable 232 Sqn
	BD892	Flt Lt J.R. Hutcheson RNZAF	Ki-56 probable att'd 266 Wing
		Sgt C.T.R. Kelly	Ki-43 258 Sqn
15/2/42	BE130	Plt Off T.W. Watson RCAF	Ki-27 232 Sqn
		Plt Off R.T. Bainbridge	Ki-27 232 Sqn
		Flt Lt I. Julian RNZAF	F1M (moored) 232 Sqn

Java

20/2/42		Flt Lt I. Julian RNZAF	Ki-27 242 Sqn
	BE230	Plt Off T.W. Watson RCAF }	Ki-27 242 Sqn
		Sgt G.J. King }	
		Sgt T.W. Young RAAF	F1M 242 Sqn
24/2/42		Plt Off J.A. Campbell (US)	CW-21B (shot down in error) 605 Sqn
		Flt Lt J.C. Hutton	Ki-21 605 Sqn
		Plt Off N.C. Sharp RNZAF	Ki-43 605 Sqn
		Sgt E.E.G. Kuhn RNZAF	Ki-43 605 Sqn
		Sgt G.J. King	Ki-21 242 Sqn
		Flt Lt I. Julian RNZAF }	242 Sqn
	BE210	Plt Off T.W. Watson RCAF }	Ki-21 242 Sqn
		2/Lt N. Anderson SAAF }	242 Sqn
25/2/42	BE322	Plt Off J.A. Campbell (US)	A6M 605 Sqn
	BE202	Sgt J.A. Sandeman Allen	C5M claimed as A6M 242 Sqn
27/2/42		Flt Lt J.C. Hutton	A6M probable 605 Sqn
1/3/42		Sgt E.E.G. Kuhn RNZAF	F1M 605 Sqn
		Plt Off M.C. Fitzherbert	2 F1M (on sea) 242 Sqn
		Sgt C.T.R. Kelly	F1M (on sea) 605 Sqn
2/3/42		Sgt J.P. Fleming RCAF	3 Ki-48 (ground) 242 Sqn
		Sgt G.J. King	Ki-27 242 Sqn
3/3/42		Flt Lt B.J. Parker	Ki-48 (ground) 242 Sqn
		Plt Off E.C. Gartrell RNZAF	Ki-43 242 Sqn

		Plt Off M.C. Fitzherbert	Ki-43 242 Sqn
		Sgt G.J. King	Ki-43 242 Sqn
4/3/42	BE239	Sgt J.A. Sandeman Allen	2 A6M, A6M Probable 242 Sqn
		Sgt G.J. King	2 A6M 242 Sqn
		Sqn Ldr R.E.P. Brooker	A6M 242 Sqn
		Flt Lt I. Julian RNZAF	A6M 242 Sqn
	Z5691	Sgt I.D. Newlands RNZAF	Ki-48 (ground) 242 Sqn
5/3/42		Flt Lt B.J. Parker	Ki-21 242 Sqn
6/3/42		Flt Lt B.J. Parker	Ki-21 242 Sqn
		Flt Lt I. Julian RNZAF	Ki-21 242 Sqn
		Plt Off E.C. Gartrell RNZAF	Ki-21, Ki-21 probable 242 Sqn
		Plt Off W.McG. Lockwood RCAF	Ki-21 242 Sqn

Summary of claims and credits

232 (P) Squadron credited with	38 destroyed	18 probables (by 31/1/42)	
232 Squadron known claims	15½	16	
242 Squadron known claims	21	2	(plus 9 on ground/water)
258 Squadron known claims	6		
605 Squadron known claims	5	1	
266 Wing known claims	½ *	1	
	86 destroyed	**38 probables + 9 on ground/water**	

* One further claim may have been made by Sgt H.P. Jenson RNZAF of 266 Wing, either at Palembang or in Java.

APPENDIX III

HURRICANE DELIVERIES & FATES

The 51 crated Hurricanes arrived at Singapore aboard HMT *Sussex* on 13 January 1942 for use by 232 (Provisional) Squadron, and were believed to have been: (2 apparently found damaged in their crates and used for spares).

BE577	to 232 Sqn shot down 21/1/42
BE579	to 232 Sqn shot down 22/1/42
BE584/P	to 488 Sqn flown 25/1/42 Tengah to Kallang; to Palembang 5/2/42; flown 28/2/42 by 232 Sqn
BE585	to 488 Sqn record of this flown 24/1/42; believed DBR on ground 27/1/42
BE587	flown 2/2/42 from Seletar to Palembang
BE588	to 232 Sqn damaged 23/1/42; destroyed on ground 27/1/42
BE589	to 232 Sqn lost 25/1/42
BE590	to 232 Sqn lost 27/1/42
BE632	to 488 Sqn record of this flown 24/1/42; believed DBR on ground 27/1/42
BE633	to 232 Sqn shot down 22/1/42
BE639	to 232 Sqn crash-landed 23/1/42
BE640	to 488 Sqn record of this flown 25/1/42; believed DBR on ground 27/1/42
BE641	to 232 Sqn lost 25/1/42
BG678	crash-landed 6/2/42
BG693	shot down 13/2/42
BG695	record of this flown at Singapore 5/2/42
BG718	to 488 Sqn flown 27/1/42
BG720	to 232 Sqn shot down 22/1/42
BG721	probably lost in sinking of *Derrymore* 13/2/42
BG722	to 488 Sqn record of this flown 25/1/42; flown to Palembang 5/2/42
BG723	to 488 Sqn flown 24/1/42; believed DBR on ground 27/1/42
BG768	to 232 Sqn crashed 12/2/42
BG796	to 232 Sqn shot down 22/1/42
BG797	to 232 Sqn shot down 9/2/42
BG798	flown 2/2/42 Kallang to Seletar
BG800	to 488 Sqn record of this flown 24/1/42; believed DBR on ground 27/1/42
BG804	to 232 Sqn shot down 22/1/42
BG807	to 232 Sqn lost 24/1/42
BG808	to 232 Sqn damaged 29/1/42
BG809	to 488 Sqn record of this flown 25/1/42; believed flown to Palembang 5/2/42
BG810	to 232 Sqn shot down 22/1/42
BG818	to 232 Sqn shot down 20/1/42
BG820	to 232 Sqn damaged 23/1/42
BG828	to 232 Sqn shot down 26/1/42
BG829	probably lost in sinking of *Derrymore* 13/2/42
BG830	to 232 Sqn lost 11/2/42
BG845	to 488 Sqn record of this flown 24/1/42; believed DBR on ground 27/1/42
BG846	to 232 Sqn shot down 23/1/42
BG847	probably lost in sinking of *Derrymore* 13/2/42
BG848	to 232 Sqn shot down 20/1/42
BG860	to 232 Sqn lost 23/1/42
BG864	to 232 Sqn crash-landed 21/1/42
BM898	to 232 Sqn shot down 23/1/42
BM899	to 232 Sqn damaged 23/1/42, repaired, to 488 Sqn; to Palembang 5/2/42
BM900	to 488 Sqn 25/1/42; flown to Palembang 5/2/42
BM901	probably lost in sinking of *Derrymore* 13/2/42

BM902	to 232 Sqn destroyed on ground 27/1/42
BM903	to 232 Sqn damaged 22/1/42
BM904	probably lost in sinking of *Derrymore* 13/2/42
BM905	probably lost in sinking of *Derrymore* 13/2/42
BM906	to 232 Sqn shot down 20/1/42

NB: 6 crated Hurricanes lost on board SS *Derrymore* when sunk by torpedo 13/2/42 en route Batavia from Singapore; probably BG721, BG829, BG847, BM901, BM904, and BM905

48 Hurricanes ex-HMS *Indomitable* 28/1/42 included:

BD891	record of this flown 5/2/42
BD892	crashed 14/2/42
BE115	232 Sqn shot down 8/2/42
BE130	232 Sqn record of this flown 14-16/2/42; shot down 3/3/42
BE158	232 Sqn shot down 9/2/42
BE160/E	232 Sqn record of this flown 8/2/42
BE163	232 Sqn record of this at Singapore 2/42
BE195	232 Sqn shot down 8/2/42
BE202/R	232 Sqn record of this flown 15/2-1/3/42
BE208/O	232 Sqn crash-landed 7/2/42; captured by Japanese following fall of Singapore
BE210	232 Sqn record of this flown 20/2/42-2/3/42
BE219	232 Sqn shot down 8/2/42
BE230/N	flown off carrier 27-28/1/42, flown 24/2/42
BE238	232 Sqn record of this flown 19/2/42
BE239	232 Sqn record of this flown 23/2-5/3/42
BE293	flown 14/2/42 Batavia to Tjililitan
BE332	shot down 24/2/42
BE365	258 Sqn flown off carrier 28/1/42
BG677/C	232 Sqn record of this flown 8/2/42; flown 15/2/42 Batavia to Tjililitan
BG687	flown of carrier 28/1/42
BG767	soc 6/2/42
Z3750	record of this flown 6/2/42
Z3754	record of this flown 5/2/42
Z5472	232 Sqn record of this flown 4/2/42
Z5481	258 Sqn record of this flown 5/2/42
Z5482	232 Sqn crashed 7/2/42
Z5485	232 Sqn record of this flown 20/2/42

NB: Apparently 232 Squadron's aircraft carried individual code letters, while 258 Squadron's aircraft did not.

It would appear that the following Hurricanes went to the Far East, but possibly some may have gone to Burma rather than Singapore/Java:

BE170, BE194, BE196, BE206, BE207, BE209, BE212, BE217, BE218, BE220, BE225, BE234, BE235, BE237, BE240, BE289, BE292, BE299, BE333, BE363, Z5317, Z5319, Z5534, Z5341, Z5343, Z5376, Z5437, Z5438, Z5442

39 crated Hurricanes arrived Java 4/2/42 ex-HMT *Athene*, and included:

Z5555	flown 13/2/42 Kemajoran to Tjililitan
Z5602	flown 17/2/42 Kemajoran to Tjililitan; 232 Sqn record of this flown 3/3/42
Z5609	flown 15/2/42 Batavia to Tjililitan
Z5616	flown 19/2/42 Tjililitan; 605 Sqn damaged 1/3/42

Z5664	flown 15/2/42 Kemajoran to Tjililitan; to Dutch 2-VlG-IV crash-landed 1/3/42
Z5667/T	232 Sqn record of this flown 8/2/42-27/2/42
Z5682	flown 15/2/42 Kemajoran to Tjililitan
Z5685	232 Sqn record of this flown 19/2/42
Z5690	605 Sqn record of this flown 22/2/42
Z5691	flown 15/2/42 Kemajoran to Tjililitan; 232 Sqn record of this flown 3/3/42
Z5693	232 Sqn record of this flown 11/2/42
Z5696	flown 16/2/42 Kemajoran to Tjililitan

It would appear that the following Hurricanes went to the Far East, but possibly some may have gone to Burma rather than Singapore/Java:

Z5546, Z5556, Z5557, Z5580-Z5584, Z5590, Z5598, Z5601, Z5611, Z5612, Z5615, Z5619, Z5620, Z5622, Z5649, Z5657, Z5666, Z5671, Z5683, Z5692

NB: 12 Hurricanes presented to NEI Air Force 10/2/42 ex-HMT *Athene* (believe Z56?? range including Z5664).

Summary

Records would suggest that a total of 138 Hurricanes reached Singapore and Java, of which at least two were found to be damaged when their crates were opened, six were lost at sea en route to Batavia from Singapore (presumably including the two damaged machines), and a dozen were transferred to the Dutch; therefore, a maximum of 120 aircraft were potentially available for use by the RAF at Singapore, Sumatra and Java. At least nine were destroyed or damaged beyond repair at Singapore during the air raid on Kallang, 27 January 1942. The last two airworthy aircraft were destroyed by 242 Squadron on 7 March 1942, although several were later repaired by the Japanese including one that crashed on 10 March, killing its Japanese pilot.

SELECT BIBLIOGRAPHY

A Gremlin on my Shoulder: Ron Cundy
Angry Skies: Mike Hayes
Battle for Palembang: Terence Kelly
Bloody Shambles Volume One: Christopher Shores, Brian Cull and Yasuho Izawa
Bloody Shambles Volume Two: Christopher Shores, Brian Cull and Yasuho Izawa
Buffaloes over Singapore: Brian Cull with Paul Sortehaug and Mark Haselden
Caged Eagles: Vern Haugland
Emperor's Guest, The: John Fletcher-Cooke
Emperor's Guest, The: Don Peacock
Epics of the Fighting RAF: Leonard Gribble
For Your Tomorrow: Errol Martyn
Flying Fever: Air Vice-Marshal S.F. Vincent
Glory in Chaos: E.R. Bon Hall
Grand Alliance, The: The Second World War Volume III: Sir Winston S. Churchill
Hawker Hurricane: Robert Jackson
Hell on Earth: Dave McIntosh
Hurricane and Spitfire Pilots at War: Terence Kelly
Hurricane over the Jungle: Terence Kelly
JAAF Fighter Units and their Aces: Ikuhiko Hata, Yasuho Izawa and Christopher Shores
Japanese Naval Aces and Fighter Units: Ikuhiko Hata and Yasuho Izawa
Last Flight from Singapore: Arthur Donahue
Life and Death in Changi: Brian Kitching
Living with Japanese: Terence Kelly
Mohawks over Burma: Gerry Beauchamp
Remorseless Road, The: James McEwan
Sea Flight: Hugh Popham
Singapore Story, The: Kenneth Attiwill
Suez to Singapore: Cecil Brown
Tattered Eagle, The: Geoffrey Rex Collis
Their Last Tenko: James Home
Unsung Heroes of the RAF: Les and Pam Stubbs
You'll Die in Singapore: Charles McCormac

Air-Britain Serial Number Registers Z1000-9999 and BA100-BZ999 proved most valuable.

Unpublished manuscripts: Untitled by Max Boyd, 488 Squadron (via Sqn Ldr Mark Haselden); *Into the Bag* by Wg Cdr Gerald Bell (via Sqn Ldr Andy Thomas); Untitled by Ting Macnamara (via John Macnamara); official report by Air Commodore Vincent entitled *History of 226 (Fighter) Group*.

MAPS OF THEATRE

ROUTES OF JAPANESE SEABORNE INVASION

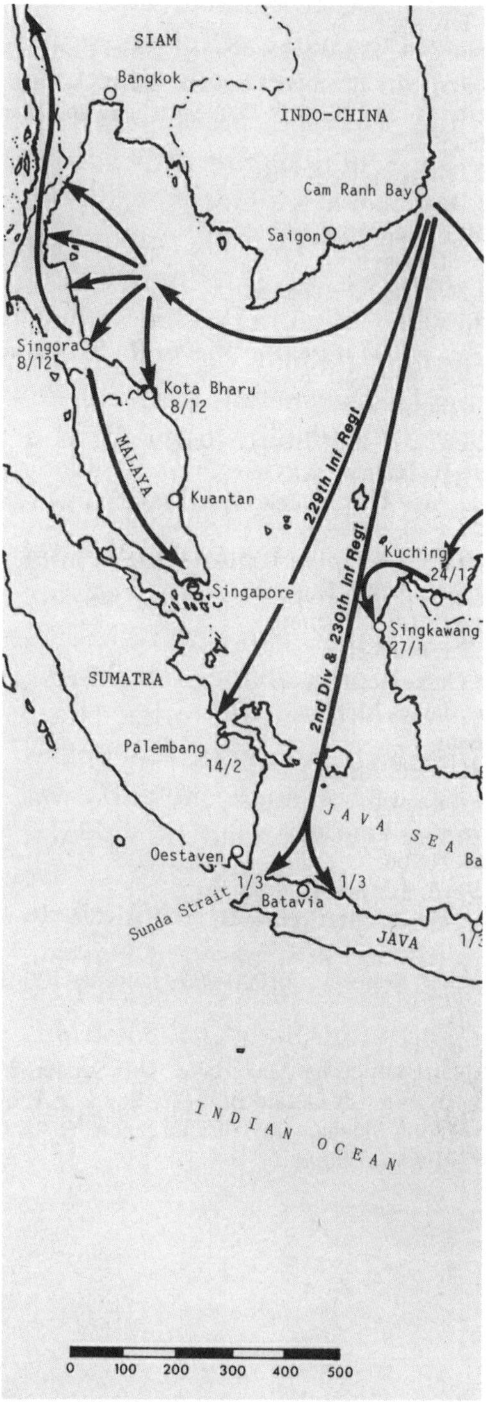

SITES OF AERODROMES ON SINGAPORE ISLAND

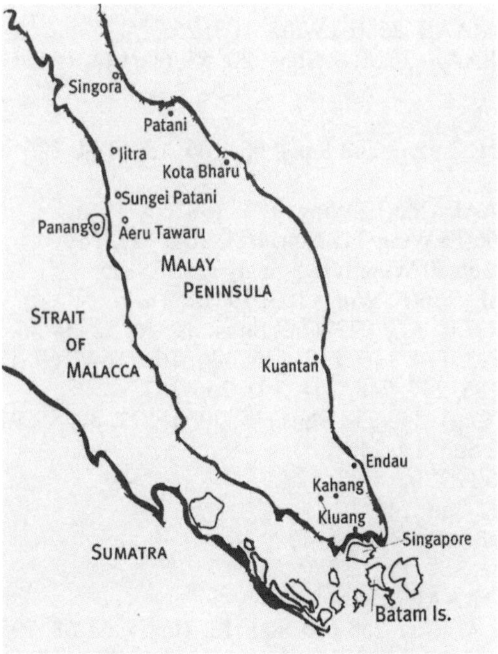

INDEX OF PERSONNEL

Hurricane Pilots – British & Commonwealth

Hurricane Pilots – NEI

Others – British & Commonwealth

Japanese

Others